New Approaches to Byzantine History and Culture

Series Editors
Florin Curta, University of Florida, FL, USA
Leonora Neville, University of Wisconsin Madison, WI, USA
Shaun Tougher, Cardiff University, Cardiff, UK

New Approaches to Byzantine History and Culture publishes high-quality scholarship on all aspects of Byzantine culture and society from the fourth to the fifteenth centuries, presenting fresh approaches to key aspects of Byzantine civilization and new studies of unexplored topics to a broad academic audience. The series is a venue for both methodologically innovative work and ground-breaking studies on new topics, seeking to engage medievalists beyond the narrow confines of Byzantine studies.

The core of the series is original scholarly monographs on various aspects of Byzantine culture or society, with a particular focus on books that foster the interdisciplinarity and methodological sophistication of Byzantine studies. The series editors are interested in works that combine textual and material sources, that make exemplary use of advanced methods for the analysis of those sources, and that bring theoretical practices of other fields, such as gender theory, subaltern studies, religious studies theory, anthropology, etc. to the study of Byzantine culture and society.

More information about this series at
http://www.palgrave.com/gp/series/14755

Adam J. Goldwyn

Witness Literature in Byzantium

Narrating Slaves, Prisoners, and Refugees

Adam J. Goldwyn
Associate Professor of English
North Dakota State University
Fargo, ND, USA

ISSN 2730-9363   ISSN 2730-9371 (electronic)
New Approaches to Byzantine History and Culture
ISBN 978-3-030-78856-8   ISBN 978-3-030-78857-5 (eBook)
https://doi.org/10.1007/978-3-030-78857-5

© The Editor(s) (if applicable) and The Author(s), under exclusive license to Springer Nature Switzerland AG 2021
This work is subject to copyright. All rights are solely and exclusively licensed by the Publisher, whether the whole or part of the material is concerned, specifically the rights of translation, reprinting, reuse of illustrations, recitation, broadcasting, reproduction on microfilms or in any other physical way, and transmission or information storage and retrieval, electronic adaptation, computer software, or by similar or dissimilar methodology now known or hereafter developed.
The use of general descriptive names, registered names, trademarks, service marks, etc. in this publication does not imply, even in the absence of a specific statement, that such names are exempt from the relevant protective laws and regulations and therefore free for general use.
The publisher, the authors and the editors are safe to assume that the advice and information in this book are believed to be true and accurate at the date of publication. Neither the publisher nor the authors or the editors give a warranty, expressed or implied, with respect to the material contained herein or for any errors or omissions that may have been made. The publisher remains neutral with regard to jurisdictional claims in published maps and institutional affiliations.

Cover image: BENEDICTUS a Sancta-Maura. Poema de bello Trojano, BNf grec 2878, fol. 195v; image courtesy of Bibliothèque Nationale de France.

This Palgrave Macmillan imprint is published by the registered company Springer Nature Switzerland AG
The registered company address is: Gewerbestrasse 11, 6330 Cham, Switzerland

For my nephews
Ari, Chase, Noam, Kallen, Levi

Acknowledgments

This book was written during my time as an Alexander von Humboldt Fellow in the Institut für Byzantinistik und Neogräzistik at the Westfälische Wilhelms-Universität Münster in 2019–21. I am grateful to the Alexander von Humboldt Stiftung for granting me the fellowship, and to the American Friends of the AvH, which provided supplementary funding through the William M. Calder III Fellowship in 2019 and 2020. This book is immeasurably improved through contact with the scholars in Münster, in particular my host Michael Grünbart, to whom I am grateful for sponsoring my fellowship and for providing the invaluable opportunity to work in such a stimulating environment. I would also like to thank the other members of the research group, and in particular Stephanos Dimitriades, Florin Filimon, and Paraskevi Toma for being φιλοξενότατοι.

Many other friends and colleagues have supported me during the writing of this book—friends and colleagues far too numerous to list here. Among them, I would like to thank Baukje van den Berg, Hendrik Dey, Dimitra Kokkini, David Konstan, Przemysław Marciniak, and Ingela Nilsson, all of whom went above and beyond the obligations of scholarship and friendship.

I would also like to express my gratitude to my colleagues at North Dakota State University for creating a welcoming and amiable academic home in which I could thrive and, in more concrete terms, taking on

viii   ACKNOWLEDGMENTS

the extra teaching and service load that allowed me to take a year of developmental leave to write.

The team at Palgrave Macmillan has also earned my deepest thanks: Allie Troyanos for welcoming the proposal; Sam Stocker for shepherding it through the various stages of publication; the anonymous peer reviewers whose contributions go unnamed but not unnoticed or unappreciated; and the editors of the New Approaches to Byzantine History and Culture series, Florin Curta, Leonora Neville, and Shaun Tougher, for creating a space within Byzantine Studies where a book like this could find a home.

Above all, I would like to thank my wife, Anastassiya Andrianova, who remains my most trusted critic and unfailing source of support. In difficult times, writing about a difficult topic, she and our daughter Freya were a limitless source of joy and delight.

PRAISE FOR *WITNESS LITERATURE IN BYZANTIUM*

"By turns reflexive and daring, Goldwyn's book is riskful thinking at its best. For medievalists, it opens up new possibilities for reading and teaching the works that matter to us most—those that somehow place us face-to-face with human Others and leave us feeling more than we can express. In Goldwyn's book, the face of the human Other presents itself, even if only briefly and in a moment of mortal danger."

— Vincent Barletta, *Stanford University, USA*

"Innovative, illuminating and daring. This theoretically sophisticated book revolutionizes the study of Byzantine literature and enriches our understanding of angst, anxiety and trauma in the middle ages. This book provides an insightful discussion of captivity in the Byzantine era and a new interdisciplinary, trans-historical understanding of narratives which will captivate scholars for years to come."

—Elena N. Boeck, *DePaul University, USA*

CONTENTS

1 Bearing Witness in Eustathios of Thessaloniki's *Capture of Thessaloniki*: Holocaust Literature and the Narration of Byzantine Trauma   1

    1.1 "The darkening of a great light": Holocaust and Genocide Studies in Byzantium   1

    1.2 Defining Witness Literature: Medieval and Modern Problems of Genre   8

    1.3 Creating the Camp in The Capture of Thessaloniki*: A Biopolitical Approach*   16

    1.4 Eustathios as Witness: Narrating the Personal in Byzantine Historiography   48

    1.5 "Alors, histoire?" Genre and Byzantine Witness Literature Revisited   57

    Bibliography   67

2 Prison Literature and Slave Narratives in Byzantium: John Kaminiates' *Capture of Thessaloniki*   71

    2.1 "I was drawn on by happy memories": Affective Narratology in Kaminiates' Letter   71

    2.2 "A narrative technique that seizes upon essential detail": Kaminiates' Principles of Selection   100

    2.3 The Subjective "I" witness and Biopolitics in Kaminiates' Principles of Selection   112

xi

xii CONTENTS

2.4	*Selektion, Biopolitics, and the Sovereign Decision in the Harbor of Thessaloniki*	122
	Bibliography	137

3 The Carceral Imaginary in Byzantium: The Komnenian Novels as Holocaust Fiction — 141

3.1	*The Shared Worlds of the Komnenian Novels and Byzantine Historiography*	141
3.2	*The Dialogic Construction of Self in the Slave Narratives of Rhodanthe and Dosikles*	166
3.3	*Selektion in* Rhodanthe and Dosikles	175
3.4	*Rhodanthe and the Voice of Female Lament in the Komnenian Novels*	183
3.5	*Completing the Cycle: Freed Slaves and Family Reunification*	195
3.6	Drosilla and Charikles *as Slave Narrative*	201
3.7	Hysmine and Hysminias: *The Symposium and the Slave Ship*	217
	Bibliography	227

4 The Refugee as Historian: Niketas Choniates and the Capture of Constantinople — 231

4.1	*Niketas as Historian and the Campaign of John II Komnenos*	231
4.2	*The Historian and the Witness: Niketas and Eustathios on the Sack of Thessaloniki*	242
4.3	*Niketas as Witness and the Sack of Constantinople*	254
4.4	*Niketas as Novelist and Hero of the Novel*	265
	Bibliography	275

5 Pleasure, Pain, Perversity: Reading Byzantine Witness Literature After Auschwitz — 277

	Bibliography	292

Index — 295

About the Author

Adam J. Goldwyn is Associate Professor of English at North Dakota State University. He received his Ph.D. in Comparative Literature at the City University of New York, was a postdoctoral fellow in Uppsala University, and has held research fellowships at the Swedish Institute in Athens and Dumbarton Oaks, and a Humboldt Fellowship at the Institüt für Byzantinistik und Neogräzistik at the Westfälische Wilhems-Universität Münster. He has also held teaching positions at Brooklyn College, the University of New York Tirana (Albania), the American University of Kosovo, and the University of Silesia in Katowice. He is the author of *Byzantine Ecocriticism: Women Nature and Power in the Medieval Greek Romance* (Palgrave Macmillan 2018), co-translator (with Dimitra Kokkini) of the twelfth-century Byzantine grammarian John Tzetzes's *Allegories of the* Iliad (Harvard University Press 2015) and *Allegories of the* Iliad (Harvard University Press 2019), and co-editor (with Ingela Nilsson) of *Reading the Late Byzantine Romance: A Handbook* (Cambridge University Press 2019).

Abbreviation of Byzantine Texts

A&K	Manasses, Constantine. *Aristandros and Kallithea.* Mazal, O. Der Roman des Konstantinos Manasses. Überlieferung, Rekonstruktion, Textausgabe der Fragmente [Wiener Byzantinistische Studien 4. Vienna: Österreichische Akademie der Wissenschaften, 1967]: 165–209. Trans. Jeffreys, Elizabeth. Four Byzantine Novels. Liverpool: Liverpool University Press, 2012, 271–338.
Chon. Hist.	Niketas Choniates. *Histories.* *O City of Byzantium, Annals of Niketas Choniates.* Trans. Magoulias, Henry. Detroit: Wayne State University Press, 1986. J. van Dieten, Nicetae Choniatae historia, pars prior [Corpus Fontium Historiae Byzantinae. Series Berolinensis 11.1. Berlin: De Gruyter, 1975]: 1–635, 637–655.
D&C	Eugenianos, Niketas. *Drosilla and Charikles.* Conca, Fabrizio. *Il Romanzo Bizantino del XII Secolo.* Turin: Unione Tipografico-Editrice Torinese, 1994, 305–498. Translation from Jeffreys, Elizabeth. *Four Byzantine Novels.* Liverpool: Liverpool University Press, 2012, 339–458.
Eust. *capta Thess.*	Eustathios of Thessaloniki. *The Capture of Thessaloniki.* Trans. Melville-Jones, John. Canberra: Byzantina Australiensia, 1988.
H&H	Makrembolites, Eumathios/Eustathios. *Hysmine and Hysminias.*

xv

xvi   ABBREVIATION OF BYZANTINE TEXTS

	In Conca, Fabrizio. *Il Romanzo Bizantino del XII Secolo.* Turin: Unione Tipografico-Editrice Torinese, 1994, 499–688. Trans. Jeffreys, Elizabeth. *Four Byzantine Novels.* Liverpool: Liverpool University Press, 2012, 157–270.
Kam. *ex. Thess.*	Kaminiates, John. *The Capture of Thessaloniki.* Böhlig, J. *Ioannis Caminiatae de expugnatione Thessalonicae.* Berlin: De Gruyter, 1973, 3–68. Trans. Frendo, David and Fotiou, Athanasios. *The Capture of Thessaloniki.* Leiden: Brill, 2002.
Men.*Rhet.*	Menander Rhetor. *Dionysius of Halicarnassus, Ars Rhetorica, Menander Rhetor.* Trans. Race, William. Cambridge, MA: Harvard University Press, 2019.
R&D	Prodromos, Theodore. *Rhodanthe and Dosikles.* Conca, Fabrizio. *Il Romanzo Bizantino del XII Secolo.* Turin: Unione Tipografico-Editrice Torinese, 1994, 63–303. Trans. Jeffreys, Elizabeth. *Four Byzantine Novels.* Liverpool: Liverpool University Press, 2012, 1–156.
Skyl.*Syn.Hist.*	Skylitzes, John. *Synopsis of Byzantine History.* J. Thurn, Ioannis Scylitzae synopsis historiarum [Corpus Fontium Historiae Byzantinae. Series Berolinensis 5. Berlin: De Gruyter, 1973]: 3–500. Trans. Wortley, John. A Synopsis of Byzantine History, 811–1057. Cambridge: Cambridge University Press, 2010.

CHAPTER 1

Bearing Witness in Eustathios of Thessaloniki's *Capture of Thessaloniki*: Holocaust Literature and the Narration of Byzantine Trauma

1.1 "THE DARKENING OF A GREAT LIGHT": HOLOCAUST AND GENOCIDE STUDIES IN BYZANTIUM

"And that day was no longer a day in its appearance, but rather it resembled night, and it seemed to suffer and to bear a gloomy appearance because of the things it saw. A thick mist spread over it, like a cloud of dust raised up by a whirlwind" (Καὶ ἦν ἰδεῖν τὴν ἡμέραν τότε οὐκέθ' ἡμέραν, ἀλλὰ νυκτὶ ἐοικυῖαν καὶ οἷον παθαινομένην καὶ σκυθρωπάζουσαν ἐφ' οἷς ἑώρα. Ὀμίχλη γὰρ αὐτὴν βαθεῖα ἐπάχυνεν, ὡσεὶ καὶ ἐκ κονιορτοῦ).[1] So begins Eustathios of Thessaloniki's description of the moment on August 24, 1185, when the Norman armies of the Kingdom of Sicily breached Thessaloniki's inner-city walls, setting off days of plunder and destruction in the second city of the Byzantine Empire. Some seven and a half centuries later, in March of 1944, a fifteen-year old Jewish boy from Sighet, Romania, was deported along with his family to the concentration camp at Auschwitz. In one of the most famous passages from his memoir, he describes his entrance into the camp: "Never shall I forget that first night in the camp, that turned my life into one long night seven

[1] Eust. *capta Thess.* 104.47; 87.

© The Author(s), under exclusive license to Springer Nature Switzerland AG 2021
A. J. Goldwyn, *Witness Literature in Byzantium*, New Approaches to Byzantine History and Culture, https://doi.org/10.1007/978-3-030-78857-5_1

2   A. J. GOLDWYN

times sealed. Never shall I forget that smoke (Jamais je n'oublierai cette nuit, la première nuit de camp qui a fait de ma vie une nuit longue et sept fois verrouillée. Jamais je n'oublierai cette fumée).[2] These parallel passages from Eustathios' *Capture of Thessaloniki* (Ιστορικόν της Αλώσεως της Θεσσαλονίκης υπό των Νορμανδών, also known by its Latin name *De Capta Thessalonica*)—which he suggests could be called "the darkening of a great light" (φωστῆρος μεγάλου ἀφάνειαν)[3]—and Elie Wiesel's *Night* (*La Nuit*)—"the ultimately canonical Holocaust memoir"[4]—demonstrate both the promise and peril of using the Holocaust as a frame of reference for conceptualizing other historical traumas and the literature of witness which is often produced in the wake.[5]

On the one hand, both Eustathios and Wiesel were eyewitnesses to the events which they relate. As such, their narratives feature significant overlap at the levels of structure, aesthetics, and style; these two passages, for instance, feature nocturnal imagery and the gathering darkness to represent the onset of suffering and destruction that run as a leitmotif through both their works. As rhetorically sophisticated works of literature, then, dealing with a similar set of experiences and affective circumstances, it is perhaps no surprise that authors as otherwise distant as a Greek Orthodox archbishop of the twelfth century and a Yiddish-Francophone

---

[2] Wiesel (2006: 34; 2007: 78).

[3] Eust. *capta Thess.* 4.31–6.1; nocturnal imagery continues at 6.21–27. Nocturnal imagery permeates the texts of witness literature that will be discussed. In *If This Is a Man*, Primo Levi describes his deportation from Fossoli to Auschwitz with similar imagery: "And night came, and it was such a night that one knew that human eyes would not witness it and survive" (E venne la notte, e fu una notte tale, che si conobbe che occhi umani non avrebbero dovuto assistervi e sopravvivere) (Levi 1959: 6; 1989: 16). Daniel Schwarz suggests that "the title motif of *Night* is moral death, or historical void. Antithetical to light and its association with understanding [. …] In *Night*, death is the antagonist, an active principle present at every moment" (231). John Kaminiates describes as "more pity inducing" (ἐλεεινότερον, translation my own) than anything else he experienced "when at night they spread leather screens over all the ships and shut up the whole unhappy lot of us in the hold, as though begrudging us light as well as everything else (ὁπότε ταῖς νυξὶν ἐφήπλουν τὰς δερματίνας δέρρεις διὰ πασῶν τῶν νηῶν καὶ πάντας εἴσω τοὺς δυστυχεῖς ἡμᾶς ἐναπέκλειον, ὥσπερ καὶ τοῦ φωτὸς ἡμῖν μετὰ τῶν ἄλλων βασκαίνοντες) (Kam. *ex. Thess.* 69.3).

[4] Franklin (2011: 9).

[5] Here I purposely summon the work of the same name by Christina Sharpe, who encourages "wake work" that speaks to the polysemous nature of the word: wake as "the keeping watch of the dead, the path of a ship, a consequence of something, in the light of flight and/or sight, awakening, and consciousness" (2016: 17–18).

1 BEARING WITNESS IN EUSTATHIOS OF THESSALONIKI'S ...

Romanian Jew of the twentieth would find recourse in similar sets of themes, narratological conventions, and literary styles—enough, perhaps, to productively conceptualize them as exemplars of witness literature. That such similarities occur throughout the works suggests that the theoretical models developed for *Night* and other Holocaust and contemporary witness testimony can help identify works written in a different time and under different circumstances as a kind of witness literature in their own right.

On the other hand, these passages, despite their seeming parallel imagery, also reveal in stark terms the inescapable difference between the representation of the two events: when Eustathios speaks of the "thick mist" (ὁμίχλη βαθεῖα) and the "cloud of dust" (κονιορτοῦ), he is deploying them in the conventional way of artful rhetoricians to heighten the emotional stakes of the moment, while for Wiesel, "the smoke" (la fumée) belongs not to the realm of metaphor, but to the literal, to describe the unprecedented reality of the crematoria. Indeed, Wiesel explicitly makes this same point himself: "the word 'chimney' here was not an abstraction; it floated in the air, mingled with the smoke. It was, perhaps, the only word that had a real meaning in this place" (Le mot «cheminée» n'était pas ici un mot vide de sens: il flottait dans l'air, mêlé à la fumée. C'était peut-être le seul mot qui eût ici un sens réel).[6] Thus, these passages also point to the limits of such an analysis, which risks slipping into simplifying comparisons that overlook or elide fundamental differences between the Holocaust and the sadly all too common experience of city-sacking in the Middle Ages (and ages past, present and, no doubt, future). For Eustathios, for instance, the moral and emotional force of his witness testimony comes not from its uniqueness, but from its very frequency; immediately after the Normans break through the inner wall, he writes: "And now the city, after our opponents had burst into it, suffered all the things that savage war enjoys doing" (Ἡ δὲ πόλις, εἰσπηδησάντων τῶν ἀντιμάχων, ἔπασχεν ὅσα φιλεῖ δρᾶν ἄγριος πόλεμος).[7] The work's English translator John Melville-Jones succinctly captures the idiomatic sense of the phrase more literally translated as "that savage war enjoys doing" by opting instead for "the usual ravages of war." Eustathios even acknowledges that the violence and destruction visited upon him was not

---

[6] Wiesel (2006: 39; 2007: 84–85).

[7] Eust. *capta Thess.* 104.31–32.

4   A. J. GOLDWYN

particularly exceptional: "And no one would consider it a novelty if, in the course of a battle, there should be a rampage through the streets of a city, or if its houses were to be damaged" (Καὶ ἀμφόδους μὲν κατατρέχεσθαι καὶ οἰκίας οὐκ εὖ πάσχειν ἂν εἰς μάχης θείη τις) he writes, noting only that the destruction of religious sites was unusual.[8] Unlike for Eustathios, for whom such events are not a "novelty" (καινοπράγημα), for Wiesel and other writers of Holocaust witness testimony, it is the uniqueness of the event which gives their narrative such force: "Only those who experienced Auschwitz know what it was. Others will never know" (Auschwitz savent ce que c'était. Les autres ne le sauront jamais).[9]

Indeed, the very question of uniqueness lies at the heart of the problem of the application of theories and methods drawn from Holocaust and Genocide Studies and related disciplines to works written under vastly different historical, political, and cultural contexts.[10] This debate orbits around two poles: on the one hand, the Holocaust as "rupture," that is, as something unique and therefore separate from everything else in human history.[11] One consequence of this way of thinking is that, as a unique and incomparable event, the Holocaust cannot serve as a locus for thinking about other historical events or theoretical or philosophical problems: "Positing the Holocaust as an ultimate rupture denies it a vital place in memory and history, leaving a space of erasure rather than inquiry."[12] The other pole is continuity, seeing the Holocaust as a product of a unique time, space, and ideological moment, and yet one woven into the broader tapestry of human history. From this perspective, the Holocaust is certainly an outlier in human history in terms of its magnitude and horror, but it remains, nevertheless, explicable within the context of human history, and thus can function as a way of thinking through other kinds of philosophical, historical, and ethical problems.

---

[8] Eust. *capta Thess.* 114.12–13. Translation my own.

[9] Wiesel (2006: 7; 2007: 13).

[10] See, for instance, Rosenbaum (2009). The question is also addressed at length by Agamben in *Remnants of Auschwitz*, originally published in Italian in 1998 and in English translation in 1999 but collected and cited throughout as Agamben (2017: 781–782).

[11] Marion (2006: 1020).

[12] Marion (2006: 1020).

Despite a lingering and justifiable fear that, in line with the view of the Holocaust as a continuity rather than a rupture, comparing the Holocaust to other historical atrocities risks shifting its focus away from the study of the fate of the Jewish people and the other victims of genocide during the Second World War, others see the broad applicability of its ethical and historical insights as essential; Michael Bernard-Donals, for instance notes that "if we see the Holocaust as one among many instances of genocide in the twentieth century and in the centuries before it, the historical stakes of the event become both lower and higher: lower because the Holocaust, on such a historical accounting, is deprived of its 'unique' status among events of history; and higher, because the lessons one can learn from studying its history have farther reaching and more contemporary implications."[13] In this reading, the Holocaust can serve as a comparator against which other acts of atrocity can be measured and understood without diminishing the Holocaust as an event or the suffering of its victims while simultaneously demanding that the suffering and deaths of other victims of atrocity be seen. In other words, the sack of Thessaloniki was not another Holocaust, but, the theoretical and methodological tools developed to study Holocaust literature and employing the models of Holocaust and Genocide Studies more broadly can illuminate otherwise obscured aspects of Byzantine literature.

At stake is a reconsideration of what kinds of atrocities constitute genocide, a fraught topic under any circumstances, but one with which scholars in Byzantine Studies have not yet engaged, even as other historical disciplines have only begun to undertake such considerations.[14] Eleni

---

[13] Bernard-Donals (2016: 43). Bernard-Donals' discussion of the issue of Holocaust uniqueness also hinges on the definition of "holocaust" and "genocide," themselves contested terms in international law and cultural studies (philosophy, literature, theology).

[14] See, for instance, the *Oxford Handbook of Genocide Studies*, which has a series of chapters in Section III, entitled "Premodern and Early Modern Genocide," that cover "Genocide in the Ancient World," "Early Medieval Europe: The Case of Britain and Ireland," and "Central and Late Medieval Europe". In his study of genocide in medieval Britain and Ireland, James Fraser argues for the ways in which the application of the codes of the United Nations' Convention on Genocide for considering medieval iterations. According to the UN

[G]enocide means any of the following acts committed with the intent to destroy, in whole or in part, a national, ethnical or religious group, as such: (a) harm to members of the group; (b) causing serious bodily injury or mental harm to members of the group; (c) deliberately inflicting on the group conditions of life

6   A. J. GOLDWYN

Kefala's *The Conquered: Byzantium and America on the Cusp of Modernity*, for instance, demonstrates the value of a comparative approach to atrocity in her pairing of the otherwise seemingly dissimilar conquests of Constantinople by the Ottomans and (seventy years later) of Tenochtitlan by the Spanish and their indigenous allies. In doing so, Kefala is able to reveal the way in which the laments produced in the wake[15] of these conquests reflect what Marianne Hirsch calls "postmemory," a concept developed for the transgenerational trauma that is the legacy of the Holocaust among survivors and their descendants but which scholars have expanded to include any cultural whose legacy includes conquest.[16] While Kefala's analysis operates two laments as exemplars of cultural trauma and transmission at the cultural level, the work of witness aims for something more intimate and personal, a reflection of the individual subjectivity.

In trying to apply the concepts of Holocaust Studies to Byzantine Studies, it is thus imperative to consider both aspects of Bernard-Donals' insight: even if medieval wars were not genocidal in intent (probably?), it does not lessen the horrors of the Holocaust to consider how insights drawn from its study might be applied to other instances of atrocity. Far from it: if such a comparison allows contemporary readers to see the otherwise nameless and faceless masses of people killed in distant periods and places, if it allows them to more fully feel the full range of emotions that Byzantine authors attempted to elicit,[17] if it makes their descriptions of human suffering more immediate, if it humanizes and enlivens

---

calculated to bring about its physical destruction in whole or in part (d) imposing measures intended to prevent births within the group; (e) forcibly transferring children of the group to another group. (Schabas 2010: 128)

Under this definition, the *Capture of Thessaloniki* surely applies.

[15] Here, again, I allude to Sharpe's consideration of the wake as a diasporic ontology and epistemology, with "wake work" as a means to "imagine new ways to live in the wake of slavery, in slavery's afterlives, to survive (and more) the afterlife of property. In short, I mean wake work to be a mode inhabiting *and* rupturing this episteme with our known lived and un/imaginable lives" (2016: 18).

[16] Kefala 50, Hirsch (2012).

[17] A point emphasized by Marc Lauxtermann in his reading of Byzantine slave letters; so often dismissed as works of rhetoric and artifice, Lauxtermann argues that their "very literariness enhanced the truth factor, the purpose of which was to garner an emotional response from the audience: tears, laughter, revulsion, sympathy, curiosity. It is modern academics who prefer cerebral detachment to sublime emotion: it is not the Byzantines, or anyone else who cares about poetry" (2014: 159).

1 BEARING WITNESS IN EUSTATHIOS OF THESSALONIKI'S ... 7

the actual historical men and women whose real suffering can only now be understood through the mediating presence of literature, then such a comparison can humanize the study of atrocities writ large.[18] For even if it is objectively true that the Holocaust surpasses the sack of Thessaloniki by orders of magnitude in terms of the scale of human suffering and death and the ultimate intention of the perpetrators, it did not necessarily seem so to those who experienced it; as he concludes his account, Eustathios writes:

> Nothing prevents me from saying this one thing before I complete this account: that if anyone says that the sun would never have seen greater sufferings in any other place, an affirmation of this kind would not be unreasonable. And if I find anyone who is about to challenge this statement, then neither the depth of my old age nor my respect for my episcopal position will restrain me from speaking.

> Τί δὲ δὴ κωλύει ἐν γοῦν τοῦτο μόνον εἰπόντα με πεπαύσεσθαι, ὡς εἴ τις ἐρεῖ μὴ ἂν ἰδέσθαι πω τὸν ἥλιον ἄλλοθι μείζω πάθη, οὐκ ἂν ἔξω λόγου ἀπισχυρίσαιτο. Καὶ εἴπερ εὑρήσω τὸν ἀντιπεσούμενον, ἀλλ' ἐνταῦθα οὐκ αἰδέσομαι εἰς λαλιὰν οὔτε τὸ βαθὺ γῆρας οὔτε τὴν ἐπισκοπήν.[19]

That is to say, people often perceive the events that happen to them as being particularly and uniquely catastrophic even if those events, from a broader perspective, do not rise to that level. Though cities always have been conquered, and though Eustathios' own lifetime saw numerous such occurrences with which he himself would have been familiar, the

---

[18] In this regard, David Konstan's "Anger, Hatred, and Genocide in Ancient Greece" serves as a useful methodological comparator. Konstan argues that his "purpose in examining ancient Greek attitudes toward the mass slaughter of noncombatant populations is to contrast the values and explanations offered by writers then, when ideas of human rights and rules of war were either non-existent or inchoate, to those that prevail now" (170–171). Despite this comparison across time, however, Konstan is careful to note that his goal is not anachronistic in attempting to transport values, even if "it is possible that this analysis may also contribute in some degree to an understanding of present-day situations in which hostilities seem especially brutal" (172). Konstan is not arguing for equivalence or likeness, but rather that modern methods can provide interpretive models for ancient and medieval atrocities.

[19] Eust. *capta Thess.* 152.18–22.

8 A. J. GOLDWYN

one that he experienced seemed by far the worst.[20] This is not to indict Eustathios as a person of narrow-minded sympathies, but to demonstrate how perception and subjectivity expand the bounds of interpretation: many events that were of smaller scope than the Holocaust nevertheless seem, to those who experienced them, to be unprecedented in their horror. These differences in positionality can thus put the narratives of the historian and the witness in tension with one another.

1.2 Defining Witness Literature: Medieval and Modern Problems of Genre

Ingela Nilsson has argued that "Eustathios' account is highly interesting from both historical and literary perspectives, especially since it presents an historical account that does not fall into any specific genre."[21] And yet, reading Eustathios' *Capture* with *Night* as a governing intertext offers a theoretically informed methodology for (re)reading the eyewitness accounts of those Byzantines who experienced and narrated their own conquest. This genre has been variously called "récits de captivité,"[22] "the *urbs capta* traditions,"[23] "poliorcetic writing,"[24] "roman de captivité,"[25] and "historical writing," yet witness literature is not the exclusive provenance of any of these.

As with any attempt to categorize according to the genre, these classifications have their strengths and weaknesses, revealing and obscuring different aspects of their significance, especially as regards considering which works fall into which genre and what the definition of that genre should be.[26] Genre, however, as with all technical terms, is itself

---

[20] Indeed, Eustathios sees the sack of his own city in geopolitical terms of reciprocal atrocity as a result of the "massacre of the Latins" in 1182 (Eust. *capta Thess.* 36.3–5).

[21] Nilsson (2013: 16).

[22] Messis (2006) further characterizes these works as "une sous-catégorie des romans ou un sous-catégorie des *récits de voyage*" (111).

[23] Papadogiannakis (2017: 190).

[24] Melville-Jones (1988a: 231).

[25] Odorico (2006: 156).

[26] Thus, for instance, where Neville would categorize Kaminiates as a work of history (Neville 2018: 4, n.7), Messis specifically excludes it (2006: 111). Further, where Messis connects Kaminiates to the Hellenistic novel (il est alors legitime d'y chercher les ressemblances les plus frappantes concernant tant le contenu qu la structure et le style), he

a contested subject within literary studies, and Byzantine Studies has long operated within its own paradigms, both those established by the Byzantines themselves (e.g. along the Aristotelian lines of epic, tragedy, comedy), and, perhaps more significantly now, the categories established by Herbert Hunger in his *Die Hochsprachliche Profane Literatur der Byzantiner* (1978). Given the seemingly definitive nature of Hunger's taxonomy, any attempt to assert the existence of a new genre within Byzantine literature will inevitably face the charge of anachronism within the rigid historicist paradigms of Byzantine Studies. Such a charge can be answered in two ways. First, Hunger's (or any other) modern taxonomy does not map exactly onto that of the Byzantines and is therefore itself an anachronism, though one organized by structuralist rather than thematic concerns. Second, diachronicity has long been an important consideration when considering genre. The immediate historical context of a work matters, and though many of the twelfth-century writers discussed in what follows would surely have read one another's works, writers of novels such as Theodore Prodromos and historiography such as his contemporary Eustathios would not have understood themselves to be writing in the same genre. And yet, acknowledging the distinctions between what medieval Greek writers thought they were doing and what modern scholars of Byzantium thought they were doing does not obviate the insights that can be gleaned from a heuristic classification of them as witness literature. Indeed, Margaret Mullett argued that Byzantinists "should have no qualms in seeking to detect the 'then meaning' as distinct from the 'now meaning.'"[27] Similar considerations of genre within Holocaust Studies have similarly emphasized that "genre is not just a way of writing: it is a way of reading, too. [...] It is necessary to think about how our ways of reading tend to assimilate texts."[28] Thus, though the Holocaust cannot change the events that occurred in the Byzantine Empire a

---

specifically precludes it from sharing the same genre, noting that "nous pouvons signaler une différence idéologique essentielle qui transforme nos récits en genre littéraire particulier: la verité ou la véracité de la narration" (2006: 112). For Eustathios' *Capture* as "un étrange mélange de genres literraires," see Odorico (2006: 165).

[27] Mullett (1992: 243); the terms come from Fowler, Alastair. *Kinds of Literature: An Introduction to the Theory of Genres and Modes.* Cambridge, MA: Harvard University Press, 256.

[28] Eaglestone (2004: 38).

10   A. J. GOLDWYN

thousand and more years earlier, it can—indeed, must—change the way we read those texts in the decades after.

The aim here, then, is not to argue that the authors under discussion were operating within a self-conscious literary tradition that was heretofore unrecognized by Byzantinists—indeed, Thomas Trezise has convincingly argued that "testimony does not respect generic boundaries" because the vastness and complexity of the events and the prismatic way in which they are experienced and remembered require all forms of representation.[29] Rather, theoretical developments in the study of the literary artifacts of the Holocaust, of slavery in the Americas, and of other iterations of genocide, conquest, and historical atrocity can help modern scholars of Byzantium (re)configure these texts as joined together in significant ways under a new theoretical paradigm.[30] In this regard, Robert Eaglestone's assertion that "texts often precede genres" shows that the problem of genre need not be subject to questions of temporality at all.[31]

In "The Holocaust as Literary Invention," Wiesel famously declared: "If the Greeks invented tragedy, the Romans the epistle, and the Renaissance the sonnet, our generation invented a new literature, that of testimony."[32] As the subsequent reading of Eustathios' *Capture* demonstrates, however, even Wiesel himself unwittingly makes a claim for uniqueness within a generic framework shared by a writer who lived eight-hundred years earlier and of whom he had never heard. Through comparison, then, of the shared methods by which authors narrate extreme human suffering and its literary depiction and, through contrast, of the different ways in which the uniqueness of the author's own circumstance and his or her political, cultural, or literary contexts shape the representation of that suffering, the juxtaposition of such otherwise seemingly unlike works can enrich readings of both works separately.

Indeed, the capture of Thessaloniki in 1185 described by Eustathios was not the first time the Byzantine city was conquered. In 904, an Arab army under Leo of Tripoli sacked the city and carried off over

---

[29] Trezise (2013: 64).

[30] Trezise (2013: 64); for a broader discussion of genre, see 32–36.

[31] Eaglestone (2004: 38).

[32] Wiesel (1990: 3). Cited widely in, for instance, Eaglestone (2004: 15) and Engdahl (2003: 3).

1 BEARING WITNESS IN EUSTATHIOS OF THESSALONIKI'S ... 11

20,000 people into slavery, an event recorded in a letter by John Kaminiates which he wrote while held in slavery (the subject of Chapter 2).[33] The centuries between Kaminiates and Eustathios were ones of turmoil and violence among the cities in the Byzantine Empire, a period which coincided with the rise of the so-called Komnenian novels (Chapter 3), which, as a form of "Holocaust fiction" use the real historical background and the conventions of witness literature to describe the imagined experience of the victims of such conquest. The sack of the capital of Constantinople in 1204 was the subject of witness testimony in Niketas Choniates' *History* (Chapter 4). Cities were not the only Byzantine institutions sacked—the eyewitness accounts of Pseudo-Nilus and Ammonius on the slaughter of monks and ascetics also provide an explicitly religious context for witness literature, as did the Ottoman conquest of the various Byzantine territories in the Peloponnese and as described by George Sphrantzes. Together, these and other works share that essential element of witnessing atrocity that binds them across otherwise disparate genres, periods, and places.

Formalist and structural approaches to defining witness literature, however, have significant limitations. Eustathios' *Capture of Thessaloniki*, for instance, was delivered as a sermon; the account by John Kaminiates, by contrast, is in the form of a letter, while Niketas' work of witness is embedded within a larger historiographical narrative; the novels, moreover, though composed in writing, were almost certainly performed orally within the social and political institution of the Byzantine *theatron*. What unites them, then, is not these formal characteristics, but other kinds of features. In this regard, subject matter is of course paramount, since they all, in one way or another, describe the individual experience of being a victim of city-sacking, though again, differences emerge, as, for instance, Kaminiates addresses only the fall of the city and the fate of the enslaved people with whom he was sent to Tripoli, Eustathios addresses the fall of the city and some broader historical and political context, while Niketas describes over a century's worth of narrative before the fall of Constantinople at the end. Focalization remains an important aspect, as first-person narration is the predominant mode, though Eustathios' narrative is mostly not about himself, and the inclusion of works like the fictional Komnenian novels would challenge this as the defining formal

---

[33] The dispute about the date and authenticity of the text are discussed in Chapter 2 (82).

12   A. J. GOLDWYN

feature (even if most of the parts that would make these qualify as "witness literature" are the first-person laments of the characters).[34]

The essential distinction between writing about atrocity (even first person, even eyewitness accounts or accounts of personal experience of atrocity) and witness literature is offered by the Holocaust survivor and witness Primo Levi. Levi's literary career as a witness began shortly after his liberation from Auschwitz and the winding journey back to his home in Italy in 1947 with *Se questo è un uomo* (translated alternately as *If This is a Man* or *Survival in Auschwitz*) and concluded with *The Drowned and the Saved* (*I sommersi e i salvati*) in 1986, a year before his suicide. In a famous passage from *The Drowned and the Saved*, Lvei, who had spent the better part of four decades writing about his experience as a witness and the broader concept of witnessing in general, wrote:

> I must repeat: we, the survivors, are not the true witnesses. [...] We survivors are not only exiguous but also an anomalous minority: we are those who by their prevarications or abilities or good luck did not touch bottom. Those who did so, those who saw the Gorgon, have not returned to tell about it or have returned mute, but they are the Muslims, the submerged, the complete witnesses, the ones whose deposition would have a general significance. [...] We who were favored by fate tried, with more or less wisdom, to recount not only our fate but also that of the others, indeed of the drowned; but this was a discourse 'on behalf of third parties,' the story of things seen close at hand, not experienced personally. The destruction brought to an end, the job completed, was not told by anyone, just as no one ever returned to describe their own death.

> Lo ripeto, non siamo noi, i superstiti, i testimoni veri. [...] Noi sopravvissuti siamo una minoranza anomala oltre che esigua: siamo quelli che, per loro prevaricazione o abilità o fortuna, non hanno toccato il fondo. Chi lo ha fatto, chi ha visto la Gorgone, non è tornato per raccontare, o è tornato muto; ma sono loro, i «mussulmani», i sommersi, i testimoni integrali, coloro la cui deposizione avrebbe avuto significato generale. [...] Noi toccati dalla sorte abbiamo cercato, con maggiore o minore sapienza, di raccontare non solo il nostro destino, ma anche quello degli altri, dei

---

[34] Messis notes that in his categorization of récits de captivité, "les textes choisis construisent une experience de mémoire autobiographique" (2006: 113). See also Hinterberger (1999: 96–117), for whom the first-person mode is the defining feature.

sommersi, appunto; ma è stato un discorso «per conto di terzi», il racconto di cose viste da vicino, non sperimentate in proprio.[35]

Though much witness literature is autobiographical in that it recounts eyewitness or lived experience, it differs from other forms of autobiography in its double focus: for Levi, the role of witness literature is "to recount not only our fate but also that of the others" (di raccontare non solo il nostro destino, ma anche quello degli altri). In this, it contrasts with the single focus of other forms of autobiography as, for instance, defined by Michael Angold in "The Autobiographical Impulse in Byzantium." In Byzantine accounts, he writes, "the basic criterion of autobiography" is "to illuminate the meaning and inner purposes of the [autobiographers'] lives."[36] But this is not the basic criterion of witness literature, even witness literature that is also autobiographical; as Levi says, "this was a discourse 'on behalf of third parties'" (è stato un discorso «per conto di terzi»). This distinction between the singular focus of autobiography and the double focus of witness literature can help distinguish among various kinds of otherwise similar life-writing. Angold, for instance, argues that the personal element in the writing of St. Symeon the New Theologian "comes close to true autobiography because it was a way of making sense of his own life and presenting it as a guide to his audience."[37] Eustathios, by contrast, does not offer his life experience as

[35] Levi (2017: 70); one of Levi's most widely quote passages, including Agamben (2017: 783). The paradoxical impossibility and yet utter necessity to witness on behalf of those who cannot is a central theme of Levi's work and, by extension, Agamben's analysis of witnessing in *Remnants of Auschwitz*: "Testimony is the disjunction between two impossibilities of bearing witness; it means that language, in order to bear witness, must give way to a non-language in order to show the impossibility of bearing witness. The language of testimony is a language that no longer signifies and that, in not signifying, advances into what is without language, to the point of taking on a different insignificance – that of the complete witness, that of he who by definition cannot bear witness. [...] It is thus necessary that the impossibility of bearing witness, the 'lacuna' that constitutes human language, collapses, giving way to a different impossibility of bearing witness – that which does not have language" (2017: 787). Esther Marion contests Agamben's position on Levi; citing this particular passage, she argues that "it is difficult to believe that [Levi] would agree with Agamben's subsequent conclusion that the 'privileged witness' (Levi, *The Drowned and the Saved* 18), the survivor, 'has nothing interesting to say,' which dismisses and silence's Levi's – and in fact all – testimony" (Marion 2006: 1011).

[36] Angold (1998: 225).

[37] Angold (1998: 230).

14   A. J. GOLDWYN

an example for others to follow, but rather to demonstrate the horror that he and others in his situation endured.

There are several other Byzantine works that address horrific experiences but which lack this crucial element of writing on behalf of those who cannot narrate for themselves. Into this category might fall a variety of surviving prison letters, among which that of Michael Glykas might be the most well-known,[38] but which would also include the prison letter composed by "an anonymous poet exiled to Malta" composed in the 1140s (about whom nothing is known beyond what is found in the letter itself) and similar lesser-known works.[39] Marc Lauxtermann's analysis of the poem and two similar prison letters points to the centrality of Levi's distinction: in suggesting they were composed in "the apologetic mode of self-writing," Lauxtermann brings out the difference between autobiographical writing which centers the self and autobiographical writing on behalf of others.[40] Lauxtermann reads this in the broader context of the cultural shift around the year 1000, after which "talking about oneself is allowed in Byzantium if one is setting oneself up as an exemplary model (as in the monastic typika) or if one has to defend oneself in public, in which case the autobiographical ego becomes a public persona."[41] The works of witness literature considered here, however, meet neither of these criteria; the authors are not offering apologia nor are they defending themselves in public. If anything, what they are doing is the opposite of showing themselves as exempla, since the tragedy of their situation is (in their view) impossible to recreate.

For this reason, too, other works might not be considered witness literature despite their centering the lives, experiences, and voices of victims of conquest and other atrocities. The progymnasmata of Nikephoros Basilakes, for instance, contain numerous *ethopoeiae* (rhetorical exercises that ask a student to practice writing by imagining what a historical figure would say) that have to do with enslaved people and prisoners: "What Joseph would say after being accused by the Egyptian woman and thrown

[38] For Glykas' prison letter, see Tsolakis (1959). For a discussion of its scholarly history and literary merits, see Bourbouhakis (2007).

[39] Lauxtermann (2014: 155).

[40] Lauxtermann (2014: 161).

[41] Lauxtermann (2014: 161).

into prison," "What David would say when, being pursued by Saul, he is held captive by the Philistines and about to be killed."[42] Basilakes' *ethopoeiae* are pseudo-autobiographical discourses about the traumatic events of enslavement, but that does not also mean they are works of witness, since neither Basilakes nor his narrators are creating discourse on behalf of others.

What defines the genre, then, is not any formal aspect, but an affective and ethical one, specifically that the authors foreground the emotional and experiential aspects of the events they describe as they impacted the author and those for whom the author as survivor must stand in as witness. They are works in which a narrator who was a victim of conquest describes the terms of their violent subjugation as representing the similar situation of the countless others with whom they shared that experience, but who did not survive to narrate it themselves. Traditionally read as histories or under other generic paradigms, reconceptualizing them through the frame of a literature of witness rather than a literature of fact, as works of subjective survivor testimony, foregrounds the importance of rhetoric, narratology, and style for their affective rather than factual content.[43]

---

[42] For Basilakes' progymnasmata, see Basilakes, Nikephoros. 2016. *The Rhetorical Exercises of Nikephoros Basilakes: Progymnasmata from Twelfth-Century Byzantium.* Edited and translated by Jeffrey Beneker and Craig A. Gibson. Cambridge, MA: Harvard University Press.

[43] Michael Levine calls this "a different, more ethical way of responding, a way of assuming co-responsibility for the act of bearing witness" (2006: 3).

1.3 Creating the Camp in *The Capture of Thessaloniki*: A Biopolitical Approach

Perhaps the most significant contemporary investigation into the ethical dilemmas of writing about the Holocaust can be found in a series of nine works written by Giorgio Agamben between 1995 and 2016 that would come to be called the "*Homo Sacer* project" (and which were collected in English translation in 2017 under the title the *Omnibus Homo Sacer*). Agamben developed a political philosophy of sovereignty and subjectivity defined by the application of state power, which he, following Michel Foucault, called "biopolitics" and which he defines variously as when "natural life begins to be included in the mechanisms and calculations of State power"[44] and "the growing inclusion of man's natural life in the mechanisms and calculations of power."[45] Agamben later expands on the definition of the term, noting that "the concept of the 'body' too is always already caught in a deployment of power. The 'body' is always already a biopolitical body,"[46] by which he means that the body is the central locus for the enactment of state power through defining, constructing, and, ultimately, controlling it through ideology, law, and violence.

The concept of biopolitics clarified for Foucault the modern turn of governments toward control of human bodies and the methods by which such control was exerted, which he called "biopower."[47] For Foucault, this control manifested itself in two ways: on the one hand, the state supported the lives of those whom it considered worthy of living through the establishment of institutions such as hospitals. On the other hand, the state disciplined and punished those lives whom it did not value through, for instance, prisons. According to Foucault, however, both biopolitics and biopower were considerations of modern governments; indeed, he argues that the development of the conception of biopolitics and the state institutions and ideologies that supported it are the very features which

---

[44] Agamben (2017: 6).

[45] Agamben (2017: 99).

[46] Agamben (2017: 152–153).

[47] Foucault defines the term in *The History of Sexuality* (1978: 140–143), though the term has since taken on a much broader significance. For a detailed investigation of the term in its Foucaultian sense and for the wide geographic, temporal, and disciplinary applicability it has achieved, see Cisney and Morar (2016).

1 BEARING WITNESS IN EUSTATHIOS OF THESSALONIKI'S … 17

define the irrevocable rupture between modernity and its antecedents, a rupture Foucault places in the seventeenth century.[48]

But despite this focus on the modern, Foucault, according to Agamben, "never brought his insights to bear on what could well have appeared to be the exemplary place of modern biopolitics: the politics of the great totalitarian states of the twentieth century. The inquiry that began with a reconstruction of the *grand enfermement* in hospitals and prisons did not end with an analysis of the concentration camp."[49] This insight became the starting point for Agamben's vast expansion of the concept of biopolitics—from both theoretical and methodological perspectives—that allowed Foucault's more explicit focus on modernity to transfer to other geographic and temporal contexts.[50]

The major feature of Agamben's revision of Foucault is his expansion of Foucault's archaeology of violence (inscribed, for instance, in the title of one of the latter's major works, *Discipline and Punish: The Birth of the*

---

[48] Agamben (2017: 853). This is the telos of the archaeology Foucault offers in Part Five of the *History of Sexuality, Vol. 1*, entitled "Right of Death and Power over Life." Despite Foucault's view that biopolitics is a phenomenon of the modern, several recent studies have made the case that a judicious application of a theory of biopolitics can elucidate the operations of sovereign power over the individual in ancient and medieval literature as well. Mika Ojakangas, for instance, begins his study *On the Origins of Greek Biopolitics* with an explicit rejection of biopolitics as a contemporary phenomenon: "It is indeed my contention in this book that Foucault's account of biopolitics as an exclusively modern idea is inaccurate. The idea of politics as control and regulation of the living in the name of security, well-being and happiness of the state and its inhabitants is as old as Western political thought itself, originating in classical Greece. Greek political thought [...] is biopolitical to the bone" (2016: 1) though he also makes clear that he is not suggesting "that the history of biopolitics would constitute a *continuum* from antiquity to the twentieth century" (2016: 7).

[49] Agamben (2017: 99). For a further description of the concept of the camp in Agamben's broader theory of biopolitics, see Minco (2011).

[50] Simon Gaunt notes that "Agamben so expands the meaning of the term biopolitics from Foucault's quite specific and limited sense (which designates modes of power prevalent in Europe from the seventeenth century) to a term that subsumes all political human life," he nevertheless argues that Agamben's revision of Foucault has important implications for a medieval biopolitics centered on autocratic rather than (as for Foucault, increasingly democratic) institutions: "if it is the power of the sovereign to include bare life in political life (or to exclude it from political life) that establishes sovereign power, it is this very act of inclusion (or exclusion) that produces (or precludes) political life" (1995: 52).

18   A. J. GOLDWYN

Prison)[51] to include the legal and extralegal mechanisms of the application of extreme forms of physical violence and mass death. Indeed, Agamben signals this focus in the title of the seminal work that would initiate the project: the eponymous *homo sacer* is he who can be killed with impunity, but may not be sacrificed, and thus paradoxically must live and die both within and beyond the reach of sovereign powers of protection and punishment.[52]

To do so, Agamben relies on a distinction between the two poles of existence that he attributes to the ancient Greeks under the terms "*zoē*, which expressed the simple face of living to common to all living beings,"[53] and "*bios*, which indicated the form or way of living proper to an individual or a group."[54] These terms are the equivalent of what Agamben later calls "bare life" (exclusion from political life and thus life as simple biological fact) as contrasted with "political existence" (inclusion in the community and thus protection under its sovereign power). The figure of the *homo sacer* thus becomes the paradigmatic figure for Agamben's consideration of how law and sovereignty both protect and harm their subjects through inclusion and exclusion within the sphere of political violence—biopolitics.

If for Foucault the hospital and the prison were the iconic forms of modern biopolitics, for Agamben it is Nazi concentration camps, represented by Auschwitz, which in some respects combine both elements into a single space—they were concerned with preserving and taking life and with incarceration and punishment.[55] In Agamben's description of the

[51] Its original French title is *Surveiller et punir: Naissance de la prison.*

[52] For which, see, for instance, McLellan (2016: 37–38).

[53] Agamben (2017: 5).

[54] Agamben (2017: 5).

[55] Foucault's view of the prison as characterizing the modern and his archaeology of the development of the bureaucratization of carceral space has been challenged by Geltner's *The Medieval Prison*: "Historians of premodern institutions in turn have faced the double challenge of explicating and predating the emergence of several allegedly modern institutions, from hospitals, to reformatories and brothels, to prisons" (2008: 104). Geltner does allow, however, that "in no case is there a convincing argument for the 'totalness' of any of these facilities, with the obvious exception of monasteries" (2008: 104). Though Geltner does not make the connection, the concentration camp from this perspective can be seen as the end result of a process that began with the medieval "proto-total" institutions he describes. Geltner notes, however, that rather than physical annihilate or otherwise eliminate the presence of social and religious deviants,

1 BEARING WITNESS IN EUSTATHIOS OF THESSALONIKI'S ... 19

consequences of Nazi biopolitics in the camps, he concludes that "insofar its inhabitants were stripped of every political status and wholly reduced to bare life, the camp was also the most absolute biopolitical space ever to have been realized, in which power confronts nothing but pure life, without any mediation" and which therefore allows the "deployments of power by which human beings could be so completely deprived of their rights and prerogatives that no act committed against them could appear any longer as a crime."[56]

Drawing from Primo Levi, Agamben thus offers a new moral insight that he argues must remain at the heart of ethical humanistic thought: "The atrocious news that the survivors carry from the camp to the land of human beings is precisely that it is possible to lose dignity and decency beyond imagination, that there is life in the most extreme degradation. And this new knowledge becomes the touchstone by which to judge and measure all morality and dignity."[57] The new knowledge that the survivors bring is "an ethics of a form of life that begins where dignity ends," and, for Agamben, Levi "is the cartographer of this new *terra ethica*."[58] Since the emergence of the historic fact of the existence of concentration camps, Agamben argues, old ways of thinking are rendered inadequate, perhaps even immoral.[59]

Though Agamben discusses the problem of biopower in concentration camps in terms of a modern rights discourse that arises from the post-medieval political concepts of the citizen and the nation-state ("the birth of the camp in our time appears as an event that decisively signals the political space of modernity"),[60] the biopolitical structures he describes and the new ethical demands they make on subsequent political and

---

various [medieval] regimes created or annexed 'marginal' institutions such as leper-houses, brothels, hospitals, and Jewish quarters" (2008: 3), thus providing a framework of the kind of sovereign exclusion later seized upon by Schmidt and the Nazis.

[56] Agamben (2017: 141).

[57] Agamben (2017: 807).

[58] Agamben (2017: 807).

[59] Esther Marion, in a broader critique of Agamben's use of the Holocaust, nevertheless agrees: "Perhaps the new ethical terrain opened by Auschwitz lies in the very challenge offered to its potential cartographers: to listen and forge responsive and responsible approaches to the ethical and human weight of this past" (2006: 1022).

[60] Agamben (2017: 143–144). The passage and its broader ramifications for narrating trauma beyond the Holocaust are discussed in Roth (2012: xix).

historical thinking has allowed these ideas to be taken up in other temporal and geographic contexts. Indeed, this insight has begun to influence how other canonical medieval texts are being interpreted. In William McLellan's *Reading Chaucer After Auschwitz*, for instance, the author makes the claim for the transferability of Agamben's conceptualization of the Holocaust in general and his readings of Levi through the prism of biopolitics in particular:

> The knowledge of the event called the Holocaust that Levi and others have imparted has equipped us to read other extreme situations. Yet, a paradox is at work here. I agree with Levi and Agamben that the event named the Holocaust is a singularity and a *unicum*, so any comparisons, strictly speaking, are not possible. Nevertheless, as Agamben argues, the Holocaust should not remain a hermetically sealed event. We need to proceed with caution and respect in this task; but, as Agamben insists, we need to proceed even if it means risking the status of the event's singularity. Our knowledge of what happened there helps us understand what happens to the subject in other situations where political power threatens or succeeds in degrading the human subject.[61]

For McLellan then, following Agamben, "after Auschwitz our moral sense has been transformed, and consequently, our reading of Chaucer has been altered. Auschwitz has initiated us into perceiving another dimension of these tales. The secret complicity between what we regarded as the tyrannical exception outside the legitimate exercise of power is, we now see, within the domain of the normal practice of sovereign power."[62] McLellan calls this the "new reception paradigm," arguing that "the traditional framework guiding our relation to the past needs to be revised so that we may better comprehend our historical situation and moral universe. It is necessary that we develop a new paradigm of reception history to account for how the Holocaust has changed our relation, not only to our present and future but also to our past as well and, consequently, to traditional texts from the past."[63]

---

[61] McLellan (2016: 14).

[62] McLellan (2016: 21).

[63] McLellan (2016: 16).

1 BEARING WITNESS IN EUSTATHIOS OF THESSALONIKI'S ... 21

Agamben himself authorizes such a reading, noting that "[i]f the essence of the camp consists in the materialization of the state of exception and in the subsequent creation of a space in which bare life and the juridical rule enter into a threshold of indistinction, then we must admit that we find ourselves virtually in the presence of a camp every time such a structure is created, independent of the kinds of crime that are committed there and whatever its denomination and specific topography."[64] And if, as he later argues, "[t]he stadium in Bari into which the Italian police in 1991 provisionally herded illegal Albanian immigrants before sending them back to their country, the winter cycle-racing track in which the Vichy authorities gathered the Jews before consigning them to the Germans, [... or] the zones d'attentes in French international airports in which foreigners asking for refugee status are detained" are "all equally [...] camps"[65] in Agamben's formulation, then certainly Thessaloniki in the immediate aftermath of the city's fall must surely qualify as well.

Indeed, Eustathios himself notes this new state of affairs, describing the treatment of the Greeks at the hands of the Latins through an animal metaphor. About the Latins, he writes,

> by their every word and action they put forward as a justification for their villainy the fact that they had taken us with the sword. In saying this they were not behaving like men, but like the lion which has seized its prey and wishes to tear it apart, not because it is hungry and longs for meat, but because of the right to do so which it has acquired from holding it in his claws.

> συχνὰ πρὸς πάντα λόγον καὶ πρὸς πᾶν ἔργον προϊσχόμενοι εἰς δικαίωσιν τοῦ κακουργεῖν πάντα λόγον καὶ πρὸς πᾶν ἔργον προϊσχόμενοι εἰς δικαίωσιν τοῦ κακουργεῖν τὸ ἀπὸ σπάθης ἡμᾶς ἑλεῖν, οὐκ ἀνθρώπινα λαλοῦντες, ἀλλ' ὡσεὶ καὶ λέων ἄγραν ἑλὼν ἐθέλει διασπᾶν αὐτήν, οὐχ ὅτι πεινώη καὶ ποθοίη σάρκας, ἀλλὰ δικαίῳ τοῦ συσχεῖν αὐτὴν ὄνυξιν.[66]

For Agamben, *bios*, or political life, is a civilized way of living that distinguishes humans from animals. But, as Eustathios says, the Latins "were not behaving like men" (οὐκ ἀνθρώπινα): they had reduced the Greeks to

---

[64] Agamben (2017: 143).
[65] Agamben (2017: 143).
[66] Eust. *capta Thess.* 130.11–14.

22   A. J. GOLDWYN

bare life, *zoē*, in the way a lion eats its prey: simply by virtue of its greater ability to enact violence. Thus, in different terms, Eustathios articulates the difference between political life and bare life through the comparison of how humans and animals behave.

If Thessaloniki then, in being "a space in which bare life and the juridical rule enter into a threshold of indistinction," can be considered from a theoretical perspective as a kind of camp, it follows that the material conditions between the two should also share some similarities. If the biopolitics of Norman-occupied Thessaloniki and Auschwitz share certain features, it follows that the descriptions of the bodies in both locations should also endure similar kinds of violence, and indeed this is reflected in the similar rhetoric of Levi and Wiesel in Auschwitz and Eustathios in Thessaloniki.

In *Night*, Wiesel describes the night the Germans arrest the Jewish leaders of Sighet as the day "the race toward death had begun" (la course vers la mort avait commencé).[67] The first incident he recounts after that is how "the Hungarian police burst into every Jewish home in town: a Jew was henceforth forbidden to own gold, jewelry, or any valuables. Everything had to be handed over to the authorities, under penalty of death. My father went down to the cellar and buried our savings" (la police hongroise fit irruption dans toutes les maisons juives de la ville: un Juif n'avait plus le droit de posséder chez lui d'or, de bijoux, d'objets de valeur; tout devrait être remis aux autorités, sous peine de mort. Mon père descendit dans la cave et enterra nos économies).[68] The Norman seizure of Greek assets on pain of death also features in Eustathios' account of the sack of Thessaloniki:

> When the owner of a house, wandering hither and thither, found the thought of his home returning to his mind, and had visions of his former possession, and desired to pass by it and approach it and glance inside [...] his reception by the barbarians would be a fatal one. They would hang him up and torture him and burn straw beneath him, and they would invent other torments to make him reveal where his wealth lay hidden and give it to them.

---

[67] Wiesel (2006: 10; 2007: 42).

[68] Wiesel (2006: 10–11; 2007: 43).

ὅτε τις τῶν οἰκοδεσποτούντων ὧδε καὶ ἐκεῖ πλαζόμενος ἀναπολήσει τὴν οἰκίαν εἰς νοῦν καὶ φαντάσεται τὰ ἑαυτοῦ καὶ ἐπιθυμήσει παρελθεῖν ἐκεῖ καὶ ἐγγίσει καὶ παρακύψει ἐντὸς [...] ἐκ τῶν βαρβάρων δεξιώματα θανατηρά· κρεμάθραι γὰρ καὶ αἰκισμοὶ καὶ ἐξ ἀχύρων καπνοὶ καὶ ἕτερα καινότροπα κακὰ ἐπὶ χρημάτων ἐκφάνσει καὶ δόσει.[69]

The hiding of such valuables, as Wiesel's father had done, also features in the description of the *Capture of Thessaloniki* in Eustathios' description of the Normans as "gold-diggers" (χρυσωρύχους)[70]:

Then the floors of the houses were disturbed and ripped up, and all of them were excavated in this way. The barbarians tunneled like hares or moles, and grubbed around like swine or any other root-eating earth-loving creature or, to use another image, like ploughmen. [...] And because they would not be satisfied with the riches which could found in the sunlight, they also planned to seize those which were beneath the earth also.

Ἐντεῦθεν δαπέδων σάλοι καὶ ἀνασχίσεις, δι' ὧν οἶκοι πάντες ἐξωρωρύχατο, ὑπονομευόντων τῶν βαρβάρων κατὰ λαγιδεῖς ἢ ἀσπάλακας ἢ καὶ χοίρους ἢ ἄλλο τι ζῷον ῥιζοφάγον γεωχαρές, εἰπεῖν δὲ καὶ ἄλλως, κατὰ ἀροτρέας. [...] Καὶ τοῖς ἀμφὶ τὸν ἥλιον μὴ ἀγαπῶντες πλουτισμοῖς, ἐπεβούλευον καὶ τοῖς κατὰ γῆς.[71]

Thus, the economic aspects of the state of exception are similarly recalled: citizens are usually protected from theft in the state of sovereign protection, but under the state of exception, such juridicial constructs no longer apply; their valuables can be taken without recourse to the law.

So, too, were the movements of the Jews of Sighet and the Greeks of Thessaloniki severely curtailed, especially after dark. Wiesel notes that, as the Germans established new laws for the Sighet ghetto, "We no longer had the right to frequent restaurants or cafes, to travel by rail, to attend synagogue, to be on the streets after six o'clock in the evening" (Nous n'avions plus le droit d'entrer dans les restaurants, dans les cafés, de voyager en chemin de fer, de nous rendre à la synagogue, de sortir

---

[69] Eust. *capta Thess.* 132.19–26.

[70] Eust. *capta Thess.* 140.3.

[71] Eust. *capta Thess.* 138.28–30; 140.1–2.

24   A. J. GOLDWYN

dans les rues après 18 heures).[72] So, too, were the Greeks made to keep off the streets after dark: "As the hour of the sun had sunk towards the west, the prudent citizen had to shut himself within his dwelling and make the doors safe with bars, since if he did not do so, there was no one who would give surety for his survival" (Καὶ τέως ἡλίου κατακλυσθέντος εἰς δύσιν, ἐχρῆν τὸν φρονοῦντα ἔσω καλύβης εἶναι, μοχλοῖς τὰς θύρας ἀσφαλισάμενον, ὡς εἴ γε μὴ οὕτως ἐποίει, οὐδεὶς ἂν ἐγγύην ἐδίδου περισωθήσεσθαι τὸν ἄνθρωπον).[73]

From the perspective of biopolitics, too, both Eustathios and Wiesel focus on the basic needs of the body—hunger, thirst, cold, fatigue, and excretion—and how these were controlled by their captors. For instance, as the first group of Jews from Sighet gather for deportation, Wiesel describes the heat as "oppressive" (intense)[74] and focuses on the thirst of children unused to such hardship:

> Children were crying for water.
> Water! There was water close by inside the houses, the backyards, but it was forbidden to break ranks.
> "Water, Mother, I am thirsty!"

> Des enfants pleuraient pour avoir de l'eau.
> De l'eau! Il y en avait, toute proche, dans les maisons, dans les cours, mais il était interdit de quitter les rangs.
> – De l'eau, maman, de l'eau![75]

Later, when it is his turn for deportation, Wiesel describes "The same hellish sun. The same thirst. Only there was no one left to bring us water" (Le même soleil d'enfer. La même soif. Mais il n'y avait plus personne pour nous apporter de l'eau).[76] When describing conditions in the cattle car which brought them to Auschwitz, Wiesel again foregrounds the lack of water: "After two days of travel, thirst became intolerable, as did the heat" (Au bout de deux jours de voyage, la soif commença à nous

---

[72] Wiesel (2006: 10; 2007: 44).

[73] Eust. *capta Thess.* 136.21–24.

[74] Wiesel (2006: 16; 2007: 52).

[75] Wiesel (2006: 16; 2007: 52).

[76] Wiesel (2006: 19; 2007: 55–56).

1 BEARING WITNESS IN EUSTATHIOS OF THESSALONIKI'S ... 25

torturer. Puis la chaleur devint insupportable).[77] This focus on thirst is preparatory for the description of the scenes in Auschwitz itself; emphasizing his own hunger and thirst, describing it as "intolerable" in the English translation, but even more powerfully in the French original— "torturer," to torture—thus increases the pathos of the description of the camp, where such deprivation was orders of magnitude greater. Indeed, Wiesel describes his relief at the hanging of the dentist who was about to pull his gold tooth:

> In fact, I was pleased with what was happening to him: my gold crown was safe. It could be useful to me one day, to buy something, some bread or even time to live. At that moment in time, all that mattered to me was my daily bowl of soup, my crust of stale bread. The bread, the soup – those were my entire life. I was nothing but a body. Perhaps even less: a famished stomach. The stomach alone was measuring time.

> J'étais même très heureux de ce qui lui arrivait: je sauvais ma couronne en or. Elle pouvait me servir, un jour, à acheter quelque chose, du pain, de la vie. Je n'attachais plus d'intérêt qu'à mon assiette de soupe quotidienne, à mon bout de pain rassis. Le pain, la soupe – c'était toute ma vie. J'étais un corps. Peut-être moins encore: un estomac affamé. L'estomac, seul, sentait le temps passer.[78]

Levi's *If This Is a Man* similarly emphasizes these basic needs: over and over again, Levi describes the deprivation of the prisoners: "We suffered from thirst and cold; at every stop we clamoured for water, or even a handful of snow, but we were rarely heard. [...] Two young mothers, nursing their children, groaned night and day, begging for water" (Soffrivamo per la sete e il freddo: a tutte le fermate chiedevamo acqua a gran voce, o almeno un pugno di neve, ma raramente fummo uditi; [...] Due giovani madri, coi figli ancora al seno, gemevano notte e giorno implorando acqua).[79] The lack of water becomes for Levi both a metaphor of the basic will to survive: "It was the very discomfort, the cold, the thirst that kept us aloft in the void of bottomless despair, both

---

[77] Wiesel (2006: 23; 2007: 62).

[78] Wiesel (2006: 70; 2007: 106).

[79] Levi (1959: 9; 1989: 25).

26   A. J. GOLDWYN

during the journey and after" (Sono stati proprio i disagi, le percosse, il freddo, la sete, che ci hanno tenuti a galla sul vuoto di una disperazione senza fondo, durante il viaggio e dopo),[80] he says, and the literal manifestation of their suffering:

> We have a terrible thirst. The weak gurgle of the water in the radiators makes us ferocious; we have had nothing to drink for four days. But there is also a tap – and above it a card which says that it is forbidden to drink as the water is dirty. Nonsense. It seems obvious that the card is a joke, "they" know that we are dying of thirst and they put us in a room, and there is a tap, and *Wassertrinken Verboten*. I drink it and I incite my companions to do likewise, but I have to spit it out, the water is tepid and sweetish, with the smell of a swamp.
> This is hell. Today, in our times, hell must be like this.

> Che sete abbiamo! Il debole fruscio dell'acqua nei radiatori ci rende feroci: sono quattro giorni che non beviamo. Eppure c'è un rubinetto: sopra un cartello, che dice che è proibito bere perché l'acqua è inquinata. Sciocchezze, a me pare ovvio che il cartello è una beffa, «essi» sanno che noi moriamo di sete, e ci mettono in una camera e c'è un rubinetto, e Wassertrinken verboten. Io bevo, e incito i compagni a farlo; ma devo sputare, l'acqua è tiepida e dolciastra, ha odore di palude.
> Questo è l'inferno. Oggi, ai nostri giorni, l'inferno deve essere così.[81]

The desperate thirst of the captives is also a feature of the Byzantines' accounts of conquest. For Eustathios, too, "the crown of the sufferings which affected us was the lack of that utter necessity, water" (τὸ δὲ δὴ κορυφαῖον ἐν τοῖς καθ' ἡμᾶς τούτοις κακοῖς καὶ ἡ τοῦ ἀναγκαιοτάτου ὕδατος ἔκλειψις ἦν).[82] Eustathios describes at length how the defenders of Thessaloniki attempted to refurbish an unused cistern, but how their leaders, through impatience and incompetence, ended up both ruining what water there was and then letting it leak out of the badly repaired cistern: "When we learned that the water was lost, our hopes vanished also; we shared out the supplies which we had gathered there, and could do nothing except

---

[80] Levi (1959: 8; 1989: 23).
[81] Levi (1959: 15; 1989: 34).
[82] Eust. *capta Thess.* 76.31–32.

1 BEARING WITNESS IN EUSTATHIOS OF THESSALONIKI'S ... 27

tremble and pray" (ἐπεὶ μάθοιμεν ἀπολωλέναι τὸ ὕδωρ, συγκατερρύημεν τὸ εὔελπι καὶ διανείμαντες ἐκεῖ τὴν συγκομιδὴν μόνου τοῦ δειλιᾶν καὶ εὔχεσθαι κατέστημεν).[83] Thus, the Thessaloniki Jews who arrived in Auschwitz with Levi would have shared the terrible fate of drinking putrid water with another victim of conquest from that city centuries before.

Indeed, thirst as a topos of witness literature is also a feature of other accounts of Byzantine witness. In his *Capture of Thessaloniki*, John Kaminiates describes the thirst of the Thessalonians under Arab occupation in terms similar to Levi's: "All were equally consumed with the same unfulfilled craving for a single drop of water, mature adults and young children: all they wanted was some short respite from the nagging pangs of thirst, yet they were denied even this" (πάντας δὲ ὁμοίως ἐφίεσθαι καὶ ἀπορεῖν ῥανίδος μιᾶς ὕδατος τούς τε ἐντελεῖς τὴν ἡλικίαν καὶ τοὺς ἔτι κομιδῇ νέους, οὐδὲν ἕτερον ἀλλ᾽ ἢ μόνον ἀναψῦξαι μικρὸν τὴν συνέχουσαν δίψαν ἐπιζητοῦντας, καὶ οὐδὲ τούτου τυγχάνοντας).[84] As a result,

> the presence of thirst consumed us no less than the proximity of the sword. Indeed, we were so violently tormented by it that we begged our guards to let us at least take some of the water that was flowing through the place and thereby gain some temporary relief. They agreed to this, not because they entertained any kindly feelings towards us (how could they who dealt in death and reveled in slaughter?) but because the water was made up of the outflow of the entire city's sewers and was capable, without any further contrivance, of proving lethal to whoever drank it. Yet each one of us joyfully put that disgusting filth to his lips as though it were a sweet, pure draught of newly-melted snow and in his imagination took the cup of stinking liquid for a cup filled with honey.

> οὐδὲν πλέον ἢ διὰ ξίφους ὡς ἡ διὰ τῆς δίψης πάντας ἀνήλισκεν, ᾗ καὶ σφοδρῶς πιεζόμενοι ἐδεόμεθα τοῖς συνοῦσι κἂν τῶν διερχομένων ὑδάτων τῷ τόπῳ μεταλαβεῖν καί τινος βραχείας μετασχεῖν ἀνοχῆς. οἰδὲ πρὸς τοῦτο ἐνένευον, οὐχ ὅτι τινὶ συμπαθείᾳ περὶ ἡμᾶς ἐκέχρηντο (πῶς γὰρ οἱ ταῖς σφαγαῖς ἐντρυφῶντες καὶ θάνατον ἀποπνέοντες;), ἀλλ᾽ ὅτι τὸ ὕδωρ ἐκεῖνο τῆς πόλεως ὃν ἁπάσης τῶν ἀφέδρων ἀπόρροια ἱκανὸν ἦν καὶ δίχα πάσης ἄλλης ἐπιβουλῆς τοὺς μετέχοντας ἀπαλλάττειν. πλὴν ὡς ἀπὸ χιόνος ἄρτι λυθείσης εἰλικρινὲς καὶ ἡδὺ πόμα, οὕτω μεθ᾽ ἡδονῆς ἕκαστος τῷ στόματι τὴν σαπρίαν

---

[83] Eust. *capta Thess.* 78.18–20.

[84] Kam. *ex. Thess.* 57.1.

ἐκείνην προσέφερε καὶ τὴν κύλικα τῆς δυσωδίας μέλιτος πλήρη τοῖς λογισμοῖς ὑπελάμβανεν.[85]

Alongside the thirst was the hunger; both Wiesel and Levi describe the lack of food in the camps in remarkably similar terms. Wiesel, for instance, describes spending his last days in the camp "in total idleness. With only one desire: to eat. I no longer thought of my father, or my mother. From time to time, I would dream. But only about soup, an extra ration of soup" (dans une oisiveté totale. Avec un seul désir: manger. Je ne pensais plus à mon père, ni à ma mère. De temps à autre, il m'arrivait de rêver. D'un peu de soupe. D'un supplément de soupe).[86] For Levi, hunger, too, becomes the chief source of his suffering. Describing how one form of suffering is replaced by another, he writes how as winter and its attendant cold gave way to spring, "we became aware of our hunger; and repeating the same error, we now say: 'if it was not for the hunger!...' But how could one imagine not being hungry? The Lager *is* hunger: we ourselves are hunger, living hunger" (noi ci siamo accorti di avere fame: e, ripetendo lo stesso errore, così oggi diciamo: «Se non fosse della fame! ...» Ma come si potrebbe pensare di non aver fame? il Lager è la fame: noi stessi siamo la fame, fame vivente).[87] Elsewhere, Levi describes the "holy grey slab which seems gigantic in your neighbor's hand, and in your own hand so small as to make you cry" (del sacro blocchetto grigio che sembra gigantesco in mano del tuo vicino, e piccolo da piangere in mano tua).[88]

Hunger is also a central theme in Eustathios' account: once the city had fallen, he describes how he was taken prisoner and lived for eight days in a garden, and how

> during this time we saw no pure bread, but we tried to satisfy our stomach's longing for good food with cakes of bran baked in the ashes of a fire, and we did not have the good fortune to experience even a sniff of wine. After this we obtained a very small quantity of a liquid masquerading as wine, literally only a drop at a time of this, and some leavened bread and a few other things.

---

[85] Kam. *ex. Thess.* 57.6–8.

[86] Wiesel (2006: 113; 2007: 196).

[87] Levi (1959: 83; 1989: 126).

[88] Levi (1959: 36; 1989: 63–64).

1 BEARING WITNESS IN EUSTATHIOS OF THESSALONIKI'S ...

ἐν αἷς ἄρτον ἀκραιφνῆ οὐδὲ εἴδομεν, ἀλλὰ τοῖς ἐκ πιτύρων ἐγκρυφίαις ἐχρεωκοποῦμεν τὸ τῆς γαστρὸς λίχνον, καὶ οἴνου δὲ μηδὲ μύρισμα εὐτυχήσαντες, μετ᾽ αὐτὰς καὶ οἴνου ψευδωνύμου ἠρέμα καὶ ὡς ἀληθῶς κατὰ στράγγα μετέσχομεν καὶ ἄρτου δὲ ζυμίτου καὶ ἄλλων δέ τινων.[89]

Though the hunger after the capture of Thessaloniki was the result of the short-term chaos of events after the catastrophe rather than part of an organized long-term strategy of genocidal liquidation, hunger plays as prominent a role in Eustathios' depiction of the suffering of the Greeks as it does in the witness testimony of Wiesel and Levi. He further describes how their captors "would give the wretched citizen a tiny loaf only as big as the circle formed by the thumb and forefinger at an exorbitant price" (Ἀρτίδιον γοῦν περιηγμένον ὡς εἰς κρίκον, ὅσον ἂν ἀντίχειρ καὶ λιχανὸς διαγράψαιεν, τριῶν χαλκῶν στατήρων ἀπεδίδου τῷ ἐλεεινῷ πολίτῃ, μόλις ὀβολοῦ ἀξιούμενον).[90] Like Levi, Eustathios' description of the size of the piece of bread is rendered in starkly sensory terms: both focus on how small the bread looks, how small it feels in the hand, thus bringing a tactile realness to the description of their starvation: "there was a rumour that the abominable Armenians were defiling our loaves, but even this was not enough to prevent these beggars from accepting what was on sale, for a terrible need brushed aside what was normally proper, and made us concentrate only on the most urgent necessities" (Οἱ δὲ ἐξώλεις Ἀρμένιοι λέγεται καὶ καταμιαίνειν ἡμῖν τοὺς ἄρτους. Ἦν δὲ αὐτὸ οὐχ ἱκανὸν τοὺς πτωχοὺς ἐκτρέπειν τοῦ προσίεσθαι τὰ πωλούμενα· δεινὴ γὰρ ἡ ἀνάγκη τὸ καθῆκον ἐκκρούεσθαι καὶ μόνου τοῦ πρὸς βίαν ἐγκειμένου γίνεσθαι).[91] In parallel with Levi's description of the polluted water the Jewish prisoners attempted to drink in Auschwitz and Kaminiates and the Thessalonians drank after the sack of the city in 904, so too does Eustathios describe in similar terms the grotesque food available to the Greek prisoners — bread mixed with feces—and the overwhelming hunger which compelled them to eat it anyway.[92]

---

[89] Eust. *capta Thess.* 110.25–28.

[90] Eust. *capta Thess.* 124.28–30.

[91] Eust. *capta Thess.* 126.11–14.

[92] Agamben articulates the ontological and political consequences of such starvation, citing Sofsky: "Power abrogates itself in the act of killing. The death of the other puts an end to the social relationship. But by starving the other, it gains time. It erects a third

30   A. J. GOLDWYN

As beings who experience bodily privation, and the necessity of sating those needs for survival, there is a certain logic to Eustathios', Levi's, and Wiesel's focus on these aspects of their time as prisoners.[93] As records of their experiences, they naturally focus in their writing on the things which consumed most of their time and mental energy during their time as prisoners. Such is the strength of this need that, as Wiesel describes, "Our first act as free men was to throw ourselves onto the provisions. That's all we thought about. No thought of revenge, or of parents. Only of bread" (Notre premier geste d'hommes libres fut de nous jeter sur le ravitaillement. On ne pensait qu'à cela. Ni à la vengeance, ni aux parents. Rien qu'au pain).[94]

As with hunger and thirst, so too does the cold—represented by clothing and its lack—form an important marker of the suffering of the victims both in Auschwitz and Thessaloniki. Terrence Des Pres terms what inmates in the concentration camps and Soviet gulags experienced "radical nakedness," by which he means in the literal sense that the inmates were stripped of their clothes but, from a biopolitical perspective (though Des Pres never uses the term), suggests the centrality of the body in a world in which all other forms of interiority are stripped: "To pass from civilization to extremity means to be shorn of the elaborate system of relationships – to job, class, tradition and family, to groups and institutions of every kind – which for us provides perhaps ninety percent of what we think we are. [...] They lost, in other words, the delicate web of symbolic identifications available to men and women in normal times."[95] In such a world, all that remains is the durability of the body: "For survivors, there is nothing else."[96]

Wiesel describes the stripping of inmates upon arrival at the camp: "Our clothes were to be thrown on the floor at the back of the barrack. There was a pile there already. New suits, old ones, torn overcoats, rags. For us it meant true equality: nakedness. We trembled in the cold" (On

---

realm, a limbo between life and death" (Sofsky 1993: 200), as cited in Agamben (2017: 792). Sofsky's phrase is much-discussed, as, for instance, in Weber (2012: 94).

[93] For the importance of food and hunger from the perspective of Nazi policy and survivor experience, see Gerhard (2015) and Singer-Genis (2011).

[94] Wiesel (2006: 115; 2007: 199).

[95] Des Pres (1976: 182).

[96] Des Pres (1976: 182).

1 BEARING WITNESS IN EUSTATHIOS OF THESSALONIKI'S ... 31

devait jeter ses vêtements au fond de la baraque. Il y en avait déjà là-bas tout un tas. Des costumes neufs, d'autres vieux, des manteaux déchirés, des loques: celle de la nudité. Tremblant de froid).[97] For Levi, too, the cold is a defining feature of life in the camp, as, for instance, to name but one of the dozens of mentions of the cold, his description of a typical night: "The dream of Tantalus and the dream of the story are woven into a texture of more indistinct images: the suffering of the day, composed of hunger, blows, cold, exhaustion, fear and promiscuity" (Il sogno di Tantalo e il sogno del racconto si inseriscono in un tessuto di immagini più indistinte: la sofferenza del giorno, composta di fame, percosse, freddo, fatica, paura e promiscuità).[98]

Levi continues by noting that, because of the cold, the struggle to find suitable clothing is a significant preoccupation of the prisoners:

> It has to be realized that cloth is lacking in the Lager and is precious; and that our only way of acquiring a rag to blow our noses, or a pad for our shoes, is precisely that kind of cutting off the tail of a shirt at the time of the exchange. If the shirt has long sleeves, one cuts the sleeves; if not, one has to make do with a square from the bottom, or by unstitching one of the many patches.

> Bisogna sapere infatti che in Lager la stoffa manca, ed è preziosa; e che l'unico modo che noi abbiamo di procurarci uno straccio per nettarci il naso, o una pezza da piedi, è appunto quello di tagliare un lembo di camicia al momento del cambio. Se la camicia ha le maniche lun- ghe, si tagliano le maniche; se no, ci si accontenta di un rettangolo dal fondo, o si scuce una delle numerose rappezzature.[99]

This desperate attempt to get better clothes, to mend the clothes they had, to find warm clothes in winter and lighter clothes in the summer resulted in prisoners assembling whatever attire they could.

Wiesel, too, describes the necessity of clothing and how this desperation resulted in odd assemblages. On the morning after the Nazis fled Auschwitz, the prisoners began to wander around the grounds "in all kinds of strange garb; it looked like a masquerade. We each had put on

---

[97] Wiesel (2006: 35; 2007: 79).

[98] Levi (1959: 67; 1989: 106–107).

[99] Levi (1959: 88; 1989: 131).

32   A. J. GOLDWYN

several garments, one over the other, to better protect from the cold. Poor clowns, wider than tall, more dead than alive, poor creatures whose ghostly faces peeked out from layers of prisoner's clothes! Poor clowns!" (d'étranges accoutrements: on eut dit une mascarade. Chacun avait enfilé plusieurs vêtements l'un sur l'autre pour mieux se protéger du froid. Pauvres saltimbanques, plus larges que hauts, plus morts que vivants, pauvres clowns dont le visage de fantôme sortait d'un monceau de tenues de bagnards! Paillasses).[100]

In Thessaloniki, too, clothes were both essential and hard to come by. Eustathios describes at length the struggles of the Thessalonians to find suitable clothing as a way to cover both their modesty and provide for their protection against the cold:

> At that time, a man might find some chance scrap of cloth thrown away by a woman after her period, or some other similar things with which the streets were littered, and would stitch them together as best he could to make some sort of a napkin, and willy-nilly he would wear this unaccustomed garment. Others devised confections of wool cardings, and joining them together managed to cover belly and back and lower parts, wrapping round their waists a rotting dirty rope of the bark of lime trees or something similar, while elsewhere the bare skin of their bodies was exposed to the air.

> Ἦν τις τότε καὶ ὃς ῥάκος εὑρηκὼς παρερριμμένον που ἀποκαθημένης τυχὸν ἢ καὶ ἀλλοῖον, ὁποίοις πολλοῖς αἱλεωφόροι κατέστρωνται, καὶ συχνὰ τοιαῦτα συγκεκρουκὼς εἰς ῥαφήν, ὡς εἶχε, καὶ λεντίου τρόπον συσκευασάμενος, ἄκων ἤθελε τὴν ἀσυνήθη περιστολήν. Ἄλλοι συνθέματα ἐρεᾶ μαδῶντα ἐξευρίσκοντες καὶ ἐναπτόμενοι, κοιλίαν μὲν καὶ ῥάχιν καὶ τὰ κατωτέρω ἔσκεπον, σχοίνῳ σαθρᾷ καὶ ῥυπαρᾷ τῇ ἐκ φιλύρας ἢ τοιοῦδέ τινος περιζωσάμενοι, τὰ δὲ λοιπὰ ἐν χρῷ κατ' αὐτὴν σάρκα τῷ ἀέρι γινόμενοι.[101]

Nor was it just clothes that covered the body that were of concern to the captives. Wiesel recalls that upon his arrival at the camp, "we all sat down in the mud. But we had to get up whenever a Kapo came in to check if, by chance, somebody had a new pair of shoes. If so, we had to hand them over. No use protesting; the blows multiplied and, in the end, one still had to hand them over" (peu à peu, nous nous assîmes tous dans

---

[100] Wiesel (2006: 83; 2007: 152). The passage is discussed in Schwarz (1998: 236).
[101] Eust. *capta Thess.* 122.11–18.

1 BEARING WITNESS IN EUSTATHIOS OF THESSALONIKI'S ...   33

la boue. Mais il fallait se lever à tout instant, chaque fois qu'entrait un kapo pour voir si quelqu'un n'avait pas une paire de chaussures neuves. Il fallait les lui remettre. Rien ne servait de s'y opposer: les coups pleuvaient et, à la fin du compte, on perdait quand même ses chaussures).[102] Levi offers a more poignant concern: "And do not think that shoes form a factor of secondary importance in the life of the Lager. Death begins with the shoes" (Né si creda che le scarpe, nella vita del Lager, costituiscano un fattore d'importanza secondaria. La morte incomincia dalle scarpe).[103] Eustathios also mentions that despite the variety of ways in which they dressed themselves, "there was one touch of holiness, albeit a distressing one, which they all shared, for as they stood upon the floor of the sacred building, all of them were set free from the footwear upon their feet" (εἶχον δέ τι πάντες οὗτοι σεμνόν, εἰ καὶ ἄλλως λυπηρόν· λελυμένοι γὰρ ἐκ τῶν ποδῶν πάντες τὰ ὑποδήματα τῶν τοῦ ἁγίου οἴκου κρηπίδων ἐγίνοντο).[104]

Eustathios also describes the many ways in which the prisoners attempted to cover their heads, though he notes that this was only possible for those with serious head wounds: "The heads of most were uncovered, a cunning imposition forced upon us by the Latins so that we might all be dressed the same" (Αἱ δὲ κεφαλαὶ τοῖς μὲν πλείοσιν ἦσαν ἀκατακάλυπτοι, τῶν Λατίνων οὕτω σκευωρησάντων, ὡς ἂν ἔχοιμεν τὸ ὁμόστολον).[105] The Latins also made a point of cutting the hair and beards of the prisoners:

> They concentrated their schemes against the heads of each of us, showing an equal dislike both for our long hair and for our long beards. It was not possible to see a man or a boy of any station in life who did not have his hair cut short all around; [...] and then a man who had been shaved in this way would also be relieved of his beard. It became a rarity to see in any place a Greek whose head was still untampered with.
>
> ἐπεβούλευον ταῖς ἑκάστων κεφαλαῖς, ἐπίσης μισοῦντες τούς τε ἀκειρεκόμας, τούς τε βαθυπώγωνας. Καὶ οὐκ ἦν ἰδεῖν ἄνδρα εἴτε καὶ παῖδα τύχης τῆς οἱασοῦν μὴ κουρίαν κατὰ κύκλον. [...]καὶ αὐτίκα καὶ ὀπώγων ἠλαφρύνετο

---

[102] Wiesel (2006: 38; 2007: 84).

[103] Levi (1959: 31; 1989: 56).

[104] Eust. *capta Thess.* 124.15–16.

[105] Eust. *capta Thess.* 122.22–24.

34   A. J. GOLDWYN

τῷ οὕτω κειραμένῳ ἀνδρί. Καὶ ἦν πάντῃ σπάνιον ἰδεῖν ἄνδρα Ῥωμαῖον ἄρτιον τὴν κεφαλήν.[106]

Wiesel notes simply that, when he arrives at Auschwitz, the Nazi barbers' "clippers tore out our hair, shaved every hair on our body" (tondeuses arrachaient les cheveux, rasaient tous les poils du corps).[107] Levi similarly describes the process of induction for new prisoners in the camp as requiring the shaving of their hair, yet his more detailed description of the scene places it in a broader narrative context which demonstrates the hair cutting as one element in a series of events meant to strip away the last vestiges of humanity and individuality in the new arrivals, thus removing from the prisoners the idea that there is any hope of sovereign protection from the harsh physical realities of bare life:

> We have to undress and make a bundle of clothes in a special manner [...]; we must take off our shoes. [...] Someone comes with a broom and sweeps away all the shoes[. ...]The outside door opens, a freezing wind enters and we are naked and cover ourselves up with our arms. [...] Now the second act begins. Four men with razors, soap-brushes and clippers burst in; [...] in a moment we find ourselves shaved and sheared.

> poi bisogna spogliarsi e fare un fagotto degli abiti in un certo modo, [...] togliersi le scarpe[. ...] Viene uno con la scopa e scopa via tutte le scarpe[. ...] La porta dà all'esterno, entra un vento gelido e noi siamo nudi e ci copriamo il ventre con le braccia. [...] Adesso è il secondo atto. Entrano con violenza quat- tro con rasoi, pennelli e tosatrici[; ...] ci agguantano e in un momento ci troviamo rasi e tosati. Che facce goffe abbiamo senza capelli.[108]

The image Eustathios depicts of the Thessalonians under Norman occupation, then, conforms to the image of prisoners in the concentration camps: wearing rags in which they all look the same, with no shoes, their hair and beards cut to create a uniform look that strips each of the prisoners of their individuated humanity, subject to beatings, starvation, cold, and thirst. Indeed, Eustathios notes that seeing the prisoners

---

[106] Eust. *capta Thess.* 130.34–132.1; 132.6–8.

[107] Wiesel (2006: 35; 2007: 80).

[108] Levi (1959: 16–17; 1989: 35–36).

was "a sight which was both painful to look upon and hard to describe. On the one hand they seemed like shadows floating up from the nether regions, and on the other hand they no longer had their natural appearance, because their blood, which made their ruddy colour blossom, had either retreated deep within them or had completely left them" (θέαμα καὶ δυσπρόσοπτον καὶ δυσείκαστον, τὸ μὲν οἷς ἐκ νερτέρων ἥκειν ἐδόκουν σκιαί τινες ἀΐσσουσαι, τὸ δ' ὅτι τοὺς κατὰ φύσιν χαρακτῆρας οὐκέτ' εἶχον διὰ τὸ ἔνδον που ἀναχωρῆσαι ἢ καὶ τέλεον ἐκλιπεῖν τὸν φίλιον χυμόν, δι' οὗπερ ἐξανθεῖ τὸ ἐρύθημα).[109] He continues, moreover, by writing that

> it was not easy to recognize among them even a very dear friend, and each asked another who he was, since in their pallor they were all alike and did not differ in any respect. One could go into the churches and observe such figures there also, and ask who among them was the rich man, who the poor and so on, and which were the priests, who was the reader and who happened to be of the laity. They all had the same appearance and form.

> Ἦν οὖν ἔργον γνωρίσαι καὶ τὸν πάνυ ἐν τούτοις φίλτατον· καὶ ἕκαστος ἀνηρώτα ἕκαστον, ὅστις ποτ' ἂν καὶ εἴη, διὰ τὸ κατὰ χρόαν πάντων ὁμοειδὲς καὶ διάφορον κατ' οὐδέν. Ἰτέον ἐπὶ τὰς ἐκκλησίας καὶ θεωρητέον τοὺς τοιούτους καὶ ἐκεῖ καὶ ἐρωτητέον τίς ἄρα ἐν τούτοις ὁ πλούσιος ἢ πένης, καὶ ὅσα τοιαῦτα. Ἀλλὰ τίς μὲν ἱέραται; τίς δὲ ἐπὶ τοῦ ἀναγινώσκειν ἐστί; τίς δὲ τοῦ λαοῦ εἶναι εἴληχε; Πάντες γὰρ εἶδος ἓν καὶ μορφὴ ἡ αὐτή.[110]

Like concentration camp prisoners, the Thessalonians "wandered about, going hither and thither in their hunger and thirst, and shivering because of the lack of clothing" (ἀπελήλαντο καὶ περιενόστουν ὧδε κἀκεῖ πεινῶντες, διψῶντες, ῥιγοῦντες, ὅτι καὶ γυμνοί).[111] Indeed, Eustathios describes how "these things, and many more like them, particularly their state of nakedness and starvation, drove the majority of the captives to a point where their spirits were near death from such harassment" (ταῦτα δὴ καὶ τούτων

---

[109] Eust. *capta Thess.* 124.3–6. Levi describes how he was summoned to one of the camp nurses, who "shows the other [nurse] the deep impression that his finger leaves in the pale flesh, as if it was wax" (fa notare all'altro la profonda incavatura che il dito lascia nella carne pallida, come nella cera) (1959: 50; 1989: 82).

[110] Eust. *capta Thess.* 124.6–8.

[111] Eust. *capta Thess.* 120.31–32.

36 A. J. GOLDWYN

ἕτερα πλείω, καὶ μάλιστα τὸ γυμνιτεύειν καὶ ὁ λιμός, τοὺς πολλοὺς τῶν αἰχμαλώτων θροοῦντα καὶ διαταράττοντα ἕως καὶ εἰς θάνατον τὰς ψυχάς).[112]

As perhaps among the only truly universal experiences of humankind, hunger, thirst, and cold are the forms of suffering to which their audiences might most easily relate and thus are markers of the transformation from *bios* to *zoē*. The affective power of such appeals draws from what Shoshana Felman and Dori Laub call the "imaginative capability of perceiving history – what is happening to others – *in one's own body*, with the power of sight (of insight) usually afforded only by one's own immediate physical involvement."[113] Through direct reference to the suffering and privations of their own bodies, Wiesel, Levi, and Eustathios call sympathetic attention to the physical hardship of their plights by emphasizing the universal experiences of hunger, thirst, and cold, recalling the reader to their own experiences of privation and then asking them to imagine those privations multiplied. But in thinking about how witness testimony can be conceptualized as a cohesive genre inclusive of works as different as *Night*, *If This Is a Man*, and the *Capture of Thessaloniki* (as well as other works that are the result of yet other atrocities), the substantial similarity in the rhetoric of sympathetic imagination demonstrates that these authors were drawn to similar sets of affective states, both because these were the real circumstances of their experience and because of the emotional force of their depiction. Robert Eaglestone calls this "reading's affect," and defines it as a "process of identification: it is the grasping, or comprehending, of another's experience as one's own by 'putting one's self in their place'."[114] This is especially necessary for Holocaust narratives, since "the events of the Holocaust are often described as incomprehensible, as ungraspable to those who did not experience them."[115] Thus, the focus on the body can create an affective identification for a reader who must assimilate events far beyond the scope of their own experience—and thus comprehension: because of the extreme nature of Holocaust testimony, "there is no stock of shared life experiences which the author and the reader share, which, as a consequences, excludes the reader."[116]

[112] Eust. *capta Thess.* 138.9–11.

[113] Felman and Laub (1992: 108); italics in original.

[114] Eaglestone (2004: 16).

[115] Eaglestone (2004: 16).

[116] Eaglestone (2004: 16–17).

1 BEARING WITNESS IN EUSTATHIOS OF THESSALONIKI'S ... 37

Indeed, Eaglestone notes that Primo Levi understood how even words that have conventional and familiar meanings are nevertheless inadequate for describing the experiences of those in the camps, citing *If This Is a Man*:

> As our hunger is not that feeling of missing a meal, so our way of being cold has need of a new word. We say 'hunger,' we say 'tiredness,' 'fear,' 'pain,' we say winter and they are different things. They are free words, created and used by free men who live in comfort and suffering in their homes. If the Lagers had lasted longer a new, harsh language would have been born; and only this language could express what it means to toil the whole day in the wind, with the temperature below freezing, wearing only a shirt, cloth jacket and trousers, and in one's body nothing but weakness, hunger and knowledge of the end drawing near.

> Come questa nostra fame non è la sensazione di chi ha saltato un pasto, così il nostro modo di aver freddo esigerebbe un nome particolare. Noi diciamo «fame», diciamo «stanchezza», «paura», e «dolore», diciamo «inverno», e sono altre cose. Sono parole libere, create e usate da uomini liberi che vivevano, godendo e soffrendo, nelle loro case. Se i Lager fossero durati più a lungo, un nuovo aspro linguaggio sarebbe nato; e di questo si sente il bisogno per spiegare cosa è faticare l'intera giornata nel vento, sotto zero, con solo indosso camicia, mutande, giacca e brache di tela, e in corpo debolezza e fame e consapevolezza della fine che viene.[117]

Thus, even if the familiar cannot be known, it perhaps remains the only possible meaning of cultivating a shared identification between writer and reader, since, beyond the demands of the body, everything else that these people experienced is entirely beyond the experiential capacity of the audience. Ruth Franklin, for instance, cites an article by George Steiner—the Jewish philologist and literary critic whose parents fled Austria due to increasing antisemitism in the early 1920s—on a Holocaust diary:

> In the Warsaw Ghetto a child wrote in its diary: 'I am hungry, I am cold; when I grow up I want to be a German, and then I shall no longer be hungry, and no longer cold.' And now I want to write that sentence again: 'I am hungry, I am cold; when I grow up I want to be a German, and

---

[117] Levi (1959: 144; 1989: 204), as cited in Eaglestone (2004: 17).

38   A. J. GOLDWYN

> then I shall no longer be hungry, and no longer cold.' And say it many
> times over, in prayer for the child, in prayer for myself.[118]

Of all the words from that child's diary, Steiner picks up on that sentence which, simply and directly, articulates these two fundamental aspects of the human experience of bare life: hunger and cold. And because he identifies with them, he identifies with the child: he wants to write those words over and over, while retaining the first-person pronoun, thus putting himself linguistically, emotionally and, in his telling, spiritually, within the experience of physical privation.

If part of the rhetoric of witness testimony is its focus on the easily relatable experiences of the body, an equally if not more affecting aspect of these authors' narratorial strategy is their focus on the uniqueness of those forms of suffering that are beyond the imaginative horizon of their audience. This violence came in myriad forms, and indeed part of the pathos of the genre comes from the sheer variety of the forms of violence, the juxtaposition between the victims' ability to endure it and the reader's inability to do so, multiplied further by those moments in which these horrific levels of everyday violence are punctured by a particularly shocking example. Indeed, Levi himself admits that before his arrival in the Lager, "to kill and to die seemed extraneous literary things to me" (e uccidere e morire mi parevano cose estranee e letterarie).[119] That is, like his audience, before Auschwitz, he was familiar only with the suffering he read about in books, much like the readers of his own testimony. Unlike them, however, he had become familiar with it experientially.

Wiesel, for instance, describes the regularity of beatings both before their arrival to the camp and during the duration of their stay. In particular, he emphasizes how quickly the prisoners adjust to this new situation. This is exemplified by the first instance of beating in *Night*, when a woman in the cattle car begins screaming. At first, "she received several blows to the head" (lui asséna plusieurs coups sur la tête), which seem to shock Wiesel, who adds, "blows that could have been lethal" (des coups à la tuer).[120] By the end of the journey, however, despite her

---

[118] Franklin (2011: 8); for which, see Steiner (1984: 258).

[119] Levi (1959: 169; 1989: 231).

[120] Wiesel (2006: 26; 2007: 66).

continued screams, "no one felt like beating her anymore" (on était fatigué de la batter"),[121] he writes—because of the other hardships of their journey: "The heat, the thirst, the stench, the lack of air, were suffocating us" (La chaleur, la soif, les odeurs pestilentielles, le manque d'air nous étouffaient, mais tout cela n'était rien, comparé à ces cris qui nous déchiraient).[122] By the next morning, Wiesel simply notes "around five o'clock in the morning, we were expelled from the barrack. The Kapos were beating us again, but I no longer felt the pain" (vers cinq heures du matin, on nous expulsa de la baraque. Des «Kapos» nous frappaient de nouveau, mais j'avais cessé de sentir la douleur des coups).[123] And yet, the frequency with which such beatings are narrated allows for some of the most poignant moments in the narrative, notably two instances in which Wiesel watches his father being beaten:

> And he began beating him with an iron bar. At first, my father simply doubled over under the blows, but then he seemed to break in two like an old tree struck by lightning. I had watched it all happening without moving. I kept silent. In fact, I thought of stealing away in order not to suffer the blows. What's more, if I felt anger at that moment, it was not directed at the Kapo but at my father. Why couldn't he have avoided Idek's wrath? That was what life in a concentration camp had made of me...

> Et il se mit à frapper avec une barre de fer. Mon père ploya d'abord sous les coups, puis se brisa en deux comme un arbre desséché frappé par la foudre, et s'écroula. J'avais assisté à toute cette scène sans bouger. Je me taisais. Je pensais plutôt à m'éloigner pour ne pas recevoir de coups. Bien plus: si j'étais en colère à ce moment, ce n'était pas contre le kapo, mais contre mon père. Je lui en voulais de ne pas avoir su éviter la crise d'Idek. Voilà ce que la vie concentrationnaire avait fait de moi...[124]

Levi, too, is matter of fact in his depiction of the beatings; upon arriving in the camp: "we new arrivals instinctively collect in the corners, against the walls, afraid of being beaten" (noi ultimi venuti ci raduniamo istintivamente negli angoli, contro i muri, come fanno le pecore, per sentirci

---

[121] Wiesel (2006: 26; 2007: 66).
[122] Wiesel (2006: 26; 2007: 66).
[123] Wiesel (2006: 36; 2007: 82).
[124] Wiesel (2006: 109; 2007: 54).

40   A. J. GOLDWYN

le spalle materialmente coperte).[125] During the course of his year in the camp, however, he learns that there is no avoiding the beatings, that they are "beaten every day" (ogni giorno percossi),[126] that some of the kapos "beat us from pure bestiality and violence, but others beat us when we are under a load almost lovingly" (ci percuotono per pura personalità e violenza, ma ve ne sono altri che ci percuotono quando siamo sotto il carico, quasi amorevolmente)[127] and that at yet other times the kapos "have no scruples about beating us up without a reason" (di quelli stessi che non hanno ritegno ad abbatterci a pugni senza perché).[128] Eventually, he comes to realize that "it is better to be beaten, because one does not normally die of blows, but one does of exhaustion, and badly, and when one grows aware of it, it is already too late" (non sa ancora che è meglio farsi picchiare, perché di botte in genere non si muore, ma di fatica sì, e malamente, e quando uno se ne accorge è già troppo tardi).[129]

Just so does Eustathios learn the same lesson: "So long as we were only pushed and struck and subjected to indignities to which we were not accustomed, we considered ourselves fortunate in our experience and prayed that this state of affairs might continue" (Καὶ ὠθούμενοι μὲν καὶ κονδυλιζόμενοι καὶ ὕβρεις οὐ τὰς ἐν ἔθει μανθάνοντες μακάριον τὸ πάθος ἐκρίνομεν, εὐχόμενοι ἐν τοιούτοις εἶναι), since the alternative was being stabbed to death.[130] Eustathios frequently returns to this theme, noting elsewhere the intersection of widespread hunger and physical abuse:

One could also survey the food which each person ate, and see that there was nothing to be got from one's fellow citizens, since all were equally famished. Some of the Latins offered us their small change, which enabled us to live in a meagre fashion, but the majority exercised their bounty only by calling anyone who begged a wretch, and by giving them an insult as their bread and a blow to season it with.

Σκοπητέον καὶ τὰς ἑκάστων τροφὰς καὶ γνωστέον ὡς ἐκ τῶν συμφυλετῶν μὲν οὐκ ἦν ὅ, τι καὶ λάβοιεν, πάντων ἐξ ἴσου πεινώντων, τῶν δὲ Λατίνων

[125] Levi (1959: 36; 1989: 61–62).
[126] Levi (1959: 141; 1989: 200).
[127] Levi (1959: 74; 1989: 114).
[128] Levi (1959: 114; 1989: 165).
[129] Levi (1959: 155; 1989: 216).
[130] Eust. *capta Thess.* 106.24–26.

1 BEARING WITNESS IN EUSTATHIOS OF THESSALONIKI'S ... 41

ὀλίγοι μέν τινες ἐχορήγουν ὀβολοὺς τοὺς παρὰ σφίσιν, ὅθεν ἦν γλίσχρως ἀποζῆν, οἱ δὲ πλείους διάβολον ἐπικαλοῦντες τὸν ἐπαιτοῦντα, τοῦτο δὴ τὸ παρ' αὐτοῖς εὐχορήγητον, ὕβρεις ἐδίδουν ὡσεὶ καὶ ψωμόν, καὶ κόνδυλον ὄψον ἐπ' αὐταῖς.[131]

More often than not, however, Eustathios describes both the regularity and the senselessness of the beatings, as when the Latins would find a Greek on the street, they "spat on us, tripped us and poured insults upon us" (συναντῶντες γοῦν κατέπτυον, ὤθουν, ἐσκέλιζον, κατέβρεχον ὕβρεις)[132] and if a Latin on horseback passed by, he "would not miss the opportunity of trampling the man and beating him, spurring on his horse to leap at him" (οὐκ ἂν ἐκεῖνος φείσαιτο καταπατῆσαι καὶ συντρῖψαι τὸν ἄνθρωπον, κεντρίζων τὸν ἵππον εἰς κατασκίρτημα),[133] and if someone smiled or laughed, "they would clench their fingers into a fist, and raising their hands would strike us repeated blows" (καὶ τοίνυν δακτύλους εἰς γρόνθον ἔπτυσσον καὶ τὴν χεῖρα γογγυλίζοντες ἐρρύθμιζον πὺξ πλήττειν).[134]

Perhaps the greatest difference between Auschwitz and Latin-occupied Thessaloniki was the function of the camp as biopolitical space. In Auschwitz, death was the end goal, and forced labor merely the by-product of that agenda. For Thessaloniki, however, plunder and conquest were the end goal, and death was the by-product. This essential difference—as with the metaphorical use of the smoke imagery in Eustathios and its horrific literality in Wiesel—points to the essentially qualitative and quantitative differences between the two spaces. And yet, regardless, both Thessaloniki and Auschwitz were sites of mass carnage, and the sight of the piles of corpses provides perhaps the most horrific and meaningful similarity among the witness testimonies from both events. Levi describes the abandoned camp through the frame of the dead:

> The ground was too frozen to dig graves; many bodies were piled up in a trench, but already early on the heap showed out of the hole and was shamefully visible from our window.

---

[131] Eust. *capta Thess.* 124.17–22.

[132] Eust. *capta Thess.* 130.2.

[133] Eust. *capta Thess.* 130.8–10.

[134] Eust. *capta Thess.* 130.22–23.

42   A. J. GOLDWYN

La terra era troppo gelata perché vi si potessero scavare fosse; molti cadaveri furono accatastati in una trincea, ma già fin dai primi giorni il mucchio emergeva dallo scavo ed era turpemente visibile dalla nostra finestra.[135]

After the passing of a few days, "the pile of corpses in front of our window had by now overflowed out of the ditch" (il mucchio di cadaveri, di fronte alla nostra finestra, rovinava ormai fuori della fossa),[136] and then again, a few days later, "we lay in a world of death and phantoms" (noi giacevamo in un mondo di morti e di larve).[137]

Eustathios, too, describes "what evils then followed" (τῶν ἐντεῦθεν κακῶν) after the sack of Thessaloniki:

As if it had not been enough when I had previously made my way on foot through the corpses still streaming with warm blood, I was now conducted on horseback among others heaped up in piles. The majority of them lay strewn before the city wall, so close together that my little horse could either find no place to set his foot, or had two or three bodies lying between his forefeet and hind legs.

Ὡς γὰρ μὴ ἀρκεσάντων τῶν νεκρῶν, δι᾽ ὧν πεζεύων ὥδευσα θερμοῖς ἀτμιζόντων αἵμασι, διὰ σωρείας ἑτέρων ἱππότης περιηγόμην, ὧν οἱ πλείους κατεστρωμένοι πρὸ τοῦ τείχους ἔκειντο οὕτω πεπυκνωμένοι, ὡς τὸ ἱππίδιον ἢ μὴ ἔχειν ὅποι γῆς θήσει πόδα ἢ ἀλλὰ μεταξὺ τῶν τε προσθίων καὶ <τῶν ὀπισθίων> ποδῶν δύο ἢ τρεῖς ἔχειν ὑποκειμένουςνεκρούς.[138]

Wiesel, too, somewhere else in Auschwitz at the same time as Levi, describes the immediate aftermath of the liberation of the camp in similar terms: "All around me, what appeared to be a dance of death. My head was reeling. I was walking through a cemetery. Among the stiffened corpses. [...] After trampling over many bodies and corpses, we succeeded in getting inside" (Autour de moi, tout paraissait danser une danse de mort. À donner le vertige. Je marchais dans un cimetière. Parmi des

[135] Levi (1959: 197; 1989: 262).
[136] Levi (1959: 201; 1989: 266).
[137] Levi (1959: 204; 1989: 270).
[138] Eust. *capta Thess.* 108.7; 7–12.

1 BEARING WITNESS IN EUSTATHIOS OF THESSALONIKI'S ... 43

corps raidis[. ...] Après avoir piétiné bien des corps et des cadavres, nous réussîmes à rentrer dans le hangar).[139]

Even within these worlds of omnipresent violence and death, these authors also draw out some paradigmatic moments of particular violence to demonstrate both the violence itself and how its specific manifestations represent the broader breakdown of social order. Among the key tropes in this regard is what Daniel Schwarz calls "the father-son tie, one that is so essential in Jewish life. Within the horrors of the Holocaust, these bonds threaten to dissolve."[140] Both *Night* and the *Capture of Thessaloniki*, for instance, describe the confusion and panic that overcomes large crowds of victims as they attempt to escape their captors or avoid death and, within this broad category, both focus on how this panic and fear separate families. Eustathios describes the Greeks' fleeing from the Normans:

> Fathers fled also, leaving behind new-born babes bereft of their mothers; and these infants wept as if begging to be rescued, but their fathers ran on without turning, and the voice of nature went unheard. And if children did turn out to join in the flight, although they did their utmost, their fathers never altered their pace, and the fear of death conquered natural love. And if a father managed to save his life, his children were trampled down and killed.

> Ἔφευγον καὶ πατέρες, νεογνὰ μητέρων ὀρφανὰ ὀπίσω ἀφιέντες. Καὶ αὐτὰ μὲν ὡς ἐπισωτηρία ἐγοῶντο, οἱ δὲ μὴ ἐπιστρεφόμενοι ἔθεον, καὶ ἡ φύσις ἐβόα κενά. Εἰ δὲ καὶ ἐξέδραμον ἐκεῖνα συμφεύγειν, αὐτὰ μὲν ἐποίουν τὸ δυνατόν, ὁ δὲ γενέτωρ ἦν ὁ αὐτὸς τοὺς πόδας, τοῦ κατὰ θάνατον φόβου τὴν φυσικὴν ἐκνικῶντος στοργήν. Καὶ εἴπερ ὁ τεκνωσάμενος περιποιήσεται ζωήν, ἀλλ᾽ αὐτὰ συμπατούμενα καὶ πρὸς βίαν σκαρίζοντα ἐξώλλυντο.[141]

More than a neutral description of events, Eustathios chooses this particular scene for its inherent pathos, an affective rhetorical strategy foregrounded by the lingering image of abandoned babies.[142] Interlaced with

---

[139] Wiesel (2006: 89; 2007: 161).

[140] Schwarz (1998: 234).

[141] Eust. *capta Thess.* 118.25–31.

[142] The death of babies rightly being considered the most emotionally affective, the particulars of how they are killed is a frequent occurrence in witness testimony; the first deaths reported in *Night*, for instance, are those of babies: "Infants were tossed into the air and used as targets by the machine guns" (Wiesel 2006: 24).

44   A. J. GOLDWYN

this narrative are Eustathios' own subtle moralizing interventions: "the voice of nature went unheard" (ἡ φύσις ἐβόα κενά), he says, and attributes the fathers' outrunning their children to "the fear of death conquer[ing] natural love" (τοῦ κατὰ θάνατον φόβου τὴν φυσικὴν ἐκνικῶντος στοργήν). Given that Eustathios was an eyewitness to the events he describes, it is almost certain that he saw scenes exactly like this play out across the city, yet, as the rest of the narrative attests, he saw all sorts of horrors, many of which he narrated in more detail and many which are left entirely unsaid. Thus, witness literature, like all kinds of literature, operates within the confines of rhetoric and generic convention. This is not to say that the events are untrue or cliché, but that people experience and narrate trauma in discursively constructed ways. Such scenes as this are not just horrifying in their own right, but somehow paradigmatic of the larger horrors for which they stand as representative examples.

Nor was the power of such a scene lost on Wiesel; one of the most affecting scenes in *Night* features the Jews leaving Auschwitz on a forced run with the retreating Germans as the Red Army advanced through Poland; those who slowed down were shot, and those who fell behind were left to die in the snow. At the end of the run, Wiesel and his father take shelter in a shed, where, soon after, "an old man appeared" (un vieillard apparut).[143] The man turns out to be Rabbi Eliahu,[144] about whom Wiesel provides perhaps the longest and certainly the most honorific description of anyone in the entire work:

A very kind man, beloved by everyone in the camp, even by the Kapos and the *blockälteste*. Despite the ordeals and deprivations, his face continued to radiate his innocence. He was the only rabbi whom nobody failed to address as 'Rabbi' in the Buna. He looked like one of those prophets of old, always in the midst of his people when they needed to be consoled. And, strangely, his words never provoked anyone. They did bring peace.

Un homme très bon, que tout le monde chérissait au camp, même les kapos et les chefs de blocks. Malgré les épreuves et les malheurs, son visage continuait à rayonner sa pureté intérieure. C'était le seul rabbin qu'on n'omettait jamais d'appeler «rabi» à Buna. Il ressemblait à l'un de

---

[143] Wiesel (2006: 90; 2007: 163).

[144] For a discussion of Rabbi Eliahu and his son and Wiesel and his father, see Schwarz (1998).

1 BEARING WITNESS IN EUSTATHIOS OF THESSALONIKI'S ...   45

ces prophètes de jadis, toujours au milieu du peuple pour le consoler. Et, fait étrange, ses mots de consolation ne révoltaient personne. Ils apaisaient réellement.[145]

This description, indeed, the scene as a whole, is not necessary for the core progression of the narrative, nor is the description of Rabbi Eliahu in any way central to any conception of the work's historiographical function; he was not an important man in the camp, and his life and death mirrored those of millions of other Jewish people during the Holocaust. But the single moment in which he appears in the text has a powerful emotional effect and contributes to Wiesel's central concern with the relationship between fathers and sons, between him and his own father, for Rabbi Eliahu had lost his son during the run and had come to inquire after him. Wiesel tells him that he had not seen him, but after Rabbi Eliahu leaves, Wiesel has an epiphany:

> But then I remembered something else: his son *had* seen him losing ground, sliding back to the rear of the column. He had seen him. And he had continued to run in front, letting the distance between them become greater. A terrible thought crossed my mind: What if he had wanted to be rid of his father? He had felt his father growing weaker and, believing that the end was near, had thought by this separation to free himself of a burden that could diminish his own chance for survival.

> Puis je me rappelai autre chose: son fils l'avait vu perdre du terrain, boitant, rétrograder à l'arrière de la colonne. Il l'avait vu. Et il avait continué à courir en tête, laissant se creuser la distance entre eux. Une pensée terrible surgit à mon esprit: il avait voulu se débarrasser de son père! Il avait senti son père faiblir, il avait cru que c'était la fin et avait cherché cette séparation pour se décharger de ce poids, pour se libérer d'un fardeau qui pourrait diminuer ses propres chances de survie.[146]

Wiesel the narrator is particularly affected by this scene because it reminds him of his own relationship with his father, and how the necessities of survival force individuals to compromise yet another of the Ten Commandments, the core values around which their lives were organized outside the Lager. In a broader way, Rabbi Eliahu's son represents all sons

---

[145] Wiesel (2006: 90, 163).
[146] Wiesel (2006: 91; 2007: 164–165).

46   A. J. GOLDWYN

in the camp, and the unique iteration of their actual individual experience also represents the breakdown of the fundamental unit of civilization, the family, as represented by the strongest of bonds within it, that of father and son.

Wiesel narrates a thematically similar scene immediately after this one: the next morning, he writes, the remaining Jews board trains moving further from the front, and there they meet Meir Katz "the strong one, the sturdiest of us all" (l'homme fort, le plus solide de nous tous).[147] But Meir Katz had lost the will to live: "His son had been taken from him during the first selection but only now was he crying for him. Only now did he fall apart. He could not go on. He had reached the end" (Son fils lui avait été enlevé lors de la première sélection, et c'est maintenant seulement qu'il le pleurait. Maintenant seulement il craquait. Il n'en pouvait plus. Au bout du rouleau).[148] The increasing frequency of the deaths of fathers and the breakdown of father–son relationships during the course of the Holocaust was surely part of Wiesel's observable reality, and thus in some sense historical. But they also belong to the seemingly opposite categories of rhetoric and narrative strategy, since they also reflect Wiesel's central preoccupation within both his lived experience of Auschwitz and his narrative of that experience, namely his relationship with his own father.

Indeed, Wiesel artfully deploys the death scenes of these peripheral fathers and sons to accentuate the central drama of his own experience—how to keep his father alive—and to build the emotional stakes for his father's eventual death. Over the course of the few days after the death of Rabbi Eliahu and Meir Katz, Wiesel's father began to suffer from an illness from which he would not recover. He persists, however, in sharing his food with his father, and one of the inmates tells him:

> Don't forget you are in a concentration camp. In this place, it is every man for himself, and you cannot think of others. Not even your father. In this place, there is no such thing as father, brother, friend. Each of us lives and dies alone. Let me give you good advice: stop giving your ration of bread and soup to your old father. You cannot help him anymore.

[147] Wiesel (2006: 102; 2007: 180).
[148] Wiesel (2006: 102; 2007: 181).

N'oublie pas que tu es dans un camp de concentration. Ici, chacun doit lutter pour lui-même et ne pas penser aux autres. Même pas à son père. Ici, il n'y a pas de père qui tienne, pas de frère, pas d'ami. Chacun vit et meurt pour soi, seul. Je te donne un bon conseil: ne donne plus ta ration de pain et de soupe à ton vieux père. Tu ne peux plus rien pour lui.[149]

Like Eustathios, Wiesel turns to the scene of fathers and sons becoming separated from one another during a mad dash because this is something he had seen and experienced during his time as an inmate. Also like Eustathios, Wiesel includes this scene because, in addition to representing their physical suffering, it also represents a larger principle of slave life: the breakdown of family bonds and the degradation of the universally normative value of honoring one's parents, and the all-important focus on food in a world of universal mass starvation.

For Wiesel, however, this scene has an added aspect absent from the *Capture of Thessaloniki*: the pathos of witness testimony is created through the same kind of discursive effects as all works of narrative, whether fiction or nonfiction and, in the case of *Night*, Wiesel builds this pathos through careful thematization and plotting. This is not to say that his work is less true on this account; the selection and ordering of real events brings out a moral truth alongside the historical one.

As he enters the camp, he sees his mother and sister sent to die in the crematoria, the major action of the narrative in Auschwitz concern his and his father's attempts to keep one another alive, and the text concludes with increasingly concentrated instances of fathers and sons betraying each other and dying, culminating in the death of his own father. These experiences were real, and in no way does the self-conscious emplotment of these kinds of themes detract from the authenticity, verisimilitude, or veracity of the narrative. Rather, it is through them that Wiesel is able to convey the emotional truth of the events which, to him is the central concern of his work. Although the reception of the *Capture of Thessaloniki* has focused almost exclusively on its historical value, reading it in parallel with *Night* reveals that Eustathios was similarly less concerned with historical comprehensiveness or utility and more concerned with transmitting the emotional truth of his experience, and marshals his narrative accordingly.

---

[149] Wiesel (2006: 110; 2007: 192–193).

1.4 Eustathios as Witness: Narrating the Personal in Byzantine Historiography

Eustathios' and Wiesel's *apologiae* are perhaps the first point of shared comparison between them in that both wrestle with the question of how to narrate horrors that are, almost by definition, beyond the affective capacity of language to articulate.[150] This is a question Wiesel wrestles with at length in the preface to *Night*, writing, for instance,

> I also knew that, while I had many things to say, I did not have the words to say them. Painfully aware of my limitations, I watched helplessly as language became an obstacle. It became clear that it would be necessary to invent a new language. But how was one to rehabilitate and transform words betrayed and perverted by the enemy? Hunger—thirst—fear—transport—selection—fire—chimney: these words all have intrinsic meaning, but in those times, they meant something else. [...] All the dictionary had to offer seemed meager, pale, lifeless. Was there a way to describe the last journey in sealed cattle cars, the last voyage toward the unknown?

> J'avais trop de choses à dire, mais pas les mots pour le dire. Conscient de la pauvreté de mes moyens, je voyais le langage se transformer en obstacle. On aurait dû inventer un autre langage. Trahie, corrompue, pervertie par l'ennemi, comment pouvait-on réhabiliter et humaniser la parole? La faim, la soif, la peur, le transport, la sélection, le feu et la cheminée: ces mots signifient certaines choses, mais en ce temps-là, elles signifiaient autre chose. [...] Les mots existants, sortis du dictionnaire, me paraissaient maigres, pauvres, pâles. Lesquels employer pour raconter le dernier voyage dans des wagons plombés vers l'inconnu?[151]

---

[150] For the problems and possibilities of the Holocaust as "unspeakable," see Trezise (2001).

[151] Wiesel (2006: 2–3; 2007: 11–12). Levi has a similar realization, though in the context of being a prisoner rather than in recording the event; upon seeing the naked bodies and shaved faces of the other inmates on their arrival in Auschwitz, he writes: "Then for the first time we became aware that our language lacks words to express this offence, the demolition of a man" (Allora per la prima volta ci siamo accorti che la nostra ingua manca di parole per esprimere questa offesa, la demolizione di un uomo) (Levi 1959: 21; 1989: 41–42). The passage is discussed at length in Fletcher (2016: 35) See also Levi (1959: 144; 1989: 204).

1   BEARING WITNESS IN EUSTATHIOS OF THESSALONIKI'S ...   49

In writing about Wiesel and others writing about the Holocaust, Alvin Rosenfeld argues that it is the affective response to the writer's perceived inability to communicate coupled with the existential imperative to do so that is the defining element of such literature, over and above any shared formal, structural, or generic aspects—more even than content: "What really is involved here is the deep anguish and immense frustration of the writer who confronts a subject that belittles and threatens to overwhelm the resources of language itself. [...] Yet to indulge in silence is to court madness or death. At just those points where, through some abiding and still operative reflex of language, silence converts once more into words – even into words about silence – Holocaust literature is born."[152] In his own way, Eustathios similarly describes the emotional consequences of the limits of language:

> Our recent experience has revealed a situation which, as much as any other in history, a person who had not been exposed to it, and was far removed from its dangers, might describe as major in its importance, unfortunate, terrible, abominable, unbearable, grievous, bringing tears to the eyes, and so on. But a person who was, so to speak, wound up in its net and, like us, trapped in the affair, would perhaps not find it so easy to sum up the disaster.

> Ἔφηνε καὶ ὁ καθ' ἡμᾶς ἄρτι χρόνος, εἴπερ τις ἕτερος τῶν πάλαι, ὑπόθεσιν, ἢν ἀπαθὴς μὲν ἄνθρωπος καὶ μακρὰν ἑστὼς τοῦ κατ' αὐτὴν κινδύνου μεγάλην εἴποι ἂν καὶ βαρυσύμφορον καὶ πάνδεινον καὶ ἀπευκταίαν καὶ οὐ ῥᾷον φορητὴν καὶ πολυπενθῆ καὶ δακρύων πηγὰς ἐθέλουσαν καὶ τοιαῦτά τινα, ὁ δὲ δικτύῳ, ὅ φασι, σπειραθεὶς καὶ καθ' ἡμᾶς ἐνειληθεὶς τῷ πράγματι ἴσως μὲν οὐκ ἂν εὐπορήσοι πρὸς ἀξίαν ὀνομάσαι τὸ κακόν.[153]

In proposing a distinction between the historian who can make sense of events and the witness who cannot do so, Eustathios presages similar problems in Holocaust Studies; Thomas Trezise, for instance, argues that "for Holocaust survivors who have chosen to bear witness, the fundamental challenge has always consisted in finding the language least poorly suited to the communication of 'that which happened' without creating

---

[152] Rosenfeld (1980: 14–15).

[153] Eust. *capta Thess.* 4.24–28, For the distinction between the ἀπαθὴς ἄνθρωπος (the person who was not there or the person who did not suffer) and the eyewitness, see below (243).

50   A. J. GOLDWYN

therewith the impression that what happened 'made sense'."[154] Thus, it follows that both writers foreground the limits of language in describing their trauma, and both emphasize that though they might use some stylistic flourishes, in the words of Wiesel, "substance alone mattered" (la substance seule comptait),[155] a sentiment echoed by Eustathios as well, if, ironically, in somewhat more florid rhetoric: "And just as such a person would not dance playfully in the midst of sorrows, so he would not add ornaments to his language. [...] He will make use of other narrative techniques with restraint" (Ὁ δ' αὐτὸς οὐδ' ἂν παίζοι χορεύων ἐν πένθεσιν, ὁποῖον δή τι καὶ τὸ πάνυ καλλύνειν τοὺς λόγους [...] Καὶ τὰ ἄλλα δὲ συγγραφικὰ εἴδη σωφρόνως μεταχειριεῖται).[156] Both writers make explicit claims about how their own rhetoric must match the subject matter of their narratives, and both agree that limits on figurative language enhance the truth value of their works—a limit they themselves transgress to great dramatic effect repeatedly throughout their narratives.

Eustathios even clarifies just what he means by this unadorned style. Returning again to the theme of *pathos*, he writes that.

> if such a person does succeed in defining this disaster in words, we would probably call it the darkening of a great light, and he will not be affecting a pathetic style (because pathos ought to be represented in a different language), but one which nevertheless expresses the magnitude of the calamity.

> εἰ δὲ καὶ δυνήσεται κατευστοχῆσαι τοῦ κακοῦ πρὸς ἔπος, ἐρεῖ ἂν αὐτὸ οὐκ ἀπεικότως φωστῆρος μεγάλου ἀφάνειαν, οὐδὲν μὲν ἐκεῖνος λέγων πρὸς πάθος (ἐχρῆν γὰρ ἄλλοις ὀνόμασιν ἐνταῦθα παθήνασθαι), τῷ μεγαλείῳ δὲ ὅμως ὀρθῶς ἐπιβάλλων τοῦ δυσπραγήματος.[157]

Eustathios' claim that whosoever is able to describe the pathos of the disaster in words must do so without using a pathetic style may perhaps seems paradoxical. Indeed, John Melville-Jones, the translator of the *Capture of Thessaloniki*, elaborates in a note on the passage that.

---

[154] Trezise (2013: 75).
[155] Wiesel (2006: 4; 2007: 14).
[156] Eust. *capta Thess.* 2.26–28.
[157] Eust. *capta Thess.* 4.30–6.3.

pathos, *pathetike lexis* and kindred expressions are used only very occasionally by Greek and Roman writers and their meaning is hard to define. The 'pathetic' style is, however, mentioned in Aristotle's *Rhetoric* (1408a-b), where it is described as the style of an angry man when there has been an outrage; the listener will, it is said, always sympathize with a person who speaks in a pathetic manner (*pathetikos*) in such a situation, even if he says nothing.[158]

Though he concedes that "some passages in Eustathios' work might deserve to be called 'pathetic' in this sense, [...] they are few in number, and the greater part of it, particularly when he is engaging in an uncomplicated narrative, would not."[159] He then rightly suggests that Eustathios might have argued against using the pathetic style because "he may have wished his description of the more dreadful moments of the capture of the city to be taken as straightforward and unadorned expressions of feeling, needing no literary artifice to produce the desired effect on the listener, and this will have been part of his claim to writing a 'syngraphy' rather than a 'history.'"[160] Eustathios here is making a stylistic distinction between two kinds of narratable events. On the one hand, there are events which are not so terrible, and therefore, in order to make them seem much worse than they actually were, the writer must adopt a pathetic style that (deceptively) heightens the emotional stakes of the event. But the sack of Thessaloniki was not one such event: there is no need for this hyperbole (though Eustathios notes that we should not blame a layman for using it anyway), nor is there a need to beautify or ornament (καλλύνειν) it: rather, he asserts that since the conquest of the city was so horrible that even narrating it in the most unadorned and straightforward manner will still convey the horrific magnitude of the event even without the aid of the pathetic style.

Eustathios' decision to narrate these events by foregrounding the suffering he experienced himself and observed in others was not inherently obvious. John Kaminiates' *Capture of Thessaloniki* forms an implicit intertext, as do both Homeric (the fall of Troy) and biblical accounts

---

[158] Melville-Jones (1988a: 163). The difficulties of translating Holocaust literature has itself become a subject of scholarly inquiry as part of the broader discourse of "untranslatability," for which, see Arnds (2015).

[159] Melville-Jones (1988a: 164).

[160] Melville-Jones (1988a: 164).

52   A. J. GOLDWYN

(the fall of Jerusalem). As a learned citizen of Thessaloniki, a Homeric scholar, and a high-ranking church official, Eustathios would be familiar with these exempla. Yet, in the twelfth-century literary circles of which Eustathios was a leading member, his decision stands out for being unique among other historiographical depictions of city-sacking.[161] Indeed, Aglae Pizzone suggests that Eustathios was aware of how "different authorial strategies [were] available to someone willing to retell the capture of a city, depending on whether he was present at the event or not. [...] While the available narrative tools are more or less equivalent, their modulation, and in particular their affective modulation, changes."[162] Pizzone's analysis demonstrates how the author's positionality contributes to their authorial self-construction in the text. As she notes, "style is a choice among suitable options," and thus the formal, aesthetic, and generic choices an author makes are reflections of how painful memories are recollected and communicated.[163]

Eustathios' positionality as a victim of conquest and violence thus results in a text that is very different than many other works of twelfth-century historiography, in which the author was not so decisively involved in the events and not so emotionally invested in the narrative itself.[164] Many Byzantine historians punctuated their work with metaliterary or metahistorical statements, and many of them acknowledged both their artifice, their (im)precision in reporting the past, and the importance of digressions and personal speculation.[165]

---

[161] To this list, one could also add similar descriptions not in the historiographical mode at all; the twelfth-century also saw a revival of the Greek novel, dormant some thousand years. Almost all of the medieval Greek novels feature barbarians sacking Greek cities and inflicting terrible suffering on the conquered populations.

[162] Pizzone (2014: 16).

[163] Pizzone (2014: 17).

[164] See, for instance, Paolo Odorico's discussion of John Kaminiates at the intersection of genres: "Caminiatès se sert, bien entendu, de la narration historique, des techniques rhétoriques de l'*ekphrasis*, des discours intercalés qui doivent résumer la situation et relever l'emotion, mais son but n'est pas de faire de l'histoire, même s'il utilise les techniques de l'historien" (2006: 159).

[165] See, for instance, the discussion of the historiographical method in Papaioannou (2010), esp. 12–21.

The historiographical debate between the eyewitness and the historian proper is a debate as old as the genre,[166] but it is significant that even as judgmental and digressive a historian as Eustathios' older near-contemporary John Zonaras never places himself and his own experience at the center of the work in the same way; indeed, in their introduction to his *History*, the translators note that "we know little about his life" save some positions he held in the imperial and ecclesiastical hierarchies. What little he does say himself is not integrally connected to the history; he describes himself as an author of history, not a participant in it. The witness, by contrast, foregrounds the self in the dramatic action; as a form of life-writing, explication of the witness' emotional and affective experience of the events is the organizing principle of the work, as opposed to the historian, for whom the events themselves are central, even if the historian frequently interjects his or her opinions. In this regard, Stratis Papaioannou's discussion of the relative importance of precision or accuracy in Byzantine historiography is telling: "In his *prooimion*, Zonaras surprisingly declares that his historiography will *not* be characterized by precision (akribeia),"[167] Eustathios, by contrast, "claims that he has narrated, in a manner of precision (*akriboun*), what has befallen their city."[168] The difference is not necessarily the distinction between the eyewitness and the historian—eyewitness observation has conferred authority on historical texts since Thucydides—but the personal trauma of those who suffer from the events.

[166] See, for instance, Thucydides' discussion of his method of including his own eyewitness record, reports of those who witnessed events he did not, and his own invention (1.22).

[167] Papaioannou (2010: 30).

[168] Papaioannou (2010: 20). Which is not to say that the account is without rhetorical flourish. Indeed, Eustathios seems to filter his experience through literary analogies; Anthony Kaldellis notes that "in Eustathios' account of the capture of Thessalonike (1185), we find far more Greek gods and creatures of mythology mentioned by name than actual Byzantines or Normans. Yet we should not dismiss this as uniformly affected and artificial. [...] Depending on their usage, the names of heroes and gods (as of Old Testament figures) allude to parallels and models by which readers could better understand or judge their present-day counterparts" (Kaldellis 2008: 246). Comparisons of the present circumstances to past exempla is part of the process of making the incomprehensible comprehensible. Levi, in fact, does something similar in *If This Is a Man* when he compares his hell to that of Ulysses in Dante's *Inferno*, an argument made most prominently and at book-length in Sodi who argues that "Levi's message is often clearest when filtered through Dante" (1990: 2).

54   A. J. GOLDWYN

Thus, while a prefatory apologia such as that appended to the *Capture of Thessaloniki* is a standard structural feature of Byzantine historiographical (and other genres of) writing, the actual content of these prefaces matters: Eustathios' preface marks his work out as a different kind of writing than that of Zonaras or other contemporary writers such as Nikephoros Bryennios or Constantine Manasses. Indeed, many of these prefaces rearticulate standard conventional ideas about Byzantine historiographical principles (that is, the difficulty of the subject matter, the proper limits of invention, and the role of adorned or unadorned language and style).[169] Yet none of the (for instance) other nine historians/chroniclers Iordanis Grigoriadis groups with Eustathios references the role of the historian as an eyewitness, as a participant, as someone who experienced the events which they are narrating.[170] This marks Eustathios as a different kind of writer than the others, who were arguing about epistemological rather than ontological questions.

The difference among these various writers lies in the relationship of the historian to the events; indeed, Eustathios makes such a distinction himself: "The capture of a city is generally reported in the same manner, whether it is recorded by a historian or by an eyewitness. But no narrator will necessarily deal with everything which has occurred, and the events which are selected will not be treated in the same way by both kinds of writer" (Πόλεων ἁλώσεις ἱστορούμεναι εἴτε συγγραφόμεναι μεθόδοις διοικοῦνται ὡς τὰ πολλὰ ταῖς αὐταῖς. Οὔτε δὲ ἁπάσας τὰς ἐπιβαλλούσας ἠναγκασμένως ὁ γράφων διαχειρίσεται, οὐδὲ μὴν τὰς ἀμφοτέρωθι χρηστὰς ὡσαύτως διοικονομήσεται).[171] Thus, though the two types of writers are writing about the same fabula, the stories they tell will be different.[172] What distinguishes the two types of narratives is precisely the positionality of the authors: historians (ἱστορούμεναι) on the one hand and eyewitnesses (συγγραφόμεναι) on the other. In an appendix to his translation of the *Capture of Thessaloniki* and in greater detail in "Eustathios as a Source

[169] For which, see Lilie (2014).

[170] Grigoriadis (1998).

[171] Eust. *capta Thess.* 2.11–14. For which, see Odorico (2006: 161).

[172] For functional definitions of these narratological terms, see De Jong and Nünlist (2007: xii–xiii) and Bal (2009): "A *narrative text* is a text in which an agent relates ('tells') a story in a particular medium[. ...] A *story* is a fabula that is presented in a certain manner. A *fabula* is a series of logically and chronologically related events that are caused or experienced by actors" (5).

1 BEARING WITNESS IN EUSTATHIOS OF THESSALONIKI'S ... 55

for Historical Information," Melville-Jones writes that Eustathios is here making a careful distinction between these two kinds of writers.[173] He makes the case that Byzantine writers used such terms interchangeably, but that Eustathios is rearticulating a distinction that

> goes back to the opening words of the *Histories* of Herodotos, and of Thoukydides's account of the Peloponnesian War. Herodotos described his work as a *historie*, while Thoukydides, although he was not trying to make a point of emphasizing the difference between himself and his predecessor, use *syngrapho* to describe what he was doing. Since the latter has always been thought of as the first and the greatest of those historians who wrote about the events of their own lifetimes, in which they had themselves played a part, the word came in due course to be used quite frequently of a historian of contemporary events, as opposed to one who writes of things which happened before his own time.[174]

Thucydides, however, never centers his own experience in the same way as Eustathios does, and perhaps this major difference between what Thucydides (and those following in that tradition) were doing and what Eustathios was doing. The historians, Eustathios says, are ἀπαθῶς γράφων, which Melville-Jones translates as "without personal involvement," but which is here perhaps better translated, given Eustathios' focus on the horrors of war, as "without suffering" (α-privative plus παθῶς), a reconsideration which perhaps gets to the heart of how personal trauma influences the narrative.[175]

Eustathios emphasizes this again a few lines later, noting that "he is speaking without having been affected by the disaster" (οἷα ἔξω πάθους λαλῶν), though πάθους here could also contain the element of

---

[173] For the former, see Melville-Jones (1988a, 2017).

[174] Melville-Jones (1988a: 230).

[175] Eust. *capta Thess.* 2.14. For Melville-Jones translating *pathos* as suffering, see the opening passage of this chapter, where παθαινομένην is translated "suffer." So too elsewhere, as in "the sufferings of the city" (κακῶν ἡ πόλις ἔπαθεν) (4.21). Pathos is a notoriously polysemous word, so it follows that it should also be difficult to translate. Martin Hinterberger's discussion of the term (2010: 126–128) notes that "that which happens to someone (or that which befalls someone)" is the word's primary meaning, thus substantiating the idea of experiential relation for which Melville-Jones aims; in parallel, however, he proposes that "the Byzantine term that is the closest equivalent of emotion is *pathos*," thus excluding the possibility that the term is purely experiential and offering its affective element as an equally crucial component.

56 A. J. GOLDWYN

personal suffering.[176] By contrast, "the eyewitness, on the other hand, who has been touched by the disaster should dwell upon the catastrophe alone" (ὁ δὲ καὶ συγγραφόμενος καὶ χρωτισθεὶς τῷ κακῷ πάντων ἐκείνων προσάψεται μὲν ἀναγκαίως μόνῳ πλεονάζειν ὀφείλων τῷ πάθει).[177] Here, too, Eustathios uses the word πάθει, suggesting the centrality of suffering. Eustathios returns several more times to the term in the introduction, each time distinguishing between the two kinds of writers: if "the writer is a layman, there is no reason to blame him if he exaggerates the pathos of his story" (τοῦ λαοῦ μὲν γὰρ ὤν, τίνα ἂν ἔχοι ψόγον εἰς κόρον παθαινόμενος).[178] Yet, he adds, this layman "would not add ornaments to his language in a manner more suited to a lament upon the stage when relating a tale of gloomy disasters" (πάνυ καλλύνειν τοὺς λόγους κομμωτικῶς ἐν σκυθρωποῖς πάθεσι).[179] This, too, he contrasts with how "a historian who was not involved in the action" (τὸν ἀπαθῆ ἱστορικὸν), where ἀπαθῆ can also mean did not suffer,[180] that is by avoiding the narrative embellishments "contrived by those writers who have played no part in the catastrophe" (οἱ ἔξω πάθους τεχνάζονται), but again couched in the language of suffering: πάθους.[181] According to Eustathios, then, the major feature which distinguishes the narrative of the historian from the eyewitness is that the latter's focus is on emotion, specifically his suffering. Having established the difference between these two kinds of writers, Eustathios begins his narrative proper by establishing his own positionality with regards to the two and thus perhaps also refining his model of what makes a witness: "the present work will soon show which kind of a writer I am" (εἰ τοίνυν καὶ ἐμὲ τοιονδέτινα ἡ παροῦσα συγγραφὴ διαδείξει, αὐτίκα φανεῖται), he writes, but again, in light of Melville-Jones' remarks in the appendix and Eustathios' own comments in his introduction, could perhaps better be translated as "what kind of witness I am": that is, in the Thucydidean vein of contemporary eyewitness.[182] Immediately after, however, he clarifies how his positionality will influence his

[176] Eust. *capta Thess.* 2.17.

[177] Eust. *capta Thess.* 2.22.

[178] Eust. *capta Thess.* 2.23–24.

[179] Eust. *capta Thess.* 2.27–28.

[180] Eust. *capta Thess.* 2.29–4.1.

[181] Eust. *capta Thess.* 4.2.

[182] Eust. *capta Thess.* 4.3–4.

narrative in this way: "The account which follows will of necessity begin with the catastrophe itself, since it is not possible for one who was himself part of these pitiful events not to treat them in tragic fashion" (Ἄρξεται δὲ ὁ ὑποτεταγμένος λόγος ἀναγκαίως ἐξ αὐτοῦ πάθους, ὅτι μηδὲ ἦν τὸν ἐν ἐλεεινοῖς ὄντα μὴ τραγικεύσασθαι τό γε πρῶτον).[183] Unlike a history, which unfolds according to chronology, the organizing principle of Eustathios' *Capture of Thessaloniki*, as of witness literature as a whole, is suffering. This is the kind of *syngrapheus* he is.

1.5 "Alors, histoire?" Genre and Byzantine Witness Literature Revisited

Eustathios was personally involved in the events he describes, and the driving force of his work is his desire to convey to his audience the depth of the catastrophe that has befallen the city, which he does by describing his own experiences and emotional states within the context of the events in which he finds himself. While there is no doubt that issues such as the dating of these texts, their historicity, and their accuracy as regards otherwise known particulars of the past are essential aspects for both understanding the texts in and of themselves and for the contributions they can make to a broader understanding of Byzantine history writ large, these works, considered as works of witness literature, offer something perhaps more rare and more valuable: insight into how Byzantine victims and witnesses of atrocity felt about those experiences, how they conceived of and remembered them, and how they coped with the aftermath of such experiences. In thus questioning the genre of the *Capture*, Paolo Odorico asks: "Alors, histoire? Oui, bien sûr, mais tout autant littérature."[184] While Odorico's underlying assumption that literature and history are discrete categories is problematic, the larger point Odorico is aiming at holds: the *Capture* is not a work whose primary purpose is to convey seemingly objective information about the past, but "il s'agit plutôt du désir d'exprimer un sentiment, qu'il soit de rage, de découragement, de tristesse ou de détresse, et c'est aussi un façon de parvenir à parler de la violence à travers ses manifestations; pour nos écrivains c'est

---

[183] Eust. *capta Thess.* 4.4–5.

[184] Odorico (2006: 51).

58   A. J. GOLDWYN

la nécessité de manifester leurs émotions qui prime."[185] Thus, articulating emotions, psychology, and subjective experience is the underlying theme that binds these otherwise disparate works together.

These generic distinctions have been further elaborated in Holocaust Studies. Robert Eaglestone, arguing that "literature seeks literary answers, history historical answers, and philosophy philosophical answers," points to how the nature of their inquiry becomes the determining aspect rather than their formal properties or subject matter.[186] For Eaglestone, moreover, the question of genre is not an abstract discussion, but rather is fundamental to the proper understanding of such texts: "Genres form horizons of understanding, interpretation, and reading, where text, readership, and knowledge come together. A genre is a way of looking at a text, implicitly connecting texts with contexts, ideas, expectations, rules of argument, and so on. Genres are vital in the act of creating texts and, more importantly, the knowledges from which texts emerge."[187] That is to say, genre prepares a reader to expect certain kinds of rhetorical figures and thus preconditions certain kinds of interpretive acts. Thus, while these works share a concern with narrating the events of the past, they are not historiography in the traditionally understood sense in which that term is used to describe the Byzantine historians, and categorizing them as such, while it allows certain aspects of the past to come to light, obscures other, perhaps more important aspects, about them, in particular their focus on the subjective individual experience, something which, by definition, is anathema to Byzantine historical writing.

If the categorization of a witness literature in Byzantium is controversial within Byzantine Studies, it is also by no means non-controversial within Holocaust Studies. Eaglestone, for instance, in the same paragraph, questions the validity of the application of the genre category to previous works: "In the case of Holocaust testimony, it is certainly true that there are accounts of horrors before (Pliny on Pompeii for example, Conrad's narrator Marlowe on the 'Grove of Death' in the Congo Free State) and it is true that these are testimonial. But they tend to be subsumed into, for example, historical accounts (an eyewitness report, an oral history) or literary accounts (novels). Literary, historical, and philosophical writing

---

[185] Odorico (2006: 51).

[186] Eaglestone (2004: 6).

[187] Eaglesetone (2004: 6).

1 BEARING WITNESS IN EUSTATHIOS OF THESSALONIKI'S …

since 1945 are involved in a new genre, testimony, with its own form, its own generic rules, its own presuppositions."[188] Though this might seem to exclude Eustathios, Eaglestone leaves open the possibility of considering earlier works as part of this tradition in some way and, therefore, of being subject to similar means of literary, historical, and philosophical investigation for explicating them: "In light of this, pre-Holocaust texts […] can perhaps be reread or reimagined or recriticized as works of testimony, and new similarities and differences can be analyzed."[189]

For others, it is not so much the content of the texts themselves as it is the reading of these texts in the long shadow the Holocaust continues to cast over the present moment. In *A Double Dying: Reflections on Holocaust Literature*, Alan Rosenfeld argues that this burden must fall on the reader as well: we should, he writes, "begin to see that Holocaust literature is an attempt to express a new order of consciousness, a recognizable shift in being. The human imagination after Auschwitz is simply not the same as it was before. Put another way, the addition to our vocabulary of the very word Auschwitz means that today we *know* things that before could not even be imagined."[190] Rosenfeld argues that as a result of the knowledge of the existence of Auschwitz, "the imagination comes to one of its periodic endings."[191] But, he suggests, the existence of an end point means that we "also stand at the threshold of new and more difficult beginnings," where the ethics of reading, thinking, and writing about the past carry the same ethical demands as all other considerations about the paradoxically simultaneous value and fragility of human life and the vital importance of remembering.[192]

Eustathios himself pauses his narration to ask: "Why should I continue to write of these things, when not even complete books written at length would be enough for me to describe sufficiently for my eager readers the woes which overtook us?" (Τί μοι πλείω γράφειν, ἔνθα οὐδὲ βίβλοι ὅλαι μακραὶ ἱκανώσαιειν ἄν με εἰς αὔταρκες διαγράφοντα τοῖς φιληκόοις ὁποῖα ἡμῖν συνέπεσε;)[193] Part of the answer may be in his answer that

---

[188] Eaglestone (2004: 6).

[189] Eagleston (2004: 6).

[190] Rosenfeld (1980: 13).

[191] Rosenfeld (1980: 13).

[192] Rosenfeld (1980: 13).

[193] Eust. *capta Thess.* 140.8–9.

60   A. J. GOLDWYN

"if anyone seems to desire to learn more concerning the omens of future events which appeared, let him now pay attention as we set them forth briefly in our history" (εἰ δέ τις ἐνταῦθα ποθῶν φαίνεται προσιστορηθῆναι καὶ οἷα σήματα τῶν μελλόντων προυφάνη, ἀκουέτω βραχυλογικῶς καὶ ταῦθ' ἡμῶν εἰς ἱστορίαν ἐκτιθεμένων).[194] His discussions of omens, however, covers only the next six paragraphs, which seems insufficient in light of the overall length and orientation of the work, suggesting the possibility of alternate reasons for its composition. Much witness literature takes as a foundational principle the Freudian idea that writing such documents is a way of healing psychological trauma through the order-bringing process of writing.[195] Elie Wiesel opens his preface to the 2008 re-publication of *Night* with this very question: "Why did I write it? Did I write it so as *not* to go mad" (Pourquoi l'ai-je écrit? Pour ne pas devenir fou), he asks, suggesting the function of witnessing as a means of psychic healing; and yet, he continues,

> or, on the contrary, to *go* mad in order to understand the nature of madness, the immense terrifying madness that had erupted in history and in the conscience of mankind? Was it to leave behind a legacy of words, of memories, to help prevent history from repeating itself?

> ou, au contraire, pour le devenir et ainsi mieux comprendre la folie, la grande, la terrifiante, celle qui avait autrefois fait irruption dans l'histoire et dans la conscience d'une humanité oscillante entre la puissance du mal et la souffrance de ses victimes? Était-ce pour léguer aux hommes des mots, des souvenirs comme moyens pour se donner une meilleure chance d'éviter que l'Histoire ne se répète avec son implacable attrait pour la violence?[196]

Though he never gives a firm answer, none of the questions could reasonably be answered with anything like to help create a positivist history of the events. Indeed, Horace Engdahl argues that one of the primary purposes of witness testimony is to refute history; they are antithetical to one another: "Historical explanations are a kind of anodyne. Feelings

---

[194] Eust. *capta Thess.* 140.12–14.

[195] See, for instance, MacCurdy (2007) for the claims of writing as therapy. For an outline of the principles of "psychoanalytic listening" as it pertains to Holocaust literature, see Budick (2015: 37–39).

[196] Wiesel (2006: 5; 2007: 9–10).

aroused by human suffering are put to rest when what happened is seen as a logical sequence of cause and effect and therefore to some extent inevitable [...] the witness talks of something that is incomprehensible in the hope that someone else will make it possible to understand and with certainty that any explanation must be rejected as inadequate," a process he describes as "the revolt against explanations."[197]

Conceiving of Eustathios' oration as a work of witness testimony rather than history foregrounds the subject and the personal over the objective and authoritative. This theoretical approach thus reframes those aspects of the narrative that are central and which are marginal or, to use Melville-Jones' own word, "essential."[198] It also opens up new ways of understanding the function and significance not just of Eustathios' text, but of the genre of witness testimony in Byzantium as a whole. Indeed, the reader of history and the reader of witness testimony may not agree on what aspects of a particular narrative are "essential" at all. For instance, the recent volume *Reading Eustathios of Thessaloniki*, perhaps the most comprehensive work on his voluminous and diverse literary output, features several chapters devoted to his commentaries on the *Iliad* and his commentary on the iambic pentecostal hymn, fitting subject matter if Eustathios is conceived of primarily as a scholar, politician, and archbishop.[199] Indeed, the one article in the volume explicitly devoted to the *Capture of Thessaloniki* exemplifies a trend in Byzantine Studies of miscategorizing the work: John Melville-Jones' "Eustathios as a Source for Historical Information" conceives of the *Capture* as Eustathios' "one historical work,"[200] which he later characterizes as his "only work of purely historical writing."[201] He thus examines the work not from a position of identification (as defined by Eaglestone), that is, trying to understand what the author wanted to relate about his subjective experience as a civilian victim of conquest and prisoner of war, but instrumentally, that is, for how it can aid the modern scholar in reconstructing an objective past. This can result in readings that are often insensitive

---

[197] Engdahl (2003: 10).

[198] Melville-Jones (2017: 301).

[199] For which, see Pontani et al. (2017).

[200] Melville-Jones (2017: 299).

[201] Melville-Jones (2017: 303).

62   A. J. GOLDWYN

and misguided. Melville-Jones, for instance, criticizes Eustathios' sense of historical perspective, arguing that he.

> spent much more time than might seem necessary on creating a biographical picture of the recently deceased emperor Andronikos I Komnenos. [… This] allowed Eustathios to vent his anger on a man of whose manner of life he evidently disapproved. [...] As an extreme example, we can see the way in which, allowing his imagination to become heated, he describes the relationship of the sixty-five year old emperor with the very young bride, Agnes-Anna of France, whom he married after arranging for the death of Alexios, to whom she had been betrothed. Of course, the reason for this 'marriage' was to prevent Agnes-Anna from being married off to any rival for power, and Andronikos certainly never lacked other female company.[202]

As a historian looking at the work of another historian, this information is unreliable, reflecting, as it does, the subjective perspective of the writer; Melville-Jones faults Eustathios for "allowing his imagination to become heated," since the positivist historian must remain at all times dispassionate and objective. Indeed, Melville-Jones faults Eustathios' own interpretation of the events through which the Byzantine writer lived; it was not, Melville-Jones suggests, due to Andronikos' sexual desire for a twelve-year-old bride ("Andronikos certainly never lacked other female company") but for purely political reasons: "of course," he writes, "it was to secure an alliance with the French."[203] Melville-Jones' substitution of Eustathios' personal impression for his own political reasoning is explicable in light of Melville-Jones' conception of Eustathios' work as history, a genre defined by its rhetoric of objectivity in which the unverifiable personal speculations of the historian are invalid. Indeed, in this light, Melville-Jones' decision as translator of the work to render *pathos* under the neutral framework of "experience" or similar rather than the more emotionally freighted "suffering" is suggestive of a view of the work as historiography rather than testimony; the process of translation thus becomes not just a transfer of languages from Greek to English but also of genre and interpretation from affective witness testimony into objective (and thus dispassionate) historiography.

---

[202] Melville-Jones (2017: 302).

[203] Melville-Jones (2017: 302–303).

1 BEARING WITNESS IN EUSTATHIOS OF THESSALONIKI'S ... 63

Eustathios, too, notes that "the events which followed could not be related by anyone without some omissions, but we can at any rate feel confident of being able to record at least a selection of them" (τὰ δ' ἐντεῦθεν οὐκ ἂν μέν τις φράσαι, ὡς μηδέν τι ἐλλεῖψαι· ὅσα δέ ἐστιν ἐπιλέξασθαι, αὐχήσωμεν ἂν καὶ αὐτοὶ ἱκανοὶ ἔσεσθαι ἀπογράψασθαι).[204] and in his description of the sufferings of the Greeks, he again notes how he must omit some—indeed, perhaps most—of the horrors he witnessed: "such were the evils – and this is only a selection from among countless others – which we suffered that day" (καὶ τοιαῦτα μὲν ἡμῖν τὰ ἡμερινὰ κακά, ἐξ ἀπείρων μέτρια καθιστορῆσαι).[205] Eustathios acknowledges the impossibility of a completely comprehensive account, and therefore also implicitly acknowledges that within his own narrative he has selected the events he chooses to narrate. He never explicitly mentions or theorizes his principles of selection in this regard, but it is significant that there is so much overlap between the kinds of scenes he chooses to narrate and those narrated by Wiesel and by the extensive *apologia* in which he describes how emotion and experience shape the eyewitness narrator's response in opposition to that of the historian. Though their circumstances were different, each appealed to a similar set of rhetorical and narratological strategies, plot conventions, and type scenes that arouse readers' sympathies. Physical privation through hunger, thirst, cold, and beatings arouse in the reader a sense of empathy, for the reader recognizes in these descriptions feelings to which they can relate but which are experienced by the narrator with far greater intensity. At the other extreme, the authors present scenes which are beyond the capacity of the reader to imagine, thus forcing the reader to recognize in the narrative levels of violence and depravity which shock by their very unrelatability.

In the introduction to his translation of the *Capture of Thessaloniki*, Melville-Jones argues that "when we come to consider the form of the whole work, it is not possible to classify it under the heading of any literary genre."[206] After a long discussion of the possible genres under which the work could be classified and the dismissal of each of these

---

[204] Eust. *capta Thess.* 120.22–24.

[205] Eust. *capta Thess.* 136.20.

[206] Melville-Jones (1988b: xi).

64   A. J. GOLDWYN

possibilities,[207] Melville-Jones concludes: "There is in fact nothing to be gained by attempting to define the form of a work which was constructed in circumstances as unusual as those in which this one was written."[208] And yet, Melville-Jones' inability to locate the genre is perhaps more the result of the genres he is willing to consider, all of which were formally prescribed Byzantine genres. In this sense, Wiesel may have been correct in arguing that "our generation invented a new literature, that of testimony," insofar as a work that was previously uncategorizable now fits into a widely accepted contemporary genre.

The question of genre and categorization has been a fraught one in Byzantine Studies since the discipline's founding, insofar as classification by genre was the principle around which Byzantine literature was organized. While Margaret Mullett's 1992 article "The Madness of Genre" exploded what she described as the long-standing and influential perception that Byzantium was a "time-free zone, in which generic prescriptions are eternally played and replayed" with the result that "Byzantine literature never really changed," she does not reject genre outright.[209] Thus, though critical of the concept of genre when considered as temporally immutable and artistically constraining, Mullett nevertheless sees value in considering genre when it opens up new ways of considering texts in relation to one another and in light of the historical periods that produced them.[210] Establishing witness literature in this regard as a genre per se is thus less important than demonstrating how categorizing these works

[207] "Some sections of it can be given individual names, but there is none which fits the whole work. It is in part a *threnos*, a sort of funeral oration or *epitaphios logos* mourning the suffering of the city, but this aspect is only a minor one. It is in part a sermon [....] It is not an encomium [....] It might on the other hand be an example of [...] *psogos* ('blame' or 'invective')... but this is only part of the story, since so much of what it includes consists of a perfectly straightforward description of the events which occurred" (xi).

[208] Melville-Jones (1988b: xi).

[209] Mullett (1992: 234).

[210] Mullett (1992: 234). See also Panagiotis Roilos' *Amphoteroglossia*, in which he writes of "established approaches to Byzantine literature in terms of immutable, fixed literary categories—approaches that go back to Krumbacher's phenomenal founding of Byzantine literary studies and only very rarely have been challenged since then" (2005: 16) and, later, of "traditional approaches to medieval Greek literature, which prefer to underscore the rigidity of inherited patterns" (2005: 19).

together under the rubric of a modern category—witness literature—that did not exist in the formal schema of either Byzantines themselves or modern scholars nevertheless allows modern readers to see shared aspects of these works that had been obscured by previous ways of configuring genre taxonomies. Traditional systems of genre classification would consider these works as history, novel, oration, epistle, and monody; in this, they represent a disparate cross-section of Byzantine genres. Considering them as works of witness gives only secondary importance to the formal characteristics by which they are typically organized, prioritizing instead the relationship of author to event, the nature of the event itself, and the affective response of the author to those events. Mullet has already suggested the potential for defining these works within what she calls "Byzantine death genres," and a new configuration of them as witness literature does not obviate their consideration within their original generic categories, but demonstrates a commonality among them that only emerges when they are allowed to read across these generic boundaries.[211]

The question, then, of how to read becomes central to such concerns, and here again the ways in which scholars of the Holocaust have engaged with these issues in theory and practice can inform a similar approach within Byzantine Studies. In this regard, Shoshana Felman and Dori Laub's *Testimony: Crises of Witnessing* (1992) holds a central position as perhaps the most influential text to engage with these questions. Felman, a literary critic, and Laub, a Holocaust survivor and psychoanalyst, outlined a model at the intersection of their disciplines for modifying the tools of listening honed in psychoanalysis to the literary listening of Holocaust survivor narratives. Laub's own contribution to the chapter points explicitly to the conflict between listening as psychoanalyst and listening as historian. In "Testimony as Historical Truth," Laub describes the testimony of a woman who saw "four chimneys going up in flames, exploding" and how at a subsequent interdisciplinary conference, a debate broke out between the historians and the psychoanalysts: "The testimony was not accurate, historians claimed. The number of chimneys

---

[211] Mullett (1992: 236). This is perhaps what Roilos is suggesting when he writes that "genre innovations and variations occur not only on the level of textual structures but also on the level of discursive textures. In other words, emphasis should rather be placed on the ways in which not only structural genre laws but also certain *discursive textures* and *modalities* are assimilated into the discursive textures of other texts" (2005: 19).

was misrepresented. Historically, only one chimney was blown up, not all four."[212] Laub, however, "profoundly disagreed" with the idea of accuracy as asserted by the historians, arguing that "knowledge in the testimony is [...] not simply a factual given that is reproduced and replicated by the testifier, but a genuine advent, an event in its own right."[213] Whereas "because the testifier did not know the number of the chimneys that blew up [...] the historian said she knew nothing," Laub, listening as a psychoanalyst of trauma, "thought that she knew more."[214] Thomas Trezise has convincingly argued that "these anonymous historians collectively constitute, for Laub, little more than a convenient straw man" and that they are "mainly informed by Laub's own questionable assumptions about history as a discipline."[215] And yet, Laub's central point remains: different methods of reading prioritize different kinds of knowledge. Read as works self-consciously describing subjective emotional experience rather than as seemingly failed works of positivist histories, the accounts of Eustathios, John Kaminiates, Niketas Choniates, and others demonstrate the ways in which an author as witness articulates authentic emotional experiences through, almost paradoxically, a conventional and limited set of rhetorical practices.

Melville-Jones argues that Eustathios' "historical work is a novel mixture (κρᾶμα καινόν), a new generic category including and combining different structural elements delivered from the tradition of history and rhetoric,"[216] but what Eustathios was doing was not in fact entirely new. That these rhetorical constructs are at once broadly shared among writers of witness literature writ large and also unique to the social, historical, and literary context in which they were produced suggests that adding Eustathios of Thessaloniki's *Capture of Thessaloniki* and the several other accounts written by Byzantine eyewitnesses before and after him may yield new insights and modes of interpretation to the growing corpus of transtemporal, transnational, and translinguistic witness literature.

---

[212] Laub (1992: 59).

[213] Laub (1992: 69).

[214] Laub (1992: 63).

[215] Trezise (2013: 13).

[216] Melville-Jones (2017: 300, n.4).

Bibliography

Agamben, Giorgio. 2017. *The Omnibus Homo Sacer*. Palo Alto: Stanford University Press.

Angold, Michael. 1998. The Autobiographical Impulse in Byzantium. *Dumbarton Oaks Papers* 52: 225–257.

Arnds, Peter, ed. 2015. *Translating Holocaust Literature*. Göttingen: V&R Academic.

Bal, Mieke. 2009. *Narratology: Introduction to the Theory of Narrative*. Toronto: University of Toronto Press.

Bernard-Donals, Michael. 2016. *An Introduction to Holocaust Studies*. New York: Routledge.

Bourbouhakis, Emmanuel. 2007. 'Political' Personae: The Poem from Prison of Michael Glykas: Byzantine Literature Between Fact and Fiction. *Byzantine and Modern Greek Studies* 31 (1): 53–75.

Budick, Emily Miller. 2015. *The Subject of Holocaust Fiction*. Bloomington: Indiana University Press.

Cisney, Vernon, and Nicolae Morar, eds. 2016. *Biopower: Foucault and Beyond*. Chicago: Chicago University Press.

De Jong, Irene, and René Nünlist. 2007. *Time in Ancient Greek Narrative*. Leiden: Brill.

Des Pres, Terence. 1976. *The Survivor: An Anatomy of Life in the Death Camps*. Oxford: Oxford University Press.

Eaglestone, Robert. 2004. *The Holocaust and the Postmodern*. Oxford: Oxford University Press.

Engdahl, Horace. 2003. Philomela's Tongue: Introductory Remarks on Witness Literature. In *Witness Literature: Proceedings of the Nobel Centennial Symposium*, ed. Horace Engdahl: 1–14. New Jersey: World Scientific.

Felman, Shoshana and Laub, Dori, eds. 1992. *Testimony: Crises of Witnessing in Literature, Psychoanalysis, and History*. New York: Routledge.

Fletcher, Alana. 2016. Transforming Subjectivity: *Se questo è un uomo* in Translation and Adaptation. In *Translating Holocaust Literature*, ed. Peter Arnds, 33–44. Gottingen: V&R Press.

Foucault, Michel. 1978. *The History of Sexuality: An Introduction*, trans. Robert Hurley. New York: Vintage Books.

Franklin, Ruth. 2011. *A Thousand Darknesses: Lies and Truth in Holocaust Fiction*. Oxford: Oxford University Press.

Gaunt, Simon. 1995. *Gender and Genre in Medieval French Literature*. Cambridge: Cambridge University Press.

Geltner, Simon. 2008. *The Medieval Prison: A Social History*. Oxford: Oxford University Press.

Gerhard, Gesine. 2015. *Nazi Hunger Politics: A History of Food in the Third Reich*. Lanham, MD: Rowman and Littlefield.

Grigoriadis, Iordanos. 1998. *A Study of the Prooimion of Zonaras' Chronicle in Relation to Other 12th-Century Historical Prooimia.* Berlin: De Gruyter.

Hinterberger, Martin. 1999. *Autobiographische Traditionen in Byzanz.* Vienna: Österreichische Akademie der Wissenschaften.

―――. 2010. Emotions in Byantium. In *A Companion to Byzantium,* ed. Liz James, 123–134. Chicester: Wiley-Blackwell.

Hirsch, Marianne. 2012. *The Generation of Postmemory: Writing and Visual Culture After the Holocaust.* New York: Columbia University Press.

Kaldellis, Anthony. 2008. *Hellenism in Byzantium: The Transformations of Greek Identity and the Reception of the Classical Tradition.* Cambridge: Cambridge University Press.

Kefala, Eleni. 2020. *The Conquered: Byzantium and America on the Cusp of Modernity.* Cambridge, MA: Harvard University Press.

Konstan, David. 2007. Anger, Hatred, and Genocide in Ancient Greece. *Common Knowledge* 13 (1): 170–187.

Laub, Dori. 1992. Bearing Witness or the Vicissitudes of Listening. In *Testimony: Crises of Witnessing in Literature, Psychoanalysis, and History,* eds. Shoshana Felman and Dori Laub, 57–74. New York: Routledge.

Lauxtermann, Marc. 2014. Tomi, Mljet, Malta: Critical Notes on a Twelfth-Century Southern Italian Poem of Exile. *Jahrbuch Der Österreichischen Byzantinistik* 64: 155–176.

Levi, Primo. 1959. *If This Is a Man,* trans. Stuart Woolf. New York: Orion Press.

―――. 1986. *I sommersi e i salvati.* Torino: Einaudi.

―――. 1989. *Se questo è un uomo.* Torino: Einaudi.

―――. 2017. *The Drowned and the Saved.* New York: Simon and Schuster.

Levine, Michael. 2006. *The Belated Witness: Literature, Testimony, and the Question of Holocaust Survival.* Palo Alto: Stanford University Press.

Lilie, Ralph-Johannes. 2014. Reality and Invention: Reflections on Byzantine Historiography. *Dumbarton Oaks Papers* 68: 157–210.

MacCurdy, Marian. 2007. *The Mind's Eye: Image and Memory in Writing About Trauma.* Amherst: University of Massachusetts Press.

Marion, Esther. 2006. The Nazi Genocide and the Writing of the Holocaust Aporia: Ethics and *Remnants of Auschwitz. Modern Language Notes* 121 (4): 1009–1022.

McLellan, William. 2016. *Reading Chaucer After Auschwitz: Sovereign Power and Bare Life.* New York: Palgrave Macmillan.

Melville, Jones. 1988a. Appendix 1: Eustathios on the Writing of History. In *The Capture of Thessaloniki,* Eustathios of Thessaloniki, 230–234. Canberra: Byzantina Australiensia.

Melville, Jones. 1988b. Introduction. In *The Capture of Thessaloniki,* Eustathios of Thessaloniki, vii–xii. Canberra: Byzantina Australiensia.

Melville-Jones, John. 2017. Eustathios as a Source for Historical Information: Decoding Indirect Allusions in His Works. In *Reading Eustathios of Thessaloniki*, eds. Filippomaria Pontani et al., 299–308. Berlin: Degruyter.

Messis, Charis. 2006. La mémoire du 'je' souffrant. Construire et écrire la mémoire personnelle dans les récits de captivité. In *L'écriture de la mémoire. La littérarité de l'historiographie*, eds. Paolo Odorico, Panagiotis Agapitos, and Martin Hinterberger, 107–146. Paris: Centre d'études byzantines, néo-helléniques et sud-est européennes.

Minco, Claudio. 2011. Camp. In *The Agamben Dictionary*, ed. Alex Murray and Jessica Whyte, 41–43. Edinburgh: Edinburgh University Press.

Mullett, Margaret. 1992. The Madness of Genre. *Dumbarton Oaks Papers* 46: 233–243.

Neville, Leonora. 2018. *Guide to Byzantine Historical Writing*. Cambridge: Cambridge University Press.

Nilsson, Ingela. 2013. Nature Controlled by Artistry: The Poetics of the Literary Garden in Byzantium. In *Byzantine Gardens and Beyond*, ed. H. Bodin and R. Hedlund, 14–29. Uppsala: Acta Universitatis Upsaliensis.

Odorico, Paul. 2006. Les trois visages de la même violence: les trois prises de Thessalonique. In *L'écriture de la mémoire. La littérarité de l'historiographie*, eds. Paolo Odorico, Panagiotis Agapitos, and Martin Hinterberger, 147–179. Paris: Centre d'études byzantines, néo-helléniques et sud-est européennes.

Ojakangas, Mika. 2016. *On the Origins of Greek Biopolitics: A Reinterpretation of the History of Biopower*. New York: Routledge.

Papadogiannakis, Ioannis. 2017. Lamenting for the Fall of Jerusalem in the Seventh Century CE. In *Greek Laughter and Tears: Antiquity and After*, ed. Margaret Alexiou and Douglas Cairns, 187–198. Edinburgh: Edinburgh University Press.

Papaioannou, Stratis. 2010. The Aesthetics of History: From Theophanes to Eustathios. In *History as Literature in Byzantium*, ed. Ruth Macrides, 3–24. London: Routledge.

Pizzone, Aglae. 2014. The Author in Middle Byzantine Literature: A View from Within. In *The Author in Middle Byzantine Literature: Modes, Functions, and Identities*, ed. Aglae Pizzone, 3–18. Berlin: De Gruyter.

Pontani, Filippo Maria, Vassilis Katsaros, and Vassilis Sarris, eds. 2017. *Reading Eustathios of Thessaloniki*. Berlin: De Gruyter.

Roilos, Panagiotis. 2005. *Amphoteroglossia: A Poetics of the Twelfth-Century Medieval Greek Novel*. Cambridge, MA: Harvard University Press.

Roth, Michael. 2012. *Memory, Trauma, and History: Essays on Living with the Past*. New York: Columbia University Press.

Rosenbaum, Alan. 2009. *Is the Holocaust Unique: Perspectives on Comparative Genocide*. Boulder, CO: Westview Press.

70   A. J. GOLDWYN

Rosenfeld, Alvin Hirsch. 1980. *A Double Dying: Reflections on Holocaust Literature*. Bloomington: Indiana University Press.

Schabas, William. 2010. The Law and Genocide. In *The Oxford Handbook of Genocide Studies*, eds. Donald Bloxham and A. Dirk Moses, 123–141. Oxford: Oxford University Press.

Schwarz, Daniel. 1998. The Ethics of Reading Elie Wiesel's *Night*. *Style* 32 (2): 221–242.

Sharpe, Christina. 2016. *In the Wake: On Blackness and Being*. Durham: Duke University Press.

Singer-Genis, Alice. 2011. *I Won't Die Hungry: A Holocaust Survivor's Memoir*. Bloomington: AuthorHouse.

Sodi, Risa. 1990. *A Dante of Our Time: Primo Levi and Auschwitz*. New York: Peter Lang.

Sofsky, Wolfgang. 1993. *The Order of Terror: The Concentration Camp*. Princeton, NJ: Princeton University Press.

Steiner, George. 1984. *George Steiner: A Reader*. New York: Oxford University Press.

Trezise, Thomas. 2001. Unspeakable. *The Yale Journal of Criticism* 14 (1): 39–66.

Trezise, Thomas. 2013. *Witnessing Witnessing: On the Reception of Holocaust Survivor Testimony*. New York: Fordham University Press.

Tsolakis, E. 1959. Μιχαὴλ Γλυκᾶ. Στίχοι οὓς ἔγραψε καθ 'ὃν κατεσχέθη καιρόν, Series: Ἐπιστημονικὴ ἐπετηρὶς φιλοσοφικῆς σχολῆς τοῦ πανεπιστημίου Θεσσαλονίκης/Epistimoniki epetiris philosophikis scholis tou panepistimiou Thessalonikis.

Weber, Elisabeth. 2012. 'Torture Was the Essence of National Socialism': Reading Jean Améry Today. In *Speaking About Torture*, ed. Julie Carlson and Elisabeth Weber, 83–98. New York: Fordham University Press.

Wiesel, Elie. 1990. The Holocaust as Literary Inspiration. In *Dimensions of the Holocaust*, 5–19. Evanston: Northwestern University Press.

———. 2006. *Night*, trans. Marion Wiesel. New York: Hill and Wang.

———. 2007. *La Nuit*. Paris: Les Éditions de Minuit.

CHAPTER 2

Prison Literature and Slave Narratives in Byzantium: John Kaminiates' *Capture of Thessaloniki*

2.1 "I was drawn on by happy memories": Affective Narratology in Kaminiates' Letter

In the summer of 904, a fleet under the Abbasid commander Leo of Tripoli sacked the second city of the Byzantine Empire, Thessaloniki, and carried off tens of thousands of people into slavery.[1] Sometime between a few weeks and a year later, one of those enslaved people, an otherwise unknown cleric named John Kaminiates, was in a prison camp in Tripoli when he received a letter from a fellow Greek slave named Gregory of Cappadocia. Gregory and Kaminiates had met in the prison camp in Tarsus before the latter was transferred to Tripoli.[2] Gregory's letter included a request that Kaminiates write him back, and this response has come down to us today under the conventional English title *The*

---

[1] For recent overviews of the history of the sack of Thessaloniki within the larger context of Byzantine history, see, for instance, Curta (2011: 166–68), Riedel (2018: 16–18); and Tougher (1997: 188–190).

[2] Messis notes that "l'historicité du personnage a été contestée et le personnage est tenu pour convention littéraire" (2006: 120, n.41). Similarly, Odorico wonders "comment considerer l'autre énonciation, commune à Caminiatès et à Anagnostès, selon laquelle ces textes auraient été composés à la demande d'un personnage particulier? S'agit-il là aussi d'un *topos* rhétorique?" (2006: 151).

© The Author(s), under exclusive license to Springer Nature Switzerland AG 2021
A. J. Goldwyn, *Witness Literature in Byzantium*,
New Approaches to Byzantine History and Culture,
https://doi.org/10.1007/978-3-030-78857-5_2

71

72   A. J. GOLDWYN

Capture of Thessaloniki.[3] But Kaminiates writes that he did not immediately respond to Gregory's letter, and he offers two reasons for his delayed response: "on the one hand there was what I considered to be the invidiousness of writing about such matters to a man of your caliber [...] and on the other hand, there was my total inability to furnish a well-written account of the subject" (τό τε πρὸς σὲ περὶ τοιούτων γράφειν ἐπαχθὲς κρίνων, ἄνδρα τοσοῦτον [...] καὶ τὸ μηδὲν δύνασθαι περὶ ὧν τὴν ζήτησιν ἐποιήσω καλῶς ἐξηγήσασθαι).[4]

Though scholars have often dismissed the value of prefaces for understanding the works to which they are attached as mere rhetoric, a reading of them within the context of Kamniates' letter demonstrates how authentic emotional experience or concerns can be conveyed through the seeming artificiality of such rhetorical conventions.[5] For Kaminiates, for instance, these concerns can be considered in two ways. The first is affective: Kaminiates does not want to recall the events both because they are ἐπαχθὲς—hateful for him to recall—and because he feels that a man of Gregory's goodness should not have to experience them, even through the representational medium of writing. The second reason is rhetorical: he worries that the style and structure of his work will not be suitable for narrating the events.

Later in the introduction, he further breaks down his concern for this rhetorical inadequacy by considering what the letter would look like at the levels of style; he notes that he did not want to "demean with the triviality of my style the magnitude of the events which you asked me to relate" (μὴ καθυβρίσαι μηδὲ σμικρῦναι τῷ λόγῳ τὸ περιφανὲς τῶν παρὰ σοῦ ζητηθέντων πραγμάτων).[6] Kaminiates knows that his diction and tone will affect how the events are perceived, and he worries that he lacks the skill to narrate them in the proper way. He offers, moreover, a more detailed description of his concerns as regards the structure of his narrative: "If I wished to

---

[3] Not to be confused with the work of Eustathios of Thessaloniki with which it shares a conventional English title. The work survives in four manuscripts, the earliest from the fifteenth century. For a brief summary of the manuscript, modern editions, and translations, see Neville (2018: 155).

[4] Kam. *ex. Thess.* 1.4.

[5] Ralph-Johannes Lilie, for instance, argues that "the preface of a Byzantine historiographer, characterized as it is by topoi, does not necessarily have anything to do with the context or style of subsequent work" (2014: 162).

[6] Kam. *ex. Thess.* 1.4.

give a full account of these events, my story would be inordinately long and needlessly long, I would be overstepping the bounds of moderation, and perhaps exhausting even your unflagging powers of concentration" (ἀλλὰ περὶ τούτων εἰ καθ' ἕκαστον ἐπεξιέναι βουληθείην, μακρὸν ἂν εἴη καὶ τῇ χρείᾳ μὴ κατάλληλον τὸν λόγον ποιήσομαι, τῆς συμμετρίας τὸν νόμον καθυπερβαίνων, ἵνα μὴ λέγω ὅτι καὶ τὴν σὴν ἀρρᾴθυμον ἀκοὴν ἀποκναίσω).[7] Kaminiates' structural concern is how to limit the length of the narrative while still conveying everything necessary, a concern that bears directly on his narratological decisions regarding his principles of selection for which events to include (or exclude) and at what level of detail (or generality) to narrate them.

These concerns guide all kinds of historical writing; as Berel Lang notes in *Act and Idea in the Nazi Genocide*, "the explanation of an historical event inevitably bears the mark of artifice. If it did not omit or compress it would be as extensive as the events it was intended to explain."[8] And yet, in the case of the survivor, they have particular valence; Wiesel would later describe the delay between the experiences described in *Night* and the writing of the text by describing the difficulties he faced:

> I knew the role of the survivor was to testify. Only I did not know how. I lacked experience, I lacked a framework. I mistrusted the tools, the procedures. Should one say it all or hold it all back? Should one shout or whisper? Place the emphasis on those who were gone or on their heirs?
>
> How does one describe the indescribable? How does one use restraint in recreating the fall of mankind and the eclipse of the gods? And then, how can one be sure that the words, once uttered, will not betray, distort the message they bear?[9]

---

[7] Kam. *ex. Thess.* 2.5.

[8] Lang (2003: 81).

[9] Wiesel (1979: 15).

74 A. J. GOLDWYN

In the terms of classical narratology,[10] these kinds of concerns and how an author like Kaminiates and Wiesel treat them fall under the broad category of "rhythm,"[11] the way an author controls the passing of time in a narrative.

Rhythm is one of the central aspects of narrative, and its manipulation by authors is one of the defining features that separate the experience of a literary representation of events from the experience of the events themselves—in real life, time moves at a static pace and everything, whether boring or exciting, important or insignificant, takes the same amount of time. In a literary representation of those events, however, the author can choose which events to include or exclude, which events to foreground or background, and which events to describe at great length and which to pass over quickly; how much narrative time (with how much text is devoted to a certain moment often used as a proxy) is determined by the author to emphasize or diminish certain events.[12] That is, authors can slow down or even pause time through more detailed description, can narrate such that time moves (roughly) at the pace of real life (such as direct reported speech), or can speed up time through elision or omission. Kaminiates, as all authors, uses all of these techniques to convey his story.

So-called "postclassical narratology"[13] builds on this structuralist model—replete with technical terminology and a scientifically schematic and taxonomic view of categorizing narrative practice—to consider how aspects seemingly external to the narrative influence the narratological decisions of an author: classical narratology sought only to reveal the

[10] By which is meant the model developed by the French structuralists (for which, see, for instance, Alber and Fludernik [2010: 2]) and Russian formalists (for which, see Bortolussi and Dixon 2003: 11, here represented by Bal [2009]). Classical narratology in this. Context has no connection to the term "classical" as referring to the study of ancient Greece and Rome, though it has been highly influential in these fields, particularly through the pioneering work of Irene de Jong, who is largely responsible for bringing the method to Classics as a discipline (de Jong 2001, 2004).

[11] Bal (2009: 98–101). For a more technical definition, see De Jong and Nünlist (2007: 10–12) and xiii in the glossary.

[12] For rhythm, see Bal (2009: 98–103). Ellipsis is frequently translated in Kaminiates as "omission," which Bal also offers as a synonym for ellipsis, defining it as "the omission of an element that belongs in the series" (2009: 217) and "an omission in the story of a section in the fabula" (2009: 100).

[13] First mentioned in Herman (1999: 14 and cited in Alber and Fludernik 2010: 1).

tools the authors used to control time, while postclassical narratology seeks to understand what issues external to a text (such as how the race, class, gender, or other identity-markers of the author) influence authorial decision-making. One such branch of this postclassical narratology focuses on how emotion impacts narratological decisions. In *Affective Narratology*, Patrick Colm Hogan argues that "story structures are fundamentally shaped and oriented by our emotion systems," by which he means that "the determination of story organization by emotion systems goes all the way down to the level of events and incidents, pervading the way in which we make causal attributions."[14] Since, as Hogan argues, "our experience of time is not uniform[,] we encode experience into hierarchized units, organizing temporality first of all by reference to emotional response," the narratological choices an author makes reflect these emotional stimuli.[15] The causality of chained events which drives narrative forward is determined by a variety of generic factors; affective narratology argues that the organizing principle that allows linked events to become a story is not (only) reason or historical causation, but the emotional response of the author as they write and the emotional response they hope to elicit from the reader. In this regard, Leonora Neville is right to suggest that just because the text "reflects real events does not entail treating it as a news dispatch. It is an artful text that we should approach as a work of rhetoric in which the author has been careful to present material in such a way as to provoke the responses he desired among his audience."[16] This could also be viewed as one of the main distinctions between historiographical writing—which is narrated according to the organizing principle of chronology—and witness literature—which is narrated according to the organizing principle of emotion.

How to write about trauma and atrocity is a difficult question that has been considered by authors ancient, medieval, and modern[17]; indeed,

---

[14] Hogan (2011: 1, 2).

[15] Hogan (2011: 66).

[16] Neville (2019: 67).

[17] This question has been particularly pressing for the study of more contemporary traumas. Patterson, for instance, begins his study of Holocaust representation by noting that "[i]n the last twenty-five years more than forty books have been published on the problem of Holocaust representation. Most of them deal with the problem of representing evil, atrocity, and trauma" (2018: 1). The ethics of writing about trauma and violence, which existed perhaps on a smaller scale across the Byzantine millennium but which was

insofar as historiography has since its beginnings focused largely on military history—that is, the study of the practice of violence, how such violence is committed and justified, and what its consequences are—narrating trauma and atrocity are, in some sense, at the heart of what it has traditionally meant to write about the past. This is difficult enough when writing about the experiences of others; it is something yet again all the more complicated when one is writing about those events which one has oneself experienced. To this, one could perhaps also add that as much as he sought to provoke certain responses in his audience, Kaminiates was as concerned with preventing them from feeling certain other emotions and, moreover, that the author's concern with feeling applied as much to him as it did to his audience. Indeed, Wiesel is explicit about the effects of emotion on his narration. Describing how he omitted some scenes from the Yiddish version when he revised it into French, he asks: "Why not include those in this new translation? Too personal, too private, perhaps; they need to remain between the lines" (Pourquoi ne pas les inclure dans cette nouvelle traduction? Trop personnels, trop intimes peut-être, ils doivent rester entre les lignes).[18] Thus, for Wiesel, the writer's own emotional experience is explicitly one of the guiding forces for what to narrate and how. Scenes that are "too personal" or "too private" are omitted.

But there is one other aspect of Kaminiates' narrative that merits consideration, specifically his position as an enslaved person who is also incarcerated in a prison camp. In *Narrating Prison Experience*, Ken Walibora Waliaula poses a series of questions that foreground how the author's positional context as a slave influences the narrative itself:

> To what extent is narrating incarceration an act of self-exploration? What are the explicit and implicit motivations for narrating incarceration? What is the relationship between the conditions of confinement and the narratives of confinement or put differently, what is the link between the context of confinement and the text narrating confinement? What are the narratological tools that narratives of confinement employ? Is form/genre relevant or irrelevant in narrativizing confinement? To what extent does the collective become embedded in the individual experience of incarceration? What

---

ultimately no less consequential for those who experienced it, has not, to my mind, been adequately theorized in Byzantine Studies.

[18] Wiesel (2006: np, 2007: 15).

is the relationship between the narration of confinement and the victim's trauma? And how does narrating confinement relate to truth claims? How do aspects of truth claims, trauma, and the I-pronoun affect the prisoner's conception of self within or without society?[19]

While his positionality as an enslaved person opens up one set of possibilities for considering the effects of subjectivity and narrative, the specifics of incarceration must also be considered. According to Waliaula, the prison itself becomes a narrative space, one that determines the author's sense of self and, insofar as the medium for transmitting that is autobiographical, their sense of the teleology of their past, present, and future.[20] In this regard, the very act of writing a letter is a form of resistance—part of what Ruth Ahnert calls "the clandestine tactics that prisoners used to express their autonomy from within disciplinary structures," though in this case there is no evidence that the tactic was clandestine, and Kaminiates' imprisonment was ontological (or perhaps economic) rather than disciplinary (by which I mean it was not meant to correct a specific behavior, as the modern penal system purports to do; rather, it was to contain his physical body and break down his sense of individual identity so he could be sold into slavery or ransomed).[21] That is to say, the act of writing itself, and particularly of autobiographical writing, resists the dehumanizing aims of incarceration. As long as a person is narrating their own life, they retain their connection to their past, and thus to their own individuality and subjectivity.

One of the major goals of the carceral system, particularly as it relates to slavery (as opposed to incarceration as rehabilitation), is the attempt to extinguish the identifiable and narratable sense of self—hence the reason for practices as diverse as the prohibition on literacy among African-American slaves and the enforced physical uniformity of prisoners in Auschwitz. Autobiographical writing thus resists the erasure of unique selfhood. This is perhaps particularly true in the case of Kaminiates;

[19] Walibora Waliaula (2013: 1).

[20] For prison autobiographies in the medieval west, see Summers (2004). Summers relies on Laurence de Looze's problematization of the seemingly neat affiliation of the historical author and the primary narrator-focalizer (the "I" voice in the text) to further distinguish among "a text may be read as 'pseudo-autobiography', 'autobiographical fiction', and 'autobiographical pseudo-fiction'" (de Looze 1997: 26–30 as quoted in Summers 2004: 7).

[21] Ahnert (2013: 30).

78   A. J. GOLDWYN

whereas the horizon of expectation of the typical African-American slave was slavery from birth to death based on the innate characteristics of their skin, Kaminiates' slavery was not enshrined in law as intrinsic to his body, but rather because of unfortunate circumstances. That is to say, unlike the average enslaved African-American, whose enslavement began at birth and whose life was therefore condition by the masters' attempt to erase the slave's individuality and humanity before they had the chance to establish them, Kaminiates had decades of freedom to establish his identity and hoped to be once again freed either through ransom or prisoner exchange.

The particular circumstances of the moment in which it was written—Kaminiates' uncertain and contingent position between past freedom and future slavery—thus determine what elements are included and excluded, how the narrator conceives of his past, and how he writes about his current moment and possible future. Kaminiates says so himself:

> And now we are at the crossroads between two expected outcomes: either we obtain our long-discussed release through the arrangement for the safe chance of prisoners or we succumb to death, which stalks us daily in the form of frequent illnesses and is in various other ways a close and constant companion of those who are in prison. Only we have no way of telling which of these we shall encounter first.

> καὶ νῦν ἐσμὲν ἐν μεθορίῳ δύο πραγμάτων ἐλπιζομένων, ἢ τοῦ τυχεῖν τῆς πάλαι θρυλλουμένης διατῆς σωτηρίου καταλλαγῆς ἀπολυτρώσεως, ἢ τῷ θανάτῳ παραπεμφθῆναι καθ' ἑκάστην ἐφεστῶτι ταῖς συχναῖς ἀρρωστίαις καὶ ἄλλως τοῖς ἐν τῇ φρουρᾷ πλησίον συνῳκισμένῳ. πλὴν οὐκ ἔχομεν ἀσφαλῶς γινώσκειν ὁποτέρῳ τούτων προτέρῳ διαλαχεῖν.[22]

Indeed, Paolo Odorico has argued that Kaminiates' diverging potential future of slavery on the one hand and freedom on the other, are the essential conditions shaping the narrative as a whole: "Il est essential de se fonder sur cette conclusion pour mieux comprendre le sens de ce texte. Un texte qui devait assouvir la curiosité de Grégoire sur le sac de Thessalonique, mais qui en réalité est bien advantage le récit des malheurs de

---

[22] Kam. ex. Thess. 78.8. Another example of the way in which emotion is systematically suppressed in the translations of both Eustathios and Kaminiates can be seen here: where Frendo and Athanassiou translate ἐλπιζομένων as "expected," it could as easily be translated as "hoped for," which would better capture Kaminiates' longing and uncertainty.

son auteur et de ses compagnons de digrâce."[23] The same fabula written by Kaminiates after he had been ransomed or after he had been sold into slavery would perhaps have produced radically different stories and texts (in the narratological sense, that is, perhaps the story would not have taken the form of a letter but a lament for his slavery or an encomium to whomever had ransomed him, for instance), as would an autobiography written just a few months earlier, when his own enslavement would have been unimaginable. Odorico thus sees in the letter "l'espoir de s'en sortir. Au fond, l'idée qu'une rançon soit payee ou qu'il fasse l'objet d'un échange de prisonnier est reprise tout au long du récit: c'est pour lui le seul moyen de s'échapper. [...] il concentre sa narration sur la brutalité des barbares qui traitent les prisonniers comme du bétail, il souligne la misère des captifs, les tourments psychologique et pyshiques auxquelles ils sont soumis, il parle des horreurs vécues et de l'attente de la deliverance. Tout est construit autour de cette dimension."[24]

As central as autobiographical writing is to the maintenance of the self, so too is the sense of what carceral theorists refer to as "community." In his discussion of slave narratives as works that construct community through narration, Ahnert draws on the work of Anthony Cohen, who "argues that community is built upon two related assumptions: that the members of a group have something in common with each other; and the thing held in common distinguishes them in a significant way from the members of other possible groups."[25] One of the defining features of incarceration, of course, is the physical (and thus ontological) separation of the incarcerated body from those who might reinforce the existing sense of self, and the replacement of those associations both with state-sanctioned associates such as fellow prisoners (or, often enough, with no one at all) and in carefully prescribed kinds of interactions that is, the strict limits on where, for how long, and in what ways prisoners can interact with other prisoners and non-incarcerated visitors.

Monika Fludernik describes this category of imprisonment as "volitional curtailment," that is, restrictions on the free exercise of the will.

---

[23] Odorico (2006: 157).

[24] Odorico (2006: 158–159). For rhetoric as fundamentally an act of persuasion, see Webb (2003: 127–128).

[25] Ahnert (2013: 75), with reference to Cohen (1985, 1988).

80 A. J. GOLDWYN

Part of this, Fludernik notes, is the "abolition of inmates' *freedom of association*—it is in the interest of the authorities to isolate prisoners or severely restrict their communication with other offenders [...] the curtailment of association strikes at another basic human need, that for communication and self-assurance by making contact with others. (In Lacanian terms, the ego is only created by the eye of the other.) In extreme forms of penal isolation, the prisoner is therefore ultimately deprived of the freedom to be him/herself, to establish and maintain their personal identity."[26] Writing, then, particularly in the form of a letter, functions as a form of resistance to the dehumanizing force of incarceration by both allowing the writer to dwell upon the unique circumstances that condition their writing on the one hand and, on the other, in allowing the incarcerated writer to choose with whom to associate.

Taken together, then, these three interlocking concerns—for affect, that is, how writing and reading such a text makes both writer and reader feel; for style and aesthetics, that is, how diction, syntax, and other similar concerns create the desired feelings in the reader (and help them avoid feeling other things the author does not want them to feel); and for structure, that is, length, order, speed, and other narratological concerns—reflect the way the author's positionality as an incarcerated slave and the subsequent emotional responses he has and wants to communicate shape the stylistic and narratological decisions he makes. Rather than, as Neville argues, "depict[ing] himself as essentially emotionless" in a "passionless self-portrayal," an analysis of these narratological, stylistic, and psychoanalytic elements demonstrates that Kaminiates frequently interrupts his recollection of the events themselves to foreground his own emotional state while he is writing about them, and in doing so delivers a series of statements on method that reveal the emotionally determined decision-making process that informs the composition of the narrative itself.[27] These authorial interruptions, moreover, show Kaminiates developing the rhetorical and narratological strategies that help him convey his trauma in the most emotionally effective and rhetorically efficient way possible.[28]

---

[26] Alber and Fludernik (2010: 8).

[27] Neville (2019: 75).

[28] Panagopoulos cites several of these authorial interruptions, arguing that "the author uses rhetorical devices and expressive means to enrich his narrative. There often appears in the course of the text a series of rhetorical questions that reflect the desperation of the

These aspects of Kaminiates' work, however, have thus far gone relatively unexamined. Indeed, perhaps the major trend in the scholarship on John Kaminiates has mostly neglected these components, focusing less on the rhetorical, psychological and emotional aspects of the text as the product of an eyewitness recalling trauma and more on what his work can offer in terms of objective knowledge about the past. Such readings, while a valuable and proper use of Kaminiates' letter, may make interpretive errors if they fail to account for the writer's role as witness or of the real human cost of the events he describes. An example of this is Florin Curta's *Edinburgh History of the Greeks c.500–1050*, which focusses on the sack of Thessaloniki exclusively from the perspective of economics: "The booty collected and the number of enslaved people were so large that Leo had to take with him a number of ships[. …] The devastation must have been serious, judging from the impression of sheer misery which Thessaloniki left on St Elias the Younger[. …] However, both the city and the surrounding countryside recovered rapidly and would witness an accelerated growth throughout the second half of the tenth and first half of the eleventh century."[29] By centering his narrative on the recovery of the city and the countryside at the expense of the actual people themselves, this interpretation tells only part of the consequences of these events, since economic growth was totally irrelevant to those killed and enslaved and was perhaps not a significant factor in the subsequent experiences of those who, though they survived themselves, suffered physical and emotional trauma or lost loved ones in the attack. A perhaps more extreme example of this can be found in Shaun Tougher's *The Reign of Leo VI: Politics and People*, in which Tougher suggests that "[i]t can be argued to a certain degree that the fate of Thessalonike in 904 was of far more significance in the psychological sphere than the physical one," a reading only possible if one asks whose psychology matters.[30] This may have been true from the perspective of Leo VI, but it certainly was a matter of far more physical concern to John Kaminiates and the men and women who were killed, maimed, or enslaved.

---

narrator in the face of tragic experiences, his inability to accomplish his writing calmly, and present in a dramatic way the hardships of the prisoners" (2014: 193).

[29] Curta (2011: 168).

[30] Tougher (1997: 189).

82   A. J. GOLDWYN

The scholarship on the work, therefore, has thus far failed to account for Kaminiates' positionality—that is, his role as an eyewitness and victim of the events he narrates and his circumstances as a prison writer writing a letter to another prisoner. Indeed, Alexander Kazhdan's "Some Questions Addressed to the Scholars, who Believe in the Authenticity of Kaminiates' *Capture of Thessalonika*," perhaps the most famous article about the *Capture*, rejects not just the author of the letter as an eyewitness to the events he recounts, but even the very historicity of the events through which he claimed to have lived.[31] Much of the scholarship on the *Capture* has been concerned with refuting Kazhdan,[32] and while there is no doubt that issues such as the dating of the text, its historicity, and its accuracy are essential aspects for both understanding the text in and of itself and for the contributions it can make to a broader understanding of Byzantine history and literature, Kaminiates' letter, considered as a work of witness literature, offers something perhaps more rare and valuable: insight into how Byzantine victims and witnesses of atrocity felt about those experiences, how they conceived of and remembered them, and how they coped with the aftermath of such experiences.

If, then, articulating his emotional experience is Kaminiates' central concern, even the historical information he describes must be seen through the lens of his personal experience and emotions: what he includes and excludes are determined as much by his psychology and emotional state as by the demands of historical writing, an insight that, while perhaps uncharacteristic of the studies of Byzantine writing about the past, has long been recognized in studies in other disciplines associated with the study of atrocity. Ruth Franklin argues that "every act of memory is also an act of narrative [....] our minds distill and pound the chaos of life into something resembling a coherent shape. From the very moment we begin the activity of remembering, we place some kind of editorial framework, some principle of selection [...] around the events of the past."[33]

---

[31] Kazhdan (1978). For a summary of the debate, see also Messis (2006: 121) and Odorico (2006: 156).

[32] See, for instance, Bakirtzis (2007: 89 n.1), Tougher (1997: 15 n.66); and the definitive rejections in Odorico (2005) and Christides (1981). For an overview of the debate, see Neville (2018).

[33] Franklin (2011: 12).

2 PRISON LITERATURE AND SLAVE NARRATIVES ...   83

This insight is not only true of Holocaust Studies; in his study of African-American slave narratives, for instance, James Olney distinguishes between autobiography as typically understood, that is, as a narrative of the past, and what he calls "autobiographical performance," by which he means "a recollective/narrative act in which the writer, from a certain point in his life—the present—looks back over the events of that life and recounts them in such a way as to show how that past history has led to this present state."[34] In this, the fact of its being recollected is the fundamental aspect of this kind of narration:

> memory creates the *significance* of events in discovering the pattern into which these events fall. And such a pattern, in the kind of autobiography where memory rules, will be a teleological one bringing us, in and through narration, and as it were by an inevitable process, to the end of all past moments which is the present. It is in the interplay of past and present, of present memory reflecting over past experience on its way to becoming present being, that events are lifted out of time to be re-situated not in mere chronological sequence but in patterned significance.[35]

While this insight is applicable to every work of writing about the past—which is by definition an ordering of events based on some principles of inclusion or exclusion—it is of primary importance for reading Kaminiates' letter. It can, moreover, provide a theoretical model for thinking narratologically about a text that, according to Neville, is concerned with "narrating personal experiences of deep horror" and thus does "not conform to the dispassionate narration normal for classicizing history"—or, indeed, "many of the conventions of Byzantine historical writing."[36] It is a work guided by affect, memory, and trauma. As a personal letter rather than a public performance, as the work of a (subjective) witness rather than a (dispassionate) professional historian, Kaminiates' *Capture* represents a different model for Byzantine writing about the past, and thus requires a different narratological and methodological paradigm for reading and interpreting it.[37]

---

[34] Olney (1985: 149).

[35] Olney (1985: 149).

[36] Neville (2018: 114).

[37] Panagopoulos similarly suggests that "the undoubted historicity of Kaminiates' narrative does not dictate the exclusive treat of it as a historiographic text, as a typical historical

84   A. J. GOLDWYN

In Holocaust Studies as well, the relationship between testimony, affect, and narrative structure has long been a constituent factor for the interpretation of such texts; scholars of Holocaust testimony have long argued for differentiating between history and testimony as two different ways of writing about the past. James Young, for instance, notes that

> the need for evidence in historical writing has always been paramount, used as it is to illustrate and justify particular renderings and explanations of events. But without understanding the constructed nature of evidence itself, and then separating the need for evidence from its actual rhetorical function as that which both naturalizes and is naturalized by a writer's governing mythos, we forfeit a deeper understanding of the interpenetration between events, narrative, and historical appreciation. That is, when we turn to literary testimony of the Holocaust, we do so for knowledge – not evidence – of events. Instead of looking for evidence of experiences, the reader might concede that the narrator has apprehended experience. [...] Narrative strategy, structure, and style all become forms of commentary on the writing act itself, now evident by the text it has produced.[38]

The first way that Kaminiates' affect and positionality influence the style and structure of the work is his relation to time, specifically the distinction between what narratologists call "simultaneous narration," that is, "the narration of events which are taking place at the moment of narration," and "subsequent narration," that is, "the narration of events which have already taken place at the time of narration."[39] From the narratological perspective, then, there are actually two different John Kaminiates in the text: there is the primary narrator who exists in his current moment— his narratorial persona as a man sitting in a slave prison writing about events that happened some time ago.[40] With the exception of the framing at the beginning of the text and the authorial interruptions that appear

source without formal aesthetic claims" (2014: 183) and later that "the work should not be compared with historical accounts, narratives of events, but exactly with the epistolographic tradition" (2014: 197).

[38] Young (1988: 37).

[39] De Jong and Nünlist (2007: xiii).

[40] In explaining this concept, de Jong uses the example of Odysseus among the Phaiakians: "The events which take place during Odysseus' ten-year journey home from Troy, but in the story a large number of these events are recounted by a secondary narrator, Odysseus, in a long embedded narrative, while the primary narrator concentrates

at crucial moments in the text to reveal this narrator's thoughts and emotional responses to the events he is narrating, the rest of the text—the narrative of the events in Thessaloniki—all occur in the past, and thus form an extended external analepsis.[41] Reading the letter thus requires an appreciation for the distinction between these two figures, for in order to understand what motivates Kaminiates to write, what he considered essential or inessential, how he chose to order and structure his text, and how he felt while writing and how these feelings influenced his composition, are properly understood only with respect to Kaminiates the primary narrator in the present, not Kaminiates the protagonist of the events in Thessaloniki, who exists only in the past.

Meaningfully distinguishing between Kaminiates the historical person, Kaminiates the character in the text, and Kaminiates the narrator of the letter is particularly fraught because of how the author's formative education within the Byzantine educational system, with its emphasis on a rhetorical tradition that subsumes authorial individuality within codified forms, shapes a work that is otherwise characterized by a radical departure from previous models in response to unprecedented trauma.[42] Reading those moments where the primary narrator interrupts his own otherwise conventional narrative, then, can reveal much about his methods, aims, and emotions.

According to Kaminiates, Gregory asked to learn about four aspects of Kaminiates' life:

> You sought through your letter to learn the way in which it had come about that we dwell in captivity, having been delivered into the hands of barbarians, how we exchanged a foreign land for our own country, where we hail from and what sort of place it is.

on the last 41 days of his return" (2001: 4). In this case, Kaminiates is like Odysseus among the Phaiakians, telling a story about his own past in the present.

[41] De Jong and Nünlist: "A flashback to an event which lies outside the time span of the **main story**" (2007: xi, bold in original).

[42] Ingela Nilsson has convincingly demonstrated with regards to Constantine Manasses that "originality should be considered rather as a skilful use of conventions, creating a tension between and careful balancing of tradition and innovation," a remark that applies more globally to the practices of Byzantine writers (Nilsson 2020: 1).

86   A. J. GOLDWYN

Ἐζήτησας μαθεῖν διὰ τῆς ἐπιστολῆς τὸν τρόπον δι' ὃν τὴν φρουρὰν οἰκοῦμεν βαρβάρων χερσὶν ἐκδοθέντες, καὶ πῶς τὴν ἀλλοτρίαν ἀντὶ τῆς ἰδίας διημειψάμεθα, ποίας τέ ἐσμεν πατρίδος, καὶ τίνα τὰ κατ' αὐτήν.[43]

To answer these questions, Kaminiates follows quite carefully the instructions laid out in the standard rhetorical treatise for the description and praise of cities attributed to Menander Rhetor in the third or fourth century CE,[44] which had become newly popular perhaps just in the period of Kaminiates' lifetime.[45] The use of Menander as a guiding rhetorical text for such an encomium would not be out of character for a writer of Kaminiates' status and education; Frendo notes "that John Kaminiates belonged to a relatively well-to-do family" and that "though belonging to the relatively low-ranking clerical grade of *anagnostes*, [he]

[43] Kam. *ex. Thess.* 2.1. These questions seem to offer another parallel between the slave narratives of Kaminiates and those of African-American slaves. In December of 1927, Zora Neale Hurston (then an undergraduate sociology major at Barnard College), traveled to Alabama to meet with Cudjo Lewis, whom she thought was the last surviving African transported to the United States to be sold into slavery. When Hurston arrives, Lewis asks her why she has come, to which she replies in words that echo Kaminiates: "I want to ask you many things. I want to know who you are and how you came to be a slave; and to what part of Africa do you belong, and how you fared as a slave, and how you have managed as a free man?" (Hurston 2018: 28). Hurston's goal is like Gregory's: to elicit an autobiographical narrative that seeks to create a coherent narrative to explain the trajectory of an enslaved person's life from their origins in freedom to their eventual enslavement.

[44] For fourth century, see, for instance, Webb (1997: 115); for the third century, see Anđelković (2019).

[45] The oldest extant manuscript of Menander is from the middle of the tenth-century, some few decades after Kaminiates wrote his letter, providing circumstantial material evidence to suggest the possibility that the latter used the former to model his encomium of the city (Anđelković 2019: 151). Martha Vinson, however, definitively proves that Leo VI, the emperor under whom the sack of Thessaloniki occurred, used Menander's model for his own speeches, "a very interesting choice," she says, "that had far-reaching consequences, to judge from the number of late ninth- and early tenth-century authors who followed his lead in using this textbook on epideictic poetry" (2004: 13). For a detailed reading of the ways in which Menander was used by John Mauropous (who lived in the early eleventh century, slightly later than Kaminiates), see Anđelković (2019: 149–169 and especially 156–163) for a comparison of the parallel passages in which Mauropous follows and elaborates on the suggested methods of Menander. Though the article is persuasive at the level of structure, the lack of Greek makes it difficult to know if passages also follow at the level of diction. Menander's influence of Michael Psellos is addressed briefly in Papaioannou (2013: 53–54) and 108; for the influence of Menander on Joseph the Philosopher in the thirteenth century, see Gielen (2017).

appears to have held the special position of Chamberlain in the bishop's household."[46] "Given this," Frendo concludes, "it is perhaps not surprising that Kaminiates should display a thorough grasp of the rudiments of rhetorical composition."[47] And, indeed, Kaminiates proves a faithful follower of Menander throughout the opening section of his work. Kaminiates' realization of Menander's instructions produces much more than a city description; in his hands, Menander's highly prescriptive rules for city description are transformed into a record of his individual experience of loss, grief, memory, and exile. That is to say, his careful adherence to a rhetorical model that is meant to be broadly applicable across a range of diverse writing contexts does not obscure the unique circumstances of its particular appropriation by this particular author; rather, it is through the adherence to tradition and formula that the text is able to articulate the author's unique experience of the city and his recollection of it in the unique circumstances of his writing.

Kaminiates' answer to the questions posed by Gregory of Cappadocia thus reflect the authorial and autobiographical strategies that Kaminiates uses to assert not just his individuality within the dehumanizing conditions of slavery and the rhetorical tradition's erasure of the unique authorial voice, but also to assert the very fact of his existence. Thus, the first of Gregory's two requests deals with the events after the arrival of Leo of Tripoli ("the way in which it had come about that we dwell in captivity" and "how we exchanged a foreign land for our own country") while the second two ask for information about the situation before Leo's arrival ("where we hail from and what sort of place it is"). Kaminiates sees the former concerns as more important, but begins his narrative with the latter two. The last request is dealt with easily enough in a single sentence, "We, dear friend, are natives of Thessaloniki" (Ἡμεῖς, ὦ φίλος, πατρίδος ἐσμὲν Θεσσαλονίκης),[48] a seemingly conventional expression which nevertheless has an added significance in light of his position as a slave writer.

By using Menander to construct an account of his capture and enslavement, Kaminiates' letter represents an appropriation of ancient rhetoric as

[46] Frendo (2000: xxxi).

[47] Frendo (2000: xxxii).

[48] Kam. *ex. Thess.* 3.

88   A. J. GOLDWYN

it does a reflection of some aspects of slave narratives. Kaminiates' beginning with this assertion of identity thus mirrors what John Olney, writing about African-American slave narratives, calls "the standard opening 'I was born,'" noting that this opening was "intended to attest to the real existence of a narrator, the sense being that the status of the narrative will be continually called into doubt, and so it cannot even begin, until the narrator's real existence is firmly established. Of course the argument of the slave narrative is that the events narrated are factual and truthful and that they all really happened to the narrator, but this is a second-stage argument; prior to the claim of truthfulness is the simple, existential claim: 'I exist.'"[49]

One example of such a claim can be seen in *The Interesting Narrative of the Life of Olaudah Equiano* (1789), an autobiography of the author's birth in West Africa, his kidnapping and sale as a child, and his life in the United States and Europe both before and after he purchased his freedom. Echoing Olney's claim of the importance of locating a slave's lost identity in deep childhood roots attached to a specific place, Equiano, like Kaminiates, includes an "I was born": "I was born, in the year 1745, in a charming fruitful vale, named Essaka."[50]

That Kaminiates begins his narrative with the same expression as at least two dozen African-American slave narratives suggests the possibility that a similar authorizing convention is at work in his text. Indeed, it is perhaps significant in this light that one of the major debates surrounding Kaminiates and his letter is the very historicity of the author and his story. Such incredulity about the viability of slave narratives, however, has been a defining feature of the reception of the genre for some time. Here again the reception of Equiano's *Interesting Narrative* also offers

---

[49] Olney (1985: 155). Significant in this regard, too, is that even the fictional slave narratives of the Komnenian novels begin in this way as well – both the embedded narratives of slaves, such as Kratandros' speech to Dosikles (Prod. *R&D*. 1.160–63) and Kleandros' speech to Charikles (2.57–59), suggesting that the novelists appropriated a shared rhetoric of self-authorization and autobiography as their counterparts in historiographical and autobiographical writing.

[50] Equiano (1999: 42). See also the opening of *Night*, in which Wiesel writes in the third sentence "of Sighet – the little town in Transylvania where I spent my childhood" (de Sighet – cette petite ville de Transylvanie où j'ai passé mon enfance) (Wiesel 2006: 3, 2007: 31). Naomi Seidman describes how one of the revisions that occurred during the process of translating the Yiddish manuscript which Wiesel originally wrote into the French version that became *Night* was the omitting of the history of Sighet with which he had originally opened the narrative (Seidman 2006: 220).

a historical parallel; it "quickly became the most popular book to date written by a black author. Nine British editions were published over the next five years, with Equiano making minor changes to each; during the same period an edition was published in the United States and translations were published in Dutch, German, and Russian."[51] And yet, despite the book's popularity and the author's personal celebrity in his own lifetime, there was an immediate backlash questioning the historical veracity of the author's claims. In 1792, Equiano responded with outrage to claims from "two London newspapers, the *Oracle* and the *Star* [that] questioned his true identity. The *Oracle* reported that 'there is no absurdity, however gross, but popular credulity has a throat wide enough to swallow it. It is a fact that the Public may depend on, that *Gustavus Vassa*, who has publicly asserted that he was kidnapped in Africa, never was upon that Continent, but was born and bred in the Danish Island of Santa Cruz, in the West Indies [now Saint Croix in the U.S. Virgin Islands]."[52] While these contemporary assertions were no doubt motivated by a desire to diminish Equiano's veracity (and thus his authority) with the ultimate goal of undermining the abolitionist aims of his autobiography, a strand of modern scholarship has also approached Equiano's narrative with skepticism on philological and historical grounds, with some scholars contending, in the words of George O'Malley, that Equiano "wrote something of a fiction for abolitionist purposes."[53]

Indeed, Equiano writes in his introduction that memoirists are confronted with a "misfortune, that what is uncommon is rarely, if ever, believed."[54] As a response to his own lack of intrinsic credibility, the autobiographical narrative portion of the text is preceded by a photograph of the author intended to affirm his reality and, perhaps more importantly, a list of "subscribers" that consists of several dozen prominent white people—led by "His Royal Highness the Prince of Wales" and "His Royal Highness the Duke of York"—all of whom lend credibility to the veracity

---

[51] Olney (1985: 30).

[52] Carretta (2005: 351). Gustavus Vassa was Equiano's baptismal name.

[53] O'Malley (2014: 32 n.4). See also Carretta (2005: 319) for the discrepancy between Equiano's description of Africa and "the external documentary evidence." Carretta bases his skepticism on documents locating his birth in South Carolina (3–5). A summary of the debate and its ramifications can be found in O'Malley (2014: 32, n.4).

[54] Equiano (1999: 41).

of the narrative and the actual existence of its author.[55] And yet, despite this, Equiano's *Interesting Narrative* still faced doubt in the author's own lifetime and in its subsequent reception, affirmation of Wiesel's assertion, in a different context, that "deep down, the witness knew then, as he does now, that his testimony would not be received. After all, it deals with an event that sprang from the darkest zone of man. Only those who experienced Auschwitz know what it was. Others will never know" (tout au fond de lui-même, le témoin savait, comme il le sait encore parfois, que son témoignage ne sera pas reçu. Seuls ceux qui ont connu Auschwitz savent ce que c'était. Les autres ne le sauront jamais).[56] The comparison with Kaminiates is, in this respect, more telling, in that the very historicity of the author and the veracity of his witness remains a subject of scholarly scrutiny, as the case of Kazhdan and others demonstrates.

This, too, is an example of how poststructural and affective narratology can reveal how authentic emotion is carried through seemingly conventional or formulaic language. Thus, for instance, Frendo's claim of Kaminiates' "initial protestations of a formal and conventional character to the effect that the task which Gregory wishes to impose upon him is beyond his limited intellectual powers" takes on a new significance when seen in the broader context of witness literature. It is a common concern across time, language, and historical context that witnesses fear that their narrative powers are insufficient. Equiano writes that "I am sensible I ought to entreat your pardon for addressing to you a work so wholly devoid of literary merit; but, as the production of an unlettered African, who is actuated by the hope of becoming an instrument towards the relief of his suffering countrymen, I trust that such a man, pleading in such a cause, will be acquitted of boldness and presumption."[57] In this, his rhetoric matches that of Kaminiates, who also worried about his "inability to furnish a well-written account of the subject" and "demean[ing] with the triviality of my style the magnitude of the events which you asked me to relate."[58] In both cases, the fear that they will not be believed is tied to their fear of the insufficiency of their narrative skills. Thus, this imprecation against their own style and literary merit is perhaps formulaic, but

---

[55] Equiano (1999: 36–39).

[56] Wiesel (2006: 3, 2007).

[57] Equiano (1999: 35).

[58] Kam. *ex. Thess.* 1, for which see above (72).

the formula stems from the lived experience of writers of witness literature and the very real reception of their work.

Before Kaminiates moves on to describing "what sort of place it is," however, he prefaces his remarks with another statement of method:

> Since you asked for detailed information about the physical layout of the city and that is in my view both a difficult enterprise and one that comes close to conflicting with the present tenor of my discourse, I shall preface my narrative with a few remarks intended to help you picture the objective reality behind my words, before turning to the saga of our misfortunes.

> ἀλλ' ἐπειδὴ καὶ τὰ κατ' αὐτὴν ἐκείνην τὴν πόλιν φιλοπόνως μαθεῖν ἐπεζήτησας, τοῦτο δὲ δυσεπιχείρη τόν τε ὡς ἐμοὶ τῇ τε παρούσῃ ὁρμῇ τοῦ λόγου παρὰ μικρὸν ἀνακόλουθον, ὀλίγα τινά, καὶ οἷς μάλιστα ἔξεστι δοκεῖν ὁρᾶν σε τῶν λεγομένων τὰ πράγματα, τῇ διηγήσει προσθεὶς ἐπὶ τὴν καθ' ἡμᾶς αὐτοὺς τραπήσομαι συμφοράν.[59]

Several aspects of this passage stand out: that his description "comes close to conflicting with the present tenor of my discourse" (τοῦτο δὲ δυσεπιχείρη τόν τε ὡς ἐμοὶ τῇ τε παρούσῃ ὁρμῇ τοῦ λόγου παρὰ μικρὸν ἀνακόλουθον)—by which, presumably, he means that his description of the city's glories contrasts with the melancholy tone that will determine the second half of the narrative after the city has been conquered, burned, and pillaged—reflects the difficulty Kaminiates faces dealing with tone. It is also significant that he considers the description of Thessaloniki not to be an essential part of the narrative itself; it is "a few remarks" (ὀλίγα τινά) that come before the main narrative and so somewhat structurally superfluous, and it is also explicitly meant to provide background: "the saga of our misfortunes" is the principle focus; the description of Thessaloniki is just meant to help concretize the images of the scenes to be described later.[60]

---

[59] Kam. *ex. Thess.* 3.7. Here the translators use "tenor of my discourse" for the Greek ὁρμῇ τοῦ λόγου; this expression occurs again later in slightly altered form—τὴν ὁρμὴν τοῦ λέγειν – and is translated as "the flow of one's narrative"; the second translation is more literal. The passage is analyzed by Panagopoulos, who considers *ekphrasis* and digression as part of Kaminiates' "need for authenticity in the presentation of events" (2014: 185).

[60] Kaminiates' insights into the economic, political, cultural, and geographic contexts of the city are discussed in Bakirtzis (2007: 102–105).

92 A. J. GOLDWYN

Kaminiates' "few remarks" begin answering Gregory's letter by describing in brief the city's history, and here he begins to adapt the rules outlined in Menander's treatise, thus offering not just city description as rhetorical topos, but articulating the way the processes of exile, loss, and memory imbue rhetoric with a personal and emotionally rich vision. He begins by following Menander quite closely and seemingly impersonally, but, as the description progresses, Kaminiates' own authorial voice begins to intrude and comment on the emotional consequences of writing about a lost home.[61]

As he comes to the end of his conventional description of the city, however, he interrupts the narrative with a comment in the first person:

> But without realizing it, I have overrun the length I had set myself initially for the account of these matters which I promised to give. Nostalgia for my native land is responsible for what has happened, because I was drawn on by happy memories, and I fondly imagined that I was present in the places I described.

> Ἀλλὰ γὰρ ἔλαθον ἐμαυτὸν μακρόν, ἢ ὡς ἀπ' ἀρχῆς ὑπεσχόμην, τὸν περὶ τούτων παρατείνας λόγον. πεποίηκε δὲ τοῦτο ὁ περὶ τὴν πατρίδα πόθος, ἡδέως τῇ τε μνήμῃ συνεφελκόμενος, καὶ ταῖς ἀνατυπώσεσιν οἷον δοκῶν συνεῖναι τοῖς λεγομένοις.[62]

This authorial interruption represents the first time that Kaminiates has deviated from the model laid forth in Menander, and the reason he does so is explicitly connected to his positionality as a slave and the circumstances of his writing in the prison. At the outset of the history and description of the city, Kaminiates had recognized that such background material was prefatory and should therefore be treated briefly, but the emotions generated during the writing process have caused him to narrate these things at greater length; that is to say, the rhythm of the narration

---

[61] For parallel passages where Kaminiates' seems to be indebted to Menander, see, for instance Menander's "How to Praise Gulfs" (πῶς δεῖ κόλπους ἐπαινεῖν) and Kaminiates' description of the gulf of Thessaloniki at 4.5, Menander's suggestion to describe the mountains and lakes of a region (Men. *Rhet.* 1.10.3) and Kaminiates' use of identical terminology at 5.1–2, and Menander's instruction to praise skilled workers in precious metals and gemstones (Men. *Rhet.* 1.16.7) with Kaminiates' mention of these same skills at 9–10.

[62] Kam. *ex. Thess.* 7.1–2.

turns out to be slower in segments that Kaminiates considered unimportant from a historical perspective but of increasing importance from the affective perspective of the remembering slave.

The reason he slows down the narrative is not because of the objective historical value of these passages, but rather because of their subjective value: the author finds pleasure in imagining the places of his past; writing provides a means of escape from the trauma of the present by immersing him in a time and place before they occurred. From this perspective, it might seem incredible that a hungry, cold slave sitting in a prison after having witnessed the death and separation of many of his family members would be able to recall the genre conventions of a third-century rhetorical treatise on city description that he may have learned about (or taught) in school many years earlier. Nostalgia, however, might explain why a letter composed in tragedy might begin with an encomium—from a literary perspective, the depth of the tragedy is increased when the destroyed city is described in all its former glory; from an affective perspective, moreover, the image of the city might increase in its splendor as it appears in the memory of a man sitting in a slave prison far away. In this way, Kaminiates' encomium on Thessaloniki marks one way in which the author innovates within the stylistic and formal constraints of the genre of city-praise. The encomium thus has an affective, emotional, and psychologically explicable function that transcends its value as a historical document, and this passage marks the initial moment in which the author's emotions, heretofore repressed beneath a dispassionate historiographical rhetoric, bubble to the surface.

In this, too, the psychological and emotional needs of John Kaminiates have much in common with Equiano. From his study of Equiano's description of his home city of Essaka, Carretta concludes that "given the number and variety of his sources, we may reasonably ask whether Equiano was experiencing recovered memory or the power of suggestion as he constructed his autobiography. A combination of personal experience, conflated sources, recovered memory, and the power of suggestion should not be surprising in a work that may be as much the biography of a people as it is the biography of an individual," an argument that perhaps holds as much for Kaminiates as for the freed African slave.[63]

[63] Carretta (2005: 7).

94   A. J. GOLDWYN

Equiano begins, like Kaminiates, with a discussion of the physical setting of his city in broad terms, narrating its geographical layout and position within the broader political world in inhabits.[64] The land itself, moreover, is, like Kaminiates' Thessaloniki, highly productive.[65] Both writers are explicit about the deeply personal reasons for offering the narrations of their homelands and, indeed, both interrupt their own descriptions to apologize for their prolixity. When Equiano completes his description, he writes: "I hope the reader will not think I have trespassed on his patience in introducing myself to him with some account of the manners and customs of my country. They had been implanted in me with great care, and made an impression on my mind, which time could not erase, and which all the adversity and variety of fortune I have since experienced served only to rivet and record; for, whether the love of one's country be real or imaginary, or a lesson of reason, or an instinct of nature, I still look back with pleasure on the first scenes of my life, though that pleasure has been for the most part mingled with sorrow."[66]

From a more theoretical perspective, the relationship between autobiography and identity under the conditions of slavery is applicable to both, as, for instance, Carretta argues that "whether [Equiano's] tale was truth or fiction, it is easy to imagine why emotionally he may have needed to tell such a story. Enslavement [...] had severed his African roots, effectively denying him a past outside of slavery. Creating or re-creating an African past allowed him to forge a personal national identity other than the one imposed on him by Europeans."[67]

And yet, there is also a significant difference between the two authors' inclusions of these scenes. Kaminiates is explicit that the overt reason was Gregory's request was of a personal nature. while its implications for identity, memory, and personal subjectivity are theoretical suppositions. Regardless, there seems to have been no broader political claim.[68]

---

[64] Equiano (1999: 45).

[65] Equiano (1999: 45).

[66] Equiano (1999: 51).

[67] Carretta (2005: 9).

[68] Kazhdan's suggestion that the work was a fifteenth-century work posing as witness leads him to suggest just such a broader political claim, arguing that it "was written as an antithesis to Anagnostes' *History*, which was marked by a latent pro-Turkish tendency" (1978: 312), a claim which Frendo dimisses: "That would make it into a sort of coded message whose purpose was to remind the reader just how badly the Turks had been

2 PRISON LITERATURE AND SLAVE NARRATIVES ... 95

Equiano's *Interesting Narrative*, by contrast, was one—though the most significant—contribution to the author's career-long engagement with abolition, a subject on which he had frequently written. Thus, Carretta writes that his "account [of Africa] was clearly intended to be part of the dialogue about the African slave trade. His representation of Igboland challenged images of Africa as a land of savagery, idolatry, cannibalism, indolence, and social disorder. Proponents of the slave trade argued that enslavement by Europeans saved Africans from such evils and introduced them to civilization, culture, industry, and Christianity."[69] In this way, both Equiano and Kaminiates use the conventions of the ekphrastic genre of description of a city or country, rhetorical imprecations of humility toward their audience, and other similar techniques that might otherwise be considered as obscuring the personal authorial voice to actually craft deeply personal narratives: for the slave Kaminiates, an appeal for his own freedom; for the freed slave Equiano, the freedom of all slaves. Indeed, in this way, Kaminiates and Equiano are both representative examples of larger groups. Just as Kaminiates represents his own suffering as the paradigmatic example of the suffering of all the Thessalonians, Equiano's sufferings serve a similar function. Carretta, for instance, distinguishes between those accounts of the Middle Passage that preceded Equiano's but which were written in the third-person by experts as studies or reports rather than first-person eyewitness records. According to Carretta, "many of these earlier accounts [of the Middle Passage] were fuller and more graphic than his own. His description [...], however, is the most frequently quoted record of the Middle Passage because it gives a voice to the inarticulate millions who suffered for it."[70]

Affective narratology also suggests that there is another psychological component to Kaminiates' unexpectedly long narration of the events before the conquest of the city. By slowing down the speed of his narration—indeed, the digression on the history and topography of Thessaloniki "pauses" the forward motion of narrative time entirely—Kaminiates delays the inevitable moment in his letter when he will have

---

behaving themselves in recent itmes by telling the story of just how beastly the Arabs had been five centuries earlier! Apart from the inherent improbability of such a notion, there seems to be no evidence of any such understanding of the text by the contemporary [... ie fifteenth-century] reader" (Frendo 2000: xxxix).

[69] Carretta (2005: 5).

[70] Carretta (2005: 33).

96   A. J. GOLDWYN

to begin relating these traumatic events.[71] De Jong defines this kind of narratological technique as "retardation," which she defines as "either (i) a slowing down of the narrative **rhythm**, or (ii) the postponement of an announced event through the intervention of other, sometimes even downright opposite events (a form of misdirection). It is used to add weight and/or create tension."[72] This example further illustrates the limits of classical narratology, which can only identify the narrative technique; postclassical narratology, by contrast, seeks to build on this foundational insight to ask why the author would make this choice, in this way, in this moment. From the perspective of affective (postclassical) narratology, then, the long introduction allows, from a more literary perspective, to "add weight" to the narrative by offering a description of a beautiful thing that the audience knows has already been destroyed. But this is not why Kaminiates himself says that he constructed such a long digression; rather, he says that the long description allowed to dwell on fond memories and to postpone the psychologically demanding task of narrating his own traumatic experience—a stylistic fulfillment of the claim made at the outset of the letter that he had delayed responding to Gregory at all.

Kaminiates quickly regains control of his emotions, however, writing "but if you think we should, let us return directly to the subject of the city" (πλὴν εἰ δοκεῖ, καὶ πάλιν ἀναδράμωμεν πρὸς αὐτὴν ἐκείνην τὴν πόλιν).[73] After a brief excursus on the city walls and the invasion of Greece by Xerxes, he concludes his previous description of the city's geography and topography by writing of its advantageous position as a coastal city with access to the best elements of both land and sea.[74] This, too, represents a rhetorical elaboration and amplification of the brief instructions

---

[71] De Jong and Nünlist define a "pause" as "a form of **rhythm** whereby no fabulatime corresponds to the story-time, i.e. the action comes to a standstill" (*Time in Ancient Greek Literature*, xiii).

[72] De Jong (2001: xvi–xvii); bold in original. De Jong offers different definitions that have functionally the same meaning in the various glossaries and writings she has compiled for narratological terms over the years. For the sake of consistency, I have generally relied on the definitions in De Jong and Nünlist (2007) except where noted, as in this instance, the term is not included in that glossary.

[73] Kam. *ex. Thess.* 7.4.

[74] Kam. *ex. Thess.* 9.4.

proposed by Menander.[75] As he comes to the end of this background material, moreover, Kaminiates interrupts his narrative again, noting the different emotions he feels as he moves from his recollections of Thessaloniki (and in particular of the beauty of the sacred hymns he remembers) to the narrative of the city's fall. In so doing, he returns again to the interrelated problems of affect, style, and narratology:

> But how can I convey in language the effect of setting words to music or the heartwarming melodies the singers sing and the zeal of those who are entirely devoted to the service of God? But how could I set down in writing a meaningful account of these matters? Up to the present point in my narrative I have been somehow carried along by the force of my words [...] But from this point onwards, especially when I recall the sweet sound of tuneful airs, I do not know what is to become of me, what direction I am to take in my narrative or which to omit of those sweetest and best ordered of melodies.

> τὰ δὲ περὶ τῆς ἁρμονίου μουσικῆς τῶν ᾀσμάτων, ἢ τῶν ἀδόντων τὰ ψυχοτερπῆ μέλη καὶ τῶν τῷ θεῷ κεκληρωμένων σπουδάσματα πῶς τῷ λόγῳ σημανῶ; πῶς δὲ τὴν τούτων διαγράψωμαι δήλωσιν; μέχρι γὰρ τοῦδε τοῦ διηγήματος οὐκ οἶδ' ὅπως τῇ ῥύμῃ τοῦ λόγου συναπαχθεὶς [...] τὸ δ' ἀπὸ τούτου, καὶ μάλισθ' ὅτι τῆς εὐρύθμου τῶν ᾀσμάτων ἐμνήσθην ἡδυφωνίας, οὐκ οἶδα τίς γένωμαι ἢ ποῖ τῷ λόγῳ χωρήσω, ποῖον δὲ παραλείπω τῶν ἡδίστων ἐκείνων καὶ εὐτάκτων μελῳδημάτων.[76]

As elsewhere, Kaminiates questions how he can describe a scene: how to recreate an actual thing when the only means available is the recollection of past events through the representational medium of words. In using the passive participle, "I have been carried along by the force of my words" (τῇ ῥύμῃ τοῦ λόγου συναπαχθεὶς), Kaminiates indicates the way that emotion has actually taken over as the guiding agent of the narrative. But in the last sentence, he switches to the active voice as he tries to take control of the narrative in a more self-determining way going forward: "what direction I am to take in my narrative" (ποῖ τῷ λόγῳ χωρήσω).

And yet, the problem of his own emotional state continues to impede and influence the narrative: first, when he recalls the happy memories of his past and, second, when he considers the misery of his current captive

[75] Men. *Rhet.* 1.10.5.
[76] Kam. *ex. Thess.* 10.4–6.

98   A. J. GOLDWYN

state, he becomes uncertain. This uncertainty is fundamentally connected with the structure of the narrative: what events to include or omit, and in what order to present them. Specifically, he is addressing the differentiation of "scene," in which "the story-time matches the fabula-time," from "summary," in which "the story-time is much shorter than the fabula-time."[77] Kaminiates' concern, therefore, as stated in the apologia, is how to limit the length of the narrative so as not to wear out the patience of his reader while also creating a factually and historically accurate account. He considers these problems through another series of rhetorical questions:

> To what lengths should we go in endeavouring to give shape to a pale reflection or in attempting through the superficial application of different colours to produce a pictorial likeness of the original, when it is in our power to get right to the heart of the matter by employing a narrative technique that seizes upon essential detail and puts the dimly apprehended into sharper focus?

> μέχρι γὰρ τίνος ὡς ἐν κατόπτρῳ τὸν ἀνδριάντα διαμορφοῦμεν, καὶ ταῖς ἔξωθεν τῶν χρωμάτων ποικιλίαις ἀπεικονίζειν πειρώμεθα τὸ ἀρχέτυπον, ἐξὸν αὐτοῖς ἐκείνοις ἐντυχεῖν διὰ τῶν καιρίων διηγημάτων τοῖς πράγμασιν, ὡς ἂν γνωριμώτερον εἴη τὸ ἀμυδρῶς πως παραδηλούμενον[78];

Kaminiates here notes that representation through writing cannot actually recreate the experience, but can only show a kind of inferior resemblance—"a pale reflection," "a pictorial likeness of the original."[79] Kaminiates also notes that literature cannot be objective in describing experience, since the author goes to some length to "give shape" to the events he describes.

[77] De Jong and Nünlist (2007: xiii).

[78] Kam. *ex. Thess.* 7.4. The desire to convey reality through literature coupled with the recognition of the limits of literature as a representational medium is also a pressing subject in Holocaust Studies. Ruth Franklin notes that "the Holy Grail of Holocaust literature" is "that forever desired and never-to-be-attained text that will provide us with a direct channel to the Holocaust. [...] And since this is clearly impossible, we are left desiring the next best thing – an authentic document, straight from the concentration camp or ghetto, that will offer us unmediated access to the experience; that will tell us, in Wiesel's words, 'how it really was'" (2011: 7).

[79] A relevant discussion for this idea can be found in Webb (1997: 115–117), where she compares Menander's *presbutikoi logoi* (*Ambassador's Speech*) with the letter of Aelius Aristides to Marcus Aurelius and Commodus.

When Thessaloniki fell again nearly three centuries later, Eustathios was dismissive of those who "adorn [their account] with descriptions of places and monuments" (τοπογραφήσει καὶ ἐκφράσεσιν ἐναγλαΐσεται),[80] which scholars such as Melville-Jones have speculated is a denunciation of Kaminiates. Melville-Jones writes that "the account of Kameniates [sic] contains a brief formal 'topography' of the city and Eustathios may have feared that the lack in his own work of any formal description of Thessaloniki, or an ekphrasis praising its many beauties, would offer an opportunity to his critics for unfavourable comment."[81] However, trauma studies and psychoanalysis may offer an alternative (or complementary) reading. In this regard, that Eustathios survived the event, that Thessaloniki was restored to Byzantine control, and that Eustathios was able to return to the city mark his experience as significantly different than that of John Kaminiates. Kaminiates was, in the words of Simon Gigliotti, a "mobile witness":

> Analyzing representations of the self and other in relation to place allows a consideration of the spatiality of testimony and the emplotment of experiences – in effect, an expansive and constricted geography of mobile witnessing. This mobile witnessing is not fixed or finite. [… P]ublic buildings are, however, more than mere backdrops in testimonies to the main themes of loss, displacement, and estrangement. Taken collectively, they constitute a memory map that marks the boundary between the familiar and the unknown. The witness's tellability of departure from ghettos, with its desperation, anticipation, and sense of motion without destination, evokes an image of a frontier or border that is to be crossed. The human and inhuman landscapes of this frontier are the central referents through which the experience of train transit is initiated, negotiated, and interpreted.[82]

Kaminiates' description of Thessaloniki, therefore, cannot be dismissed as simply a piece of rhetoric; rather, it must be understood within the broader categories of his own positionality and subjectivity. He himself tells us that he has been carried away by nostalgia, that the memories of his native land so overwhelm him that he loses control of the flow of

---

[80] Eust. *de Capta* 2.16.

[81] Melville-Jones (1988: 232–233).

[82] Gigliotti (2009: 65).

100   A. J. GOLDWYN

his narrative. In light of Gigliotti's notion that the recollection of specific architectural features anchors the transported witness to the place from which they were deported, Kaminiates' elaborate and lengthy depiction of the city takes on added significance as part of the author's overall work of witnessing. Memory and emotion are anchored to place, and the description of place is constructed through rhetorical conventions. For the "mobile witness" who had, like Eustathios, experienced the privations of city-sacking but who, unlike Eustathios, had also been transported from the city, the topographical survey demonstrates how affect can influence narratives: "the civic architecture provides initial locations and places from which to ground the witness's emerging dialogue with loss of the familiar, especially one's accommodation and family."[83]

2.2   "A NARRATIVE TECHNIQUE THAT SEIZES UPON ESSENTIAL DETAIL": KAMINIATES' PRINCIPLES OF SELECTION

Kaminiates' meditation on how to give shape to a story is also one narratologists have attempted to answer through the tripartite division of "fabula," "story," and "text," that is, the events that happened, the ordering of those events in a specific way, and their presentation through a particular medium.[84] The problem he faces, therefore, is how to choose which events to include or omit, and in what order to put them to create the desired effect. This, too, can be put in terms of modern narratology: Kaminiates is wrestling with the question of "patterning," which Bal defines as the "the attention paid to the various elements" and which, according to her, "gives us a picture of the vision of the fabula communicated to the reader."[85] To solve the question of selectivity in narration, Kaminiates develops what he calls καιρίων διηγημάτων (a narrative technique that seizes upon the essential detail) or, a few lines later, τὴν τῶν καιρίων ἐξήγησιν (an account of the things that really matter), as the

---

[83] Gigliotti (2009: 66).

[84] For functional definitions, see de Jong and Nünlist (2007: xii–xiii) and Bal: "A *narrative* text is a text in which an agent relates ('tells') a story in a particular medium[. ...] A *story* is a fabula that is presented in a certain manner. A *fabula* is a series of logically and chronologically related events that are caused or experienced by actors" (2009: 5).

[85] Bal (2009: 99).

best method for conveying the affective experience of witness while also narrating.[86] Alternate translations might modify "essential detail" somewhat; "relevant stories" or "timely stories" could be construed as more literal renderings, but would not necessarily change the fundamentals of the expressions: in either case, they point to a self-consciousness as regards principles of selection: the entirety is impossible to narrate, and thus some representative examples must be chosen as a limiting device for the near-infinite possible events to narrate. In this, he builds upon an earlier programmatic statement, "the account of what will be said proceeds truthfully, and in a manner alien to all falsehood and fiction" (ἀληθῆ δὲ μᾶλλον καὶ παντὸς ἀλλοτρίαν καὶ ψεύδους καὶ πλάσματος τὴν τῶν ῥηθησομένων προβαίνουσαν συγγραφὴν).[87] Focusing on the essential detail/relevant story becomes the crucial method for creating a coherent story (in the narratological sense) out of the effectively infinite number of possible events (the fabula) that occurred in the harbor that day—while also being true. Though Kaminiates cannot narrate all the events, he can choose an individual example that serves as a representative of the whole, a kind of synecdoche of witness, or, in narratological terms, a form of iterative narration: "when repeated events are told only once."[88]

This method becomes crucial for describing the human suffering in which he was both participant and witness. For example, shortly after the city had fallen, Kaminiates describes how he and the other survivors were.

> forcibly separated and herded on to the ships, which were large enough to hold great numbers of people [...] In this way all the ships (fifty-four of them in all as I pointed out) were loaded up. But there was still a large number of people left over who had been designated for transportation. Accordingly, the barbarians got together the ships belonging to the city, which our merchants occasionally used for importing grains, and also those which we had sunk at the entrance of the harbour.

> βιαίως οὕτως ἐξ ἀλλήλων διαιρεθέντες φύρδην ταῖς ὁλκάσιν εἰσήχθησαν, εὐρείαις τε οὔσαις καὶ ἱκαναῖς πλήθεσι πολλοῖς ἐξαρκεῖν [...] Πᾶσαι δὲ αἱ νῆες τῷ τρόπῳ τούτῳ πεπλήρωντο· τέτταρες γὰρ οὖσαι, καθὼς ἔφαμεν, καὶ πεντήκοντα. ἔτι δὲ πλῆθος ἦν περιττεῦον, ἄξιον καὶ αὐτὸ κρινόμενον τῆς

---

[86] Kam. *ex. Thess.* 7.4, 5.

[87] Kam. *ex. Thess.* 1.6.

[88] De Jong and Nünlist (2007: xii).

102   A. J. GOLDWYN

ἀποδημίας. οἱ οὖν βάρβαροι συναγαγόντες τὰς νῆας τῆς πόλεως, αἷς ἐχρῶν τό ποτε πρὸς τὸ τὸν σῖτον ἐπικομίζειν οἱ καθ᾽ ἡμᾶς ἔμποροι, ἔτι δὲ καὶ ἃς ἦμεν βυθίσαντες κατὰ τοῦ πορθμοῦ τοῦ λιμένος.[89]

When this, too, proved insufficient for the number of captives, they dredged up the ships that the defenders of the city had sunk to block the entrance to the harbor. Concluding this description, he writes: "It was impossible for anyone who paused to consider them individually not to break down at the sight of their misfortune" (οὓς ἄν τις καθ᾽ ἕνα λογιζόμενος κατεκλᾶτο, μὴ σθένων ὁρᾶν τὰ καθ᾽ ἕκαστον αὐτῶν ἀτυχήματα).[90] Kaminiates knows that, with all of these people, narrating the entirety of their individual horrors would not only be impossible, but it would dilute the emotional response of the reader, who counterintuitively finds the misfortune of the individual, narrated in detail, to be more affecting than the narration of that suffering on a massive scale in general terms. Thus, the narrated sufferings of one individual come to stand in as representative of the unnarrated sufferings of everyone else.[91]

The actual rhetorical strategies that Kaminiates uses to allow his reader to consider the plight of the suffering individual within the broader context of mass suffering can be seen in his description of very first moments of the city's fall. He begins his narrative from an almost omniscient perspective: "The population of the city broke up into numerous groups which huddled together in stunned bewilderment and confusion, not knowing how to save themselves or how to fend off disaster" (τὸ δὲ πλῆθος τῆς πόλεως εἰς πολλὰ μέρη τμηθὲν διεθρυλλεῖτό τε καὶ συνείχετο, οὐκ ἔχον ὅπου περισωθείη ἢ τὴν συμφορὰν διακρούσεται).[92] Having established that a large number of people are suffering, Kaminiates slowly begins to zoom in on individual figures. He uses what narratologists call "embedded focalization," to place the reader directly in the moment, as though they were there: "One could see people drifting about aimlessly like ships without a rudder, a pitiful

---

[89] Kam. *ex. Thess.* 60.7, 61.1–3.

[90] Kam. *ex. Thess.* 61.5.

[91] Alex Haley explicitly stated a similar goal when writing *Roots*: "I began to realize that the biggest challenge I had was to try and write a book which, although [sic] was the story of my family would symbolically be in fact the saga of Black people in this country" (Lambert 2019: 27 n.24).

[92] Kam. *ex. Thess.* 35.4.

2 PRISON LITERATURE AND SLAVE NARRATIVES ... 103

sight; men, women and children throwing themselves on each other, clinging to one another and exchanging that last and most piteous parting embrace" (ἦν γὰρ ἰδεῖν τότε τοὺς ἀνθρώπους ὡς ἀκυβέρνητα σκάφη τῆδε κἀκεῖσε περιφερομένους, ἐλεεινὸν θέαμα, ἄνδρας γυναῖκας νήπια, ἀλλήλοις συμπίπτοντας, ἀλλήλων ἐκκρεμαμένους, ἀσπαζομένους τὸν οἴκτιστον ἐκεῖνον καὶ τελευταῖον ἀσπασμόν).[93] In this instance, the verb ἰδεῖν enables the audience to see through the eyes of the narrator, a form of explicitly embedded focalization that "describ[es] the content of perception."[94] Kaminiates, moreover, describes the scene as ἐλεεινὸν θέαμα (a pitiful sight), further reinforcing the guiding principle of the work—to narrate that which will make his audience feel most pity/sympathy.[95] Having surveyed the entirety of the scene and having purposefully directed the audience's perception, Kaminiates then moves to the narration of individual suffering: "If somewhere in their midst there was an elderly father he would throw his arms around his son's neck and set up a dreadful wailing, and would be unable to bear the separation. Instead, he would hold fast to his beloved son and feeling the pangs of natural affection before he felt the pain of the sword, would break into an improvised lament" (εἴ πού τις καὶ πατὴρ ἐν αὐτοῖς πρεσβύτης, ἐπιπεσὼν τῷ τραχήλῳ τοῦ παιδὸς δεινὸν ἐπεκώκυε, τὸν χωρισμὸν οὐ φέρων, ἀλλὰ τὰ μέλη κατέχων τοῦ φιλτάτου, καὶ πρὸτοῦ ξίφους τῷ φυσικῷ νυττόμενος πάθει τὸν θρῆνον ἑαυτῷ διετίθει).[96] Thus, Kaminiates brings the narrative from the very general level ("the population of the city") to the level of the individual person (the father speaking to his son). In order to do so, however, Kaminiates must narrate something essentially fictional yet also essentially true: there was no actual father who said the exact words of the long lament that Kaminiates then puts in his mouth, but rather Kaminiates is inventing a composite character who stands in for the actual individuals

---

[93] Kam. *ex. Thess.* 35.5.

[94] De Jong (2004: 38). De Jong elaborates on this idea by adding that "explicit embedded focalization involving the perceptions of characters can be triggered off in the *Iliad* by the following verbs: (see, look at): νοέω, ὁράω, δράω, δέρκομαι" and other similar verbs (2004: 38). Kaminiates' ἰδεῖν is the aorist infinitive of ὁράω, thus indicating that the passage is focalized through the conquered people of Thessaloniki.

[95] For "sensory witnessing" and the (problematic) priority of sight for articulating experience, see Gigliotti (2009: 128–168). The phrase also appears in the *History* of Niketas Choniates, 65 and 349.

[96] Kam. *ex. Thess.* 35.6.

104   A. J. GOLDWYN

in the city.[97] In so doing, Kaminiates stretches the boundaries between fiction and nonfiction, inserting a rhetorical *ethopoeia* of the type what a father might say upon lamenting his son.[98] In his analysis of the form and function of *ethopoeia*, Panagiotis Roilos argues that they are largely a literary phenomenon, that is, they have as their referent other works of literature or rhetoric and not the actual world of lived experience and uttered speech (though in their original functions they were used for court recitation as "real" voices having nothing to do with rhetoric of fiction). Thus, for instance, speaking about the "pathētikai ēthopoiia-laments," he writes: "Like their ancient Greek models, the Komnenian novels, too, are replete with laments that draw primarily on the dramatic and rhetorical threnodic traditions" and "must be viewed therefore not only in relation to their ancient literary models but also in terms of their connections with the literary and performative practice of their contemporary rhetorical laments."[99] He concludes by noting that "the ways in which the Komnenian novelists construct the speeches of their characters bespeak a careful reworking of the established conventions of *progymnasmata*, and specifically of the genre of ēthopoiia (character study). [...] By manipulating inherited modes of rhetorical expression the Komnenian novelists articulate highly self-referential fictional discourses that respond creatively first to their ancient literary models, second to one another, and, finally, to the horizon of expectations of the rhetorically trained members of their audience."[100] Nowhere in this analysis is an accounting of lived experience: what grieving people actually said. This may suffice for an analysis of fictional works, but it complicates any potential reading of John Kaminiates' ostensibly nonfictional text. Kaminiates' use of the rhetoric of *ethopoeia* here, as elsewhere, demonstrates that the expression of authentic emotion often flows through otherwise seemingly rigid and conventional

[97] Panagopoulos argues that the lament of the father for his son and the husband for his wife (for which, see below), reflect "the influence of another rhetorical *progymnasma*, that of the *ethopoeia*[. ...] This is precisely what rhetoric was aiming at with *ethopoeia*: what such-and-such a man said, whether it be about a particular person or about a man who is identified only by the situation in which is found, in a particular circumstance" (2014: 199–200).

[98] For ethopoeia in general and in the Komnenian novel in particular, see Roilos (2005: 79–110).

[99] Roilos (2005: 79).

[100] Roilos (2005: 112).

2 PRISON LITERATURE AND SLAVE NARRATIVES ... 105

structures. In that they do not, therefore, originate within a modern romantic paradigm of originality, they may seem inauthentic, and yet, the laments of Kaminiates and others suggest that authentic emotional experience is often communicated through pre-established generic and rhetorical forms.

The insufficiency of a pure rhetoric separate from lived experience for explaining Kaminiates' inclusion of seemingly fictional *ethopoeia* in a text that is otherwise committed to the highest demands of verisimilitude suggests that Kaminiates at least believed that genre and rhetoric could nevertheless convey something, as he says "truthfully and in a manner alien to all falsehoods and fictions" (ἀληθῆ δὲ μᾶλλον καὶ παντὸς ἀλλοτρίαν καὶ ψεύδους καὶ πλάσματος τὴν τῶν ῥηθησομένων).[101] Indeed, the connection between rhetoric and lived experience might offer a psychoanalytic reading that connects Kaminiates' own invented laments with his experience at the harbor, for he himself suffered the fate that he puts in the mouths of another: he notes that during their initial period of separation, one of his children died during the sea voyage.[102] Perhaps Kaminiates transferred his own laments for this dead child into a more representative and less personal form, a way of separating himself from his own trauma that would be in line with both Neville's view of him as having "created a rhetorical self in the text that was more a witness to tragedy than a sufferer. He described the anguish of others, but scrupulously avoided first-person expressions of grief."[103] It would also be in line with the traumatic recollection of witness literature, as when Wiesel notes that he omitted some aspects of the narrative because they were "too personal, too private" (trop personnels, trop intimes)."[104]

Kaminiates uses this strategy of inventing a representative example from among a real crowd to describe other kinds of grieving that occurred in the initial moments after the defenses failed, and again, this lament draws from the rhetorical tradition and has a potential real-life referent. He offers the fictional but representative lament of "some other man who happened to be standing near his wife" (ἄλλος τις τῇ συννόμῳ γυναικὶ

---

[101] Kam. *ex. Thess.* 1.6.

[102] Kam. *ex. Thess.* 73.11.

[103] Neville (2019: 69).

[104] Wiesel (2006: 70; 2007: 15).

106   A. J. GOLDWYN

προστυχών), thus providing a different example of severed familial relations; this man "would groan loud and deep, shake his head, change expression, run up to her, embrace her and give tragic utterance to his grief" (βύθιόν τι καὶ μέγα στενάξας, τὴν κεφαλήν τε κινήσας καὶ τὴν μορφὴν ἀλλοιώσας, προσδραμὼν αὐτῇ καὶ περιπλακεὶς τὴν συμφορὰν ἐτραγῴδει) and then begins another monologue that focuses on the specific sufferings of the separated husband and wife.[105] But, this, too, is what happened to Kaminiates' brother: "My brother's wife was among those sold, an occurrence which caused considerable anguish" (ἐν οἷς ἔτυχεν ἐκδοθεῖσα καὶ ἡ τοῦ ἐμοῦ ἀδελφοῦ σύζυγος, οὐ μετρίαν ἡμῖν ὀδύνην περιποιήσασα).[106] Thus, when Kaminiates writes of trying to make his reader pause to consider each of these people individually, he is speaking of the plight of real people, but in order to direct the reader's attention in this way within the constraints of mimetic language, his method is to invent hypothetical figures whose suffering nevertheless represents the suffering of all those in similar situations throughout the city. This is, in a sense, one method by which Kaminiates' uses a kind of fictionality within a narrative defined by a rhetoric of adherence to truth to produce witness literature as Levi's "discourse on behalf of others." Indeed, here the translation seems to downplay the emotive aspect of the Greek: translating οὐ μετρίαν as "considerable" understates the dimension of the suffering. "Considerable" denotes something that is within the capacity of the human mind to know—it can be considered—whereas a more literal rendering of the Greek phrase would be "overwhelming" or "immeasurable," that is, the anguish or suffering is beyond human understanding.

When Kaminiates asserts that speaking about the entire group (summary) is less effective at creating an emotional response in his readers (sorrow or grief, as represented through crying) than of seeing these events from the perspective of a single figure, he is also referring obliquely to the one individual whose suffering is narrated in greatest detail throughout the letter and from whose perspective Gregory (and, by extension, subsequent readers) witness the conquest of Thessaloniki and its aftermath: Kaminiates himself. Kaminiates as author and witness is the paradigmatic example: he cries when he considers the scene. But, by focalizing the sufferings through his own perspective, Kaminiates also makes

---

[105] Kam. *ex. Thess.* 36.1.

[106] Kam. *ex. Thess.* 73.10.

2 PRISON LITERATURE AND SLAVE NARRATIVES ... 107

the audience stop to consider him as an individual and, as the narrative progresses, the individuals who suffering he then narrates. For Kaminiates, then, the job of the survivor as writer and witness is to consider the unique iteration of one individual's suffering as both a mimetic transcription of that person's actual experience and, simultaneously, for that individual's experience to stand as the paradigmatic example of the experiences of those who shared in it but who could not—through death or other circumstances—bear witness themselves.

As much as writing witness literature in this way is a matter of narratology in terms of focalizing through individual experience, it is also a question of order: in describing the heart-rending scenes of family separation and chaos in the harbor of Thessaloniki before they were put on the ships, for instance, Kaminiates pauses his narration to ask two rhetorical questions as he recalls the chaos of activity spread out before him: "But which of these things shall I relate first? Which incident shall I single out as having a better claim on one's sympathy?" (ἀλλὰ ποῖον τούτων πρῶτον ἐξείπω; ποῖον δὲ κατ' ἀξίαν ἐλεεινότερον κρινῶ;)[107] In asking such a question, Kaminiates is responding directly to the rhetorical tradition embodied in Menander, who uses the verb κρίνω (here translated as "single out" but in Race's translation of Menander as "evaluate")[108] to introduce new topics for encomiastic inquiry, ἀξίαν as the measure of what is or is not worth writing about,[109] and ἐλεεινότερον (here "sympathy" but in Race's translation as "pity").[110]

In this, too, Kaminiates shares a narrative aim with Equiano, who implores his readers in similar terms: "Permit me, with the greatest deference and respect, to lay at your feet the following genuine Narrative; the chief design of which is to excite in your august assemblies a sense of compassion for the miseries which the Slave-Trade has entailed on my unfortunate countrymen."[111] Both aim to instill in their readers a sense of sympathy or compassion in order to induce them to support, on the one

---

[107] Kam. *ex. Thess.* 60.4. For Eustathios and pity, see, for instance, 8.5: "the most pitiable of all was that even infants lay among those who fell in one manner or another" (Ἐλεεινότατον δὲ ὅτι καὶ βρέφη συνέκειντο τοῖς παντοδαπῶς πίπτουσι).

[108] Κριτέον: Men. *Rhet.* 1.11.11; κρίνομεν: Men. *Rhet* 1.10.1.

[109] As, for instance, that one should praise a festival by saying "it is dignified and worthy of great admiration" (ὅτι σεμνὴ καὶ ὅτι θαύματος ἀξία πολλοῦ) (Men. *Rhet.* 2.13.4).

[110] For the significance of this word, see below, p. 256.

[111] Equiano (1999: 35).

108   A. J. GOLDWYN

hand, the abolition of slavery as a whole and, on the other, the ransoming of one particular slave.

Kaminiates, therefore, is asking a rhetorical question—that is, he is attempting to evaluate which elements of the story will have the most powerful emotional impact by using the concepts and diction set forth in the rhetorical treatises. But, for Kaminiates, these narratological choices are not simply stylistic but will have important ramifications for the interpretation of the text: "But how from this point on shall I describe to you, o most cultured of men, our misfortune or outline the sequence of so many painful events? Which shall I select for first mention, thereby relegating the rest to second place?" (Ἀλλὰ πῶς ἄν σοι τοῦ λοιποῦ τὴν καθ' ἡμᾶς συμφοράν, ὦ ἀνδρῶν λογιώτατε, ἢ τὴν ἐπαλληλίαν τῶν τοσούτων ἀνιαρῶν διαγράψωμαι; ποῖον τούτων πρῶτον εἰπὼν τοῖς ἄλλοις δευτερεύειν παραχωρήσω;)[112] The concern is both stylistic (that is, his concern with how to describe) as well as narratological (that is, with principles of selection and with the sequencing of events). But more importantly, he seems to recognize here that, given that each person in the harbor had different experiences, the ordering of these events is also a statement of ideology or values: whichever one comes first is more important than whichever one comes second.

And yet that ordering is essential, and these kinds of decisions must be made, for without them, there could be no narrative, and thus no remembrance, at all for those victims. And yet, just as he must narrate something, he cannot narrate everything, lest he wears out his reader: if no one reads the work, then the events are just as forgotten as if he had never written them down. Thus, style and structure are essential elements of the process of memory. Kaminiates returns to the connection between style, structure, and memory when he describes the conditions on the slave ships, he writes:

> If I wished to furnish a detailed narrative of the hardships and over-crowding to which we were continually subjected during that voyage, most people would think that I was romancing and departing from that strict adherence to truth that I promised at the outset of my account would be the guiding principle of my writing. Accordingly, having deliberately omitted most of what took place and confined myself so far to that which lies within my mental capacity to convey, and having done so with a view

[112] Kam. *ex. Thess.* 37.1–2.

2 PRISON LITERATURE AND SLAVE NARRATIVES … 109

to providing you, Gregory, o wisest and most learned of men, with an account that is reliable in every particular, let me now observe the same procedure in dealing with the remaining part of my narrative.

εἰ γὰρ ἀπαριθμῆσαι θελήσω καθ' ἓν ὅσα κατὰ τὴν περίοδον ἐκείνην τοῦ πλοὸς ὑπέστημεν καὶ μεθ' ὅσης στενοχωρίας, μύθους δόξω τοῖς πολλοῖς ἐξηγεῖσθαι καὶ τῆς ἀληθείας ἐκτρέπεσθαι, καθ' ἣν ἐν ἀρχῇ τοῦ λόγου πάντα γραφῇ παραδοῦναι καθυπεσχόμην. διά τοι τοῦτο τὰ πλεῖστα τῶν πεπραγμένων ἑκὼν παραδραμών, οἷς ἂν ἐδόκουν μάλιστα τὴν ἡμετέραν ἐξαρκεῖν διάνοιαν μέχρι τοῦ νῦν προσδιατρίψας, ὡς ἐν ἅπασι τὸ πιστόν σοι παρασχεῖν, ὦ σοφώτατε ἀνδρῶν καὶ φιλομαθέστατε Γρηγόριε, κατὰ τὸν αὐτὸν τρόπον πάλιν καὶ περὶ τῶν λοιπῶν διεξίω.[113]

At the level of style, Kaminiates must convince his audience that he is not as the translator says in a telling and yet anachronistic rendering, "romancing" (μύθους δόξω […] ἐξηγεῖσθαι), perhaps more meaningfully translated as "narrating [false] stories", or "departing from that strict adherence to truth" (τῆς ἀληθείας ἐκτρέπεσθαι) and thus the work would not stand as a work of witness. Thus, he comes to the question of structure, in which, ironically, "omit[ing] most of what took place" (τὰ πλεῖστα τῶν πεπραγμένων ἑκὼν παραδραμών) or focusing on the essential detail, becomes the most comprehensive and accurate means of narration.[114] In this way, the verb ἀπαριθμῆσαι takes on added significance, for what the translators propose as "if I wished to furnish a detailed narrative" might be more literally translated "if I wished to enumerate" or "count" all that happened, suggesting that the sheer number of events would be overwhelming.

For Kaminiates, moreover, these are not just abstract decisions of narrative choice: these decisions memorialize or condemn to obscurity the

---

[113] Kam. *ex. Thess.* 74.9–10.

[114] For omission, see Bal (2009: 100–104). Leonora Neville similarly notes that "John maintained a dual narrative, on the one hand describing the experiences and suffering of the people of the city in a general abstract sense, and on the other, revealing what happened to himself and his family" (Neville 2019: 68), thus recognizing the distinction between the mass of people and the individual narrator. However, she concludes from this that "[i]t is in this division in the subject of his story and the separate treatment of the two narrative strands that we see most clearly his attempt to craft a self-portrayal in which he maintains control over himself (2019: 69), I argue that his authorial interruptions demonstrate a rhetorical strategy which prioritizes the author's lack of emotional self-discipline in order to cultivate his audience's sympathy and cope with his own trauma.

110   A. J. GOLDWYN

suffering of individual people whom he himself knew; indeed, Kaminiates describes his experience observing the carnage of the conquest as he was marched from the upper city where he had been captured to the harbor down below:

> We gazed intently as we passed, and whenever we recognized a late acquaintance or friend, we confined ourselves to pointing him out to one another with a whispered sigh. There was no time to mourn him or to bestow some token of grief appropriate to the circumstances of our past friendship. Faced, therefore, with the impossibility of giving the dead man a funeral, we could only turn back sorrowfully to our own concerns.

> παριόντες οὖν ἐσκοποῦμεν, καὶ εἴ πού τινα τῶν ποτε γνωρίμων ἢ φίλων μεταξὺ τῶν ἄλλων νεκρῶν ἀπηκριβωσάμεθα, ἠρέμα μόνον τοῖς στεναγμοῖς πρὸς ἀλλήλους τοῦτον διεσημαίνομεν. σχολὴ δ' οὐκ ἦν ἢ θρηνῆσαι τοῦτον ἢ χαρίσασθαί τι τῆς ποτε φιλίας τῷ καιρῷ χρήσιμον· ἀλλ' ἢ μόνον ἄπρακτα τῷ κειμένῳ περιαλγήσαντες πάλιν περὶ τῶν καθ' ἑαυτοὺς ἐσκεπτόμεθα.[115]

Thus, when Kaminiates wonders how to order the sequence of events from his fabula into a particular story, when he wonders what to include and what to omit entirely, he is also asking by extension which of his friends' lives is more deserving of narration—whose suffering was greater, or more representative, or more extreme—even as he is choosing who among them will be remembered and who forgotten. Indeed, the very narrative of his walking to the harbor is a stylistic enactment of the very principles that Kaminiates struggled with: he does not give the names of any of the friends or acquaintances he passes. As there was no time to mourn them then, there is no time to mourn them now. The consequences of this decision are that those people's lives and life stories are lost forever; in omitting the stories of the unique iteration of their suffering, however, Kaminiates is able to effectively create the story of one among them who survived, Kaminiates himself, and his individual story thus also serves as a representative or paradigmatic example of all the lost and unmemorialized ones.

Here, then, the narratological distinction between summary and scene has important ramifications for the act of witnessing, since the witness ultimately decides who will be remembered and who will be forgotten.

---

[115] Kam. *ex. Thess.* 54.11–12.

2 PRISON LITERATURE AND SLAVE NARRATIVES ... 111

Kaminiates thus gestures toward what Primo Levi calls the "lacuna" in every example of witness testimony and on which Giorgio Agamben dwells at length, concluding: "There is another lacuna in every testimony: witnesses are by definition survivors and so all, to some degree, enjoyed a privilege. ... No one has told the destiny of the common prisoner, since it was not materially possible for him to survive."[116]

As elsewhere in the narrative, however, because the primary narrator-focalizer is himself also a witness, these narratological decisions cannot be separated from his lived experience of the events. In his description of the gathering of the survivors at the harbor, for instance, the text itself is influenced both by the author's intention but, perhaps more significantly, by the emotions he feels as he begins to actually write:

> The recollection of events drives me to distraction. I seem to see actually happening all over again the things that I am about to relate and am, in consequence, not insensible to the difficulty of embarking on such a narrative. For the representation of events as if they were actually occurring portrays danger to the mind's eye through the immediacy of recollection, and reshaping reality by means of the imagination, forcibly arrests the flow of one's narrative.

> ἐξιστᾷ γάρ μου τὸν νοῦν ἡ μνήμη τῶν γεγονότων, καὶ οἷον ὁρᾶν πάλιν δοκῶν τῶν λεχθησομένων τὰ πράγματα δυσεπιχείρητον τὴν περὶ τούτων ἐξήγησιν ἐπαισθάνομαι. ἡ γὰρ ἀνατύπωσις τῶν γεγονότων ὡς ἄρτι πραττομένων τῇ ψυχῇ διὰ τῆς μνήμης τὸν κίνδυνον εἰκονίζουσα καὶ διαμορφοῦσα τῇ φαντασίᾳ τὰ πράγματα, τὴν ὁρμὴν τοῦ λέγειν ἐπέχειν βιάζεται.[117]

Kaminiates explicitly ties the emotional experience of the recollection of traumatic events to the ordering and construction of the narrative. These psychotraumatic struggles, moreover, manifest themselves in a particular way; the act of remembering "forcibly arrests the flow of one's narrative." The rhythm of the narrative is affected by the emotional pain of the writer recollecting the events: he stops his narration rather than relive the emotional trauma of the experience through writing it out. The narrative

---

[116] Agamben (2017: 783).

[117] Kam. *ex. Thess.* 37.3–4. For φαντασία (imagination) in Menander Rhetor and the rhetorical tradition, see Webb (1997: 117–120).

112   A. J. GOLDWYN

as constructed by the witness must therefore be different than the narrative constructed by those who did not experience it, since both kinds of writers are operating under different affective circumstances.

2.3 THE SUBJECTIVE "I" WITNESS AND BIOPOLITICS IN KAMINIATES' PRINCIPLES OF SELECTION

John Kaminiates frequently interrupts the narrative thread of his letter to discuss the difficulties of relating the traumatic events of which he was a part: "But why do I try to furnish an account of these things, when I am incapable of conveying even a tiny fraction of the events that took place on that occasion?" (ἀλλὰ τί μάτην τὴν ἐπὶ τούτοις ἐπιχειρῶ συγγραφήν, οὐδὲ τὸ πολλοστὸν μέρος τῶν τότε πεπραγμένων ἱκανὸν παραστήσασθαι;)[118] he asks, later adding "If anyone wished to record their misfortunes he would be like a man trying to arrive by guesswork at the precise number of grain of sands on the seashore" (ὧν εἰ θελήσοι τις τὰς συμφορὰς ἀναγράφεσθαι, ὅμοιος εἶναι δόξει τῷ τὴν παραλίαν ψάμμον ἐκμετρεῖν εἰκαίως τοπάσαντι).[119] Knowing that a complete list of the horrors he witnessed and which were visited upon him would require a narrative of impossible length, he had to apply a variety of narratological strategies, including elision, summary, narrative delay, and others that allow for the reconstruction of lived reality in the mimetic form of narrative without allowing the narrative to go on too long. He thus settles upon a method that will "omit most of what took place" and instead employ "a narrative technique that seizes upon the essential detail," a limiting strategy of narrative synecdoche in which a narrated part of the sufferings that occurred on that day stand in for the (unnarrated and unnarratable) whole of the sufferings—a principle in line with the kinds of epideictic texts modeled in Menander: "The epideictic orator was not therefore simply stating the obvious, but was selecting evidence from a certain interpretation of events from a multifarious reality which could be subject to competing interpretations."[120] Thus, Kaminiates shapes the events to create a larger teleological narrative thread, increasing the piteousness of

---

[118] Kam. *ex. Thess.* 71.15.

[119] Kam. *ex. Thess.* 78.3.

[120] Webb (2003: 134–135).

2 PRISON LITERATURE AND SLAVE NARRATIVES ... 113

the destruction of the city by preceding it with a list of the city's glories, a method suggested by Menander in *The Ambassador's Speech*.[121]

Despite these frequent authorial interruptions in which Kaminiates describes his method, he never states what he considers the essential detail to be nor by which principle(s) he chooses which events to include or omit, though two rhetorical questions posed during his narrative reveal his principles of selection for not just what events to include and how to narrate them, but what order in which to place them: "But which of these things shall I relate first? Which incident shall I single out as having a better claim on one's sympathy?" For Kaminiates, the principle of inclusion is to choose, from among all those endured by all those in the city, the individual events which most arouse his readers' "sympathy;" a rhetorical decision that follows what Menander calls in *The Ambassador's Speech* ἐλεεινολογησάμενος (appeals to pity).[122]

Thus, though he never articulates his principles of selection in terms of what makes an event arouse more or less sympathy, a close reading of the letter with careful attention to what kinds of scenes are depicted (and how) allows for an inductive reading to create the general principles by which he deems an episode to meet the threshold of narratability.

This inductive process reveals that what appears to Kaminiates as most sympathetic—and thus most narratable—are those events which reveal the fundamental workings of Agamben's theory of biopolitics. The idea of "bare life and sovereign power" that Agamben used to define the contexts and manifestations of the application of state violence offers a framework for thinking about how Kaminiates organizes his exemplary narratives. Taken together, the incidents Kaminiates recounts demonstrate

---

[121] "Here you should develop two topics. The first consists of amplifying the opposite case. For example, 'The city of Ilium was once illustrious and the most famous of all cities under the sun, and it held out long ago against attacks from Europe.' The second consists of a vivid description, in which you elaborate the present misfortune, saying how the city has fallen to the ground" (ἐν δὲ ταύτῃ δύο τόπους ἐργάσῃ, ἕνα μὲν τὸν ἀπὸ τῆς τοῦ ἐναντίου αὐξήσεως, οἷον· ἦν ποτε τὸ Ἴλιον πόλις λαμπρὰ καὶ ὀνομαστοτάτη τῶν ὑφ' ἥλιον πασῶν, καὶ ἀντέσχεν πρὸς τοὺς ἀπὸ τῆς Εὐρώπης πολέμους τὸ παλαιόν· εἶτα τὸν ἐκ διατυπώσεως, ἐν ᾧ καὶ διασκευάσεις τὴν παροῦσαν τύχην, ὅτι πέπτωκεν εἰς ἔδαφος) (Men. *Rhet.* 2.12.2).

[122] Men. *Rhet.* 2.12.2. The Greek root ἐλεεινό- is the same, though the respective translators of Kaminiates and Menander opt for sympathy in the former case and pity in the latter. The passage is discussed in Webb (1997: 115).

114   A. J. GOLDWYN

the catastrophic human consequences of the sudden move from a political existence (inclusion in the community and thus protection under its sovereign power) to bare life (exclusion from political life and thus life as simple biological fact) under what Agamben calls the "state of exception," the moment when "man as a living being presents himself no longer as an *object* but as the *subject* of political power,"[123] the moment when he changes sovereignty.[124] Biopolitics—perhaps more precisely, biopower as the imposition of state power over the life and death of the individual—becomes the central concern of such narratives.[125]

Kaminiates' concern, then, focuses on what happens to the bodies of the people of Thessaloniki as they move from Byzantine sovereignty—under which they were able to have *bios*, that is, sovereign protection from violence—to the sovereignty of their captors, under which they had only *zoē*, bare life.[126] During this period, they lived in the state of exception as a kind of *homo sacer*: no law protected them. And, for Kaminiates, articulating the consequences of this threshold state were those that seemed to him to most arouse his reader's sympathy and thus merit narration as "the essential detail."

The first moments after the breach of the wall were previously analyzed from a narratological perspective, that is, how Kaminiates focalized a representative set of horrors that were afflicting all those in the city through the individual examples of the hypothetical people who endured them. This same scene, however, can also be usefully analyzed for demonstrating what kinds of scenes merit narration for Kaminiates:

> Once these barbarians were inside, they slew all those whom they found writhing about on the ground in the vicinity of the wall, regardless of whether they found them prostrated or paralyzed with fear and so unable

---

[123] Agamben (2017: 11).

[124] With Agamben defining the sovereign here, following a Nazi legal scholar, as "he who decides on the state of exception," that is, he who decides who can and cannot be killed with impunity (2017: 13).

[125] For one approach to the distinction between biopolitics and biopower and an archaeology of the latter term, see Cisney and Morar (2015). They define it as follows: "Biopower exposes the structures, relations, and practices by which political subjects are constituted and deployed, along with the forces that have shaped and continue to shape modernity" (2015: 1).

[126] For Agamben's use of these terms, see above, p. 18.

2 PRISON LITERATURE AND SLAVE NARRATIVES ... 115

to move or languishing around without any hope of flight owing to the injuries they had sustained during their earlier falls.

οἳ καὶ ἔνδον γενόμενοι πρῶτον μὲνοὖς εὗρον ἔτι περὶ τὸ τεῖχος ἐνστρεφομένους, εἴτε τῷ φόβῳ βληθέντας καὶ κινηθῆναι μὴ δυναμένους παρεθέντος αὐτοῖς ἐκ τοῦ φόβου τοῦ σώματος, εἴτε πάλιν τοῖς ῥηθεῖσι πτώμασι συνθλασθέντας καὶ πρὸς τὴν φυγὴν καὶ πρὸς τὴν φυγὴν ἀπελπίσαντας, τούτους τὸ τάχος ἀνεῖλον.[127]

From this first instance, Kaminiates demonstrates the way the state of exception allows for a different biopolitics: where once people would have been protected from slaughter, now they are slaughtered. Where once conquered people who were prostrate or wounded might be spared, here they are killed without consequence. In bare life, there is no mediating institution—material, juridicial, or cultural—that limits the application of biopower. The right to kill is absolute, without limits, and without consequences.

The next scene depicted is that of family separation: "One could see people drifting about aimlessly like ships without a rudder, a pitiful sight; men, women and children throwing themselves on each other, clinging to one another and exchanging that last and most piteous parting embrace" (ἦν γὰρ ἰδεῖν τότε τοὺς ἀνθρώπους ὡς ἀκυβέρνητα σκάφη τῇδε κἀκεῖσε περιφερομένους, ἐλεεινὸν θέαμα, ἄνδρας, γυναῖκας, νήπια, ἀλλήλοις συμπίπτοντας, ἀλλήλων ἐκκρεμαμένους, ἀσπαζομένους τὸν οἴκτιστον ἐκεῖνον καὶ τελευταῖον ἀσπασμόν).[128] The family, which is the core unit of social organization, becomes the first thing sundered in the state of exception. Furthermore, in terms of Kaminiates as the representative of all Thessalonians, the passage introduces the theme of family separation, which will become the most significant theme in Kaminiates' narration of his own plight. Using the "interlace technique,"[129] Kaminiates alternates between a general view of the falling city as a whole and the specifics of his own experience, with each mirroring the other at different levels of narration. His narrative of his own experience focuses

---

[127] Kam. *ex. Thess.* 35.3.

[128] Kam. *ex. Thess.* 35.5.

[129] "The technique of interweaving different storylines or scenes through regular switches between them" (De Jong 2001: xiv).

116   A. J. GOLDWYN

on the increasingly dire situation of his own family and their increasingly desperate and ultimately futile attempts to remain alive and together.

Kaminiates offers the specific example of the father who sees his son— a powerful affective theme in witness literature—and the focus of the father's lament is on the reversal from political life to bare life. The rhetoric of the lament that the father delivers, moreover, gives a tragic pathos to the transition from political life to bare life. He begins by singing of the blessings the son brought to the father: "So that when I expected to be considered fortunate in having been blest with children and to be envied for the pride I took in you [...] is it just at such a moment that I must gaze upon this disaster and this most unhappy separation?" (ἵν' ὅτε προσεδόκων ζηλωτὸς μὲν εἶναι τῇ εὐπαιδίᾳ, ἐπίφθονος δὲ τῇ ἐπὶ σοὶ καυχήσει [...] τότε κατ' ὀφθαλμοὺς ἰδέσθαι τὸν ὄλεθρον τοῦτον καὶ δυστυχέστατον ἀπὸ σοῦ χωρισμόν;).[130] Kaminiates, then, in offering an invented lament, offers insight into what he considers to be the most sympathy-inducing aspects of the conquest, which he reveals to be those situations which show the starkest inversion of personal circumstances, with particular regard to the shifting power dynamics by which the father, who could once protect his son, is now unable to do so:

And have I been kept alive till now with this unhappy head of grey hair simply that I may behold your body disfigured by barbarians, and the beloved limbs I long to embrace pitilessly hacked asunder by the executioner's sword?

καὶ διὰ τοῦτο μέχρι τοῦδε τῇ δυστήνῳ ταύτῃ τετήρημαι πολιᾷ, ἵν' ὑπὸ βαρβάρων ἴδω κατακιζόμενόν σου τὸ σῶμα καὶ τὰ φίλτατά μοι καὶ παμπόθητα μέλη τῷ ξίφει τοῦ δημίου ἀνηλεῶς δια-σπώμενα[131];

The father himself, moreover, becomes a figure of great sympathy as he reflects upon his own circumstances: "Alas, what is to become of me? With what eyes shall I look upon these happenings? What funeral dirge shall I utter on your account?" (οἴμοι, τίς γένωμαι; ποίαις ὄψεσι ταῦτα κατίδω; ποῖον ἐπὶ σοὶ ποιήσωμαι θρῆνον;)[132] Having shifted the focus of

---

[130] Kam. *ex. Thess.* 35.8.
[131] Kam. *ex. Thess.* 35.9.
[132] Kam. *ex. Thess.* 35.10.

2 PRISON LITERATURE AND SLAVE NARRATIVES ... 117

the lament from the misfortunes that have befallen his son, the father now focuses on his own plight, wishing for his own death:

> Would that I might find an executioner who would first slay me with his sword, so that I should not live on to feel on your account pains sharper than the sword inflicts! On this score alone I shall acknowledge a debt of gratitude to the foul murderer, if he but begin his work of execution with my aged neck.

> εἴθε τοιούτου τύχοιμεν δημίου ὃς ἐμὲ πρῶτον τῇ μαχαίρᾳ διέλοι, ἵνα μὴ καθυστερήσας δριμυτέρας τοῦ ξίφους ἐπὶ σοὶ τὰς ἀλγηδόνας αἰσθήσωμαι. ἑνὶ τούτῳ τῷ μιαιφόνῳ χάριτας ὁμολογήσω, εἴ γε τῆς σφαγῆς ἀπὸ τοῦ ἐμοῦ κατάρξηται γηραιοῦ τραχήλου.[133]

The ultimate way in which Kaminiates narrates the essential detail as the paradigm for the unrepresentable suffering of everyone is in his depiction of himself: Kaminiates himself is a synecdoche for every Thessalonian—one resident of the city of Thessaloniki whose experiences and sufferings stand in for the unnarratable experiences and sufferings of every Thessalonian.

Thus, for instance, Kaminiates narrates the destruction at the numerous gates of the city:

> How dreadful a calamity occurred at the so-called Golden Gate! How badly those people who had flocked to the spot and who wished to open it a little failed in their attempt. Scarcely had they managed to ease the wings of the gate apart when they forced them to slam shut against through the sheer weight of their own congested numbers. Finding them in this condition, the enemy no longer slew them one at a time with their swords but when they saw them crowded and clinging together and unable to get out of the way they came down with their swords on their heads. Each blow resulted in the severing of someone's head and mutilated bodies jostled with their fellows and even after death were not allowed to fall to the ground but were held up in the general throng of bodies, until all were slain.

> Οἷον γὰρ ἐγεγόνει κακὸν κατὰ τὴν καλουμένην Χρυσέαν πύλην! πῶς παρανοῖξαι ταύτην βουληθέντες μικρόν, ὅσοι τοῦ δήμου τῷ τόπῳ συνέρρευσαν, διήμαρτον τῆς ἐπιχειρήσεως! μόνον γὰρ ὅτι τὰς πύλας ἀλλήλων

---

[133] Kam. *ex. Thess.* 36.11–12.

118   A. J. GOLDWYN

διέστησαν, καὶ τῷ ἰδίῳ πιλήματι πάλιν ἐν ἑαυταῖς συνδραμεῖν αὐτὰς
κατηνάγκασαν· οὕτω δὲ ἔχοντας αὐτοὺς καταλαβόντες οἱ δυσμενεῖς οὐκέτι
καθ᾽ ἕνα τοῖς ξίφεσιν ἀνῄρουν, ἀλλ᾽ ὡς εἶδον συνεσφιγμένους ἀλλήλων τε
ἐχομένους καὶ ἐκτραπῆναι μὴ δυναμένους, κατὰ κόρρης αὐτοὺς τοῖς ξίφεσιν
ἔπαιον, ὡς μετὰ τὴν πληγὴν διαιρεῖσθαι τοῦ προστυχόντος τὴν κεφαλήν,
καὶ τοῖς ὁμοίοις τῇδε κἀκεῖσε τὰ μέρη συμπίπτειν, καὶ μηδὲ μετὰ θάνατον
τῇ γῇ δίδοσθαι ἀλλ᾽ ἔτι παρακρατεῖσθαι τοῖς λοιποῖς σώμασιν, ἕως πάντων
ἀναιρεθέντων.[134]

The carnage at the Golden Gate is paradigmatic for what was happening
in the rest of the city; rather than narrate all of it again, however, Kaminiates simply notes "exactly the same thing happened at the other gate,
known as the Litaia Gate" (τὸ δ᾽ αὐτὸ τοῦτο καὶ περὶ τὴν ἄλλην πύλην,
ἣν καλοῦσι Λιταίαν, πραχθῆναι συνέβη) and then narrates the scene at the
other gates, "as we pointed out" (καθὼς γὰρ ἔφαμεν) earlier in the narrative.[135] He then describes the scene at "the gate near the Acropolis" (τῆς
κατὰ τὴν ἀκρόπολιν πύλης) where the Thessalonians were also trapped.[136]
Having thus given a panorama of human carnage at the gates and in the
neighborhoods all across the city, Kaminiates himself enters the narrative:

Along with my father and my brothers (I have two younger brothers who
up to now have been my companions in captivity and distress) I myself
also happened to be in that place at that time, as were a not inconsiderable
number of other people from the city, as were a not inconsiderable number
of other people from the city.

κἀγὼ γὰρ αὐτὸς σὺντῷ πατρὶ καὶ τοῖς ἀδελφοῖς (δύο δέ μοί εἰσιν οὗτοι
νεώτεροι, τῆς ἐμῆς ἡλικίας ὑποβεβηκότες, οἱ μέχρι τοῦ δεῦρο τῆς τε φρουρᾶς
καὶ τῶν λοιπῶν ἀλγεινῶν μοι συγκοινωνοῦντες) κατ᾽ αὐτὴν τὴν ὥραν παρόντες
εὑρέθημεν ἐν τῷ τόπῳ μετὰ καί τινων ἄλλων τῶν ἀπὸ τῆς πόλεως οὐκ
ὀλίγων.[137]

---

[134] Kam. *ex. Thess.* 40.1–5.

[135] Kam. *ex. Thess.* 41.1, 2.

[136] Kam. *ex. Thess.* 41.4.

[137] Kam. *ex. Thess.* 42.2. Messis write that "À partir du chapitre 42 de cette unité,
l'intérêt de la narration se focalise sur l'auteur et son sort: les faits concernant la ville
passent à l'arrière-plan et ses efforts pour éviter la mort et pour s'assurer de sa propre
captivité ainsi que celle de sa fammile á premier" (2006: 120).

2 PRISON LITERATURE AND SLAVE NARRATIVES ... 119

Kaminiates thus differentiates one Thessalonian from among the many gathered not just at the gate near the Acropolis, but among all the gates of the city. In this way, he sets himself up as a representative example of the kind of suffering experienced there: his is one of the many stories of Thessalonians trapped at the gates throughout the city. As the disaster there unfolds, Kaminiates further contextualizes his own experience within those of the other Thessalonians: "My father then decided, and so did we, that since the barbarians had not yet reached us, we should go up for the time being on to one of the towers surmounting the inner wall" (ἔδοξεν οὖν τῷ τε πατρὶ καὶ ἡμῖν, μήπω πεφθακότων πρὸς ἡμᾶς τῶν βαρβάρων, εἴς τινα πύργον τῶν κατὰ τὸ ἐνδότερον τεῖχος ἀνιέναι τέως).[138] Having thus spoken in a general way about the conditions of the citizenry, Kaminiates narrows in on his own experience, and this method switching back and forth from the very dilated perspective of the people as a whole to the very concentrated focalization of his own individuated experience—from the summary narration of the group to the scenic narration of his own situation—enable him to articulate the entirety of the horrors through the use of the representative example set against the entirety of that which he represents.

Thus, when Kaminiates and his party have finally found a moment of respite by taking refuge on a temporarily unoccupied rampart,[139] his father delivers another lament. This lament mirrors in many ways the rhetoric of the lament of the hypothetical father in the harbor; Kaminiates, however, not having experienced a lament of that kind by virtue of his having been on the rampart rather than in the harbor, invents a hypothetical one with representative significance. In this case, however, he includes a father's lament—his own father's—presenting it not as hypothetical but in the form of direct narration. In so doing, Kaminiates, moreover, also demonstrates how the discourse of the father, like that of the son, is influenced by affect; indeed, they use the same words; Kaminiates writes to Gregory: "But without realizing it, I have overrun the length I had set myself initially for the account of these matters which I promised to give" (Ἀλλὰ γὰρ ἔλαθον ἐμαυτὸν μακρόν, ἢ ὡς ἀπ᾽ ἀρχῆς ὑπεσχόμην, τὸν περὶ τούτων παρατείνας λόγον).[140] Now, his father interrupts his own narrative

[138] Kam. *ex. Thess.* 42.4.
[139] Kam. *ex. Thess.* 43.
[140] Kam. *ex. Thess.* 7.1–2.

120 A. J. GOLDWYN

with the same words: "But, dear children, I have, without realizing it, strayed far from what I ought to have said" (Ἀλλὰ γὰρ ἔλαθον ἐμαυτόν, ὦ φίλτατα τέκνα, πόρρω τοῦ δέοντος πλανηθεὶς καὶ ἅπερ οὐκ ἔδει τοῖς θρήνοις συνεξειπών).[141] Both describe losing the thread of their narration because they were overwhelmed by emotion, and yet, for Kaminiates, it is "nostalgia for my native land" (τὴν πατρίδα πόθος), while for his father, it is the "misfortune, and the general calamity" (τῷ κακῷ, καὶ ἡ πάνδημος συμφορὰ) of his current predicament.[142]

After narrating this moment of individuated experience, Kaminiates then zooms back out to the general plight of all those gathered there. "While he was speaking to us in this way" (Ἐν ὅσῳ δὲ ταῦτα πρὸς ἡμᾶς διελέγετο) Kaminiates writes, marking the simultaneity of his individual experience of these moments against the background of the broader scene in the city, "some barbarians, a considerable number in fact, suddenly appeared on the scene. [...] they pounced on those who had turned back with us after the criminal incidence involving the locking of the gates, and who now stood there huddled up along the wall, only to be dispatched by their swords" (ἰδοὺ δὴ καὶ τῶν βαρβάρων κατεφάνησάν τινες ἀνιόντες, τὸν ἀριθμὸν οὐκ ὀλίγοι, [...] τοὺς μεθ᾽ ἡμῶν ὑποστρέψαντας ἀπὸ τῆς τῶν πυλῶν κακούργου συγκλείσεως, αὐτοῦ που παρὰ τὸ τεῖχος εἰλουμένους, τοῖς ξίφεσιν ἐκείνοις διεχειρίσαντο).[143] In thus dilating his narration from the speech of his father to the general scene of death and destruction, Kaminiates heightens the pathos of both narrative frames: on the one hand, Kaminiates' individual experience, focalized here through his father's speech, becomes all the more poignant in that it is being delivered in the midst of the mass slaughter he is describing. On the other hand, having heard one iteration of a father's lamentation for the death of his impending sons, the general frame also becomes more emotionally fraught, as the speech serves as a representation of the many other similar speeches that must have been given at that same moment by others in the massed crowd. The emotional power of the scene is also enhanced by the sensory nature of the narration, focalized again through Kaminiates: he heard the speech directly from his father's mouth, but he summons the general din of the indistinct suffering of everyone else through auditory focalization as

---

[141] Kam. *ex. Thess.* 44.1.

[142] Kam. *ex. Thess.* 44.2.

[143] Kam. *ex. Thess.* 45.1, 45.2.

2 PRISON LITERATURE AND SLAVE NARRATIVES ...   121

well: "And in so huge a crowd of people nothing could be heard save the swish of swords and the sound of blood spurting out in torrents" (οὐδὲν δὲ ἕτερον ἦν ἀκούειν ἐν οὕτω παμπληθεῖ καὶ πολυανθρώπῳ δήμῳ, ἀλλ' ἢ μόνον τὸν συριγμὸν τῶν ξιφῶν καὶ τῶν τοῦ αἵματος ὀχετῶν τὴν μετὰ βίας ἔκρυσιν).[144] The narrative then picks up with another temporal deixis, marking again the transition from summary (the treatment of the whole population) to scene (narration of Kaminiates' own experience): "In a short time they all lay dead" (Οὐ πολὺ δὲ τὸ ἐν μέσῳ καὶ πάντες ἔκειντο)[145] he writes, and then comments on how these events can be focalized visually through the narrator's own eyes: "a fitting spectacle for abundant wailing and lamentation" (θέαμα πολλῶν ὀδυρμῶν καὶ θρήνων ἐπάξιον).[146] He then transitions the narrative gaze from those whom he saw to himself—"When the slaughter reached us," (ὡς δὲ καὶ πρὸς ἡμᾶς ἔφθανεν ἡ τομή)—and the narration at this point becomes much more detailed.[147] The mass slaughter of the other people at the gate is narrated summarily, but his own survival is narrated in great detail, as Kaminiates describes in superlative detail how the tower in which he and his family had taken refuge, down to the number of planks that spanned the gap between the wall and the tower—"only two planks lay suspended across the middle" (δύο γὰρ μόνα κατὰ μέσον ξύλα ἐναπηώρηντο).[148]

Kaminiates then moves on to describe his own actions, how he approached the barbarians and offered them money to spare his life; when they make as if to kill him, he says: "Do not do this! You will make yourself and your companions lose a great deal of money" ("μὴ τοῦτο πράξῃς" εἶπον, "ἐπεὶ πολλῶν χρημάτων σεαυτὸν καὶ τοὺς περὶ σὲ ζημιοῖς").[149] And then, to distinguish this form of narration from the hypothetical words elsewhere narrated, he adds: "Those were my actual words" (Οὕτως ἔτυχον εἰπών).[150]

From the moment of his capture, the narrative begins to exhibit many of the same methods of affective narration as the accounts described

[144] Kam. ex. Thess. 45.7.
[145] Kam. ex. Thess. 46.1.
[146] Kam. ex. Thess. 46.1.
[147] Kam. ex. Thess. 46.2.
[148] Kam. ex. Thess. 46.5.
[149] Kam. ex. Thess. 46.13.
[150] Kam. ex. Thess. 47.1.

122   A. J. GOLDWYN

in the previous chapter. Like the Wiesel family, the Kaminiates "had, in fact, taken the fortunate and almost prophetic decision of storing away in advance in a secret place of deposit all our personal possessions and valuables" (ὑφ᾽ ἑνὶ γάρ τινι κρυφιώδει ταμείῳ, ὅσοιπερ ἂν ἦμεν κατὰ συγγένειαν ἀγχιστεύοντες, προαποθεῖναι τὰ ἑαυτοῦ ἕκαστος, ὥσπερ τοῦ μέλλοντος μαντευόμενοι, συμφερόντως ἐβουλευσάμεθα).[151] This decision buys them their lives for the moment but, also like many of the Wiesels, it does not save them in the long term, as some are led off to captivity and others either killed or, like John Kaminiates, left with fates unknown.

Like Wiesel and Levi in Auschwitz, Kaminiates also sees piles of corpses as he makes his way from the upper city down to the harbor: "The bodies of the slain lay still dripping with blood, a gruesome spectacle, persons of every age all condemned alike to a single sentence of death by the sword and all alike bereft of burial" (ἔκειντο γὰρ τὰ σώματα τῶν ἀνῃρημένων ἔτι τοῦ λύθρου ἐναποστάζοντα, φρικτὸν ὅραμα, πᾶσα ἡλικία τῶν ἀνθρώπων μιᾷ ψήφῳτὸν διὰ ξίφους κατακριθεῖσα θάνατον καὶ μετὰ τῶν ἄλλων καὶ ταφῆς ἀμοιροῦσα).[152] Kaminiates' own life is thus contrasted with those of the corpses. The emotional pathos of the scene, moreover, is heightened by the author's exposure to mass death—the end consequence of the state of bare life.

2.4   SELEKTION, BIOPOLITICS, AND THE SOVEREIGN DECISION IN THE HARBOR OF THESSALONIKI

As the walls of Thessaloniki fall and the barbarians rush in, the residents of the city "now stood there huddled up along the wall, only to be dispatched by the swords" (αὐτοῦ που παρὰ τὸ τεῖχος εἱλουμένους, τοῖς ξίφεσιν ἐκείνοις διεχειρίσαντο).[153] As the Thessalonians move from *bios* to *zoē*, they also move from the state of political protection to a state of exception—any form of physical violence (or none at all), may be visited upon them with impunity. Kaminiates describes how the barbarians actually made these decisions, classifying the different ways in which the inhabitants of the city were killed at the whim of the conquerors:

[151] Kam. *ex. Thess.* 54.2.
[152] Kam. *ex. Thess.* 54.9.
[153] Kam. *ex. Thess.* 45.2.

2 PRISON LITERATURE AND SLAVE NARRATIVES ...   123

If the murderer felt some compunction at the obedient manner in which the victim surrendered himself and bowed down to receive the death blow, he would aim a mortal stroke and put him out of his misery. But if he did not soften in his heart of stone and wished instead to revel in his madness, [...] he would mutilate the victim's body limb by limb and cause the unfortunate wretch to suffer many deaths in one disaster.

εἰ γὰρ τῷ εὐπειθεῖ τοῦ ἑαυτὸν προδόντος καὶ πρὸς τὸν θάνατον ὑποκλίνοντος ὁ φονεὺς κατενύγη, καιρίαν ἄγων θᾶττον αὐτὸν τῶν ἀλγηδόνων ἀπήλλαττεν· εἰ δὲ μὴ ἐμαλάχθη τὴν λιθώδη καρδίαν, ἀλλ' ἤθελεν ἐντρυφᾶν τῆς μανίας, [...] μεληδὸν κατήκιζε τὸ προστυχὸν σῶμα καὶ πολλῶν θανάτων φορὰν ἐν μιᾷ συμφορᾷ τῷ δειλαίῳ παρείχετο.[154]

The passage serves a variety of functions in the text: first, what could be called a historical function: it describes an actual event which he witnessed and which he believes deserves to be preserved through his testimony. But, considering again the infinite number of possible stories within a fabula, it also has a function as a piece of affective narratology: Kaminiates calls it "an utterly horrendous spectacle" (καὶ ἦν ἰδεῖν τὸ πραττόμενον ἐκπλήξεως γέμον), emphasizing the visual as a means of arousing his readers' sympathy and thus fulfill one of his main narratorial objectives. It also has a plot function, heightening the suspense of the subsequent narrative of Kaminiates' own individual actions by laying them against a backdrop of prolific, gruesome, and all-encompassing violence.

But this scene also perhaps inadvertently reveals how biopower operated within the biopolitical space of the conquered city. In one of his most widely discussed passages, Foucault writes that "the sovereign exercised his right of life only by exercising his right to kill, or by refraining from killing; he evidenced his power over life only through the death he was capable of requiring. The right which was formulated as the 'power of life and death' was in reality the right to take life or let live [faire vivre ou laisser mourir]. Its symbol, after all, was the sword."[155] Though Foucault certainly did not have Kaminiates in mind when he was writing these lines, it is significant that Kaminiates notes that the barbarians had the complete power "to take life or let live" over the Thessalonians as well. Indeed, in words that coincidentally but significantly echo those

---

[154] Kam. *ex. Thess.* 45.6.

[155] Foucault (1978: 136).

124 A. J. GOLDWYN

of the proto-Nazi political philosophers of eugenics Karl Binding and Alfred Hoche, Kaminiates notes that those who "were to be considered worthy of having their lives spared" (σωτηρίας τε ἀξιοῦσθαι) were sent home, while, for those without sufficient wealth, "it was a matter for the sword to deal with" (τῆς μαχαίρας γενέσθαι).[156] Indeed, Leo of Tripoli, who embodies the sovereign decision, uses almost the exact wording of Foucault: noting (with the use of the royal we) that "we can deliver a verdict," a reflection of the sovereign decision, "either to let them live or make the die!"[157] And, if Foucault is right that the symbol of this sovereign power was the sword, then the harbor of Thessaloniki, the site of decapitations and mutilations so numerous that "in so huge a crowd of people nothing could be heard save the swish of swords and the sound of blood spurting out in torrents," is a fitting locus for considering the application of sovereign power and biopolitics in Kaminiates' account.[158]

Indeed, the most detailed and specifically autobiographical part of the letter concerns the moments when Kaminiates' own life hangs in the balance, relying only on the arbitrary decision-making of his captors. Kaminiates, his father, two brothers, and uncle hide in part of a tower where the floor has given way and "only two planks lay suspended across the middle."[159] Kaminiates and his family are trapped, but the barbarians hesitate to cross for fear of falling off the planks, and so Kaminiates makes a heroic decision and goes to greet the barbarians across the two planks. Again, the imagery of the threatening sword of sovereign decision looms over the scene; the barbarians were "holding up their right hands and making as if to come down with their swords on my head" (τὰς δεξιὰς ἀνατείναντες, τάς τε μαχαίρας κατὰ τῆς ἐμῆς κορυφῆς ἐπαγαγεῖν σχηματισάμενοι) and, when he engages them to talk, "one of the Ethiopians [...] tried to fetch me a blow on the forehead with his sword" (εἷς τις τῶν Αἰθιόπων [...] κατ' ἐμὲ γενόμενος ἐπεχείρει μοι

---

[156] Kam. *ex. Thess.* 58.5. Agamben discusses the ethical and political ramifications of their 1920 work *Authorization for the Annihilation of Life Unworthy of Being Lived* (*Die Freigabe der Vernichtung lebensunwerten Lebens*), indeed making that the title of *Homo Sacer I* 3.1: "Life That Does not Deserve to Live" (2017: 113–118).

[157] Kam. *ex. Thess.* 63. Odorico's French translation echoes Foucault's: "laisser vivre, ou les tuer" (2005: 121).

[158] Kam. *ex. Thess.* 45.7.

[159] Kam. *ex. Thess.* 46.5. See above, p. 121.

τὴν μάχαιραν κατενεγκεῖν τῷ μετώπῳ).[160] Kaminiates, however, dissuades them by telling them of the buried money and giving them a small amount with promises of more later. For a moment, the distinction between *bios* and *zoē* is laid bare: the barbarians have complete power to kill them, but, because they have some money, they decide not to; one of the barbarians says to them "Take heart [...] dismiss all thoughts of death" (θαρσεῖτε [...] καὶ τοῦ θανάτουτῆς ἐννοίας ἀπόσχεσθε).[161] Thus, in terms of Foucaultian biopolitics, the barbarians opt to "faire vivre" rather than "laisser mourir."

During the walk from the upper city through the harbor, Kaminiates' narration emphasizes the contingent nature of this decision, what Judith Butler calls states of "precarious life" and "corporeal vulnerability."[162] Noting how the group was "stepping over the corpses of those who had already been slaughtered" (ἐπάνω τῶν σωμάτων τῶν ἤδη ἀναιρεθέντων βαδίζοντες), Kaminiates offers the contrasting image of those who had been let live like himself and those who had been killed—the corpses he sees.[163] Moreover, the lives of the Kaminiates group was only partially protected, since other groups of Ethiopians were not bound by the decision of the group that had spared them: though they had more power than Kaminiates, his captors were not ultimately sovereign themselves either. When another group of Ethiopians comes, his captors tell them to leave him alone and "they dispersed and withdrew" (σκεδασθέντες ὑπανεχώρησαν).[164] One of them, however, does not accept the determination, and he "managed somehow to drag me [Kaminiates] away from the others without being noticed, and once he was a little distance away, tried to kill me" (ὑποσῦραι τῶν ἄλλων ἐμὲ καὶ μικρὸν ἀποστὰς ἀνελεῖν ἐπεχείρει).[165] Kaminiates thus oscillates between two different decisions—the one to take life, the other to let live—and though we know that the man who will write the letter in which the events are narrated must ultimately survive, the scene nevertheless dramatizes the precarious state of

---

[160] Kam. *ex. Thess.* 46.11, 46.12.

[161] Kam. *ex. Thess.* 48.4.

[162] Butler (2004: 29–30).

[163] Kam. *ex. Thess.* 49.1.

[164] Kam. *ex. Thess.* 49.4.

[165] Kam. *ex. Thess.* 49.6.

126   A. J. GOLDWYN

bare life under the state of exception. Only the intervention of Kamini-ates' father, who alerts his captors that his son is about to be killed "stayed the barbarian's hand just as it was stretched out and poised to deal the death blow" (ἐπιστάντα τῷ τόπῳ τὴν δεξιὰν κατασχεῖν τοῦ βαρβάρου τεταμένην οὖσαν καὶ τὴν σφαγὴν σχηματίσασαν).[166] Kaminiates is thus spared for the moment, but later the same barbarian does indeed manage to stab him, though not fatally, and Kaminiates notes that "to this day my back displays the violence of the hand that dealt it" (τὴν καὶ μέχρι νῦν δεικνῦσαν τῆς δεξιᾶς τὴν ἐπίτασιν).[167] Thus, though they seem to be afforded some protection, their lives are still in a contingent and precarious situation.

All this changes, however, when they come to the nunnery which is occupied by one of the commanders of the invasion. There, the precarity of their situation is again emphasized, as they saw "a barbarian seated on a high chair with a frown on his face and a sword in his hand" (ὁρῶμέν τινα βάρβαρον σκιμποδίῳ ἐγκαθεζόμενον, ἀνασπάσαν τά τε τὰς ὀφρύας ξίφος τε κατέχοντα γεγυμνωμένον).[168] Again, Kaminiates and his family come to a moment of decision where again it will be determined whether they will be let live or made to die, symbolized by the sword the commander holds in his hand: "His minions stood watching him intently as though to signify that, should he want anything done, they were ready to spring into action" (καὶ ἀτενὲς τοὺς ἑστῶτας βλέποντας εἰς αὐτόν, εἴ τι καὶ βούλοιτο πράττειν, ἑτοίμους εἶναι ταῖς ὁρμαῖς ὑπεμφαίνοντας).[169] But the commander here, too, decides to spare their life:

Turning his sword round, he struck each of us once with the blunt edge on the back of the head. Then he told us to take hear. "Now that you have received this token of your safety," he said, "you have nothing, I assure you, about which you should be apprehensive in the future."

ὁ δὲ τὸ ξίφος, ὅπερ ἔτυχε ταῖς χερσὶ κατέχων, ἑτέρως ἢ ὡς πέφυκε τέμνειν ἀνθυποστρέψας, ἐπάταξε ταῖς κάραις ἐφάπαξ καθ' ἕνα ἡμῶν. εἶτα ἀνίστασθαι

---

[166] Kam. ex. Thess. 49.7.
[167] Kam. ex. Thess. 49.16.
[168] Kam. ex. Thess. 51.4.
[169] Kam. ex. Thess. 51.4.

2 PRISON LITERATURE AND SLAVE NARRATIVES ... 127

καὶ θαρρεῖν ἐκέλευε, καὶ "τοῦτό" φησι "τῆς ἀσφαλείας τεκμήριον ἔχοντας μηδὲν τοῦ λοιποῦ δεινὸν ὑμᾶς ὑποπτεύειν παρεγγυῶ."[170]

But though Kaminiates and his family are spared, he again emphasizes how the decision to let live or make die is based entirely on the decision of the sovereign; indeed, right after sparing Kaminiates and his family, he surveys the other Greek captives in the church and "signaled to the barbarians to start a massacre. With the speed of savage wolves falling upon their prey they butchered their unhappy victims without mercy" (νεύματι τοῖς βαρβάροις ἀνελεῖν ἐκείνους προσέταττεν. οἳ δὴ τὸ τάχος καθάπερ ἀτίθασοι λύκοι θήρας ἐπιτυχόντες, οὕτως ἠπειγμένως καὶ ἀνηλεῶς τοὺς ἀθλίους κατέτεμον).[171] Thus, "even though we were the sole survivors of such massive and indiscriminate slaughter" (ὡς ἐν τοσαύτῃ πανολεθρίᾳ μόνοι διαφυγόντες τὸν θάνατον),[172] Kaminiates is not certain of his survival even when they are brought into the presence of Leo of Tripoli, who decrees that they should be spared if they can produce the promised money, otherwise "they were to hack each one of us to death with their swords" (τοῖς ξίφεσιν ἕνα ἕκαστον ἐκεῖσε διελόντας τῆς ζωῆς ἀπαλλάξαι)[173] Thus, they remained "in a state of uncertainty and suspense" (Ἀλλ' οὔπω ταῦτα βεβαίως ἔχοντες σκοπεῖν) as to whether they would live.[174] Leo of Tripoli, as the one who has ultimate authority to make live or let die, embodies the sovereign power of the new biopolitical context in which Kaminiates finds himself.

Agamben begins *Sovereign Power and Bare Life* with a consideration of the very kind of moment in which Kaminiates finds himself. Agamben's concern with the state of exception stems from his reading of Carl Schmitt's *Politische Theologie*, published in 1922. Schmitt's work provided the theoretical justification for dictatorial regimes, and thus was central to Nazi political ideology; Schmitt himself was a member of the party during the war and an unrepentant advocate of Nazi politics until his death in 1985. Schmitt was thus committed to interrogating the nature of dictatorship and sovereign power, and the passage Agamben cites is

---

[170] Kam. *ex. Thess.* 51.7–8.

[171] Kam. *ex. Thess.* 52.4–5.

[172] Kam. *ex. Thess.* 52.11.

[173] Kam. *ex. Thess.* 53.6.

[174] Kam. *ex. Thess.* 54.1.

128   A. J. GOLDWYN

Schmitt's thesis for the justification and exercise of such power: "The sovereign creates and guarantees the situation as a whole in its totality. He has the monopoly over the final decision. Therein consists the essence of State sovereignty, which must therefore be properly juridicially defined not as the monopoly on sanction or to rule but as the monopoly to decide [...] The decision reveals the essence of State authority most clearly. Here the decision must be distinguished from the juridicial regulation."[175] Agamben refers to this as the "sovereign decision," to which he frequently refers throughout the *Homo Sacer* Project,[176] but which, perhaps most relevant for the consideration of Foucault's distinction between the power to let live and make die as it pertains to John Kaminiates, is that it "suspends law in the state of exception and thus implicates bare life within it."[177] While Kaminiates thus stands before Leo of Tripoli in a very literal sense, he also stands more theoretically at the threshold of indistinction between the states of exception and inclusion, between *bios* and *zoē*, between life and death, in states of corporeal vulnerability and precarious life. If, as Foucault describes it, biopolitics is the systems of power that determine who will live or die, then the encounter between sovereign and slave becomes the paradigmatic moment where this power dynamic is most clearly visible.

For Foucault, the sword-wielder who determines who lives and dies is a model of biopolitical sovereignty of a pre-modern age; he summons this figure to distinguish this model from the modern model of hospitals, public health politics, and other life-organizing institutions that arose in the seventeenth century and continue to define modern state power. Agamben, however, is concerned with one particular manifestation of Foucaultian biopolitics, that is, its application of sovereign power under the Nazis: the sovereign decision, he notes, rests in the body of the Führer; indeed, Agamben suggests, "By virtue of this identity, his every word is immediately law [...] and he recognizes himself immediately in his own command."[178] That is to say, the sovereign knows he is the sovereign by his power to decide. Agamben's great insight was that the entire world was not a concentration camp, but the politics of certain kinds of historical

---

[175] As cited in Agamben (2017: 18).

[176] See for instance, Agamben (2017: 20, 21, 55, and *passim*).

[177] Agamben (2017: 70).

[178] Agamben (2017: 150).

and present circumstances could be made legible through the understanding of the biopolitical power dynamics of the camp, particularly as it bears on the determination of life unworthy of being lived.

Thus, the scene in which the captive meets the sovereign represents the two meetings of the people at the furthest remove from one another: the one who makes the sovereign decision and the one upon whom the decision is made; the one who is the subject of biopower and the one who is its object. The narration of this type-scene is thus one of the most compelling and generically common in witness literature. In the Holocaust, the moment in which the sovereign decision to let die or make live was called "Selektion," and it is among the central concerns of the narratives. Levi describes the moment of sovereign decision when the captives arrive at Auschwitz:

> A dozen SS men stood around, legs akimbo, with an indifferent air. At a certain moment they moved among us, and in a subdued tone of voice, with faces of stone, began to interrogate us rapidly, one by one, in bad Italian. They did not interrogate everybody, only a few: "How old? Healthy or ill?" and on the basis of the reply they pointed in two different directions.

> Una decina di SS stavano in disparte, l'aria indifferente, piantati a gambe larghe. A un certo momento, penetrarono fra di noi, e, con voce sommessa, con visi di pietra, presero a interrogarci rapidamente, uno per uno, in cattivo italiano. Non interrogavano tutti, solo qualcuno. «Quanti anni? Sano o malato?» e in base alla risposta ci indicavano due diverse direzioni.[179]

Levi notes how, at the time, they did not know what happened to those who were separated, but now he knows that the first Selektion was the moment of sovereign decision: "of our convoy no more than ninety-six men and twenty-nine women entered the respective camps of Monowitz-Nuna and Birkenau, and that of all the others, more than five hundred in number, not one was living two days later" (del nostro convoglio, che novantasei uomini e ventinove donne, e che di tutti gli altri, in numero di più di cinquecento, non uno era vivo due giorni più tardi).[180]

[179] Levi (1959, 1989: 27–28).

[180] Levi (1959, 1989: 30).

130   A. J. GOLDWYN

Such is the significance of Selektion that when Levi describes the liberation of the camp, it is the second thing he thinks of: "To anyone who stopped to think, it [liberation] signified no more Germans, no more selections" (A porvi mente con attenzione voleva dire non più tedeschi, non più selezioni, non lavoro, non botte, non appelli, e forse, più tardi, il ritorno).[181] For Wiesel, too, Selektion is depicted as the ultimate act of sovereign decision: "An SS man would examine us. Whenever he found someone extremely frail—a 'Muselman' was what we called those inmates—he would write down his number: good for the crematorium" (Nous savions ce que cela voulait dire. Un S.S. allait nous examiner. Lorsqu'il trouverait un faible, un «musulman», comme nous di- sions, il inscrirait son numéro: bon pour le crématoire.).[182] Indeed, Wiesel understands the sovereign decision in the stark terms of making live or letting die; as the first Selektion approaches, he thinks to himself: "One more hour. Then we would know the verdict: death or reprieve" (Une heure de délai. Dans une heure, nous allions connaître le verdict: la mort, ou le sursis).[183] Perhaps as significantly, in his preface to the new translation, Wiesel asks "how was one to rehabilitate and transform words betrayed and perverted by the enemy?" (Trahie, corrompue, pervertie par l'ennemi, comment pouvait-on réhabiliter et humaniser la parole?) and then lists several words which have particular relevance to how the biopolitics of the camp changed everyday language: "Hunger – thirst – fear – transport – selection – fire – chimney" (La faim, la soif, la peur, le transport, la sélection, le feu et la cheminée).[184] In the context of the concentration camp, Selektion is thus the moment where the distinction between *bios* and *zoē* is most heightened, where the distinction between the bare life of the prisoner and the power of the sovereign is at its most starkly apparent.

As with the Nazi Selektion at Auschwitz, the prisoners are brought before the sovereign and interrogated; Kaminiates writes that "we reached the harbour and stood near the tyrant" (Ἤδη δὲ φθασάντων ἡμῶν τὸν λιμένα παρέστημεν τῷ τυράννῳ) the equivalent moment of the prisoners arriving at the concentration camps and seeing the SS men and the

---

[181] Levi (1959, 1989: 266).

[182] Wiesel (2006: 70, 2007: 132).

[183] Wiesel (2006: 70, 2007: 133).

[184] Wiesel (2006: np, 2007: 12).

2 PRISON LITERATURE AND SLAVE NARRATIVES ... 131

Lagerkommandant.[185] Leo of Tripoli then questions Kaminiates and his father—"He gave orders to his attendants to have us brought before him. When we had been brought there, he began to question my father" (ἀχθῆναι ἡμᾶς κατὰ πρόσωπον τοῖς ἐφεστῶσι διεκελεύσατο. ὡς οὖν ἤχθημεν, ἐπυνθάνετο τὸν πατέρα)[186]—before ultimately rendering the sovereign decision: "I want you to rid yourselves completely of your worst suspicions" (πάσης ὑμᾶς πονηρᾶς ὑποψίας ἐκτὸς εἶναι βούλομαι) he says,[187] noting that "the vast amount of treasure that has been displayed to my view ha[s] granted you your life, a rare boon that most men may not hope for, and you have no further grounds for fearing death" (τὸ νῦν ἐν ὄψεσι ταῖς ἐμαῖς προτεθὲν χρημάτων πλῆθος τὴν ζωὴν ὑμῖν, ἥτις δυσέλπιστός ἐστι τοῖς πολλοῖς, ἐχαρίσαντο, καὶ οὐκ ἔστιν ὑμῖν ὑπόνοια τοὐλοιποῦ θανάτου ἐξ ἐπιβουλῆς).[188] The sovereign decision has been rendered, and twice Leo says that such is the force of his decision that the Kaminiates group has no need to fear death.[189]

Levi also describes the arrival at the gathering point at Auschwitz upon his arrival as the site of family separation:

Someone else did not want to leave his wife [. ...] Many mothers did not want to be separated from their children[. ...] But Renzo stayed an instant too long to say goodbye to Francesca, his fiancée, and with a single blow they knocked him to the ground. It was their everyday duty. In less than ten minutes all the fit men had been collected together in a group. What happened to the others, to the women, to the children, to the old men, we could establish neither then nor later.

qualche altro non voleva lasciare la moglie [...] molte madri non volevano separarsi dai figli [...] ma Renzo indugiò un istante di troppo a salutare Francesca, che era la sua fidanzata, e allora con un solo colpo in pieno viso lo stesero a terra: era il loro ufficio di ogni giorno. In meno di dieci minuti tutti noi uomini validi fummo radunati in un gruppo. Quello che accadde

[185] Kam. *ex. Thess.* 55.1.

[186] Kam. *ex. Thess.* 55.1–2.

[187] Kam. *ex. Thess.* 55.12.

[188] Kam. *ex. Thess.* 55.12.

[189] Though it will later turn out that the sovereign guarantee is not foolproof, since many of Kaminiates' family members die on the transport ships or are sold into slavery anyway.

132   A. J. GOLDWYN

degli altri, delle donne, dei bambini, dei vecchi, noi non potemmo stabilire allora né dopo.[190]

The scene was baffling to Levi at the time—he did not know what happened to those who were separated. In hindsight, however, he understands that it was a moment of sovereign decision, when the Nazis determined whose life was unworthy of being lived: "Today, however, we know that in that rapid and summary choice each one of us had been judged capable or not of working usefully for the Reich" (Oggi però sappiamo che in quella scelta rapida e sommaria, di ognuno di noi era stato giudicato se potesse o no lavorare utilmente per il Reich), and that the rest were killed.[191] Wiesel describes a similar scene in more personal terms:

An SS man came toward us wielding a club. He commanded:

"Men to the left! Women to the right!"

Eight words spoken quietly, indifferently, without emotion. Eight simple, short words. Yet that was the moment when I left my mother. There was no time to think, and I already felt my father's hand press against mine: we were alone. In a fraction of a second I could see my mother, my sisters, move to the right. Tzipora was holding Mother's hand. I saw them walking farther and farther away; Mother was stroking my sister's blond hair, as if to protect her. And I walked on with my father, with the men. I didn't know that this was the moment in time and the place where I was leaving my mother and Tzipora forever.

Un gradé S.S. vint à notre rencontre, une matraque à la main. Il ordonna:

- Hommes à gauche! Femmes à droite!

Quatre mots dits tranquillement, indifféremment, sans émotion. Quatre mots simples, brefs. C'est l'instant pourtant où je quittai ma mère. Je n'avais pas eu le temps de penser, que déjà je sentais la pression de la main de mon père: nous restions seuls. En une fraction de seconde, je pus voir ma mère, mes sœurs, par- tir vers la droite. Tzipora tenait la main de

---

[190] Levi (1959, 1989: 28–29).
[191] Levi (1959, 1989: 29).

maman. Je les vis s'éloigner; ma mère caressait les cheveux blonds de ma sœur, comme pour la protéger et moi, je continuais à marcher avec mon père, avec les hommes. Et je ne savais point qu'en ce lieu, en cet instant, je quittais ma mère et Tzipora pour toujours. Je continuai de mar- cher. Mon père me tenait par la main.[192]

The scene in the harbor at Thessaloniki shares these aspects with the collection place at Auschwitz; Kaminiates notes that Leo orders his men "to embark first the young people of both sexes, not keeping those who were related together but splitting them up so that in this matter too they should suffer, in terms of physical separation" (τὴν νεάζουσαν κήραν τοῦ πλήθους ἀρρένων τε καὶ θηλειῶν πρῶτον ταῖς ναυσὶν εἰσενεγκόντας, μὴ κατὰ συγγένειαν ἀλλὰ διακεκριμένως, ἵν' ἔχωσι κἂν τούτῳ τιμωρίαν οὐ τὴν τυχοῦσαν, τὴν φυσικὴν ἐξ ἀλλήλων διαίρεσιν).[193] Kaminiates focalizes this scene through both auditory and visual means: "one confused and universal cry of lamentation rose to such a climax as all natural ties were severed and close relatives called out to one another and voiced their indignation at being parted" (ὁπότε συμμιγής τις καὶ σφοδρὸς ἀνήγερτο θρῆνος διχοτομουμένης τῆς φύσεως, ἀλλήλους τοὺς ἀγχιστεῖς ἀνακαλουμένους καὶ τὸν χωρισμὸν δυσχεραίνοντας),[194] he says, describing the sound, and, for the visual: "one could see the frenzied victims of misfortune, men, women, youths, children letting out terrible screams and tearing at themselves" (καὶ γὰρ ἦν ἰδεῖν τοὺς τῷ πάθει συγκεχυμένους, ἄνδρας γυναῖκας, ἀκμάζοντας παῖδας, ὁμοῦ πάντας δεινὸν ἀλαλάζοντας καὶ ἑαυτοὺς διαρρηγνύντας).[195] Nevertheless, they were "forcibly separated and herded on to the ships" (ὡς γὰρ βιαίως οὕτως ἐξ ἀλλήλων διαιρεθέντες φύρδην ταῖς ὁλκάσιν εἰσήχθησαν).[196]

Kaminiates, moreover, is among those who suffer family separation; his mother and one of his brothers are brought back to the rest of the group, he writes,

> But my wife, along with my three small children and our youngest sister, together with a large number of other relatives, they either did not find or,

---

[192] Wiesel (2006, 2007).

[193] Kam. *ex. Thess.* 60.1.

[194] Kam. *ex. Thess.* 60.5.

[195] Kam. *ex. Thess.* 60.6.

[196] Kam. *ex. Thess.* 60.7.

134   A. J. GOLDWYN

if they did find them, they were unwilling to bring them to us. Instead of this they languished, some in one place some in another, struck down by the shafts of common misfortune and buffeted by the chill wind of their separation from us.

ὁμόζυγα δὲ τὴν ἐμὴν σὺν τρισὶ νηπίοις καὶ τὴν ὑποβεβηκυῖαν κατὰ τὴν γέννησιν ἡμῶν ἀδελφὴν μετὰ καὶ ἄλλου πλήθους τῶν προσηκόντων οὔτε ἀνευρεῖν ἠθέλησαν, οὔτε δὲ ἀνευρόντες ἴσως ἀγαγεῖν πρὸς ἡμᾶς ἐβουλήθησαν, ἀλλ' ἦσαν ἄλλος ἀλλαχῇ τῷ κοινῷ πάθει καὶ ταῖς νιφάσι τῆς ἐξ ἡμῶν βαλλόμενοι διαιρέσεως. ὅμως ἐκαρτεροῦμεν ὡς ἐν δεινοῖς καὶ τὴν ἐξ ἀλλήλων κατατομήν, εἰ καὶ ὅτι παντὸς ἀνιαροῦ πεῖραν τὰ καθ' ἡμᾶς ὑπερέβαλλεν.[197]

In line with his broader method of moving between the narrative of his own individuated experience and the more general narrative of those who suffered as he did, Kaminiates returns to the theme of family separation among the rest of the Thessalonians again:

If, say, a mother had an infant that was still being breast-fed, then only that child was to stay with his mother[. ...] Everybody else, on the other hand, was to be separated from his family all over again, so that people were simply herded together and then callously sorted out[. ...] Son was dragged away from father, daughter from mother, brother from brother. What must they all have felt in such a situation, when they were being led off to slavery in a foreign land, where the worship of our faith is treated as an abomination and the most senseless passions are revered, where whoredom is held in high repute.

καὶ εἴ πού τις μήτηρ, φησίν, ἐν αὐτοῖς νήπιον ἔχουσα τοῦ γάλακτος προσδεόμενον, τοῦτο μόνον πρὸς τὴν τεκοῦσαν μένειν οἱ δυσσεβεῖς κατεθέσπισαν[. ...] τοὺς λοιποὺς δὲ τῶν συγγενικῶν συναφειῶν καὶ αὖθις διαιρεθέντας ἀναμὶξ καὶ ἀδιαφόρως τοῖς κλήροις ἀποδοθῆναι. [...] καὶ γὰρ ἀπεσπᾶτο πατρὸς μὲν υἱός, μητρὸς δὲ θυγάτηρ καὶ ἀδελφὸς ἀδελφοῦ. ἐν οἷς τί πάσχειν εἰκὸς τούτους ἅπαντας, ὁπότε πρὸς δουλείαν ἤγοντο εἰς γῆν ἀλλοτρίαν, ὅπου τὸ μὲν σέβας τῆς καθ' ἡμᾶς πίστεως ὡς ἐναγὲς ἐνυβρίζεται, πάθη δὲ τιμᾶται ἀλογώτατα, ὅπου πορνεία σεμνύνεται.[198]

---

[197] Kam. *ex. Thess.* 65.5–6.
[198] Kam. *ex. Thess.* 72.4, 72.7, 72.8.

2 PRISON LITERATURE AND SLAVE NARRATIVES ... 135

Kaminiates focuses on family separation no doubt because it was among the most horrific and sympathetic kinds of trauma experienced by the citizens of Thessaloniki after the conquest. His language, moreover, evokes the oppositional nature of the two cultures: where Thessaloniki is noted for its piety "εὐσέβια,"[199] the barbarians are described as "impious," using a word that changes the honorific prefix εὐ- for the pejorative δυσ- in δυσσεβεῖς.

The narrative's switching back and forth from the detailed depiction of Kaminiates' own family to the general plight of families being separated is also an effective method for choosing the "essential detail" as the means for narrating mass suffering: with each of the movements back and forth, the plight of his own family gets more and more dire, mirroring the general plight of the Thessalonians as a whole. And, indeed, in the concluding section of the letter, Kaminiates' reveals in the dry language of emotional depletion and understatement the conclusion of his own family's story, delivered as an interwoven narrative against the fall of the city as a whole:

> My brother's wife was among those sold, an occurrence which caused us considerable anguish. But my mother and my wife together with two children (the third child had perished at sea) and also my poor unhappy brother and our youngest sister happened by some dispensation of Providence to be in a ship from Sidon and consequently destined for transportation to Syria.

> ἐν οἷς ἔτυχεν ἐκδοθεῖσα καὶ ἡ τοῦ ἐμοῦ ἀδελφοῦ σύζυγος, οὐ μετρίαν ἡμῖν ὀδύνην περιποιήσασα. ἡ δέ μοι μήτηρ καὶ ἡ γαμετὴ σὺν δυσὶ τέκνοις (τὸ γὰρ ἕτερον ἔργον ἦν γενόμενον τῆς θαλάσσης), ἔτι δὲ καὶ ἐλεεινὸς ἄθλιος ὁ τλήμων ἀδελφὸς καὶ ἡ τῷ χρόνῳ πάντων ἐφυστερίζουσα ἀδελφή, ἔκ τινος θεϊκῆς προνοίας εἰς μίαν Σιδωνίαν ἔτυχον ναῦν, τῆς πρὸς Συρίαν ἀποδημίας τηρούμενοι.[200]

Thus, Kaminiates' note that "whoredom is held in high repute" is a general statement about the plight of the Thessalonian women generally, but one which is derived from the specific circumstances of the author's

---

[199] For which, see also below, p. 218.

[200] Kam. *ex. Thess.* 73.10.

136   A. J. GOLDWYN

own suffering—his sister-in-law's being sold—while his general description of family separation matches his own experience at a more universal level.

At last, given the narrative's focus on fathers and sons, the final act of suffering is also the most painful:

> We fared no better in Tripoli during the time we spent there; indeed, from my own point of view, we fared considerably worse since it was there that I lost my dear father (and finding myself without him was like the start of a fresh round of disasters).

> καὶ οὐδὲν κρεῖττον οὐδ' ἐν αὐτῇ τῇ Τριπόλει, παρ' ὅσον ἐν αὐτῇ διετρίψαμεν χρόνον, γενόμενοι, ἀλλὰ μόνον ὅσον τὸ κατ' ἐμὲ καὶ μοχθηροτέροις τισὶν ὁμιλήσαντες (ἐκεῖσε γὰρ ἐγὼ καὶ τοῦ καλοῦ πατρὸς ἀπωρφανίσθην, καθάπερ ἄλλην ἀρχὴν τῶν δεινῶν τὴν ἐκείνου στέρησιν ἐφευράμενος).[201]

As in *Night*, so too in the *Capture of Thessaloniki*: the father, who had repeatedly been the source of comfort and support, dies at the end, a death foreshadowed in both works by the constant interweaving of the father–son theme and the deaths of other fathers and sons throughout. Indeed, though the theme can be read as a topos of witness literature, postclassical narratology can allow for a reading by which the literary topos is appropriated for deeply personal reasons: Kaminiates and Wiesel chose this structure and thematic element because the loss of their father was the organizing emotional principle of their recollection of their experience. Because their own fathers died, the foreshadowing of their fathers' deaths and the other father–son relationships (and the severing of those relationships) stand out in their minds as the experience around which their memories organize their time in captivity. The literary topos thus provides a structural framework for narrating the lived experience of a certain kind of trauma.

[201] Kam. *ex. Thess.* 78.7.

BIBLIOGRAPHY

Agamben, Giorgio. 2017. *The Omnibus Homo Sacer*. Palo Alto: Stanford University Press.

Ahnert, Ruth. 2013. *The Role of the Prison in the Sixteenth Century*. Cambridge: Cambridge University Press.

Alber, Jan, and Monika Fludernik. 2010. Introduction. In *Postclassical Narratology: Approaches and Analyses*, ed. Jan Alber and Monika Fludernik, 1–32. Columbus: Ohio State University Press.

Andelković, Jovana. 2019. Mauropous as Menander's Student of Rhetoric. In *Transmitting and Circulating the Late Antique and Byzantine Worlds*, eds. Mirela Ivanova and Hugh Jeffery, 149–169. Leiden: Brill.

Bakirtzis, Charalambos. 2007. Imports, Exports and Autarky in Byzantine Thessalonike from the Seventh to the Tenth Century. In *Post-Roman Towns, Trade and Settlement in Europe and Byzantium, vol. 2: Byzantium, Pliska, and the Balkans*, ed. Joachim Henning, 89–118. Berlin: DeGruyter.

Bal, Mieke. 2009. *Narratology: Introduction to the Theory of Narrative*, 3rd ed. Toronto: University of Toronto Press.

Bortolussi, Maria and Dixon, Peter. 2003. *Psychonarratology: Foundations for the Empirical Study of Literary Response*. Cambridge: Cambridge University Press.

Butler, Judith. 2004. *Precarious Life: The Powers of Mourning and Violence*. New York: Verso.

Carretta, Vincent. 2005. *Equiano, the African: Biography of a Self-Made Man*. New York: Penguin.

Christides, V. 1981. Once Again Caminiates' 'Capture of Thessaloniki'. *Byzantinische Zeitschrift* 74 (1): 7–10.

Cisney, Vernon, and Nicolae Morar, eds. 2015. *Biopower: Foucault and Beyond*. Chicago: Chicago University Press.

Cohen, Anthony. 1985. *The Symbolic Construction of Community*. London: Routledge.

———. 1988. Of Symbols and Boundaries, or, Does Ertie's Greatcoat Hold the Key? In *Symbolising Boundaries: Identity and Diversity in British Cultures*, 1–21. New York: Palgrave Macmillan.

Curta, Florin. 2011. *The Edinburgh History of the Greeks, c. 500 to 1500*. Edinburgh: Edinburgh University Press.

De Jong, Irene. 2001. *A Narratological Commentary on the Odyssey*. Cambridge: Cambridge University Press.

———. 2004. *Narrators and Focalizers: The Presentation of the Story in the* Iliad, 2nd ed. Bristol: Bristol Classical Press.

De Jong, Irene and René Nünlist. 2007. *Time in Ancient Greek Narrative*. Leiden: Brill.

138 A. J. GOLDWYN

De Looze, and Laurence. 1997. *Pseudo-Autobiography in the Fourteenth Century: Juan Ruiz, Guillaume de Machaut, Jean Froissart, and Geoffrey Chaucer.* Gainesville: University of Florida Press.

Equiano, Olaudah. 1999. The Interesting Narrative of the Life of Olaudah Equiano, or Gustavus Vassa, the African. In *I Was Born a Slave: An Anthology of Classsic Slave Narratives,* vol. 1, ed. Yuval Taylor and Charles Johnson, 29–179. Chicago: Lawrence Hill Books.

Foucault, Michel. 1978. *The History of Sexuality: An Introduction,* trans. Robert Hurley. Vintage Books.

Frendo, David. 2000. Introduction Part One: John Kaminiates and His correspondent. In *The Capture of Thessaloniki,* John Kaminiates, xxvii–xl. Perth: Byzantina Australiensia.

Franklin, Ruth. 2011. *A Thousand Darknesses: Lies and Truth in Holocaust Fiction.* Oxford: Oxford University Press.

Gielen, Erika. 2017. Joseph the Philosopher, an Outstanding Outsider: Philosophy and Rhetoric at the Court of Andronicus II. In *Basileia: Essays on Imperium and Culture in Honour of E.M. and M.J. Jeffreys,* eds. Geoffrey Nathan and Lynda Garland, 205–215. Leiden: Brill.

Gigliotti, Simone. 2009. *The Train Journey: Transit, Captivity, and Witnessing in the Holocaust.* New York: Berghahn Books.

Herman, David. 1999. *Narratologies: New Perspectives on Narrative Analysis.* Columbus: Ohio State University Press.

Hogan, Patrick Colm. 2011. *Affective Narratology: The Emotional Structure of Stories.* University of Nebraska Press: Lincoln.

Hurston, Zora Neale. 2018. *Barraccoon: The Story of the Last "Black Cargo."* New York: Amistad.

Kazhdan, Alexander. 1978. Some Questions Addressed to the Scholars, who Believe in the Authenticity of *Kaminiates' Capture of Thessalonika. Byzantinische Zeitschrift* 71: 301–314.

Lambert, Raphaël. 2019. *Narrating the Slave Trade, Theorizing Community.* Leiden: Brill.

Lang, Berel. 2003. *Act and Idea in the Nazi Genocide.* Syracuse: Syracuse University Press.

Levi, Primo. 1959. *If This Is a Man,* trans. Stuart Woolf. Orion Press: New York.

———. 1989. *Se questo è un uomo.* Torino: Einaudi.

Lilie, Ralph-Johannes. 2014. Reality and Invention: Reflections on Byzantine Historiography. *Dumbarton Oaks Papers* 68: 157–210.

Messis, Charis. 2006. La mémoire du 'je' souffrant. Construire et écrire la mémoire personnelle dans les récits de captivité. In *L'écriture de la mémoire. La littérarité de l'historiographie,* eds. Paolo Odorico, Panagiotis Agapitos, and Martin Hinterberger, 107–146. Paris: Centre d'études byzantines, néo-helléniques et sud-est européennes.

Melville-Jones, John. 1988. Appendix 1: Eustathios on the Writing of History. In *The Capture of Thessaloniki, Eustathios of Thessaloniki*, 230–234. Canberra: Byzantina Australiensia.

Neville, Leonora. 2018. *Guide to Byzantine Historical Writing*. Cambridge: Cambridge University Press.

———. 2019. Pity and Lamentation in the Authorial Personae of John Kaminiates and Anna Komnene. In *Emotions and Gender in Byzantine Culture*, ed. Stavroula Constantinou and Mati Meyer, 65–92. New York: Palgrave Macmillan.

Nilsson, Ingela. 2020. *Writer and Occasion in Twelfth-Century Byzantium: The Authorial Voice of Constantine Manasses*. Cambridge: Cambridge University Press.

Odorico, Paolo. 2005. *Thessalonique: Chroniques d'une Ville Prise*. Toulouse: Anacharsis.

———. 2006. Les trois visages de la même violence: les trois prises de Thessalonique. In *L'écriture de la mémoire. La littérarité de l'historiographie*, eds. Paolo Odorico, Panagiotis Agapitos, and Martin Hinterberger, 147–179. Paris: Centre d'études byzantines, néo-helléniques et sud-est européennes.

Olney, James. 1985. 'I was Born': Slave Narratives, Their Status as Autobiography and as Literature. In *The Slave's Narrative*, eds. C. Davis and H.L. Gates, Jr., 148–174. Oxford: Oxford University Press.

O'Malley, George. 2014. *Final Passages: The Intercolonial Slave Trade of British America*, 1619–1807. Chapel Hill: North Carolina Press.

Panagopoulos, Spyros. 2014. Técnicas Narrativas en *De Expugnatione Thessalonicae* de Juan Kaminiates"/"Narrative Techniques in John Kaminiates' *De Expugnatione Thessalonicae. Byzantion Nea Hellas* 33: 181–202.

Papaioannou, Stratis. 2013. *Michael Psellos: Rhetoric and Authorship in Byzantium*. Cambridge: Cambridge University Press.

Patterson, David. 2018. *The Holocaust and the Nonrepresentable: Literary and Photographic Transcendence*. Albany: SUNY Press.

Riedel, Meredith. 2018. *Leo the VI and the Transformation of Byzantine Christian Identity*. Cambridge: Cambridge University Press.

Roilos, Panagiotis. 2005. *Amphoteroglossia: A Poetics of the Twelfth-Century Medieval Greek Novel*. Cambridge, MA: Harvard University Press.

Seidman, Naomi. 2006. *Faithful Renderings: Jewish-Christian Difference and the Politics of Translation*. Chicago: University of Chicago Press.

Summers, Joanna. 2004. *Late-Medieval Prison Writing and the Politics of Autobiography*. Oxford: Oxford University Press.

Tougher, Shaun. 1997. *The Reign of Leo VI (886–912): Politics and People*. Leiden: Brill.

Vinson, Martha. 2004. Rhetoric and Writing Strategies in the Ninth Century. In *Rhetoric in Byzantium: Papers from the Thirty-fifth Spring Symposium*

140   A. J. GOLDWYN

of Byzantine Studies, Exeter College, University of Oxford, March 2001, ed. Elizabeth Jeffreys, 9–22. London: Routledge.

Waliaula, Walibora, and Ken. 2013. *Narrating Prison Experience: Human Rights, Self, Society, and Political Incarceration in Africa*. Champaign, IL: Common Ground Publishing.

Webb, Ruth. 1997. Imagination and the Arousal of Emotion in Greco-Roman Rhetoric. In *The Passions in Roman Thought and Literature*, eds. Susanna Braund and Christopher Gill, 112–227. Cambridge: Cambridge University Press.

———. 2003. Praise and persuasion: Argumentation and audience response in epideictic oratory. In *Rhetoric in Byzantium: Papers from the Thirty-fifth Spring Symposium*, ed Elizabeth Jeffreys, 127–136. London: Routledge.

Wiesel, Elie. 1979. *A Jew Today*, trans. Marion Wiesel. Albany: SUNY Press.

———. 2006. *Night*, trans. M. Wiesel. New York: Hill and Wang.

———. 2007. *La Nuit*. Paris: Les Éditions de Minuit.

Young, James Edward. 1988. *Writing and Rewriting the Holocaust: Narrative and the Consequences of Interpretation*. Bloomington: Indiana University Press.

CHAPTER 3

The Carceral Imaginary in Byzantium: The Komnenian Novels as Holocaust Fiction

3.1 THE SHARED WORLDS OF THE KOMNENIAN NOVELS AND BYZANTINE HISTORIOGRAPHY

In his discussion of the literary historical context for Eustathios' *Capture of Thessaloniki*, John Melville-Jones argues that Eustathios' narrative did not have an obvious literary antecedent or model, since "there was in fact no established genre of poliorcetic writing as such in Byzantine literature, and most accounts of sieges appear as chapters in larger works."[1] This may be true within the context of nonfictional literature, but in fact, by the time Eustathios was writing, there was indeed at least one genre that could serve as a model for Eustathios: the Komnenian novels, a twelfth-century revival of the ancient Greek novels that survives in four exemplars, one of which survives only in fragments.[2] Though the dating remains subject to some speculation, recent scholarship has dated the first of them,

---

[1] Melville-Jones (1988: 231). By "poliorcetic," Melville-Jones means that genre of Byzantine literature that narrates sieges such as the two tenth-century military instructional manuals attributed to Heron of Byzantium and translated into English under the title *Siegecraft: Two Tenth-Century Instructional Manuals by "Heron of Byzantium"* (Sullivan 2000).

[2] The ancient Greek novels are collected in English translation in Reardon (2008).

© The Author(s), under exclusive license to Springer Nature Switzerland AG 2021
A. J. Goldwyn, *Witness Literature in Byzantium*,
New Approaches to Byzantine History and Culture,
https://doi.org/10.1007/978-3-030-78857-5_3

142 A. J. GOLDWYN

Theodore Prodromos' *Rhodanthe and Dosikles*, to the 1130s,[3] and the last, Niketas Eugenianos' *Drosilla and Charikles*, to 1156.[4] The plots of the novels have been variously summarized to emphasize their amorous aspects; in the introduction to her translation, for instance, Elizabeth Jeffreys writes that their "plots deal with the trials of a pair of well-born lovers who are separated by dramatic misfortunes but eventually emerge unscathed to be united in marriage,"[5] while Roderick Beaton defined them as "tales of love, death and adventure."[6] Though the unbreakable love bond of the lovers is the organizing principle of the plot, the plot itself details the frequent and manifold ways in which that love is tested through the lovers' separation and reunion, and one of the frequent plot devices used to bring about this separation and reunion is the lovers' capture, imprisonment, and slavery. First-person narration is also a prominent feature of the extant corpus of novels: *Hysmine and Hysminias* is told in the first-person voice of its protagonist, while *Rhodanthe and Dosikles* and *Drosilla and Charikles*, though told in the third person, feature numerous long sections of first-person character narration. Given that these narratives feature deep explorations of the suffering caused by being the victims of military conquest, a consideration of them within the framework of Holocaust Studies can redeem the moral and ethical force of works that have been, at worst, dismissed as "insipid, mildly pornographic imitations of their classical models with no intrinsic interest" and at best as having only historical value for being "pivotal in the transmission of

---

[3] Jeffreys (2014: 9). For the complicated dating situation of *Rhodanthe and Dosikles*, particularly as it relates to the priority of that work or of Eumathios Makrembolites' *Hysmine and Hysminias*, see Jeffreys (2014: 161–165). The novels' chronology is also discussed by Roilos, who concludes that "the sequence of the three texts discussed so far must have been: Prodromos, Makrembolites, Eugeneianos" (2005: 10). Ingela Nilsson suggests *Hysmine and Hyminias* may be the earliest (2014: 61). For our purposes here, the exact dating and order of composition is less important than that the novels were all products of the mid-twelfth century and thus would have been known to both Eustathios of Thessaloniki (Chapter 1) and Niketas Choniates (Chapter 4).

[4] Jeffreys (2014: 342–343).

[5] Jeffreys (2014: ix). Some further generic distinctions can be found in Goldwyn (2018: 31–32 and Goldwyn and Nilsson 2019: xviii).

[6] Beaton (1996: xiii).

the concept of fictional writing from the ancient to the modern world."[7] Specifically, seeing them as a kind of Byzantine "Holocaust fiction," a well-attested subgenre in literature after the Second World War and one that has been carefully theorized in contemporary literary studies, can foreground how fiction can open a window into those experiences that nonfictional testimony cannot.

While one trend in this scholarship argues for the impossibility at best or immorality at worst of writing fiction about the Holocaust—immortalized in Theodor Adorno's famous and frequently misunderstood dictum that "nach Auschwitz ein Gedicht zu schreiben, ist barbarisch" (to write poetry after Auschwitz is barbaric)[8]—some scholars have also seen the ways in which such fiction can provide access to a more elusive kind of truth; Emily Miller Budick, for instance, argues in *The Subject of Holocaust Fiction* that "in a way that historical and documentary accounts do not and perhaps cannot, fictions also highlights the centrality of subjectivity or subject position in the processes by which we know – or think we know – the quotidian realm of eternal facts and events."[9] That is to say, fiction allows for the exploration of individual experience and interiority rather than examining (only) verifiable and observable exteriors. This is what Dorrit Cohn calls "the singular power possessed by the novelist: creator of beings whose inner lives he can reveal at will."[10] Indeed, Sue Vice goes so far as to suggest, following her reading of Bakhtin, that "the defining characteristic of the novel is not its fictionality but its inclusion of the multiple, conflicting voices of dialogism," thus rendering the

---

[7] Jeffreys (2014: x). For a consideration of their adaptation and appropriation of their classical sources, particularly the ancient Greek novels, see Nilsson (2014, especially 72–74).

[8] Adorno (1983: 34). A detailed discussion of the phrase itself, the context in which it was produced, and the way it "has been cited often enough to produce the numbing effect of a seriously overworked platitude," see Trezise (2013: 63–121), including Adorno's later modification—perhaps retraction—of the phrase: "it may have been wrong to say that after Auschwitz you could no longer write poems" (as quoted in Trezise 2013: 66), and his subsequent return to his original position: "I do not want to soften my statement that it is barbaric to continue to write poetry after Auschwitz" (Trezise 2013: 67).

[9] Budick (2015: 3). For the historical dimension of the Holocaust novel and authorial claims to authenticity while writing self-conscious fabrications, see Lang (2003: 131–137).

[10] Cohn (1978: 4).

144   A. J. GOLDWYN

fraught relationship between fact and fiction irrelevant in determining the relationship of novel and history.[11]

Though writing with specific regard to fictional works about the Holocaust, Budick argues that Holocaust fiction thus has both an ethical and an epistemological component: "fiction renders the faceless millions as discrete human beings, both reversing the Nazis' intention of making the Jew disappear and simultaneously restoring to each person the uniqueness and specificity that often becomes attenuated even after the war," an insight that also applies to the Komnenian novel, which demonstrates the costs and consequences of war on the intimate level of the emotional experience of the individual person. Thus, though historiography is generally conceived of as being factual and novels as being fabrications, Budick argues that the novel allows for the articulation of a kind of truth—individual, subjective—that historiography can't access, even as historiography can offer broader political and cultural contexts that novels cannot.

This may be especially true in the case of the Komnenian novels, which are set in both real places (Rhodes and Cyprus in *Rhodanthe and Dosikles*) as well as realistic but imaginary locations set within the real world (Eurykomis, Aulikomis, Daphnepolis, and Artykomis in *Hysmine and Hysminias*, for instance, are fictional cities, but the marble that adorns the gardens is from Chios, Lakonia, Thessaly, and Chalkidike, all real places).[12] The question then becomes less which genre conveys truth,

[11] Vice (2000: 91).

[12] For the marble, see *H&H* 1.5.7–1.6.1. Jeffreys notes that "the place names in *H&H* all have suggestive etymological elements [...], but attempts to see these as symbolizing Alexandria, Constantinople, Ephesus and Antioch are not supported by the narrative" (2014: 177, n. 2). In distinguishing the genre of les récits de captivité (e.g., explicitly Kaminiates and Palamas, but also presumably Eustathios, Choniates, and others) from "le roman Hellenistique" (and presumably, though only implicitly, the Komnenian novels), Messis argues: "Soit nos récits relatent un espace reel et un temps reel avec des personages reels soit nos auteurs viest à créer *une convention* de verité" (2006: 112). This is, however, complicated by the seeming imprimatur of reality within the Komnenian novels and the incorporation of fictional conventions and modes in the nonfictional accounts (i.e., *ethopoieae*/invented laments presented as having actually happened). Bourbouhakis notes that the novels are set "imprecise time designed to evoke an almost generic, and in the case of the Byzantine narratives, notably *pagan* Antiquity" allows the authors to "free[] the plots from nominal Christian stricutres regarding subject matter" (Bourbouhakis 2009: 218).

but what aspects of truth are foregrounded or elided by each.[13] Indeed Emmanuel Bourbouhakis makes just this kind of case for the Komnenian novels: "One interesting consequence of fiction is that it can sometimes cast *fact* into greater relief. Reality may be enhanced, or diminished, in a manner of speaking, by comparison with fiction."[14] The Komnenian novels, therefore, read as a kind of historical fiction describing the experience of family separation, slavery, sexual assault, and physical privation, can be seen as a commentary on the historical context in which they were produced, showing, if in a fictional way, the experience of certain individuals within the broader context of an empire at war.

The necessity of serious consideration of the Komnenian novels as fictional accounts of a recognizable lived experience is given further urgency by the lack of other means of gleaning insights into slaves' lives in Byzantium. Unlike witness testimony after the Holocaust or the well-attested genre of slave narratives in the antebellum United States, there are no Byzantine accounts of the lives of slaves as described by the slaves themselves.

Though it might seem incongruous to compare works as seemingly different as novels and historiography, historians and literary critics alike have long noted the interpenetration of these modes of writing.[15] Scholars of the Holocaust, too, have long noted the porous boundary between fiction and nonfiction; as James Edward Young writes in the context of witness testimony and histories of the Holocaust on the one hand and novels and other imaginative genres set during the period on

---

[13] For a discussion of the Byzantine perspective on the relationship beween "l'histoire, le récit et « la vérité»," see Nilsson (2014: 87–90). Nilsson argues that "bref, nous devons apprendre à lire les textes historiques d'une manière qui nous permette de «percer» les procédés rhétoriques et littéraires et d'extraire les informations historiques, mais, en même temps, d'apprécier la forme en soi et ce qu'elle peut nous dire de l'époque et de la culture dans lesquelles se situe le texte" (90).

[14] Bourbouhakis (2009: 218).

[15] In a Byzantine context, Panagiotis Roilos writes that "rather than an inclusion of several distinct genres within the 'super-genre' of the novel, I prefer to speak of a subtle interweaving of different discursive textures drawn from a number of genres" (2005: 20). Though he speaks explicitly of "the rhetorical, allegorical, and comic modulations in the Komnenian novels" (2005: 20), there is no reason why historiography could not function as a similar discursive texture. Similarly, Ralph-Johannes Lilie (2014) has amply demonstrated the ways in which Byzantine historians invented stories to entertain their audiences and make political arguments; Goldwyn (2015) and Nilsson (2004) have addressed the ways in which novelistic forms appear in the historiographical tradition.

146 A. J. GOLDWYN

the other, "if there is a line between fact and fiction, it may by necessity be a winding border that tends to bind these two categories as it separates them, allowing each side to dissolve occasionally into the other."[16] As much as fiction draws from nonfiction to grant it verisimilitude and thus authorize its insights, nonfiction too draws from fiction to give it a recognizably archetypal structure. In his influential article on the rhetoric of Holocaust literature, Hayden White describes how "the ideology of modern realism has it that an artistic, poetic, or literary treatment of real events constitutes a kind of category mistake. Real events of the past are properly treated by history, which eschews any interest in the imaginary, invented, or fantastical events of literature."[17] And yet, as he shows in his analysis of *If This is a Man*, the emotional effect and historical truth values of Levi's work of witness are enhanced by his use of Dante's *Inferno* as an intertext. According to White, understanding and interpreting the literary and rhetorical devices which go into the making of witness testimony, therefore, is not a mistake at all, but rather a reflection of what he calls Levi's "figural realism," which reflects a different kind of truth, not the historian's positivistic attempt to draw out the objective historical facts visible beneath layers of rhetoric, but to see that rhetoric as a form of truth itself, the subjective truth of individual experience: the "meaning [of witness testimony] resides in large measure in the extent to which it copies the plot-structure of a poetic fiction."[18] That is to say, the style, plotting, figurative language, and all the other ostensibly literary effects of witness testimony do not obscure the fundamental experiential truth of the author's lived experience, but rather "shows how even the most rigorously [sic] objective and determinedly 'clear' and literal language cannot do justice to the Holocaust without recourse to myth, poetry, and 'literary' writing."[19]

One strand of Byzantine scholarship offers just this sort of causal relationship between the increasingly volatile situation on the borders of the Byzantine Empire and the resurrection of the ancient novel in the twelfth century as a way of exploring these problems. Beaton, for instance,

---

[16] Young (1988: 52).

[17] White (2004: 122).

[18] White (2004: 117).

[19] White (2004: 118).

suggests that the defeat at the Battle of Manzikert in 1071 and other territorial losses at the end of the eleventh century had as one consequence that "the educated Byzantine of the late eleventh and twelfth centuries found himself having to think again about himself and his place in society, and the place of that society in the cosmos."[20] In this reading, then, the resurrection of the genre of the novel, with its capacity to plumb interiority and emotion in a world at best uncertain and at worst entirely lawless, became a vehicle for responding to increasing external chaos. Beaton calls this "a symptom of the times."[21] Similarly, David Holton argued that "we may usefully ask why works of secular fiction suddenly appear again in Greek after a hiatus of many centuries. [...] In Byzantium too the twelfth century was an era of major social, economic and political upheaval. The romance, with its tendency to idealise (but also to instruct), with its invocation of a past age or a socially remote world, and above all with its escapism, provides entertainment and wish-fulfilment in an uncertain world."[22] Thus, if Byzantine authors of the twelfth century were looking for a genre that would allow them to explore more intimate narratives of conquest and the affective interiority of conquered people in a way that other genres of medieval Greek literature such as historiography could not, the turn to fiction, specifically through the resurrection of the ancient novel under the Komnenian dynasty, would provide a suitable genre. Such a causal reading, however, has been called into question by Ingela Nilsson, who challenges Beaton's assertion that the revival occurred as a result of, in her summary of his argument, "the intellectual *Angst* of Byzantine society in the late eleventh century."[23] Rather, she argues that "it is, however, hard to prove that such a crisis ever existed."[24] Though Beaton's and Holton's narrative of historical causality is an ultimately inconclusive if nevertheless tempting explanation linking the territorial decline in the empire and the rise of the Komnenian novel, what yet remains is the central uniqueness of this corpus (as much as can be understood, anyway, from four surviving exemplars, one

[20] Beaton (1996: 9).

[21] Beaton (1996: 12).

[22] Holton (1991: 207).

[23] Nilsson (2001: 32).

[24] Nilsson (2001: 32).

148   A. J. GOLDWYN

in fragmentary form): a fiction that explores the interiority of characters as they traverse social boundaries (from aristocrat to slave and back) and geographical ones. Thus, Budick's central premise, that "the work of fiction […] is to complicate the relationship between the fictional representation and the world that the text purports to be representing," can still illuminate the distinction between historiography and novels in the Byzantine context.[25]

This task is in many ways simpler for considering the Holocaust, insofar as such novels are often explicit about the grounding of their fictions in the specifics of time and place. The action of the extant Komnenian novels, by contrast, is set in explicitly imaginary geographies in an unidentifiable yet pointedly distant past. And yet, a careful examination of the real-world settings which are the source of the imaginary ones of the novels can demonstrate the ways in which, while the geography might be invented, the situational contexts—and thus affective states—in which the characters of the novels find themselves are firmly grounded in the lived reality of the period (or, at least, the lived reality as expressed through the discourse of historical writing). Reading the novels against roughly contemporaneous historiographical texts reveals how both the real and fictional locations of the novels reflect the reality of the period as understood by its most authoritative historians. The novels were composed just after the period covered in John Skylitzes' *Synopsis of History*, produced in the late eleventh century and covering the ninth to eleventh centuries, and squarely within the period described in Niketas Choniates' *History*, written in the beginning of the thirteenth century and covering the twelfth and early thirteenth centuries.

Within the broad contours of these histories, which cover a variety of major events and themes in Constantinople and throughout the empire, for the purposes of considering the settings of the novels, these centuries were ones during which, according to Niketas, "pirates rule the seas and the Roman maritime provinces are harassed by pirate ships" (θαλασσοκρατοῦσιν οἱ πειραταὶ καὶ κακῶς πεπράγασι ταῖς λῃστρίσιν αἱ παραθαλαττίδιοι Ῥωμαίων χῶραι).[26] Indeed, the plundering of the Roman maritime provinces, represented in nonfictional works like Eustathios' *Capture of Thessaloniki* and John Kaminiates' letter, serves as the opening

[25] Budick (2015: 4).
[26] Chon. *Hist.* 55.

3 THE CARCERAL IMAGINARY IN BYZANTIUM: THE KOMNENIAN ... 149

of two of the romances. The barbarian pirate assault on Rhodes that opens *Rhodanthe and Dosikles*, moreover, begins, as in Eustathios, at night, just as after the sun

> had traversed the earth with its swift-running circuit
> and, dipping beneath it, was bringing on the shades of evening,
> leaving the air around us darkened.

> τὴν γῆν διελθὸν εὐδρόμῳ περιδρόμῳ,
> ταύτην ὑπελθὸν ἐγνόφου τὴν ἑσπέραν,
> λιπὸν σκοτεινὸν τὸν καθ' ἡμᾶς ἀέρα.[27]

Prodromos then describes the arrival of the enemy fleet:

> a trireme from the pirate fleet
> was the first from the entire expedition to dart forward
> and put in to the harbor of Rhodes.
> It attacked the estates along the shore-line
> and was ravaging all the area round about.

> καὶ ναῦς τριήρης ληστρικῆς ναυαρχίας
> πρώτη προπηδήσασα παντὸς τοῦ στόλου
> ἐλλιμενίζει τῆς Ῥόδου τῷ λιμένι.
> καὶ τοῖς ἐπ' ἀκτῆς ἐμβαλοῦσα χωρίοις
> ἐβόσκετο ξύμπαντα τὸν πέριξ τόπον.[28]

The opening of the novel thus emulates a kind of historical event frequently narrated in the histories of the middle Byzantine period—and indeed pushes even more deeply into the Greek literary past in both Homer and Heliodorus. This allusion to fictions of the past, however, does not diminish the connection of the novel to its historical present.

Indeed, John Skylitzes' *Synopsis of History*, which covers the period from 811 to 1057, the centuries immediately preceding the production of the extant novels, is full of pirate fleets and hostile navies sacking and conquering cities across the Byzantine coastline. Indeed, many of these scenes match the one in *Rhodanthe and Dosikles* in specific and detailed

---

[27] *R&D* 1.2–4.
[28] *R&D* 1.6–8.

150   A. J. GOLDWYN

ways. In one such scene, Skylitzes describes how "the Hagarenes inhabiting the western gulf of Iberia facing onto the [Atlantic] ocean, the ones called Spaniards, had become too numerous" (οἱ τὸν ἑσπέριον κόλπον τῆς Ἰβηρίας οἰκοῦντες Ἀγαρηνοί, πρόσχωροι τῷ Ὠκεανῷ ὄντες [Ἰσπάνους τούτους κατονομάζουσιν], εἰς εὐανδρίαν ἑληλακότες)[29] and so asked their commander to plunder Byzantine cities. Skylitzes writes that

> this fleet was permitted to ravage the eastern isles which are ours. Thus he was able to assuage the hunger of his subjects by filling them with others' bread, while spying out whether there was one of the islands suitable for them to colonise. He sailed out in springtime and attacked several islands without finding anybody to oppose him. The islands were all destitute of help as the fleet which usually defended them was away fighting with Thomas. Thus he was able to reap much gain from every island he attacked. One day he came to Crete, overran it and took as many prisoners as possible.

> τῶν πρὸς τὴν ἕω κειμένων νήσων καὶ ἡμετέρων ἐτράπετο, ὁμοῦ μὲν τὸ τοῖς ὑπηκόοις ὀρεκτὸν ἐκπληρῶν καὶ ἐκ τῶν ἀλλοτρίων αὐτοὺς κορεννύς, ὁμοῦ δὲ κατασκεψόμενος, εἴ τίς ἐστιν εὔφορος τῶν νήσων καὶ πρὸς μετοικίαν ἐπιτηδεία αὐτοῖς. ποιησάμενος δὲ τὸν ἀπόπλουν ἔαρος ὥρᾳ, καὶ πολλὰς ἐπιὼν τῶν νήσων, οὐδένα εὕρισκε τὸν ἀντιπαρατασσόμενον. ἐχήρευον γὰρ πᾶσαι βοηθείας, τοῦ εἰωθότος φυλάττειν στόλου παντὸς συστρατευομένου τῷ Θωμᾷ. διὸ καὶ μεγάλας ὠφελείας ἐκ πασῶν, αἷς καὶ προσώρμιζεν, ἐκαρποῦτο. ἦκε δέ ποτε καὶ εἰς Κρήτην καὶ ταύτην καταδραμὼν καὶ ἀνδραποδισάμενος.[30]

The opening of *Rhodanthe and Dosikles* thus places its characters in the recognizable world of barbarian pirate raids along with the Byzantine maritime provinces and the taking of captives and plunder described in Skylitzes' historical work.

When the pirates in *Rhodanthe and Dosikles* land, moreover, "the barbarians rushed out immediately | they trampled the grapes and tore down the vines" (οἱ βάρβαροι γὰρ ἐξιόντες αὐτίκα | βότρυς ἐπάτουν καὶ

---

[29] Skyl. *Syn.Hist.* Mich2.16.

[30] Skyl. *Syn.Hist.* Mich2.16. Anna Komnene's *Alexiad* similarly features coastal invasion, most prominently those of Tzachas, a Seljuk Turkish naval commander who raided the coasts of Asia Minor before his defeat by a Byzantine fleet and subsequent murder by his Turkish son-in-law. For a philological history of ἀνδραποδισάμενος, "andrapodizing," see Gaca (2010), with brief reference to Kaminiates.

3 THE CARCERAL IMAGINARY IN BYZANTIUM: THE KOMNENIAN ...   151

κατέκλων ἀμπέλους)[31] a small detail that nevertheless offers a hint of historical verisimilitude, since the destruction of agriculture is something that Niketas mentions frequently in his description of similar raids. During the 1142 siege of Antioch, for instance, John I Komnenos allowed his troops to plunder the outlying lands, such that "not even the fruit-bearing trees were left unharmed, but were given over to the flames for cooking" (μηδὲ τὰ καρποφόρα τῶν δένδρων ἀσινῆ παρεώμενα, ἀλλὰ καὶ ταῦτα τῷ πυρὶ τῆς διαίτης παραδιδόμενα).[32] During the campaigns of the Emperor Alexios Angelos against the Turks, too, "piles of fruit and wheat fields were burned to ashes" (θημωνίαι τε καρπῶν καὶ λήϊα πυροφόρα κατηθαλώθησαν).[33] Later, he describes how the failed usurper Theodore Mangaphas gathered an army and "ravaged the draft animals and in countless ways maltreated the Laodikeians and Phrygians and even the inhabitants of my own city of Chonai, burning and destroying the grain fields in summertime" (τῶν ζώων ἐλυμαίνετο τὰ ὑπὸ ζυγὸν καὶ τοὺς Λαοδικεῖς δὲ Φρύγας μυριαχῶς ἐκάκωσεν, ὥσπερ καὶ τοὺς τῶν Χωνῶν τῶν ἐμῶν οἰκήτορας, τὰς ἅλωνας κατὰ τὸν θέρειον καιρὸν πυρπολῶν).[34] As in *Rhodanthe and Dosikles*, moreover, the raid that began with burning crops also ends with the taking of captives: "An incursion into Caria brought him many captives there whom he delivered to the barbarians to be led away into captivity" (ἐμβαλὼν δὲ τῇ Καρίᾳ καὶ πολλοὺς προνομεύσας τῶν ἐκεῖ τοῖς βαρβάροις ἐκδέδωκεν εἰς ἀπαγωγήν).[35]

Indeed, crop burning must have been a common military tactic, since Niketas describes a Turkish general named Arsan, who "habitually plundered the Romans provinces" (οἳ ληστεύειν τὰ Ῥωμαίων εἰώθασιν) and was given the epithet "the Crop-Burner" (καυσαλώνης) because "he laid waste the planted fields" (μάλιστα δὲ τὰς ἅλωνας ἐλυμαίνετο) with strategic frequency.[36]

The initial moments after the fall of the city echo the accounts in both historiographical texts and those in witness literature:

---

[31] *R&D* 1.10–11.

[32] Chon. *Hist.* 40.

[33] Chon. *Hist.* 504.

[34] Chon. *Hist.* 400.

[35] Chon. *Hist.* 400. Slightly modified from Magoulias' translation.

[36] Chon. *Hist.* 421.

152   A. J. GOLDWYN

> They burned the cargo-carrying hulks,
> tearing the cargo out of their holds,
> and incinerated the crew together with the vessels.

> τὰς φορταγωγοὺς ἐξεπίμπρων ὁλκάδας,
> τὸν φόρτον ἁρπάσαντες ἐκ τούτων μέσων,
> καὶ τοὺς ἐν αὐταῖς συνεπίμπρων ναυτίλους.[37]

Prodromos account of the capture and burning of the ships and crew echo, for instance, Skylitzes' description of the Byzantine naval victory over Thomas:

> the fleet came quickly and anchored off a place called Berydes, three hundred and fifty warships and supply vessels in all. When the commanders of the imperial fleet learned of their arrival, they attacked by night while the enemy ships were riding at anchor. So sudden was the attack that they were able to capture several panic-stricken vessels, crews and all, and to burn other ships with Greek fire.

> καὶ τὸ μὲν ναυτικὸν εὐθυπλοῆσαν ταχέως ἀνάγεται καὶ τῷ χωρίῳ προσορμίζεται τῷ Βηρύδων, ἐκ πεντήκοντα καὶ τριακοσίων συνιστάμενον πλοίων πολεμικῶν τε καὶ σιταγωγῶν. οἱ δὲ τοῦ βασιλικοῦ στόλου κατάρχοντες τὴν τούτων ἐπεγνωκότες ἔλευσιν νυκτὸς ἐπιτίθενται ναυλοχοῦσι τοῖς ἐναντίοις, καὶ τῷ αἰφνιδίῳ καταπληξάμενοι πολλὰς μὲν αὐτάνδρους ἔσχον τῶν νηῶν, τινὰς δὲ καὶ τῷ σκευαστῷ πυρπολοῦσι πυρί.[38]

Similarly, during the raid that opens *Rhodanthe and Dosikles*, Prodromos describes the mass slaughter of the inhabitants after the city falls, noting that, amid the general carnage,

> some of the inhabitants died by the sword
> but others died beforehand from fear of the sword.
> Some, fearing the barbarian's bitter hands,
> hurled themselves into ravines and glens,
> thinking it better to be deprived of life
> than to succumb to piratical heartlessness.
> Others they [the barbarians] chained by the neck.

---

[37] *R&D* 1.12–14.

[38] Skyl. *Syn.Hist.* Mich2.10.

3 THE CARCERAL IMAGINARY IN BYZANTIUM: THE KOMNENIAN ... 153

τῶν γὰρ κατοίκων οὓς μὲν ἔκτεινε ξίφος,
οὓς δὲ προαπέκτεινε τοῦ ξίφους φόβος·
οἳ μὴν τρέμοντες βαρβάρων πικρὰς χέρας
ἔρριπτον αὐτοὺς εἰς φάραγγας, εἰς νάπας,
κρεῖττον κρίνοντες ζημιοῦσθαι τὸν βίον
ἢ ληστρικῇ γοῦν ἐμπεσεῖν ἀστοργίᾳ.
ἄλλους δὲ δεσμήσαντες ἐκ τῶν αὐχένων.[39]

This, too, has its precedent in previous accounts of city-sacking; John Kaminiates, for instance, recounts a similar scene. As the Thessalonians awaited the onrush of the surging barbarians, some awaited their death serenely while others panicked, and "most of these threw themselves off the wall without stopping to think. They either died from the fall or delivered themselves into the hands of the barbarians" (πλεῖστοι πρὸς τὸ ἐκτὸς τοῦ τείχους ἀσυλλογίστως ἑαυτοὺς ἀκοντίσαντες ἢ τῷ πτώματι τὴν ζωὴν συνεπέραναν ἢ τοῖς ἐκεῖσε στρεφομένοις βαρβάροις ἑαυτοὺς ἐνεχείρισαν).[40] Eustathios, too, describes a similar scene:

> What can I say of those who leaped down from the roofs of their houses in search of death when the catastrophe began to ensnare them also? They could not fly into the ether, although they might have wished to do so, and so they suffered the fate of all naturally heavy things as they hurled themselves through the mid-air to crash to their deaths below.

> Τί ἂν λέγοιμι τοὺς τῶν τεγέων οἴκων ἄνωθεν καθαλλομένους ἐπὶ μελέτῃ θανάτου, ὅτε τὸ μέγα κακὸν καὶ αὐτοὺς περιεστοίχιζεν; Οἳ πτερύξασθαι εἰς αἰθέρα μὴ ἔχοντες, οὗπερ ἐφίεντο ἄν, τὸ τῶν βαρέων ἔπασχον καὶ ἐλάκουν εἰς θάνατον ἐκ μετεώρου κατασκήπτοντες.[41]

Thus, between "history proper" in works such as those by John Skylitzes and Niketas Choniates, in works of fiction like the Komneninan novels, and in works of witness literature like those by John Kaminiates and Eustathios of Thessaloniki that blur the boundary between them, certain kinds of scenes that reflect the lived experience of the inhabitants of the Byzantine Empire are repeated, thus demonstrating that each of these works, though generically distinct, nevertheless depict a shared universe.

---

[39] *R&D* 1.27–33.
[40] Kam. *Ex. Thess.* 37.
[41] Eust. *De capta Thess.* 118.

154   A. J. GOLDWYN

Despite these similarities, the overall aim of the works is different, as reflected in the various levels of detail that characterize each of their descriptions of falling cities. For instance, whereas Niketas and Skylitzes are content simply to note the pirate raids and move on, Prodromos, like Eustathios and Kaminiates, has a different concern: narrating the emotional and physical experiences of the individuals who were involved in these events. The ensuing narration thus demonstrates the power of the novels to narrate experience and emotion at the level of scene rather than the summary in ways that would not conform with history proper but are appropriate—indeed, required—for the novel: the captured Greeks, bound in chains and fetters, are led into slavery and confined in the inner recesses of the pirate ship. Among these are the eponymous heroes of the novel, Rhodanthe and Dosikles. Unlike Niketas, for whom the fact of being conquered and taken into captivity was sufficient, the genre of the novel allows Prodromos to follow the captives into the prison camp where they are held: "But what of the multitude confined within that space?" (Τί γοῦν τὸ πλῆθος τῶν συνεγκεκλεισμένων;) Prodromos asks, indicating a focus on the slaves in the prison camp.[42] This is a question with which the writers of history were not concerned. And yet, the plight of the individual is precisely the concern of the writers of both witness testimony and novels, and what follows is a survey of the fates of the men and women who were in that ship, often told from their own perspective, and including the voices of both men and women.[43] Prodromos thus opens the novel within the recognizable historical world of the twelfth-century Byzantine coastline in general. In particular, moreover, the early part of the novel takes place among the prisoners inside the slave prison, thus opening up the possibility of reading it through the broader discourses of

[42] *R&D* 1.83. I have emended Jeffreys' translation of "held within" with a stronger (and I believe more accurate) term for their incarceration.

[43] Lambert argues that *Roots* has a similar function: "Haley devotes six chapters of *Roots* to the terrifying experience of crossing the Atlantic. He uses verisimilitude to do so and spares his readers not a single detail: the darkness and the exiguity, the bewilderment, the fear, the despair, the heat, the sweat, the vomit, the feces, the blood, the stench, the beatings, the deaths, the suicides, the sexual violence, the rats, the lice, and the epidemics" (Lambert 2019: 32).

3 THE CARCERAL IMAGINARY IN BYZANTIUM: THE KOMNENIAN ...   155

carceral studies and prison literature. Indeed, in the context of African-American slave narratives, Paul Youngquist calls this "listen[ing] to the voices of the lower deck."[44]

In *The Self in the Cell: Narrating the Victorian Prisoner*, Sean Grass, for instance, argues for the significance of the prison setting for interpreting first-person fictional slave narratives produced during the nineteenth century in ways that could yield new insights for thinking about analogous fictional prison literature in Byzantium: "By embracing and even mimicking the explicit and implicit narrative aims of the prison," he writes, "Victorian novelists recognized that they could engage in deliberate psychological invention without compromising the apparent legitimacy or integrity of their realist fictions."[45] The fictional construction of an ostensibly nonfictional setting, that is, the close verisimilitude between reality as perceived by the reader and that reality as reflected in the novels suggests that the other aspects of the novel with which the reader is not familiar—in this case, the depiction of life in a slave ship and the interior lives of the slaves themselves—must have a similar verisimilitude. According to Grass, "Reading and narrating prisoner bodies and texts, insisting thematically upon the prisoner's solitude, adopting the form of self-narration undertaken from the cell – these modes all became part of Victorian novelists' repertoires in accounting for the struggling through solitude to narrate a private and idiosyncratic experience of the cell."[46]

Here, too, an insight from Victorian prison literature is transferrable to the context of the Komnenian novels: the novelists' realization that "the Victorian prison in each of its forms clearly demanded fictional treatment as a place of powerful psychological – rather than just physical – moment," coupled with the recognition that "solitude and confinement are necessary preconditions to the self-ordering, self-exposition, and narrative self-invention that occupy the heart of the text" opened up these spaces for inquiry.[47] But this could not be done through the genre of history, which required devotion to provable exteriorities; it was

---

[44] Youngquist (2011: 15).

[45] Grass (2003: 9).

[46] Grass (2003: 10).

[47] Grass (2003: 9).

156   A. J. GOLDWYN

thus unable to interrogate the psychological and emotional components—equally real, but harder to articulate without the happenstance survival of a witness account. Given, moreover, Levi's insistence that the survivor is not the true witness,[48] the novel allows the voices of those who did not survive or who, having survived, did not survive within the material conditions that would allow them to produce and transmit that experience, the novel becomes perhaps the only locus for transmitting such experience.[49] Grass sees just such an operation at work in Victorian prison fiction:

> By treating prisoner bodies and self-accounts as texts for interpretation, Victorian prison novels both imitate the prison's narrative logic and presage Freud's desire to account fully for maimed selves incapable of speaking the truth about their own identity and desire. More, they do so even as they insist – in opposition to Foucault – that the prisoner contains an essential subjectivity, which must be silenced and circumvented narratively by both the prison and the novel. We see in the prison novel (as in the prison) less a negation of subjectivity than an obliteration of the self's power to account for its subjectivity.[50]

The prison, therefore, can serve as an essential locus for narrating the self, and thus for analyzing how prison writers construct the self in response to the self-obliterating (through physical and psychological violence) and narrative-obliterating constraints of the slave ship. This is especially true in fiction, which must create such a feeling without undermining their core argument: that they represent a high degree of external verisimilitude and can thus offer an interior verisimilitude which cannot be found in other kinds of texts.

The inaccessibility of nonfiction to the actual experiences of captivity has also undergirded literary theoretical innovations into a literary genre which also corresponds to Byzantine witness literature, namely the African-American slave narrative.[51] In arguing for the importance of fictional slave narratives over historical ones; Raphaël Lambert argues

---

[48] For which, see above, p. 12.

[49] Levi (1989: 83–84) as quoted in Agamben (2017: 783).

[50] Grass (2003: 10).

[51] For the relation of African-American slave narratives to Byzantine witness literature, see above, p. 83.

3 THE CARCERAL IMAGINARY IN BYZANTIUM: THE KOMNENIAN ... 157

that historical slave narratives "steer[] clear of subjectivity and pathos. This is where fiction becomes relevant as it uncovers territories that have remained either untapped or inaccessible to historians."[52] As with Holocaust novels, the relationship between truth and fiction in African-American slave literature has also been the subject of much debate; indeed, Alex Haley described his novel *Roots: The Saga of an American Family* (1976) as "faction," a portmanteau combining both fiction and fact.[53] As in the case of John Kaminiates, scholars and critics attempted to determine which parts of *Roots* were historical and which were fabrications, which were fictional, and which nonfictional.[54] Haley, however, resisted such critiques, arguing that such a distinction was fundamentally untenable: certain aspects of the slave experience can only be interrogated through a mixing of fact and fiction.

Haley's "faction" can also be said to be the determining genre of perhaps the most famous slave novel, Toni Morrison's *Beloved* (1989), based on the life of an actual slave named Margaret Garner.[55] Dennis Childs argues that *Beloved* represents a new kind of text that follows what he terms the "Middle Passage carceral model."[56] Though Childs' model is largely concerned with how the depiction of African-American slavery and incarceration[57] is rooted in the particulars of the African-American experience, the concept of the Middle Passage carceral mode has, in other respects, broad applicability to the Komnenian novels as slave novels. Childs notes that "the resurfacing of the chain-gang cage in her novel [...] exemplifies the centrality of architectures such as the slave-ship hold [...] with respect to U.S. Empire,"[58] an insight that also bears on the spatiality of the Komnenian novels, where the slave ship and the

---

[52] Lambert (2019: 2–3).

[53] Lambert (2019: 27). For the application of "faction" as a literary concept, see Vice's analysis of the relationship between literary invention and historical fidelity in the novel *Schindler's List* (2000: 89–115).

[54] Lambert (2019: 27).

[55] For Morrison's use of the textual witnesses of Garner's life as an intertext for *Beloved*, see Smith (2012).

[56] Childs (2015: 28).

[57] Childs begins his book by noting that he took his inspiration from a sentence fragment from within Angela Davis' larger revision of Foucault: "*Within the institution of slavery, itself a form of incarceration*" (2015: 1, 2, italicized in the original both times).

[58] Childs (2015: 28).

158   A. J. GOLDWYN

symposium function as inverted models of human existence, what Childs calls the ways in which the cage serves as a "lens" for the "remapping of the carceral" and the "formations of spatial violence."[59] And though Childs' "Middle Passage carceral model" is "a paradigm of racial capitalist internment and violence" and thus specific to the North American political and historical contexts, his argument that this model "necessitates a shift of white-subject-centered penal historiography"[60] offers a useful theoretical repositioning of subjectivity within the Komnenian novels, foregrounding slaves rather than free people, and foregrounding the slave experience within the broader narratives of romance and adventure. Perhaps most importantly, Childs argues that "*Beloved* represents as much of an epistemic intervention as a narrative one – how it can be conceived as offering a kind of black diasporic counter-penology that [...] disinters largely unheard aspects of the unhistorical predicament of early black neoslavery."[61] In this way, too, the Komnenian novels open up a narrative space for the "unheard" lives of Byzantine slaves.

Thus, when Prodromos refuses to skip past the conquest of Rhodes and move on to some other possible story within the fabula he has established, that is, by following the characters into the slave prison, Prodromos illuminates a part of Byzantine society that had remained invisible in the kinds of elite Constantinopolitan literary circles where the novels were originally performed. This suggests the importance of the spaces of incarceration as central to the novel's narrative configuration of incarceration and offers a counter-penology that focuses not on conquerors but on the conquered. At first, Prodromos scans the entirety of the interior of the prison camp:

> They slept (sleep of a kind – it was very disturbed),

---

[59] Childs (2015: 28).

[60] Childs (2015: 28).

[61] Childs (2015: 28). Childs also argues that *Beloved* makes a political argument about the carceral politics of its own time, that it "also offers a fundamental reassessment of the present moment of mass (in)human entombment through its centering of chattel slavery and the chain gang as primary sources of modern racial capitalist misogynist imprisonment" (Childs 2015: 28). While I do not dispute this in the case of *Beloved*, I see no evidence that the Komnenian novels had any similar what one might call "abolitionist" function in the original sense in which it was used in the antebellum United States or in the contemporary anti-carceral sense of, for instance, Michelle Alexander's *New Jim Crow* (Alexander 2010).

3 THE CARCERAL IMAGINARY IN BYZANTIUM: THE KOMNENIAN ... 159

Lying on the ground for a bed,
As night covered all after the setting of the sun.

ὕπνωττον (οἷον ὕπνον, ὡς κακὸν λίαν),
εἰς γῆν κατακλιθέντες ὡς οἷα κλίνην·
νὺξ γὰρ τὸ πᾶν κατέσχε δύντος ἡλίου.[62]

In doing so, takes his audience closer to the experience of the captive than his contemporary historiographers. The only other comparable nonfictional text to do so is indeed none other than Eustathios' *Capture of Thessaloniki*, in which the author describes the lack of sleeping quarters, and how he thus had to "lay[] ourselves down on the bench of the tiny bath house with only a simple layer of straw between us, we passed eight days" (ἐπιδόντες ἑαυτοὺς πεσσουλίῳ τοῦ ἐκεῖσε βραχυτάτου λοετροῦ ἐκείμεθα, χόρτον ἄμικτον ὑποβεβλημένοι, καὶ ὅτι ὀκτὼ μετρήσαντες ἡμέρας).[63] The specific sleeping conditions of captives and slaves are central to their individual experience; more importantly, the prison camp full of sleeping slaves also becomes the narrative space, serving as a framing device for, first, one character's (Dosikles') lament followed by a dialogic exchange of autobiographies by two of the prisoners (Dosikles and Kratandros). Dosikles' lament allows Prodromos to begin plumbing the interiority of his characters, exploring their thoughts and emotions by conceding narration to a secondary narrator-focalizer.[64]

As his lament opens, Dosikles articulates the grief, fear, and uncertainty of the experience:

Where are you taking me? To what end will you send me?
You have compelled me to migrate from the land that bore me,
you have condemned me to flight and wanderings,
you have separated me from kinsmen, friends and loved ones,
from my beloved mother, from my dearly loved progenitor.

ποῦ με προάγεις, εἰς τί με στήσεις τέλος;
ἄποικον εἰργάσω με τῆς γειναμένης,

---

[62] *R&D* 1.84–86.

[63] Eusth. *De capta Thess.* 110.

[64] For lamentation in the novels, see Nilsson (2017), though her analysis focuses on the ways in which lament foregrounds the marriage plot rather than the slave narrative.

160   A. J. GOLDWYN

φυγήν με κατέκρινας ὡς δὲ καὶ πλάνην,
ἀπεξένωσας συγγενῶν, γνωστῶν, φίλων,
μητρὸς ποθεινῆς, προσφιλοῦς φυτοσπόρου.[65]

Though Prodromos gives us the lament of a single imprisoned slave, these are the fears that no doubt plagued all of them, as they must have plagued all the enslaved and displaced persons the historians describe, articulating as they do fears of family separation, of exile, and a future whose certainty is only marked by hardship. Dosikles' lament, therefore, can be seen in the context of the imaginary possibilities opened up by fiction but precluded by genres such as history and witness literature, whose claims to authority rest upon the presumption of articulating only facts.

Thus, Prodromos is building on the omissions within previous kinds of narratives. John Kaminiates, for instance, writes that parents "would mingle with their children, set up a chorus of lamentation and steel themselves against the moment of separation. Brother met brother, friend friend, the one category bewailing their kinship, the other their close association" (εἶτα τοῖς τέκνοις ἀναμιχθέντες καὶ τὸν θρῆνον χοροστατήσαντες τὴν διαίρεσιν ἐκαρτέρουν. ἀδελφὸς δὲ πάλιν ἀδελφῷ συναντήσας καὶ φίλος φίλῳ, ὁ μὲν τὴν συγγένειαν ὁ δὲ τὴν μακρὰν συνήθειαν ἀπεκλαίετο).[66] Kaminiates further notes that "simply by virtue of the immense number of individual laments, the air was filled with a meaningless babel of voices" (καὶ ἁπλῶς τῇ ἀμετρίᾳ τῶν κατὰ μέρος θρήνων κραυγῆς ἀσήμου πάντα πεπλήρωτο)[67] thus preventing any individual lament from coming into focus. The novel solves this problem through the use of fiction: like witness literature, novels can isolate one voice from among the many to give a more individualized portrait of the experience, and yet the novel has yet one more advantage, so to speak, in this regard: whereas the witness can narrate one voice, it must be his own. Kaminiates' narration focuses only on what he himself experienced or observed. The novelist, by contrast, can isolate any voice he wants, thus allowing Prodromos to choose any particular individual experience he wanted; indeed, where the narrative of the witness is bound by his own lived circumstances, the novelist can invent whatever circumstances are most suitable for

[65] R&D 1.89–93.
[66] Kam. Ex. Thess. 36.7–9.
[67] Kam. Ex. Thess. 36.9.

3 THE CARCERAL IMAGINARY IN BYZANTIUM: THE KOMNENIAN … 161

conveying the kind of emotional experience he wants to communicate through his fiction.

As Dosikles' lament and other examples from among the corpus of witness literature demonstrate, chief among these emotional experiences was the suffering of family separation. Whereas John Kaminiates (and Elie Wiesel) focus on the severing of the father–son bond, the Komnenian novels foreground a different kind of family separation, that of lovers and husbands and wives. Indeed, here too, the interpenetration of the genres of history, witness, and novel reflect three different ways of considering this unique iteration of this particular form of suffering. In his description of the scene at the harbor, John Kaminiates writes that the first captives led onto the slave ships were

> the young people of both sexes, not keeping those who were related together but splitting them up so that in this matter too should they suffer, in terms of physical separation, no ordinary punishment. […] So all the young were led away, their only crime being the bloom of youth and the beauty of their faces. […] Indeed for many it was their beauty that had provided the pretext which delivered them to disaster.

> τὴν νεάζουσαν κήραν τοῦ πλήθους ἀρρένων τε καὶ θηλειῶν πρῶτον ταῖς ναυσὶν εἰσενεγκόντας, μὴ κατὰ συγγένειαν ἀλλὰ διακεκριμένως, ἵν' ἔχωσι κἂν τούτῳ τιμωρίαν οὐ τὴν τυχοῦσαν, τὴν φυσικὴν ἐξ ἀλλήλων διαίρεσιν […] ἤγετο οὖν τὸ νεάζον πρόσωπον ἅπαν, τοῦτο μόνον κατηγορίαν ἔχον, τὸ ἀνθηρὸν τῆς ἡλικίας ἢ τῶν προσώπων τὴν ὡραιότητα. […] καὶ πρόφασις ἦν τοῖς πολλοῖς τὸ κάλλος, ἐν τοῖς δεινοῖς αὐτοὺς προδιδόμενον.[68]

Niketas Choniates, too, in describing the naval raids of the Sicilian king Roger II Guiscard in the spring of 1147 on Greece proper, notes that his captain "encamped in the land of Kadmos, and, plundering the towns along the way, he came to Thebes of the Seven Gates, which he took by storm, treating her inhabitants savagely" (τὰ ἀμφιβοσκόμενα τῇ Καδμείᾳ γῇ παρενέβαλε καὶ τὰς ἐν μέσῳ κωμοπόλεις ὁδοῦ πάρεργον λῃσάμενος ταῖς ἑπταπύλοις Θήβαις προσέβαλεν, ὧν καὶ γενόμενος ἐγκρατὴς ἀπανθρώπως τοῖς ἐκεῖ προσηνέχθη, ὧν καὶ γενόμενος ἐγκρατὴς ἀπανθρώπως τοῖς ἐκεῖ προσηνέχθη.)[69] Thus, the conquest itself is treated in a cursory fashion, a

---

[68] Kam. *Ex. Thess.* 60.1–2. See p. 133.

[69] Chon. *Hist.* 74.

162   A. J. GOLDWYN

single passing line, while another line addresses the general horrors befell the inhabitants, which must have been similar to the events that befell Eustathios and John Kaminiates. Niketas, however, does elaborate more on one aspect of the prisoners' treatment:

> He did not refrain from keeping his hands off the bodies of those whom he had gleaned, but took captive and sailed off with the most eminent according to birth and merit and chose those women who were comely and deep-girded in form, and who had often bathed in the running waters of Dirce's beautiful spring, and who had styled their tresses and had mastered the weaver's art.

> οὐδὲ τῶν σωμάτων αὐτῶν τῶνὑπ' αὐτοῦ καλαμωθέντων ἀπέσχετο, ἀλλὰ καὶ τούτων ἀριστίνδην τὸ προὖχον συλλαβὼν τῶν τε γυναικῶν ἀποκρίνας ὅσαι τὸ εἶδος καλαὶ καὶ βαθύζωνοι καὶ τοῖς νάμασι πολλάκις τῆς καλλικρούνου Δίρκης λουσάμεναι καὶ τὰς κόμας διευθετισάμεναι καὶ τὴν ἱστουργικὴν κομψότητα καλῶς ἐπιστάμεναι οὕτως ἐκεῖθεν ἀνάγεται.[70]

Here, Niketas describes how the invasion of the Byzantine coastal cities by pirates resulted in the mass kidnapping of local prominent men and women, with particular emphasis on the physical beauty of the captured women. As with the heroines of the Komnenian novels, beautiful captive women are the most valuable prize in conquering cities. The Sicilian captain's particular penchant for capturing elite men and beautiful women is repeated again when he conquers Corinth: he did not put out to sea again until he "had enslaved the Corinthians of illustrious birth, and had taken captive the most comely and deep-bosomed women" (τοὺς γένει λαμπροτάτους τῶν Κορινθίων ἐδουλαγώγησεν, ἐξηχμαλώτισε δὲ καὶτῶν γυναικῶν ὅσαι κάλλισται καὶ βαθύκολποι).[71] Thus, both Kaminiates and Niketas focus on the physical beauty and youth of the captives. Whereas Niketas, writing in a historiographical mode, merely narrates the observable fact of their capture and moves on, Kaminiates, writing in the mode of witness, notes the emotional context of their capture, that it was "no ordinary punishment" and that its main purpose was "that they should suffer." But both of these authors are bound by the mandates of

[70] Chon. *Hist.* 74.
[71] Chon. *Hist.* 76.

3 THE CARCERAL IMAGINARY IN BYZANTIUM: THE KOMNENIAN ... 163

their respective genres to maintain the illusion of narrating only verifiable fact, and this prevents them from describing the experience of these things. Prodromos, by contrast, is explicitly concerned with this experience, and the genre of the novel allows him to imaginatively enter into the slave ship, to imagine the responses of people in this situation.

That Rhodanthe was beautiful is indeed the central fact about her: the first mention of her in the narrative proper (as opposed to the author's dedication)[72] is an elaborate ekphrasis on her exceptional physical appearance:

> The girl's beauty was something extraordinary,
> an august figure, a replica of a divine image,
> wrought in the form of Artemis.

> Ἦν οὖν τὸ κάλλος τῆς κόρης χρῆμα ξένον,
> ἄγαλμα σεπτόν, εἰκόνος θείας τύπος,
> εἰς εἶδος Ἀρτέμιδος ἀπεξεσμένον.[73]

This is followed by seventeen lines that describe in detail each of her physical features from head to toe, from the beauty of her eyebrows (46), nose (48), cheeks (49), and mouth (55) down to the posture of her ankles.[74] Nor is her beauty only expressed in terms of this ekphrasis; even secondary focalizers such as the barbarian captain Gobryas acknowledge it:

> The maiden was so excellent to look at
> that that the predatory robber Gobryas
> suspected it was a goddess who had been captured.

> Οὕτως ἀρίστη τὴν θέαν ἡ παρθένος,
> ὡς καὶ τὸν ἀγρεύσαντα λῃστὴν Γωβρύαν,
> θεὰν ὑποπτεύσαντα τὴν ἠγρευμένην.[75]

---

[72] Though there, too, her beauty is the central aspect of her character, as is the youth and beauty of Dosikles; she is "the silvery girl Rhodanthe" and he "the comely youth Dosikles" (Dedication 17–18).

[73] *R&D* 1.39–41.

[74] *R&D* 1.58. For the novelistic tradition of ekphraseis of women as statues, see the note to *R&D* 1.41).

[75] *R&D* 1.61–63.

164   A. J. GOLDWYN

Thus, Prodromos takes a historical phenomenon—the traumatic separation of beautiful youths bound for slavery—and uses the genre of the novel to dramatize their suffering in a way that other genres cannot, thus making an individual character for whom one can feel sympathy out of a historical phenomenon affecting thousands with which one cannot. Dosikles' lament continues with him noting that his fears of family separation from his parents and exile from his native land are "small matters" (μικρά)[76] compared to the fate he fears awaits his beloved Rhodanthe. Indeed, when later in the narrative Dosikles and Kratandros are captured again by another barbarian captain named Byraxes, who "intended to offer a sacrifice to the gods of the region" (ταῖς γὰρ ἀπαρχαῖς τοὺς θεοὺς τιμητέον) he says, and "had nothing better than Dosikles | and Kratandros, the handsome couple" (οὐδὲν δὲ κρεῖττον εἶχε τοῦ Δοσικλέος | καὶ τοῦ Κρατάνδρου, τῆς καλῆς συζυγίας).[77] The primary narrator then offers an authorial interruption in their own voice:

> Oh shameful beauty, oh evil gift from the gods;
> May no one be beautiful in life
> If they are to be slaughtered because of their beauty.

> ὦ κάλλος αἰσχρόν, ὦ θεῶν κακὴ χάρις·
> μὴ γὰρ καλοὶ γένοιντό τινες ἐν βίῳ,
> ἂν εἰ κατασφάττοιντο τοῦ κάλλους χάριν.[78]

Prodromos thus acknowledges the role of physical beauty in slaves, giving fictional form to a feature of captivity that is also attested in historical accounts of the period during which the novels were composed.

Though it suits his literary purposes—one of the major themes of the novel is the unflagging determination of the lovers to be reunited—Prodromos' imagining of Dosikles' lament also makes an unsupportable and unverifiable presupposition about the captive mentality: Dosikles is not concerned with himself—"perhaps I would survive the violence [...] for I am a man reared in battles" (Κἀγὼ μὲν ἴσως καρτερήσω τὴν βίαν [...] ἀνὴρ γάρ εἰμι καὶ μάχαις συνετράφην)[79]—but with his beloved: "But

[76] R&D 1.98.
[77] R&D 7.326, 327–328.
[78] R&D 7.329–331.
[79] R&D 1.113, 116.

3 THE CARCERAL IMAGINARY IN BYZANTIUM: THE KOMNENIAN ... 165

how will Rhodanthe endure the pain?" (ἀλλ' ἡ Ῥοδάνθη πῶς ὑποίσει τὸν πόνον;)[80]

Dosikles' concern thus turns from his own plight toward that of the family from whom he has been separated:

> For perhaps when the robber chief sees the girl
> he will immediately succumb to the fire of love
> and will kindle a burning flame in his heart
> and will force Rhodanthe into marriage.
> [...]
> If it does not [happen], then there is death for the maiden Rhodanthe,
> for barbarians are hot for love
> and when thwarted quick turn to murder.

> ἰδὼν γὰρ ἴσως τὴν κόρην ὁ λῃστάναξ
> ἔρωτος εὐθὺς ὑποδέξεται φλόγα
> καὶ πῦρ ἀνάψει λάβρον ἐν τῇ καρδίᾳ,
> βιάσεται δὲ τὴν Ῥοδάνθην εἰς γάμον.
> [...]
> εἰ δ' οὐ τύχῃ, θάνατος εἰς τὴν παρθένον·
> θερμὸν γάρ ἐστιν εἰς ἔρον τὸ βάρβαρον
> καὶ μὴ τυχὸν πρόχειρον εἰς φονουργίαν.[81]

Given the fate that Niketas describes for beautiful women in the *History* and given the novel genre's focus on beautiful women, it is no surprise that Dosikles' greatest fear is the sexual violation of his beloved.[82] But, compared to Niketas' *History*, in which such behavior is simply listed before the narration moves on, Prodromos dwells on the emotions of the individuals who find themselves in such situations. Here, too, however, we come to another distinction between novels and histories: Niketas, ostensibly committed to verifiable fact or some notion of historical objectivity,

---

[80] *R&D* 1.118.

[81] *R&D* 1.102–105, 1.109–111. The passage is discussed in the broader context of gender-based violence in the Komnenian novels in Goldwyn (2018: 87–88).

[82] African-American slave narratives testify to this kind of violence when sexual advances are refused. Youngquist, for instance, reports on the 1792 trial of Captain John Kimber for the murder of a slave girl during the Middle Passage: "The alleged reason for his violence: the girl would not 'dance.' That's slaver parlance for exercise, but who knows what Kimber had in mind. The fact was, however, that the anonymous female would not oblige his command, refused to dance, and in a fit of pique, Kimber strung her up" (2011: 1). Kimber was acquitted (Youngquist 2011: 3–4).

166   A. J. GOLDWYN

perhaps refrains from speculating about the goings-on inside the minds of the captives in the holds of Robert Guiscard's ships because he himself could not verify them—this kind of speculative empathetic imagination is reserved for the novel, not the history. Indeed, through first-person narration and various sub-narrators, the genre of the novel allows for a closer psychological examination of the very real fear of rape, forced marriage, and other forms of sexual violence on the people whose loved ones experience these traumas.

3.2   THE DIALOGIC CONSTRUCTION OF SELF IN THE SLAVE NARRATIVES OF RHODANTHE AND DOSIKLES

Given the tight quarters of the prison ship, it is no surprise that his lament is overheard by one of the other prisoners. Narration from within the prison ship, therefore, shapes not only the content and context for the delivery of the speech, but also its reception:

> While the young man was bewailing in this way,
> a youth, goodly in appearance, stood beside him:
> he had been captured earlier, I think, and imprisoned previously.

> Οὕτως ἀποιμώζοντι τῷ νεανίᾳ
> ἐφίσταται παῖς ἀγαθὸς τὴν ἰδέαν,
> οἶμαι προληφθεὶς καὶ προεγκεκλεισμένος.[83]

The prison is thus not just a space of community and communal grief and consolation. Indeed, the fellow prisoner begins in just this way, urging Dosikles to "Cease your groans" (παύθητι [...] τῶν στεναγμῶν).[84] He continues:

> You have been banished from your own country: bear up,
> For you have us who have been banished with you.
> You are restrained through the greed of harsh robbers:
> We have all been restrained by the barbarians' weapons.
> You dwell in a prison: we are fellow prisoners.

[83] R&D 1.132–134.
[84] R&D 1.137.

3 THE CARCERAL IMAGINARY IN BYZANTIUM: THE KOMNENIAN ... 167

ἀπεξενώθης τῆς ἐνεγκούσης· φέρε·
ἔχεις γὰρ ἡμᾶς συναπεξενωμένους.
λῃστῶν ἀπηνῶν ἁρπαγῇ κατεσχέθης·
πάντες κατεσχέθημεν ὅπλοις βαρβάρων.
οἰκεῖς φυλακήν· συμπεφυλακίσμεθα.[85]

Kratandros thus engages with his fellow prisoner in a spirit of shared community-making: he identifies Dosikles' condition—"you have been banished" and "you are restrained"—and then shares its similarities with those of the others in the new community—"us who have been banished with you" and "we have all been restrained." Kratandros then offers what Elizabeth Jeffreys calls a piece of "sententious moralizing" but which, given the context of the slave ship as a space of loneliness and grief, could also be read as a sympathetic welcome and valuable piece of advice to a new slave:

> [...] to share miseries
> brings comfort to the sufferer,
> lightens the burden of pain
> and quenches the furnace of distress,
> sprinkling the water of consolation.

> [...] ἡ κακῶν κοινωνία
> φέρει παρηγόρημα τῷ πεπονθότι,
> ἐλαφρύνει δὲ τοῦ πόνου τὴν φροντίδα
> καὶ τῆς ὀδύνης τὴν κάμινον σβεννύει,
> ὕδωρ ἐπιστάξασα παραμυθίας.[86]

This act of community-making sets up the prison as a dialogic space for the crafting of Dosikles' new sense of self as a prisoner and slave through

---

[85] R&D 1.139–143. Constantine Manasses' *Aristandros and Kallithea* expresses a similar sentiment, though since the novel survives only in fragments, the exact context cannot be ascertained: "If members of this species encounter each other | as fellow prisoners or fellow toilers or fellow captives, | they share the dangers and disasters with each other, | they groan together, they weep together, and they mourn with each other" (εἰ δέ τινες ὁμογενεῖς ἐντύχοιεν ἀλλήλοις | συμφυλακῖται, σύμμοχθοι, συναιχμαλωτισθέντες, | κοινοῦνται καὶ τὰς συμφορὰς καὶ τοὺς ἀλλήλων πόνους, | συστένουσι, συγκλαίουσιν, ἀλλήλοις συμπενθοῦσιν) (A&K fr. 17, 1.48–54).

[86] R&D 1.144–148.

narrative[87]; Kratandros encourages Dosikles to "recount your unfortunate fate | for you will tell it to a yet more unfortunate man" (τὰς σεαυτοῦ δυστυχεῖς τύχας λέγε· | εἴποις γὰρ αὐτὰς ἀνδρὶ δυστυχεστέρῳ).[88] That Dosikles is both relieved and consoled by this is evident from his immediate response: "A Hellene, saviour gods, this stranger is | a Hellene" (Ἕλλην, θεοὶ σωτῆρες, οὗτος ὁ ξένος, | Ἕλλην).[89] Raphaël Lambert notes that for African slaves, the hold of the slave ship was also a multicultural space in which "slave-ship captives, dazed and exhausted, chained in the hold, often came from very different geographic, cultural, and linguistics horizons. It was difficult for them to communicate [...] yet, driven by a basic need for survival, and perhaps interpreting their common dehumanization as a rallying sign, captives did engage in mutual support."[90] Maurice Rediker takes a similar approach, arguing that the slave ship represented the first phase of "a new community in formation. [...] Here was the alchemy of chains mutating, under the hard pressure of resistance, into bonds of community. The mysterious slave ship had become a place of creative resistance."[91] Thus, the recognition by Dosikles of another Hellene with whom he shared a language and culture marks the slave prison as a location of community building and, in allowing the slaves to speak to one another without the supervision of the slavers themselves, to cultivate a new shared sense of identity that formed the foundation of their resistance to their own desubjectification. Indeed, Olaudah Equiano notes a similar feeling when he writes of the slave ship that "in a little time after, amongst the poor chained men, I found some of my own nation, which in a small degree gave ease to my mind."[92] Equiano therefore attests, in a nonfictional context, to the importance of community formation in slave spaces.

Indeed, these sentiments are also part of the Byzantine slave narrative as well. John Kaminiates, for instance, writes to Gregory of Cappadocia in the beginning of his letter that "a common urge tends to inevitably hold

---

[87] Ingela Nilsson argues that this passage demonstrates how "the act of exchanging sad stories becomes a central narrative device" (2017: 294).

[88] *R&D* 1.152–153.

[89] *R&D* 1.153–154.

[90] Lambert (2019: 5).

[91] Rediker (2007: 307).

[92] Equiano (1999: 58).

3 THE CARCERAL IMAGINARY IN BYZANTIUM: THE KOMNENIAN ... 169

in a common bond of compulsion both listener and narrator. And in fact, neither sight nor hearing will easily be parted from what they most enjoy, nor will the speaker abate his ardour until he has told his tale" (φιλοῦσι γὰρ ἀεὶ τὰ ποθούμενα τῶν πραγμάτων ἀνάγκης δεσμοῖς καὶ τὸν λέγοντα περὶ αὐτῶν κατέχειν καὶ τὸν ἀκούοντα· καὶ οὐκ ἂν οὕτως εὐχερῶς καὶ ῥᾳδίως οὔτε ὄψις τῶν ἡδίστων θεαμάτων οὔτε ἀκοὴ τῶν τερπνῶν ἀποστήσεται ἀκουσμάτων, οὔτε λόγος ἡδὺς τῆς ὁρμῆς ἀνακοπήσεται, μέχρις ἂν φθάσῃ τὸ πέρας πρὸς ὃ κατ᾽ ἀρχὰς ἐπείγεται).[93] At the end of the letter, Kaminiates restates this shared experience: "And indeed, ever since that occasion on which you showed sympathy and shared in our suffering by manifesting your concern to hear the full story of these events, it is clear that you have been deeply moved by our fate and uncommonly sensitive to our misfortunes" (ἐξ οὗ δὴ καὶ αὐτὸς συμπαθήσας τότε καὶ ἐν τούτῳ κοινωνήσας ἡμῖν τοῦ πάθους ἐν τῷ περὶ πολλοῦ ποιήσασθαι μαθεῖν τὴν περὶ τούτων ἀκολουθίαν, ἔκδηλος ἐγένου τῇ λύπῃ πληγεὶς καὶ πέρα τοῦ μετρίου τὴν καρδίαν ὀδυνηθείς).[94] Indeed, in this regard, John Kaminiates' use of συμπαθήσας and πάθους indicate just the kind of affective connection between audience and listener that Eustathios noted as the element that distinguishes his work of witness from that of the historiographers. And yet, if the sentiment at least is shared in *Rhodanthe and Dosikles*, Constantine Manasses' *Aristandros and Kallithea* uses the exact word: "The tale of another's suffering can shed | some drops of comfort on one who is faring badly" (Οἶδε καὶ γὰρ ἀναψυχῆς ψεκάδας ἐπιστάζειν | διηγηθὲν ἀλλότριον τῷ δυσπραγοῦντι πάθος).[95] Because *Aristandros and Kallithea* survives only in fragments, it is impossible to understand the context in which these words were uttered. Though it seems tempting to suggest that one slave is telling them to another, this is ultimately unknowable; what is certain, however, is that this sentiment is shared by both writers of eyewitness testimony and novels, an indication that two genres that ostensibly differ in their approach to narrating truth nevertheless have a shared interest in the mimetic narration of emotion and suffering.

In both the *Capture of Thessaloniki* and *Rhodanthe and Dosikles*, two Greek slaves commiserate about their misfortunes and swap autobiographies of incarceration and slavery, with the emphasis being on the shared

---

[93] Kam. *Ex. Thess.* 7.

[94] Kam. *Ex. Thess.* 78.

[95] *A&K* fr. 16, 1.46–147.

170   A. J. GOLDWYN

misfortune of their situation—"And in fact you too were yourself at that time destitute and enduring the same misfortune as us" (καὶ γὰρ ἔτυχες τότε καὶ αὐτὸς ἀλητεύων κατὰ τὴν αὐτὴν ἡμῶν συμφοράν).[96] Thus, though the only surviving remnant of the meeting between Kaminiates and Gregory is a letter, Kaminiates reveals that they too spoke of their shared miseries while held in the prison, just as Dosikles and Kratandros. In this regard, it significant that Kaminiates specifically references their συμπαθεστάτῃ φιλίᾳ, what Melville-Jones translates as "sympathetic friendship," but which, given the importance of *pathos* as a defining feature of both the witness as narrator and the dialogic nature of shared experience (*sym-*), might be better understood as their shared experience of (extreme, since the word is in the superlative) suffering, thus creating the possibility of witness testimony as autobiographical narrative and dialogic construction of identity.

Figures like Gregory of Cappadocia and Kratandros are thus central features of witness literature. These are important figures in witness literature; Michael Levine calls them the "*supplementary* witness,"[97] the "witness to the witness,"[98] or "the addressable you."[99] Levine argues that the "listener, interviewer, or reader [of] the testimonial act [...] implicitly commits himself to the task of assuming *co*-responsibility for an intolerable burden, for the crushing weight of a responsibility which the witness had heretofore felt he or she bore alone and could therefore not carry out."[100] The witness to the witness, therefore, eases the psychological burden— a feature of witness which Kratandros evidently understands when he claims speaking will give Dosikles comfort. Levine traces an ontological argument within the debate of Holocaust Studies by which the Nazis "extinguished philosophically the very possibility of address, the possibility of appealing, or of turning to, another," thus severing the individual from the broader communal contexts in which they lived[101] as a simultaneous process with the severing of the individual from their own self,

---

[96] Kam. *Ex. Thess.* 2.

[97] Levine (2006: 7, italics in original).

[98] Levine (2006: 2). For this term, see also Hartman (2004: 92).

[99] Levine (2006: 3).

[100] Levine (2006: 7).

[101] Levine (2006: 8).

3 THE CARCERAL IMAGINARY IN BYZANTIUM: THE KOMNENIAN ... 171

which he calls "the loss of the capacity to be a witness to oneself" and the capability to be "a witness from the inside."[102] He considers these dual losses "perhaps the true meaning of annihilation, for when one's history is abolished one's identity ceases to exist."[103] Levine concludes that "it is the *mutual recognition* of speaker and listener, and the essential possibility of the one dialogically exchanging places with the other, that maintain within each 'I' the space of an internal 'you,' that hold open the space of an inner dialogue in which one can 'say "thou" ... to oneself.'"[104] Indeed, in her analysis of Primo Levi, Alana Fletcher argues that "the experience of the Lager is monologic as opposed to dialogic: it exiles addressivity from language."[105] Following Levine, then, this "testimonial alliance"[106] allows for the reconstitution of the traumatized witness into an individual again, preserving (or reconnecting) the body to its past, to its memories, emotions, and sense of subjectivity. For Levine, moreover, it is through the "*chance encounter*" that "this 'I' dialogically constitute[s] itself first and foremost as an act of language, an act of witnessing."[107] Thus, the chance encounter of Gregory and John Kaminiates in the slave prison in Tripoli and the chance encounter of Dosikles and Kratandros in the slave ship off the coast of Rhodes open up the possibility of a dialogic space in which the speaker can become a witness by telling his story to someone else, thus easing his own burden and reconstructing the individuated subjective self that the material, institutional, and internal effects of slavery and incarceration seek to annihilate.

Despite this fortuitous circumstance, however, Dosikles initially refuses the offer, saying

> You should rather tell your story first,
> for perhaps by telling it you will excise the pain
> and relieve me of long lamentations.

---

[102] Levine (2006: 8).

[103] Levine (2006: 8).

[104] Levine (2006: 8, italics in original).

[105] Fletcher (2016: 36).

[106] Levine (2006: 9).

[107] Levine (2006: 4).

172   A. J. GOLDWYN

σὺ τὰς σεαυτοῦ προφθάσας μᾶλλον λέγοις·
λέγων γὰρ ἴσως ἐξεώσεις τὸν πόνον
καὶ κουφιεῖς με τῶν μακρῶν στεναγμάτων.[108]

Dosikles, too, recognizes the possibility of dialogic autobiographical narration for easing pain, but does not himself have a concept of how to tell it. He does not know how to tell a slave narrative, which is what his autobiography must now be. Kratandros, however, a more experienced slave, knows how to self-narrate in this genre, and in recounting his own life, both constructs his own identity and teaches Dosikles how to narrate his own life—and thus understand his new subject position and identity as a slave. In this, trauma studies and psychoanalysis can play a crucial role in understanding how identity is constructed through dialogical autobiographical narration: "psychoanalytic thinking also attends to the way a story told to another person might nonetheless be primarily a story told to the self."[109] This, then, is how and why the construction of the self in the slave prison becomes a dialogic act: it is in the shared physical space of the prison that the shared narrative space also emerges in which new slaves can form community through cultivating a shared generic sense of self.

Indeed, Kratandros' response conforms in a broad way to that of John Kaminiates' letter to Gregory of Cappadocia from two centuries earlier: "You sought through your letter to learn the way in which it had come about that we dwell in captivity, having been delivered into the hands of the barbarians, how we exchanged a foreign land for our own country, where we hail from and what sort of place it is" (Ἐζήτησας μαθεῖν διὰ τῆς ἐπιστολῆς τὸν τρόπον δι᾽ ὃν τὴν φρουρὰν οἰκοῦμεν βαρβάρων χερσὶν ἐκδοθέντες, καὶ πῶς τὴν ἀλλοτρίαν ἀντὶ τῆς ἰδίας διημειψάμεθα, ποίας τέ ἐσμεν πατρίδος, καὶ τίνα τὰ κατ᾽ αὐτήν).[110] This, too, becomes the overarching framework for Kratandros' speech to Dosikles and, like Kaminiates, Kratandros begins with the last question first: "I had, Dosikles, Cyprus for my homeland, | Kraton as my progenitor, Stale as my mother" (ἐγώ, Δοσίκλεις, Κύπρον ἔσχον πατρίδα, | φυτοσπόρον Κράτωνα, μητέρα

---

[108] R&D 1.155–157.

[109] Budick (2015: 45).

[110] Kam. *ex. Thess.* 2.1.

3 THE CARCERAL IMAGINARY IN BYZANTIUM: THE KOMNENIAN ...   173

Στάλην).[111] He then begins his narrative of the second part, "the way in which it had come about that we dwell in captivity," as Kaminiates put it. He delivers a long speech about the death of his own beloved Chrysochroe, how he was wrongly convicted of the crime, and how he fled Cyprus aboard a ship which was then captured by a barbarian pirate fleet. At this point, a marginal gloss in the manuscript reads "Capture" (Ἅλωσις) and the fleet, which fell upon them,

> having already looted a thousand ships.
> Thereupon, it went back towards its own country,
> Having shut the captives in nether hell
> (as I call this cell common to us both),
> And turned to a second bout of pillage.

> ἔχων προσυληθέντα μυρία σκάφη.
> στραφεὶς δὲ τηνικαῦτα πρὸς σὴν πατρίδα
> καὶ τοὺς ἁλόντας ἐν μέσῳ κλείσας ζόφῳ
> τὸν κοινὸν ἀμφοῖν τοῦτον οἰκίσκον λέγω
> εἰς δευτέραν γοῦν ἁρπαγὴν ἀντετράπη.[112]

As every autobiography, slave narrative, or work of witness testimony, Kratandros' narrative includes and omits, varies its rhythm, and uses tools of narrative art to create a single story from the infinite number of possibilities within any given fabula. Kratandros' principles of selection conform to the genre of slave narratives: it begins by establishing the subjectivity of its narrator, establishes his geographic and familial origins, and then describes a series of events in a teleological way that interpret his past as a series of incidents that inevitably and inexorably lead to his current position as a slave.

Kratandros' narrative thus adheres to a model of identity construction legible through contemporary theories of psychoanalytic identity formation. In this regard, the use of first-person narration as much represents Kratandros showing Dosikles who he is as much as how he can come to understand himself within this new identity. Judith Butler argues that "we become conscious of ourselves only after certain injuries have been inflicted. Someone suffers as a consequence, and the suffering person or,

---

[111] *R&D* 1.160–161.

[112] *R&D* 1.420–424.

rather, someone acting as his or her advocate in a system of justice seeks to find the cause of that suffering and asks us whether we might be that cause. It is in the interest of meting out a just punishment to the one responsible for an injurious action that the question is posed and that the subject in question comes to question him or herself."[113] It is significant in this regard, then, that Kratandros' narrative is in fact a criminal one, one in which he attempts to acquit himself of the accusation of murdering his beloved. But for Charikles, it is in the movement from *bios* to *zoē* (the movement between ethical norms governing the life of the free aristocracy and the ethical norms governing the lives of slaves) is the moment when he first catches a glimpse of himself outside of the social context in which he understands himself, and thus can see himself for the first time. According to Butler:

> The "I" does not stand apart from the prevailing matrix of ethical norms and conflicting moral frameworks. In an important sense, this matrix is also the condition for the emergence of the "I," [...] when the "I" seeks to give an account of itself, an account that must include the conditions of its own emergence, it must, as a matter of necessity, become a social theorist. The reason for this is that the "I" has no story of its own that is not also the story of a relation—or set of relations—to a set of norms.[114]

First-person narration, therefore, is not only a means for explaining the self to the other, but as significantly, a means for discovering the self. Kratandros' narrative humanizes and grants him, in the eyes of himself as narrator, Charikles as listener, and the reader/listener of the text, a subject positionality: he is given a chronological depth that allows him to reveal the emotional depth of a character who might otherwise appear as but one in an otherwise anonymous and undifferentiated mass. With specific regard to the narration of Holocaust testimony, Thomas Trezise defines the dialogical nature of identity construction as "the 'I' as inextricable from the 'you' (and, since these pronouns are universally available, from third persons as well)" and concludes that "we find that the identity of the self derives from alterity, its sameness from difference, its interiority from an 'outside' without which no relation to itself—in this instance, no listening to itself or, in keeping with the holism of the model, to others as

---

[113] Butler (2005: 10).

[114] Butler (2005: 7–8).

3 THE CARCERAL IMAGINARY IN BYZANTIUM: THE KOMNENIAN ... 175

others—would even prove conceivable."[115] Dialogue is thus the minimal necessary condition for testimony as regards both communicating one's experience to the other and understanding one's experience as related to one's own coalescing sense of identity in the face of its potential collapse.

In Prodromos' telling, the captives are not just a group or a deracinated collective, but are, in fact, made up of unique individuals who, though they share a physical space and position of subjugation, nevertheless each has their own backstory, personal experiences, motivations, and life trajectories that, in sum, define them beyond the circumstances of their slavery. Kratandros' narrative thus ends with the present moment, its consolatory and pedagogical function achieved, for as he finishes, Dosikles suggests they go to sleep.

3.3   SELEKTION IN *RHODANTHE AND DOSIKLES*

Kratandros and Dosikles do not have much time to themselves, however; their sleep is interrupted, when

> Mistylos (for he was the robber chief)
> Came out of his own lodging at dawn
> And ordered the barbarians under his command
> To bring out the imprisoned captives.
> Gobryas went into the prison
> And immediately brought out all those who were inside
> And presented them to the emperor Mistylos.

> ὁ Μιστύλος δέ (τοῦτο γὰρ ὁ ληστάναξ)
> ἔωθεν ἐκβὰς τῆς φίλης κατοικίας
> τοὺς αἰχμαλώτους τοὺς πεφυλακισμένους
> ἄγειν κελεύει τοῖς ὑπ' αὐτὸν βαρβάροις.
> τὴν γοῦν φυλακὴν εἰσιὼν ὁ Γωβρύας
> ἅπαντας αὐτοὺς ἐκτὸς εὐθὺς ἐξάγει
> καὶ τῷ βασιλεῖ Μιστύλῳ παριστάνει.[116]

In this way, Prodromos introduces the moment of Selektion that was so central to the Holocaust memoirs of both Elie Wiesel and Primo Levi and which, in a more directly precedential way, was featured in John

---

[115] Trezise (2013: 29).

[116] *R&D* 1.434–440.

176   A. J. GOLDWYN

Kaminiates' letter. Indeed, the morning roll call, the gathering of all the prisoners, and their presentation to the commander who will determine their fate echo even the specifics of these narratives. From the perspective of Foucaultian biopolitics, the definitive act of sovereign power is contained in the sovereign decision: the ability to decide who will be allowed to live and who made to die. In *Rhodanthe and Dosikles*, the prison serves the function of the Appelplatz, as each of the captives passes before the sovereign, Mistylos, who decides the fates of the prisoners, determining not only who will live and die, but how and under what circumstances each will do so. First,

> The robber chief saw Dosikles,
> And then saw Rhodanthe immediately afterwards.
> He could not have been more astonished,
> For both were so handsome in appearance.

> Ὁ ληστάναξ δὲ τὸν Δοσικλέα βλέπων
> καὶ τὴν Ῥοδάνθην εὐθέως μεταβλέπων,
> οὐκ εἶχεν οἷον ἐκπλαγήσεται πλέον·
> ἄμφω γὰρ ἤστην ἀγαθὼ τὴν ἰδέαν.[117]

Because of their youth and physical beauty, Mistylos decides that "I shall make them temple attendants on the gods" (δώσω γὰρ αὐτοὺς τοῖς θεοῖς νεωκόρους).[118] He then proceeds to deliver his decision for the remaining slaves individually and as a group:

> "This snivelling old man
> (weeping all the time for fear of being executed),"
> Pointing to Stratokles, "send him back to his own country,
> Freed from a slave's bitter fate.
> Those four huddled over there,
> Whose appearance shows them to be sailors,
> Kill them and pour their blood out as a libation to the gods.
> [...]
> All others, if they have been ransomed by their progenitors
> Or brothers or loving children,
> Let them return to their own countries,

[117] *R&D* 1.441–444.
[118] *R&D* 1.449.

3 THE CARCERAL IMAGINARY IN BYZANTIUM: THE KOMNENIAN ...   177

Or else let them experience a slave's fate.

'τοῦτον δὲ τὸν κλαίοντα, τὸν γηραλέον
(κλαίει δὲ πάντως τὴν σφαγὴν ὑποτρέμων)',
δείξας Στρατοκλῆν, 'πέμψον εἰς τὴν πατρίδα,
ἐλευθερώσας δουλικῆς πικρᾶς τύχης.
τοὺς τέτταρας δὲ τοὺς κεκυφότας κάτω,
οὓς ἡ θέα δείκνυσιν εἶναι ναυτίλους,
κτανὼν δὸς αἷμα τοῖς θεοῖς πεπωκέναι.
τοὺς γὰρ προνοίᾳ τῶν θεῶν σεσωσμένους
[...]
ἄλλοι δὲ πάντες, εἰ μὲν ἐκ φυτοσπόρων
ἢ γοῦν ἀδελφῶν ἢ φιλοστόργων τέκνων
λυθῶσιν, ἐλθέτωσαν εἰς τὰς πατρίδας
ἢ δουλικῆς γοῦν πειραθήτωσαν τύχης.'[119]

As with Selektion, the sovereign decision determines who will live, and
who will die: "Stratokles | was sent on his way home" (Ὁ γοῦν Στρατοκλῆς
[...] | τὴν ἀπάγουσαν εἰς τὸν οἶκον ἐστάλη), but the four sailors are
sentenced to death.[120] Rather than conclude the scene there, however,
Prodromos summarizes the laments of three of the sailors:

One bewailed a wretched infant,
Tiny, new-born and still nursing;
Another wept for his aged father,
He cried out, he wailed loudly;
Another pitifully lamented his wife,
The lovely young bride of a young groom.

ὁ μὲν γὰρ ἐξῴμωξεν ἄθλιον βρέφος,
μικρόν, νεογνὸν καὶ γεγαλακτισμένον·
ἄλλος δὲ τὸν τεκόντα, τὸν γηραλέον
ἔκλαυσεν, ὠλόλυξεν, οἰμώξας μέγα·
ὁ δ' οἰκτρὸν ἐθρήνησε τὴν ὁμευνέτιν,
καλὴν νεαροῦ νυμφίου νύμφην νέαν.[121]

---

[119] *R&D* 1.451–457, 462–465.
[120] *R&D* 1.473–474.
[121] *R&D* 1.479–484.

178   A. J. GOLDWYN

Though he does not narrate exactly what it is they said, the scene is reminiscent of the hypothetical laments described in John Kaminiates' letter, in which a father laments for his son (an inversion of the sailor lamenting his father here),[122] and the lament of the husband for his wife,[123] as well as the separation of parents from infants. Even though they are unnamed, Prodromos emphasizes that they had their own unique, individual concerns and sorrows—wives, children, parents—and thus, in showing the sorrows they experience, he increases the sorrow of the readers/listeners who learn of their fate. The fourth sailor, however, a certain Nausikrates "hastened to his slaughter as though to a symposium" (εἰς τὴν σφαγὴν ἔσπευδεν ὥσπερ εἰς πότον) and Gobryas "pitifully slew the fair Nausikrates" (ἔκτεινεν οἰκτρῶς τὸν καλὸν Ναυσικράτην).[124] Thus, Prodromos' narration of the type scene of the captive meeting the sovereign, the moment that exposes most starkly the difference between subjectivity and objectivity, between *bios* and *zoē*, between political inclusion and bare life, resolves differently for each of the characters. The three unnamed sailors die each lamenting some person that they love—parents, children, wives. Rhodanthe, Dosikles, and Kratandros, by contrast, are spared because of their beauty and made temple attendants. The power of sovereign decision, however, is most clearly indicated in the differing fates of the other two named characters. Unlike the three sailors, two of the other prisoners are named: Stratokles and Nausikrates. One is set free, and the other walks boldly to his own execution. Thus, in one Selektion, Prodromos describes the differing fates of eight characters—freedom, death, slavery—all at the arbitrary whim of the sovereign. After this, the scene—and Book 1—ends with Dosikles, Kratandros, and Rhodanthe returning again to the prison and Dosikles now telling his own backstory.

Dosikles' autobiography begins an extended external analepsis, that is to say, it begins the night before the pirate raid with which Book 1 opened and, in doing so, contrasts the horrors of their present enslaved situation with the pleasures of the freedom which they have just lost. Where Book 1 opened with the arrival of the pirate fleet in Rhodes, Book 2 opens with the arrival of the ship carrying Rhodanthe and Dosikles— "our ship moored well, unaffected by evil, safe and sound" (Ἡμῖν μὲν

---

[122] Kam. *Ex. Thess.* 35.

[123] Kam. *Ex. Thess.* 36.

[124] *R&D* 1.486, 1.498.

οὖν εὔορμον ἦλθε τὸ σκάφος, | κακῶν ἀθιγές, ὑγιές, σεσωσμένον), Dosikles says, heightening the contrast between the openings of Books 1 and 2.[125] The opening of the passage, moreover, also features a perhaps surprising revelation: that this safe arrival was "thanks to the skill of the captain Stratokles" (τοῦ ναυτιλάρχου τῇ τέχνῃ Στρατοκλέος), the very same man who had been set free by Mistylos during Selektion at the end of the previous book.[126] Thus, the analepsis of Book 2 offers significant biographical information on not just the primary characters, but the secondary ones as well and, in so doing, shows the full humanity and deeply individuated backstory of the characters whom we have just seen at their moment of greatest dejection.

If one of the purposes of Holocaust fiction is to render individually human the mass of faceless people who suffered and died during the Holocaust, then Stratokles' appearance in the narrative serves a similar function. After safely piloting the ship to shore, Stratokles leads the group to the house of Glaukon, a merchant friend of his, who immediately asks him: "Are your babies well, | my good Stratokles? Is Panthia in good health?" (σώζεταί σοι τὰ βρέφη, | καλὲ Στρατόκλεις; ὑγιὴς ἡ Πανθία;).[127] Stratokles replies that though

> A kindly fortune directly my life,
> [...]
> my son Agathosthenes has died
> a pitiful death.

> Εὔνους κυβερνᾷ τὴν ἐμὴν ζωὴν Τύχη,
> [...]
> ὁ παῖς δέ μοι τέθνηκεν Ἀγαθοσθένης
> θάνατον οἰκτρὸν.[128]

This simple exchange enriches the previous scene when Stratokles cries while facing the possibility of execution or enslavement by Mistylos: he has recently lost his son, and hopes to be able to return to his other children and wife. The contrast between the first glimpse of Stratokles

---

[125] *R&D* 2.21–22.
[126] *R&D* 2.28.
[127] *R&D* 2.36–37.
[128] *R&D* 2.38, 41–42.

180   A. J. GOLDWYN

"snivelling" and "weeping" before Mistylos contrasts with Dosikles' depiction of him in Book 2: he is a skillful sailor piloting a ship through dangerous waters, he has a deep family background full of sadness and joy, and, at the symposium on the last night before his capture, "he tunefully began a splendid song" (ᾠδῆς ἀγαθῆς ἐμμελῶς ἡγουμένῳ).[129] Prodromos thus uses the temporal dislocation of the story-order of the fabula to offer a rounded portrait of the man and to show just what he stands to lose during his execution. Dosikles' narration here thus offers a kind of dramatic irony, since Dosikles, Kratandros, and the audience of the novel all know what will happen to Stratokles the next day, though Stratokles at the symposium does not know.

The contrast that this dramatic irony reveals is even more pronounced in the case of the other guests at the symposium: as he narrates Stratokles' singing, Dosikles reveals the presence of the other named prisoner from the preceding book: "Immediately Nausikrates got up from the symposium | and began a somewhat nautical dance" (εὐθὺς δ' ἀναστὰς τοῦ πότου Ναυσικράτης | ὄρχησιν ὠρχήσατο ναυτικωτέραν).[130] In that the action of Book 1 takes place after the action of Book 2 (though, since Dosikles is narrating them from the prison, the narration of those actions occurs in chronological sequence), the audience—in this case both Kratandros and the listeners/readers of Prodromos' novel—know that he dies. This gives added emotional context to Dosikles' description of Nausikrates' dance: " [Nausikrates'] twistings and turnings | were more desirable than the melody" (ἐραστὸν τῆς μελῳδίας πλέον | τὸ στρέμμα καὶ λύγισμα τοῦ Ναυσικράτους) and "a little rustic perhaps (for it was only Nausikrates!), | but not lacking in humour and charm" (ἀγροικικὸν μέν [τί γὰρ ἢ Ναυσικράτους!], | οὐ μὴν γελώτων ἐνδεὲς καὶ χαρίτων).[131] Though Nausikrates' dance is depicted as carefree and happy, the dramatic irony inherent in the audiences' knowledge of his death casts a pall of sorrow over this otherwise almost comical moment. Indeed, the last glimpse Dosikles offers of Nausikrates is such that, when he hears it, Kratandros remarks that "Hilarity, Dosikles, in the midst of misery is coming over me" (Γελᾶν, Δοσίκλεις, ἐν κακοῖς ἔπεισί μοι).[132] Nausikrates, Dosikles

[129] R&D 2.108.
[130] R&D 2.109–110.
[131] R&D 2.115–119.
[132] R&D 3.34.

3 THE CARCERAL IMAGINARY IN BYZANTIUM: THE KOMNENIAN ... 181

says, passes out drunk, but even in his dream seems to still be drinking wine, the sign of a happy man having his last night of peaceful rest before his execution.[133] In this way, too, Nausikrates' last words, seemingly incongruous with the situation in which he finds himself, come to have a greater significance in light of Dosikles' subsequent analeptic narration. Unlike the other three unnamed sailors who lament their deaths and the loss of their families, Nausikrates shows neither fear nor sadness, saying

> Greetings, banquets and symposia of this life
> and the delicacies of the table.
> Nausikrates has had his fill of you
> and goes gladly to the abode of Hades,
> and will investigate the symposia of the dead
> and will view the festivities of the underworld.

> χαίροιτε, δεῖπνα καὶ πότοι τῶν ἐν βίῳ
> καὶ τῶν τραπεζῶν ἡ πολυτελεστέρα·
> πλησθεὶς γὰρ ὑμῶν εἰς κόρον Ναυσικράτης
> κάτεισιν εἰς Ἅιδος ἄσμενος δόμον,
> καὶ τῶν θανόντων ἱστορήσει τοὺς πότους,
> ἐπόψεται δὲ νεκρικὰς εὐωχίας.[134]

The revelation that Nausikrates had spent the previous evening at a symposium—perhaps the paradigmatic marker of civilization in the Greek world—epitomizes the tragic and fatal change in his circumstances from life as a happy, drunk, and free citizen to an executed prisoner.

Thus, in the first book of *Rhodanthe and Dosikles*, Prodromos shows the fate of a group of eight slaves and shows their differing fates: freedom, slavery, death. In the second book, he uses a secondary narrator-focalizer, Dosikles, to narrate an external analepsis that shows the happy dispositions and last free moments of the prisoners whose fates are most divergent—the executed Nausikrates, the freed Stratokles, and the enslaved Rhodanthe and Dosikles. But there was one other named character among those present at the symposium whose fate remains unaccounted for, since he did not appear at the Selektion: the host, Glaukon. But Dosikles narrates his fate as well, telling Kratandros that

---

[133] *R&D* 3.19–43.
[134] *R&D* 1.488–493.

182 A. J. GOLDWYN

Glaukon (alas, alas, the inhumanity of Fate)
Has died, slain by fear before the sword reached him,
Gaining no benefit from his kindness to strangers.

Γλαύκων δέ (φεῦ φεῦ, τῆς ἀπανθρώπου Τύχης)
θνήσκει φονευθεὶς τῷ φόβῳ πρὸ τῆς σπάθης,
μὴ κερδάνας τι τῶν φιλοξενημάτων.[135]

The opening of *Rhodanthe and Dosikles* thus shows a kind of cross-section of Byzantine society: young people like Dosikles on the cusp of marriage and aged people like Stratokles who have already married, had, and lost children; various kinds of professions such as merchant, sailor, captain, and aristocrat.[136] Each of the characters is shown having their own rich interiority and particular history. Their fates, too, show the same level of variety: Glaukon dies during the initial assault, Nausikrates is executed during Selektion, Stratokles is released, and Dosikles is enslaved.

All this narrative, moreover, takes place in the prison camp, as both Dosikles and Kratandros construct their relational slave identities through dialogue with one another. Indeed, Prodromos then intervenes in the narrative to argue for the significance of the prison as a space of community building:

Association in many hazards can thus
unite those are clearly alien
and strong desire can develop more easily,
and also an unshakeable affection, in the midst of grief
than amid superabundant banquets
of overbrimming wine bowls.

οὕτω τὰ πολλὰ συμφορῶν κοινωνία
οἶδε ξυνάπτειν τοὺς σαφῶς ἀλλοτρίους,
καὶ ῥᾷον ἂν γένοιτο καρτερὸς πόθος
καὶ φίλτρον ἀκράδαντον ἐν λύπαις μέσαις
ἢ τῶν τραπεζῶν ταῖς πολυτροφωτέραις
καὶ τῶν κρατήρων τοῖς ὑπερχειλεστέροις.[137]

---

[135] *R&D* 3.122–124.

[136] In this, Prodromos offers a novel twist on what Papadogiannakis calls "the listing of ages and social classes – from guards to women and babies – [a]s a trope that city lament uses to register the magnitude of the catastrophe at every level" (2017: 191).

[137] *R&D* 3.135–140. Cf. also *A&K* fr. 56, 3.38: "Tribulation tests the reliability of friendship" (Τῆς γὰρ φιλίας τὸ πιστὸν ὁ πειρασμὸς ἐλέγχει).

3 THE CARCERAL IMAGINARY IN BYZANTIUM: THE KOMNENIAN ... 185

for the mother is more rare. Equally unusual is the description of violence against women independent of rape, as when Prodromos describes how "Wealthy women (oh, bitter fate) | had their rings cut off with their fingers" (Αἱ πλούσιαι γυναῖκες [ὦ πικρᾶς τύχης] | χεῖρας συνε<κ>τέτμηντο τοῖς δακτυλίοις).[143] Taken together, then, this description of the looted city, though seemingly conventional, points the audience toward women's experiences. In so doing, the novel transitions from focalization through Dosikles to focalization through Rhodanthe, a major shift.

The themes of sexual violence and rape permeate slave narrative fiction, foregrounding as it does one of the major forms of trauma experienced by incarcerated women. This is as true in the Komnenian novels as it is in fictional African-American slave narratives such as *Beloved*. Patrick Elliot Alexander, for instance, argues that "it is the unchecked sexual violence that most fundamentally circumscribes the carceral lives of Black women and girls who appear in [...] *Beloved*."[144] Alexander further argues that "the state-sanctioned disciplinary use of sexual violence on the Black female body – a distinctly *gendered* form of Transatlantic Slave Trade terror and slavery-era social control [was] designed to wound Black women and girls psychically, debase them corporeally, and exploit them capitalistically,"[145] and indeed, this is the very situation in which Rhodanthe and her fellow women captives find themselves. Mass rape during conquest becomes a genre convention,[146] with the central heroine of the romance spared that fate, only to live for the remainder of her period of incarceration under the constant threat of rape. Her position as slave also marks her as a capital good—Rhodanthe is the only character whose monetary value is discussed, and her price is given three times: first when Gobryas tries to buy her from Mistylos for twenty *minai*,[147] then when the merchants who rescue her sell her to Kraton for thirty *minai*,[148] and again when Dosikles calls that "a bargain price"

---

[143] *R&D* 6.134–135.

[144] Alexander (2018: 62).

[145] Alexander (2018: 63).

[146] See, for instance, Papadogiannakis for what he calls "the *urbs capta* traditions" (2017: 190).

[147] *R&D* 3.177–180.

[148] *R&D* 6.251–253.

186 A. J. GOLDWYN

(κερδαλέον τὸ χρῆμα).[149] In this, Rhodanthe's experience supplements the cursory narration of the sale of female slaves in narratives such as Kaminiates' letter. Putting in at Bolbos, Kaminiates sees some men "wishing to buy certain particular women, whom the barbarians quickly took off their ships and sold, receiving much gold for them" (ῥητάς τινας γυναῖκας ὠνήσασθαι θέλοντες, ἃς τὸ τάχος οἱ βάρβαροι τῶν νηῶν ἐξενεγκόντες ἀπέδοντο, πολὺ χρυσίον ὑπὲρ αὐτῶν κομισάμενοι).[150] Of these women, however, Kaminiates makes no further mention. Thus, the narration of the life and experience of the fictional slave girl Rhodanthe gives a face and a voice to the historical women of Thessaloniki whose lives Kaminiates did not.

Sexual violence against Rhodanthe haunts much of the novel; it is Dosikles' primary fear when they are initially taken captive, and one of the major subplots of the first five books is Gobryas' attempt to rape Rhodanthe and Dosikles' attempts to foil him. Dosikles, for instance, when taken captive, decries being separated from his family and homeland before saying that "these are small matters" (ταῦτα μικρά)[151] compared to his fear that Rhodanthe will be raped:

> For perhaps when the robber chief sees the girl
> he will immediately succumb to the fire of love
> and will kindle a burning flame in his heart
> and will force Rhodanthe into marriage.

> ἰδὼν γὰρ ἴσως τὴν κόρην ὁ ληστάναξ
> ἔρωτος εὐθὺς ὑποδέξεται φλόγα
> καὶ πῦρ ἀνάψει λάβρον ἐν τῇ καρδίᾳ,
> βιάσεται δὲ τὴν Ῥοδάνθην εἰς γάμον.[152]

The novel, however, prioritizes Dosikles' fear; Prodromos offers nothing of Rhodanthe's. Indeed, Dosikles describes her sufferings in the prison with him—"you sleep on the ground and [you are] worn down by hunger" (ἐν γῇ καθεύδεις καὶ λιμῷ τετηγμένη)—and he even notes that she is speaking a lament herself—"you have Dosikles on your lips. You

---

[149] R&D 9.164.
[150] Kam. *Ex. Thess.* 67.
[151] R&D 1.97.
[152] R&D 1.102–105.

3 THE CARCERAL IMAGINARY IN BYZANTIUM: THE KOMNENIAN ... 187

call out frequently" (ὅμως Δοσικλῆν ὑπάγεις ὑπὸ στόμα)[153] Yet, Rhodanthe's own speech is never reported; she sleeps during the entirety of the initial scene of their captivity, when facing Mistylos during the sovereign decision, and when they are taken back to the hold of the ship. Such is the narrative silencing of Rhodanthe that when Dosikles finishes his initial lament, the sleeping Rhodanthe is not mentioned, and Dosikles engages Kratandros, a complete stranger, in conversation. Later, when Dosikles finishes his tale, Prodromos again indicates Rhodanthe's silent participation, though even though she is now awake, she still does not speak: "[he] partook of food, not without the maiden's participation, | and with the stranger Kratandros joining them both" (τροφῆς μετέσχεν οὐκ ἄνευ τῆς παρθένου, | συνόντος ἀμφοῖν καὶ Κρατάνδρου τοῦ ξένου).[154] In fact, the first time Rhodanthe speaks in the text is not until Book 2, when she insists that she not enter Glaukon's symposium for fear of being immodest.[155] Even this speech, however, is not directly hers, since it is embedded within Dosikles' analeptic speech to Kratandros, as are the next several times she speaks.[156]

Indeed, the fear of rape and the preservation of chastity are of such cardinal importance that two of her first three speeches as reported by Dosikles have to do with her modesty and sexual reserve. Unlike Dosikles and Kratandros, who speak on a variety of subjects, Rhodanthe's reported speech for the majority of the novel concerns her sexuality alone. The first time she speaks in her own voice in the narrative present is not until Book 3, when the barbarian Gobryas, disobeying his master Mistylos' command that Rhodanthe not be married to him, nevertheless attempts to rape her: "Come here and embrace me as your bridegroom | and do not be disturbed by my sleeping with you" (ὦ δεῦρο τὸν σὸν ἄσπασαί με νυμφίον | καὶ μὴ ταραχθῇς τὴν ἐμὴν συνουσίαν) he says, before forcibly kissing her.[157] She escapes, however, and runs back to Dosikles, uttering her first lines in the novel:

---

[153] R&D 1.124–125.

[154] R&D 3.133–134.

[155] R&D 2.61–75.

[156] When she is carried off by Dosikles: R&D 2.475–479; when they meet under the vines and he tries to kiss her: R&D 2.66–75.

[157] R&D 3.274–275.

188   A. J. GOLDWYN

"Save me," she said, "from the brutish barbarian,
Save, Dosikles, your dear maiden,
Rescue me from the robberly brute.
You have destroyed me; make haste, indeed I am ruined."

καὶ 'σῶσον' εἶπεν 'ἐκ τυράννου βαρβάρου,
σῶσον, Δοσίκλεις, τὴν φίλην σοι παρθένον·
ἀπόσπασόν με ληστρικῆς τυραννίδος.
ἀπώλεσάς με· σπεῦσον, ἦ μὴν ᾠχόμην.'[158]

Rhodanthe's first directly reported character speech marks her as the iconic damsel in distress, her virginity threatened, seeking help from her beloved. Rhodanthe speaks again at 3.504–505 to urge Dosikles to tell her why he is upset, and then, in another short speech that closes out Book 3—her last speech until Book 7—again pledges her virginity to Dosikles on pain of death: "May I be kept pure and preserved either for you | or for the sword, but not for Gobryas" (ἢ σοὶ φυλαχθῶ καθαρῶς τηρουμένη, | ἢ τῷ ξίφει γοῦν, οὐ γὰρ ἂν τῷ Γωβρύᾳ).[159] The silencing of Rhodanthe continues throughout Book 6; Prodromos reports that she speaks—"Rhodanthe was distressed, she uttered a great lament | As she saw Dosikles in chains" (ἤλγει Ῥοδάνθη, θρῆνον ἐθρήνει μέγαν | ὁρῶσα δεσμηθέντα τὸν Δοσικλέα)[160]—but does not report the lament in direct speech. Instead most of Book 6 is given over to another of Dosikles' laments, which comprises 6.264–415 and 479–494. Though women slaves presumably had the same sense of grief and loss of their homelands, family, friends, and personal freedom as their male counterparts, the only speaking slave woman in *Rhodanthe and Dosikles* seems, unlike the male slaves, to have no concern for such things.

Nevertheless, the novel continues to focus on women's experiences after the second capture, if from a limited perspective. Until the second capture, all the slaves had been held together; afterward, however, "they were all taken to somewhere near the harbour" (ἤγοντο πάντες ἀμφί που τὸν λιμένα), which serves as another kind of Umschlagplatz or barracoon for sovereign decision.[161] There,

---

[158] *R&D* 3.290–293.

[159] *R&D* 3.521–522; her speech in total comprises lines *R&D* 3.519–525.

[160] *R&D* 6.165.

[161] *R&D* 6.172.

3 THE CARCERAL IMAGINARY IN BYZANTIUM: THE KOMNENIAN … 189

Artapes [the barbarian captain] separated the prisoners into two groups
and he filled one vessel with the men
and the other with the women.

διχῆ διαιρεῖ τοὺς ἀλόντας Ἀρτάπης,
καὶ τῶν μὲν ἀνδρῶν ὁλκάδα πληροῖ μίαν
καὶ τῶν γυναικῶν ἀτέραν πάλιν μίαν.[162]

The scene of family separation and separation by gender evokes in
Dosikles the same response that Levi witnessed and reported at a similar
moment at Auschwitz when "Renzo stayed an instant too long to say
goodbye to Francesca, his fiancée, and with a single blow they knocked
him to the ground"[163]; Prodromos reports that

When Dosikles realized the division
He said, "But if you tear me away
From my maiden sister, leader of the satraps
I shall put an end to the drama of my fate
By throwing myself into the midst of the sea."
As he said this an uncouth barbarian
Who was standing nearby, a huge ruthless giant,
Struck the handsome young man in the face
And threw him against his will into the middle of the vessel.

ταύτην Δοσικλῆς τὴν διαίρεσιν φθάσας,
'ἀλλ' ἤν με' φησί 'τῆς ἀδελφῆς παρθένου
ταύτης διαρπάσειας, ἀρχισατράπα,
ἐγὼ τὸ δρᾶμα τῆς ἐμῆς λύσω τύχης
βαλὼν ἐμαυτὸν εἰς μέσον πόντου στόμα.'
Ἔλεξε ταῦτα, καί τις ἑστὼς πλησίον
βάρβαρος ὠμός, νηλεὴς μέγας γίγας,
κατὰ προσώπου τὸν καλὸν παίσας νέον
ἄκοντα ῥιπτεῖ πρὸς μέσην τὴν ὁλκάδα.[164]

The lovers are separated, Dosikles is beaten, and the ships set sail in the
same direction. As they are out at sea, however, a great storm appears, and

---

[162] *R&D* 6.174–176.

[163] Levi (1959: 11). See also above, p. 131.

[164] *R&D* 6.177–185.

190   A. J. GOLDWYN

while the ship carrying all the men sails off to safety, the ship carrying all
the women

> Was dashed against a concealed rock
> And broken in pieces, disgorging its cargo.
> And immediately the whole throng of women
> Who were crammed into the bitter hull
> Found the sea (alas, the suffering) a common grave,
> Apart from Rhodanthe.

> τινὶ προσαραχθεῖσα μυχίῳ πέτρᾳ
> συνθρύπτεται μέν, τὸν δὲ φόρτον ἐξάγει.
> ἅπαν γὰρ εὐθὺς τῶν γυναικῶν τὸ στίφος,
> ὅσας τὸ πικρὸν ἐμπεφόριστο σκάφος,
> τὸν πόντον εὗρε (φεῦ πάθους) κοινὸν τάφον,
> ἐκτὸς Ῥοδάνθης.[165]

Rhodanthe floats alone for some time on the sea until she sees a merchant
fleet; that she speaks is narrated—"she begged the merchants who were
sailing | in them to rescue her" (καὶ τὴν ἑαυτῆς λιπαρεῖ σωτηρίαν | ἐκ τῶν
ἐν αὐταῖς ἐμπλεόντων ἐμπόρων)[166]—but the actual content of the speech,
much less what if anything she said while on board the ship, goes unnarrated. Eventually she reaches Cyprus, where she is sold again; the narrator
concludes the episode as follows: "And so Rhodanthe embraced a slave's
fate | and the light of slavery rather than that of freedom" (Ἡ μὲν Ῥοδάνθη
ταῦτα καὶ δούλην τύχην | ἔστεργε καὶ φῶς δοῦλον ἀντ' ἐλευθέρου).[167]
Despite the trauma that Rhodanthe suffers—family separation, shipwreck,
witnessing mass drowning, and being sold into slavery—the narrator
remains unconcerned with Rhodanthe's interiority, for immediately after
this, the focalization shifts again with an authorial interruption posed as
a rhetorical question: "But what voice, what human speech | is capable
of describing Dosikles' grief?" (ποία δὲ φωνὴ καὶ τίς ἀνθρώπου λόγος |
εἰπεῖν τὸ πένθος ἀρκέσει Δοσικλέος;)[168] The author answers the question with 150 lines of lamentation in Dosikles' direct reported speech;
of Rhodanthe's grief, however, he reports nothing.

[165] R&D 6.227–232.
[166] R&D 6.241–242.
[167] R&D 6.254–255.
[168] R&D 6.256–257.

3 THE CARCERAL IMAGINARY IN BYZANTIUM: THE KOMNENIAN ... 191

It is not until Book 7 that Rhodanthe's lament is given in direct speech. Though Rhodanthe is largely silent through the first six books, almost all of Book 7 is devoted to Rhodanthe speaking. As such, it represents a longer and more sustained interrogation of female sorrow than is to be found in the works of Kaminiates, Eustathios, or Niketas Choniates. Moreover, immediately following her lament, she delivers an autobiographical narrative of nearly sixty lines, which thus forms the only female slave narrative up to that point. Indeed, though the text is fictional, and though the writer who composed Rhodanthe's speeches is male and thus ventriloquizing female lament, Rhodanthe's speeches in Book 6 are the closest glimpse that Byzantine literature offers of women's slave narratives.[169] When looked at from this perspective, however, it becomes clear that while the voices of female slaves are sometimes relevant, the subjectivity of the speaking woman is less so. Thus, for instance, in Book 1, both men and women are taken captive, and yet it is only the men who are allowed to trade stories with one another; the prison may be a space for community building, but it is a community of men.[170]

In this regard, it is significant that Rhodanthe does not get to exchange stories with another slave, as Dosikles (and John Kaminiates) had; rather, she tells her story to the slaver Myrilla who, seeing Rhodanthe lament for Dosikles, asks not about her, but about him: "what was the sorrow for which she wept, | who was Dosikles, where was he from and how did he die" (πυνθάνεται τὸ πένθος, ἐξ οὗ δακρύει, | καὶ τίς Δοσικλῆς καὶ πόθεν καὶ πῶς θάνοι).[171] She is asked not to tell her own story, but that of another, and she obliges, inverting the conventional trope of the beginning of the slave's narrative:

---

[169] For the problems of male authorship of female laments in the Komnenian novels, see Goldwyn (2018: 129, n. 107), and especially Katharine Haynes' argument that, as almost all ancient and medieval texts are male-authored, ignoring the evidence of women's lives that they present would effectively "dismiss[] most of Classical literature at one stroke" (2003: 12).

[170] I have elsewhere dealt with the problem of male authorship of female lament and the inability of the novel and the romance as genres to adequately plumb the psychological depths and establish the subjectivity of women characters. I referred to this as "ecofeminist narratology" (Goldwyn 2018: 85–145), defining it as "the lack of female narration and the consequences of this silencing both for women as theoretical subjects and for their embodied experience of physical pain and mental anguish" (Goldwyn 2018: 127).

[171] R&D 7.190–191.

192   A. J. GOLDWYN

About my family or country or begetters
or abundant gold or prosperous hearth
or everything else that belongs to yesterday and my prosperity
it is superfluous and long-winded for you to hear.

γένη μὲν ἢ πατρίδας ἢ φυτοσπόρους
ἢ χρυσὸν ἁδρὸν ἢ μεγίστας ἑστίας
ἢ τἄλλα τῆς χθὲς ἢ πρὸς εὐετηρίας
περιττὸν ἀκοῦσαί σε καὶ πολὺς λόγος.[172]

By comparison, Dosikles and Kratandros both begin their narratives with exactly this sort of information, giving them a subjective identity grounded in their own history and sense of their current self as the teleological result of a cumulative past. Myrilla's questions demand the decentering of the narrator from her own story in almost exact opposition to how Gregory's questions demand John Kaminiates center himself. Understanding how Myrilla has framed the question and given the inherent and alienating power dynamic between slaver and slave, Rhodanthe elides as much of herself from her own speech as she can.

Thus, the majority of Rhodanthe's speech is not about Rhodanthe at all; the first part is comprised of a long ekphrasis on Dosikles' physical appearance (*R&D* 6.213–238) before she describes her own backstory:

he seized me and put me in a freighter
and sailed in flight as far as Rhodes.
There a robber fleet attacked us,
whose emperor was Mistylos and under him was Gobryas;
Mistylos captured us and put us in a vessel
and carried us off to his own country;
and we endured chains and prison and darkness.

καὶ ξυλλαβών με καὶ βαλὼν ἐν φορτίδι
φυγὰς καταπέπλευκεν ἄχρις εἰς Ῥόδον.
ἐνταῦθα ληστρικός τις εἰσπεσὼν στόλος,
οὗ βασιλεὺς Μιστύλος, ὑφ' ὃν Γωβρύας,
κατέσχεν ἡμᾶς καὶ βαλὼν ἐν ὁλκάδι
εἰς τὴν ἑαυτοῦ ξυμμετῆρε πατρίδα,
καὶ δεσμὸς ἡμῖν καὶ φυλακὴ καὶ σκότος.[173]

[172] *R&D* 7.207–210.
[173] *R&D* 7.244–250.

3 THE CARCERAL IMAGINARY IN BYZANTIUM: THE KOMNENIAN ... 193

This is the entirety of the backstory that Rhodanthe is allowed to give, for immediately following she mentions that, in the prison with them was "a young man, Kratandros by name, who boasted of Cyprus as his homeland, | child of his father Kraton and mother Stale" (κλῆσιν Κράτανδρος, Κύπρον αὐχῶν πατρίδα, | πατρὸς Κράτωνος καὶ Στάλης μητρὸς τέκνον).[174] At this point, Myrilla cuts her off—"she sprang up from the ground and went to Stale" (ἄνεισι τῆς γῆς, ἔρχεται πρὸς τὴν Στάλην)[175]—since it turns out that Kratandros was her long-lost and presumed dead brother. Thus, Rhodanthe's interlocutor showed no interest in her history, specifically asking her not to describe it, but to describe her lover instead, and then cuts off her speech at its beginning.

Indeed, Rhodanthe's own syntax matches the decentering of her own agency in her own past; each of her autobiographical sentences features her as the object: ξυλλαβών με (he seized me), βαλὼν ἐν ὁλκάδι (threw [me] in a freighter), κατέσχεν ἡμᾶς ([Mistylos] captured us), βαλὼν ἐν ὁλκάδι ("put [threw us] in a vessel,") and ξυμμετῆρε (carried us off). In a moment of stylistic enactment, the final line contains no verb at all: entirely the passive agent, only three nouns: δεσμὸς (chains), φυλακὴ (prison), σκότος, (darkness). By contrast, one of the major aims of the slave narrative is to center the slave and articulate the slave's subjectivity in the face of the dehumanizing forces of slavery. Kratandros' narrative, for instance, differs fundamentally from Rhodanthe's at this syntactic level; in every moment, he is the active agent. Whereas Rhodanthe declines to describe her past, Kratandros begins with a strong articulation of his own identity with the first-person pronoun ἐγώ: "I had [...] Cyprus for my homeland" (ἐγώ [...] Κύπρον ἔσχον),[176] syntactically taking control over the sentence with the personal pronoun and the active verb. This continues throughout the narrative; each of the several verbs with which the narrative opens have him as the subject: ἥλων ἐκείνης (I succumbed to her),[177] ἁλοὺς δὲ τὴν ἐνοῦσαν (when I succumbed I revealed),[178]

---

[174] R&D 7.252–253. It remains unclear how Rhodanthe, who was sleeping the entire time that Kratandros was telling this story, could know this.

[175] R&D 7.266.

[176] R&D 1.160.

[177] R&D 1.163.

[178] R&D 1.166.

προσῆλθον τῇ πύλῃ (I approached the gate),[179] ἀνέῳξα τὰς θύρας (I opened the doors),[180] ἔσπευδον (I hastened),[181] οὐ λέληθα (I did not escape).[182]

Having revealed the name of Kratandros, moreover, the slaver loses all interest in the slave's narrative, and when Rhodanthe is asked to continue, it is no longer about her at all: "All begged Rhodanthe to say indeed | where Kratandros was and what life he was living" (πάντες Ῥοδάνθην ἠξίουν ἦ μὴν λέγειν | ὅποι Κράτανδρος καὶ τίνα ζῇ τὸν βίον).[183] Thus, Rhodanthe is again not allowed to tell her own story; in the first half of her speech, her narrative, at the request of her interlocutor, centered around Dosikles; in this second speech, also at the request of her interlocutor, she is also marginalized. Instead of her own story, she again tells the story of another male slave. Thus, where Dosikles and Kratandros' dialogue in the opening section of the work allows them to construct their own identities as slaves and find solace in their companionship, Rhodanthe is never given the chance to have such a dialogue. When she does get the chance to narrate, it is not to her equal, but to her mistress, and she is frequently interrupted. Alexander writes in regard to Toni Morrison's narrative choices in *Beloved* that "by depicting women in her novel who craft and exchange testimonial narratives in which they condemn their subjection to disciplinary rape, Morrison reveals these captive women's will to survive, reclaim their bodies, and build community in the midst of such gendered social control."[184] The men are given this capacity in *Rhodanthe and Dosikles*, but the women—who surely spoke with one another on the crowded and sex-segregated slave ships described in the novel—by virtue of the focalizing decisions made by Prodromos, are not. Indeed, this female silencing by male authors is central to the narrative structures of the novels; Corinne Jouanno notes how male speech is prioritized over women's speech not just qualitatively (that is, in what contexts they narrate and the things they are and are not allowed to say about

[179] *R&D* 1.173.
[180] *R&D* 1.174.
[181] *R&D* 1.177.
[182] *R&D* 1.178.
[183] *R&D* 7.273–274.
[184] Alexander (2018: 65).

3 THE CARCERAL IMAGINARY IN BYZANTIUM: THE KOMNENIAN ... 195

themselves) but also quantitively (that is, in terms of how many lines they get to speak):

> whereas Dosikles' speeches amount to around 1160 lines, Charikles' to 1043 and Hysminas' to 520 (within the first person narrative), Rhodanthe's direct addresses cover no more than 376 lines, Drosilla's 393 and Hysmine's 190. And in Prodromos' and Eugenianos' novels, even if we do not take the heroes' retrospective narrative into account, the disproportion between the sexes remains important, with 540 lines to Dosikles and 347 to Rhodanthe, 611 lines to Charikles and 393 to Drosilla.[185]

In this, the silencing of female characters in *Rhodanthe and Dosikles* marks it as a significantly different kind of slave narrative from the perspective of gender. Whereas in *Beloved*, "testimony [...] is thus a radical act of subjectification" for the women in the novel, Rhodanthe's narrative never allows her to claim her own subjectivity because she speaks to men and other social superiors and because she is frequently interrupted. As a result, where "women in *Beloved* experience revelation, survival, and healing by uniting to create narrative that is at once interlocutory and evasive—unreservedly dialogic among its practitioners," Rhodanthe never gets this chance.[186]

And yet, the novel's gesture in the direction of women's experience and navigation is still a marked difference from the narratives of either Eustathios of Thessaloniki or John Kaminiates, the latter of whom mentions a sister-in-law, sister, and wife—none of whom are heard from at all. Kaminiates is not entirely blind to the experiences of women, but because of his limited perspective as a witness, Kaminiates cannot focalize his narrative through their eyes nor can they function as secondary narrator-focalizers.

3.5 COMPLETING THE CYCLE: FREED SLAVES AND FAMILY REUNIFICATION

Reading *Rhondathe and Dosikles* as a romance foregrounds the reunification of the lovers as the completion of the plot arc that began with their

---

[185] Jouanno (2006: 145).

[186] Alexander (2018: 85).

196   A. J. GOLDWYN

falling in love and elopement, proceeded to their separation (from society and from one another) and trials, and concludes with their marriage and reintegration into society as a happy couple surrounded by families. The symbol of this reunion is an embrace by the lovers and their fathers, which Prodromos, in an authorial intervention, describes as a tetraktys, a being in which "four bodies could be seen | beneath what appeared to be the one head" (ὡρῶντο γὰρ τέτταρες ἄνθρωποι κάτω | ὡς εἰς κεφαλὴν προσπεφυκότες μίαν).[187]

Reading *Rhodanthe and Dosikles* as a slave narrative, however, fore-grounds the plot cycle of free people who become enslaved and are then set free again. In this way, the novel offers insight into an aspect of slaves' lives absent from the historiographical sources. In contrast with the nonfiction slave life of John Kaminiates, who is still enslaved at the end, who does not know what will happen to his family, and whose hopes for a ransom conclude the letter with a lingering uncertainty, the novel, as a work of fiction, is structured as a self-contained narrative with a clearly defined conclusion. It offers a perspective on the life of a slave that Kamniates, by virtue of his being a prisoner cannot. *Rhodanthe and Dosikles*, by contrast, shows a number of different emotional states: those of the families of captured slaves when they think their loved one is enslaved, those of the family when they are reunited, and those of the slave themselves being ransomed.

After hearing that his son might still be alive, Kratandros' father, Kraton "set off to Pissa in quest of his son" (εἰς Πίσσαν ἐξώρμησε τοῦ παιδὸς χάριν), a statement of plot fact which is then followed by Prodromos' own authorial intervention: "O paternal compassion, O fatherly heart, | there is nothing greater than a father's affection" (ὦ σπλάγχνα πατρός, ὦ τεκόντος καρδία, | ὡς κρεῖττον οὐδὲν πατρικῆς εὐστοργίας).[188] In adding this, Prodromos emphasizes the importance of the father–son bond as the emotional foundation of witness testimony (at least as written by male witnesses) as in the novels but also in, for instance, the letter of John Kaminiates. Kratandros and Dosikles, meanwhile, face a second Selektion, this time with Bryaxes, their new captor, who "summoned both young men to him" (ἄμφω κεκληκὼς εἰς ἑαυτὸν τοὺς νέους),

---

[187] *R&D* 9.318–319. For a further description, see 9.315–354, with the note by Jeffreys. See commentary in Goldwyn (2018: 103–105, 201–207).

[188] *R&D* 7.310, 311–312.

3 THE CARCERAL IMAGINARY IN BYZANTIUM: THE KOMNENIAN ... 197

thus turning the city into a kind of Appelplatz where the sovereign decision is made.[189] Indeed, Bryaxes justifies his decision to sacrifice Dosikles and Kratandros—the sovereign decision here described as "the decree of violence" (νόμος βίας)[190]—in terms that recall the Foucaultian dichotomy of making live and letting die and the Agambenian dichotomy of *bios* and *zoē*:

> That a prisoner's fate is yours
> (whoever you are and from whatever family),
> It is not necessary to teach you who know from your circumstances –
> Nor that the masters are permitted to take any action,
> Nor that might is right where the defeated are concerned.

> ὅπως μὲν αἰχμάλωτος ὑμῖν ἡ τύχη
> (οἵπερ ποτ' ἂν εἴητε κἀξ οἵου γένους),
> οὐ χρὴ διδάσκειν γνόντας ἐκ τῶν πραγμάτων·
> οὐδ' ὡς ἐφεῖται πάντα δρᾶν τοῖς δεσπόταις,
> οὐδ' ὡς τὸ κρατοῦν τοῖς κρατουμένοις νόμος.[191]

Bryaxes argues that their previous state of *bios* is irrelevant—their family and place of origin—and that now they live in a state of *zoē*—prisoners. Because of this, they are subject to sovereign violence—biopower—with no other political or juridical recourse to shield them from this violence. In this, Bryaxes' claims echo those of the Nazi political theorist Carl Schmitt, whose work on the justification of autocratic power legitimized the genocidal politics of the Third Reich:

> There is no rule that is applicable to chaos. Order must be established for juridical order to make sense. A regular situation must be created, and sovereign is he who definitely decides if this situation is actually effective. All law is "situational law." The sovereign creates and guarantees the situation as a whole in its totality. He has the monopoly over the final decision. Therein consists the essence of State sovereignty.[192]

---

[189] *R&D* 7.356.

[190] *R&D* 7.332.

[191] *R&D* 7.358–362.

[192] Agamben (2017: 1).

198   A. J. GOLDWYN

Bryaxes makes a similar appeal to sovereign power and the sovereign decision as a kind of natural law ("you obey the natural order of things" [τῇ φυσικῇ πεισθέντας ἀκολουθίᾳ])[193] undergirding a society of order rather than chaos:

> For if all things lived together in the one fate,
> And no one was slave but everyone was free,
> There would be no rule, no measure, no standard of life,
> No overall command, no discipline,
> Everything would be in confusion and corrupted.
> Since natural reason controls everything,
> It is necessary that there should be slaves and masters.

> εἰ γὰρ μιᾷ τὰ πάντα συνέζη τύχῃ,
> καὶ δοῦλος οὐδείς, ἀλλὰ πᾶς ἐλεύθερος,
> οὐκ ἦν κανών, οὐ μέτρον, οὐ στάθμη βίου,
> οὐ ξυνταγὴ ξύμπαντος, οὐκ εὐταξία,
> τὸ πᾶν δὲ κατέστραπτο καὶ παρεφθάρη.
> ἐπεὶ δὲ πάντα φυσικὸς τάττει λόγος,
> δούλους ἀνάγκη τυγχάνειν καὶ δεσπότας.[194]

The hierarchical distinction between slave and master, in Bryaxes' view, is the founding binary for order against chaos. The foundational sovereign power—and thus order itself—is constructed by the sovereign who has the power to exclude slaves from the political order he establishes. Thus, the sovereign exception which allows for the killing of the slave is both an exclusion of the slave from the law and, "not," according to Agamben, "on account of being excluded, absolutely without relation to the rule. On the contrary, what is excluded in the exception maintains itself in relation to the rule in the form of the rule's suspension. The rule applies to the exception in no longer applying, in with drawing from it." Thus, just as Kratandros and Dosikles had constructed their identities as members of a slave community in dialogic relation with one another, the dialogue between them and Bryaxes demonstrates how the scene of Selektion also provides for the dialogic construction of the sovereign identity as well.

The tension of the Selektion scene is heightened by the simultaneous action of Kraton's voyage to ransom his children and the long dialogue

---

[193] *R&D* 7.363.

[194] *R&D* 7.364–370.

3 THE CARCERAL IMAGINARY IN BYZANTIUM: THE KOMNENIAN ... 199

between Bryaxes and the slaves. As Book Eight opens, Prodromos maintains the suspense by showing the sovereign decision actually as a moment of indecision: "Bryaxes pondered what was to be done; | knotting his eyebrows in a frown, he sat in silence for no short time. | While he was debating what he should do" (Τῷ μὲν Βρυάξῃ σκέψις ἦν τοῦ πρακτέου· | κατεσπακὼς γὰρ τὴν τάσιν τῶν ὀφρύων | καθῆστο σιγῶν οὐ βραχύν τινα χρόνον), however, Kraton arrives, upending the parameters by which Bryaxes was considering his decision.[195]

Kraton then delivers a speech which Elizabeth Jeffreys characterizes as an example of an ethopoeia of the type "on what should be said if threatened with sacrifices, with response from the prospective victim, the victim's friend and now the victim's father."[196] This is certainly true, and also recalls the use of *ethopoeia* in Kaminiates' laments during the scenes of family separation at the harbor,[197] but Jeffreys goes on to note that "The exemplification of rhetorical exercises is arguably the purpose of Prodromos' novel," a claim which perhaps misconstrues the nature of *ethopoeia*. Whereas Jeffreys' would have the *ethopoeia* serve a purely rhetorical function, Prodromos' inclusion of rhetorical set-pieces throughout *Rhodanthe and Dosikles* represents the application of rhetorical practice to recreate the otherwise unrecorded laments of fathers over their enslaved sons with some semblance of verisimilitude and emotional gravity.

Prodromos' novel has shown a variety of outcomes for prisoners during Selektion: executed prisoners like Nausikrates and the three sailors; freed prisoners like Straton; enslaved prisoners like Kratandros, Rhodanthe, and Dosikles; and now, finally, ransomed prisoners. Prodromos thus narrates a scene of family reunification, showing the reactions of the individual characters as well as the general scene in the city celebrating their return.[198] Yet, in choosing to follow the genre conventions of the romance and end his narrative on a happy note of marriage and family reunification, Prodromos narrates the experiences of privileged slaves. From within the established fabula, Prodromos could have chosen any of the other

---

[195] *R&D* 8.1–3.

[196] See note 243 to *R&D* 8.16. The subject of *ethopoeia* in the novels is discussed at length from formal, rhetorical, and intertextual perspectives in Roilos (2005, especially Chapter 2).

[197] For which, see above, p. 103.

[198] *R&D* 8.150–170.

200 A. J. GOLDWYN

prisoners: those who threw themselves from the walls or died during the initial assault on Rhodes, the three sailors who were executed, the women prisoners who were raped during the fall of the cities or those who drowned during the shipwreck; indeed, the narrative could even have been organized around the families of those prisoners who never returned: the experiences of Kratandros, Rhodanthe, and Dosikles, in all of these regards, are not those of the typical slaves, whose stories remain untold and whose deaths are narrated in a perfunctory way, if at all. By choosing to follow these characters and to narrate according to the genre conventions of the romance, the very fictionality of the novel protects the reader from the worst consequences even as it exposes them to a level of human suffering from which historiography traditionally shies away.

Prodromos' narratological decisions in this regard, however, are made legible through the theoretical paradigms of Holocaust literature. Budick, for instance, singles out the *Diary of Anne Frank*, which, though nonfictional, exposes audiences to suffering of a certain kind and only up to a certain limit:

> As the diary of a thirteen-year-old girl in hiding, which ends before her incarceration and death in a concentration camp, the *Diary* necessarily stops short of portraying either the harrowing experience of the camps or the extermination of the Jews. Furthermore, as the narrative of an adolescent girl falling in love for the first time, fighting with her parents, and fantasizing about who she will become after the war, the book offers itself up (especially for younger readers, of whom there are many) as an object of easy identification.[199]

This, too, applies to *Rhondathe and Dosikles* and the Komenian novels as a whole: though the lovers at the heart of the story are put through often harrowing suffering, the audience always remains confident that, due to the constraints of the genre, they will never die and that they will end up united in the end. Like the *Diary of Anne Frank*, the sweetness of the descriptions of the budding of first love give dubious justification for the suffering of the lovers at the center of the plot; moreover, and perhaps more importantly, Anne-as-narrator of the diary is spared the horrors that occurred after the diary's last entry on August 1, 1944: Anne the historical person was transported to Auschwitz, where she performed slave

---

[199] Budick (2015: 19).

labor digging pits and carrying rocks before eventually dying of typhus in Bergen-Belsen concentration camp. Rhodanthe and Dosikles, too, are pushed right to the edge of actual catastrophe, but they never suffer, for instance, the rape or death that is the fate of most of the unnarrated prisoners with whom they shared the prison. By focusing on those who will survive the horrors of war, conquest, and captivity, so too are the lovers at the center of the Komnenian novels spared the full extent of the suffering inflicted on the other anonymous characters in the novels and histories, a narratological strategy that shields the audience from the most graphic and disturbing violence in these texts.

Nevertheless, *Rhodanthe and Dosikles* shows a relatively comprehensive cycle of the existence of slaves and prisoners: it begins with the moment of capture, uses analepses to show how the characters got there, shows the various fates of the captives with attention to both men and women, shows the sorrows of the families who have lost loved ones, and then shows the ransom and reunification of slaves with their families. These are all scenes which would have occurred in real life, but through the empathetic imagination available to the writer of the novel as opposed to the historian or eyewitness, Prodromos is able to humanize these events through the more palatable backdrop of the struggles of the lovers at the center of the work.

3.6 DROSILLA AND CHARIKLES AS SLAVE NARRATIVE

Niketas Eugenianos' *Drosilla and Charikles* begins in a fashion similar to the *Rhodanthe and Dosikles* of his teacher Theodore Prodromos: again there is a raid by sea and the familiar account of conquest that includes execution— "some they put to the sword" (Τοὺς μὲν γὰρ ἐσπάθιζον)[200]— and mass enslavement—"others they took away bound in chains" (τοὺς δὲ προῆγον δεσμίους κρατουμένους),[201] and the small detail again of the destruction of agriculture: "In their excess they cut down every tree, | although they saw they were heavy with fruit" (Πᾶν συγκατέκλων δένδρον ἐξ ἀπληστίας, | καίτοι βρῖθον βλέποντες ἐξ εὐκαρπίας).[202] The specifically gendered nature of conquest is emphasized in the most piteous manner,

---

[200] *D&C* 1.23.

[201] *D&C* 1.25.

[202] *D&C* 1.26–27.

202   A. J. GOLDWYN

as Eugenianos describes how "They dragged off women who dragged off their infants with them" (Γυναῖκας εἷλκον αἳ συνεῖλκον τὰ βρέφη)[203] and how the infants could not nurse because the milk "was turned into a stream flecked with blood" (εἰς αἱματοστάλακτον ὄμβρον ἐτράπη).[204] Having conquered the city and rounded up loot and prisoners, the Parthians sailed away from Barzon with their captives (including the eponymous couple Drosilla and Charikles) in the hold of the ship and, after five days at sea, arrived at their homeland. There they "consigned the captives to prison, | mixing them with the wretched prisoners | already confined there" (εἰς φυλακὴν ἔδοντο τοὺς κρατουμένους, | μίξαντες αὐτοὺς τοῖς προεγκεκλεισμένοις | ἐκ πρωτολείας αἰχμαλώτοις ἀθλίοις).[205] Thus, the description of conquest and its aftermath echoes not just the fictional account of Theodore Prodromos, but also that of John Kaminiates, transported by ship to a slave prison.

Just as for Kaminiates and Dosikles, moreoever, the prison for Charikles becomes a communal space where he can mingle with prisoners from other conquests and thus learn both more about his new identity and find solace from his woes through dialogue with them. His first thought turns to his beloved, Drosilla, and he wonders what hardships she is facing, or even if she is dead. Quickly, however, his thoughts turn to sexual violence:

> Are you happy or sad or afraid? Do you not fear the sword?
> Are you in pain or being beaten or suffering? Surely you are not enduring rape?
> Which satrap's bed are you sharing?

> Χαίρεις; Θλίβῃ; Δέδοικας; Οὐ φοβῇ ξίφος;
> Ἀλγεῖς; Κροτῇ; Πέπονθας; Οὐ πάσχεις φθόρον;
> Τίνος μετέρχῃ λέκτρον ἀρχισατράπου;[206]

[203] D&C 1.30.
[204] D&C 1.35.
[205] D&C 1.208–210.
[206] D&C 1.235–237. Jeffreys notes the similarities to R&D 1.88–131.

3 THE CARCERAL IMAGINARY IN BYZANTIUM: THE KOMNENIAN ...

His lament is interrupted by another prisoner, whom the narrator describes as "a fine young man" (τις ἀγαθὸς νεανίας) and, moreover, "a fellow prisoner, a foreigner in the same prison" (συναιχμάλωτος, συμφυλακίτης ξένος) who "hastened to console his fellow prisoner" (παρηγορεῖν ἔσπευδε συμπεπονθότα).[207] This youth, Kleandros, expresses the consolatory nature of the prison as communal space for autobiographical reflection:

> Speak to me, and make a reply,
> So that you may relieve the main weight
> Of despondency by a spontaneous discussion.
> For speech is the remedy for all grief.

> ἐμοὶ λόγον δός, ἀνταπόκρισιν λάβε,
> ὡς ἂν τὸ πλεῖστον τῆς ἀθυμίας βάρος
> ἐκ προσλαλιᾶς κουφίσῃς αὐθαιρέτου·
> λύπης γάρ ἐστι φάρμακον πάσης λόγος.[208]

In this way, Kleandros offers himself as the supplementary witness or the witness to the witness, offering to hear the story of his fellow prisoner: afflictions, he says, cannot be extinguished "unless [one] expresses the cause of the affliction to another | who is able to console the afflicted" (εἰ μὴ πρὸς ἄλλον ἐξαγάγῃ τὸ θλίβον, | παρηγορεῖν ἔχοντα τοὺς λυπουμένους).[209] Charikles is immediately calmed by these words, and immediately falls asleep, with the promise that he will tell Kleandros his story the next morning.

Elizabeth Jeffreys notes that "at the comparable point in *R&D* 1.138 the hero's newly found companion embarks on a lengthy narrative of the past," but this does not happen in *Drosilla and Charikles*.[210] Rather, the narrator shifts the location to simultaneous action elsewhere in the world: foregrounding the women's experiences that had been elided in the nonfictional texts of Eustathios, Kaminiates, and the historians, Drosilla's

---

[207] *D&C* 1.260, 262, 264. Jeffreys notes that "the definition of 'foreigner' (ξένος) in this context offers many possibilities, ranging from lack of acquaintance or kinship ties ('stranger') to different ethnicity ('foreigner')."

[208] *D&C* 1.266–269.

[209] *D&C* 1.272–273.

[210] *D&C* 1.290–291.

204 A. J. GOLDWYN

lament is given in direct discourse. It is significant, however, that of all the varieties of women's traumatic experiences referenced in the novels, there is no example of direct discourse of a mother lamenting her children, a frequent subject of grief mentioned conventionally in the descriptions of city-sacking like the one that opens *Drosilla and Charikles* and also occurred in real life in, for instance, John Kaminiates' account of the sack of Thessaloniki. The one woman allowed to speak thus cannot represent all women—especially given, as the novel notes, the vastly different treatment of virgins and nonvirgins in captivity (as, for instance, in the virginity test at Artemis' Spring in *Hysmine and Hysminias*, in which the nonvirgins are drowned but the virgins are spared or the "symposium of blood" in which the nonvirgins are serially raped but the virgins are not). Nevertheless, Drosilla's lament can offer some insight into the mind of one woman (albeit a fictional woman as imagined by a male author), and thus merits analysis as a close approximation of a variety of contemporary women's experiences of slavery. As the lament opens, for instance, Drosilla begins with the hardship of uncertainty caused by family separation; calling Charikles "my husband" (ἄνερ) she addresses him directly: "You are now asleep in some corner of the prison" (σὺ μὲν καθυπνοῖς τῆς φυλακῆς εἰς μέρος).[211] This forced separation leads to her rumination on her worst fear, that he has abandoned and forgotten her, that he is "without the slightest thought in your mind for Drosilla, | but, as a result of your evil situation, you have forgotten" (Δροσίλλαν εἰς νοῦν οὐδὲ μικρὸν εἰσφέρων, | ἀλλ' ἀμελήσας ἐκ κακῶν προκειμένων) their marriage vows.[212] She worries that "Fate" (Τύχη) will "break asunder our indissoluble conjunction | and divide us in two" (ὡς τὴν ἀδιάρρηκτον ἀλληλουχίαν | ἡμῶν διασπᾶν καὶ μερίζειν εἰς δύο).[213] Drosilla's lament is thus principally concerned with the particular trauma of family separation. Drosilla returns to this theme in several different variations over the course of the next several lines; she laments that her circumstances are made all the more unbearable by Fate "imprisoning me apart from Charikles" (ἀλλ' ἐκτὸς ἐγκλείεις με τοῦ Χαρικλέος),[214] that she would rather be in prison than free "if I had been condemned to stay with Charikles" (εἰ συγκαθῆσθαι

---

[211] *D&C* 1.289; 291.
[212] *D&C* 1.292–293.
[213] *D&C* 1.301, 304–305.
[214] *D&C* 1.309.

Χαρικλεῖ κατεκρίθην),[215] and she urges Charikles to resist forgetting her "even if Fate strives | so hard to divide friends | and contrives the separation of a couple" (κἂν τοσοῦτον ἡ Τύχη | ἀντιστρατεύῃ πρὸς διάστασιν φίλων | καὶ μηχανᾶται συμμερισμὸν τῶν δύο).[216] Following this more literal lament, Drosilla offers an elaborate metaphor for their separation, saying "that she should never be divided from Charikles" and they are symbiotic in the same way as "Ivy is inseparable from oak" (Κισσὸς γὰρ εἰς δρῦν δυσαποσπάστως ἔχει).[217] Thus, Drosilla's lament focuses not just on the physical horrors of captivity, but its emotional and social ones as well: separation from her beloved, fear, uncertainty, despair. As such, it is the lament of a particular woman (a beautiful virgin of the urban aristocracy on the violent edge of the empire), but shares the social and emotional themes that the glimpses of female lament elsewhere in Byzantine witness literature suggest were common to female slaves more broadly.

In contrast with Charikles, however, Drosilla does not find any consolation among the other prisoners; rather she offers a solitary lament through the night, until

> day returned to the captives
> who were sleeping wretchedly in prison,
> although the cell's pitch blackness
> prevailed and darkened the day.

> τοῖς αἰχμαλώτοις ἀντεπῆλθεν ἡμέρα
> τοῖς ἐν φυλακῇ δυστυχῶς κοιμωμένοις,
> κἂν καὶ τὸ ταύτης ὡς βαθύτατον σκότος
> κατακρατοῦν ἦν καὶ ζοφοῦν τὴν ἡμέραν.[218]

Drosilla must lament alone, and therefore there is no consolation, no supplementary witness to ease her suffering, and she laments all night, unlike Charikles, for whom the appearance of a friendly stranger soothes. Indeed, Drosilla, not finding the possibility of a community in slavery,

---

[215] *D&C* 1.311.

[216] *D&C* 1.313–315.

[217] *D&C* 1.324. The use of this metaphor in this passage and as conventional across the Komnenian novels is discussed in Goldwyn (2018: 109).

[218] *D&C* 1.355–358.

206   A. J. GOLDWYN

cries out "Come hither, Sleep, and overcome me a little, | in the hope that a dream may appear and calm me" (Ὦ δεῦρο, μικρόν, Ὕπνε, συγκάτασχέ με, | εἴ που φανεὶς ὄνειρος ἐγκαθηδύνει).[219] For Charikles, calm comes through a friendly fellow slave; Drosilla must soothe herself, and places her hope in dreams.

The next day, the scene shifts back to Kleandros and Charikles and the telling of autobiographies. Kleandros and Charikles are thus transformed into witnesses, and in doing so, both articulate the value of the sharing of autobiographical narratives as a form of consolation. Kleandros says that in Charikles' telling his own story,

> Thus you will lighten your own
> groans by revealing to me what grieves you,
> and you will also relieve me, your fellow inmate
> Kleandros, from my own sufferings.

> Καὶ γὰρ σὺ σαυτὸν κουφιεῖς στεναγμάτων
> ἐμοὶ παριστῶν δῆλα τὰ θλίβοντά σε
> καὶ τὸν Κλέανδρον τὸν συνεγκεκλεισμένον
> ἐλαφρυνεῖς με τῶν ἐμῶν παθημάτων.[220]

While acknowledging the consolatory nature of shared witnessing, however, Charikles, like Dosikles, defers: "Tell me about your circumstances, tell me the suffering we share" (Λέγοις τὰ σαυτοῦ, ταυτοπάθειαν λέγοις).[221] In this way, as with Dosikles, Charikles can learn how to craft a slave narrative: one that focuses on shared suffering, ταυτοπάθειαν, as its central element.

Kleandros thus begins, and his answer again echoes both the fictional Dosikles, the nonfictional Kaminiates, and, indeed, the openings of texts of witness literature and slave narratives as geographically and temporally diverse as Elie Wiesel and Olaudah Equiano, by beginning with his origins: "Charikles, I had Lesbos as my country; | I came from responsible and respectable parents – | my mother is Kydippe and my father is Kallistias" (Ἐγώ, Χαρίκλεις, Λέσβον ἔσχον πατρίδα· | σεμνῶν προῆλθον

---

[219] D&C 1.347–348.
[220] D&C 2.36–39.
[221] D&C 2.54.

κοσμίων φυτοσπόρων | μητρὸς Κυδίππης καὶ πατρὸς Καλλιστίου).[222] The novel then switches to a first-person narrative, as Kleandros assumes the role of narrator, and the remainder of the book and the beginning of the next, almost four hundred lines, are presented as the direct discourse of one slave telling his life to another in a slave prison, beginning with the love affair which caused him to leave Lesbos, the storm that blew their ship into Barzopolis, and his separation from his beloved Kalligone, who hid in the bushes during the raid in which he was taken captive. Thus, the narrative covers his life from his origins and parentage in Lesbos to his "the present day" (τῆς παρούσης ἡμέρας)[223] imprisoned "in a gloomy dungeon" (εἱρκτὴν [...] τὴν κατεζοφωμένην).[224]

For Kleandros, Charikles serves as the supplementary witness, or the witness to the witness, not only listening, but also offering sympathy and compassion; in the reciprocal nature of community building within the carceral space, the two then switch roles, and Charikles begins to speak. In so doing, his narrative adopts a similar structure and phrasing as the one he had just heard, beginning with the conventional origins of parents and geography which he had just learned as the method for opening a slave narrative from listening to Kleandros: "My mother was Krystale, my father Phrator, | from a family not lacking in repute, my homeland was Phthia" (Μήτηρ μὲν ἦν μοι Κρυστάλη, πατὴρ Φράτωρ, | οὐκ ἐκ γεναρχῶν ἀκλεῶν, πατρὶς Φθία).[225]

Where Kleandros, however, moved immediately to a discussion of his love affair and its consequences, Charikles expounds at length on a physical description of Phthia and its environs. While Elizabeth Jeffreys consistently connects this description to "a paradisiacal setting, which has its origins in Alkinous' garden (*Odyssey* 7.112–132 and a long history in European literature as *locus amoenus* (pleasant place),"[226] a comparison of this description with John Kaminiates' demonstrates that the referent here is not purely literary, but also a reflection of the psychology, and thus

---

[222] *D&C* 2.57–59.

[223] *D&C* 3.37.

[224] *D&C* 3.39.

[225] *D&C* 3.51–52.

[226] Note 61 to *D&C* 3.65.

208   A. J. GOLDWYN

the narrative representation, of past lost places in the memory of enslaved people; Charikles as "mobile witness."[227]

As with Kaminiates' description of Thessaloniki, Charikles' description of his past, both in terms of the idyll of his upbringing and the physical beauty and material abundance of the land suggest an environment markedly at odds with his current situation. Thus, newly enslaved and separated from his loved ones, many of whose fates are, like Drosilla's, unknown to him. Indeed, considering that the devastation of the city matches the description in Kaminiates, it is likely that his family, friends, and other loved ones are either captive or killed. Thus, in this uncertainty, an autobiographical narrative imbued with a deep sense of nostalgia would not be out of place. Charikles' statement that "I was happy in the company of the young men with whom I associated" (μείραξι συνέχαιρον οἷς προσωμίλουν) adds an affective element to a narrative imbued with a deep sense of loss and sorrow.[228] Additionally, he recalls during this happy youth participation in a series of aristocratic events which it is likely, given his shift in circumstances, he will never participate in again: "I rode, I joined in sports, as is customary for young men, | I hunted hare, I became a skilled equestrian" (ἵππευον, ἀμφέπαιζον, ὡς νέοις νόμος, | λαγὼς ἐθήρων, εὐφυῶς ἱππηλάτουν).[229]

This sense of nostalgic hyperbole also infuses his description of the land itself: "trees that were always blooming as if in spring, | brimming with fruit and burgeoning leaves" (ἀεὶ τὸ δένδρον οἷον ἀνθοῦν εἰς ἔαρ | βρῖθόν τε καρπῷ καὶ τεθηλὸς φυλλάσι)[230]; the water from the river Melirrhoe was "sweet to see and even more delightful to drink" (ἰδεῖν μὲν ἡδὺς καὶ πεπόσθαι βελτίων)[231]; Charikles recalls that "a kind of golden plane tree | flourished with vigorous golden leaves" (Τούτου παρ' ὄχθαις χρῆμα χρυσῆς πλατάνου | ἐν θαλλεραῖς ἔθαλλε χρυσαῖς φυλλάσιν).[232] In the primary narration of *Drosilla and Charikles*, the natural world is depicted in a recognizably realistic way; it is only in Charikles' embedded character

---

[227] For the mobile witness, see p. 99.

[228] *D&C* 3.55.

[229] *D&C* 3.56–57.

[230] *D&C* 3.66–67.

[231] *D&C* 3.69.

[232] *D&C* 3.83–84.

3 THE CARCERAL IMAGINARY IN BYZANTIUM: THE KOMNENIAN ... 209

speech that the natural environment is imbued with such otherworldliness. Thus, the unrealistic aspects of the description of Phthia offered here by Charikles cannot be accepted as an objective description of the world as it was; rather, it can only be understood as a subjective description of a lost world as he understands it through memory and narrative within the context of his speech as a slave to a fellow slave in a slave prison.

Indeed, Charikles himself makes the case for this, albeit in a different way. He describes how he was unschooled in love, and how at this festival he sat down with his friends and "rejoiced with those with whom I ate: | such is the heart which is unaware, | when it rejoices, of future evil" (Ὅμως πάλιν ἔχαιρον οἷς συνετρύφων. | Τοιοῦτόν ἐστιν ἀγνοοῦσα καρδία | κακὸν τὸ μέλλον ἐν χαρᾷ καθημένη).[233] Though here explicitly speaking of the joys of a youth who does not yet understand the pains of love, the context of the remark gives weight to it with the significance of a second meaning. The idyllic picnic with his friends also seems delightful because he is unaware not just of the future pain love will cause him, but also the future evil of the conquest and enslavement which lead him to be narrating this memory to Kleandros in the first place. The circumstantial disparity between the events being narrated and the context in which they are being narrated further heightens the dramatic and emotional stakes. As in the slave ship, Charikles and a male companion are sharing stories and lamenting their woes, but the contrast of the severity of the woes of the slave ship and the amorous woes lamented during the picnic in the garden, even as the songs and communal dances described contrast with the imprisonment of the teller.

As in other examples of witness literature, the initial capture of the prisoners leads to Selektion, with the same arbitrary exercise over the power of life and death by the sovereign, in this case "the barbarian Kratylos" (Ὁ βάρβαρος δὲ Κρατύλος).[234] The morning after Charikles and Kleandros' meeting, "those who had been imprisoned by the laws of captivity | he bade bring from the gaol. | [...] | The Parthian ruler contemplated them as they stood there" (καὶ τοὺς ἁλόντας αἰχμαλωσίας νόμοις | ἐκ τῆς φυλακῆς ἐγκελεύεται φέρειν | [...] | Ἑστηκότας γοῦν εἰσορῶν ὁ Παρθάναξ).[235] As in previous instances, the sovereign makes a decision based entirely on his

---

[233] D&C 3.125–127.

[234] D&C 4.71.

[235] D&C 4.74–75, 86.

210   A. J. GOLDWYN

own whims, and Eugenianos, like Prodromos, describes the various and
varied fates of the prisoners:

> some he distributed to the satraps under him,
> [...]
> some he dismissed to gaze on the light of freedom,
> others he returned miserably to prison,
> to be freed by gifts from their begetters.
> Many he doomed to the sword.

> οὓς μὲν μερίζει τοῖς ὑπ' αὐτὸν σατράπαις
> [...]
> οὓς δὲ προπέμπει φῶς ἐλεύθερον βλέπειν,
> ἄλλους πρὸς εἱρκτὴν δυστυχῶς ἀντιστρέφει,
> δώροις ὅπως λυθεῖεν ἐκ γεννητόρων·
> πολλοὺς δὲ καὶ δίδωσι μοῖραν τῷ ξίφει.[236]

As in previous instances, the decision over life and death is solely in
the hands of the sovereign, but, from a narratological perspective, how
Prodromos and Eugenianos narrate these analogous scenes is different.
Where Eugenianos narrates this scene in a summary fashion, Prodromos
treats it more scenically: where the latter author showed individuals from
different social and economic conditions, narrated some of the decision-
making process of the sovereign, and the various responses of some of the
captives to their fates, the former provides some details only as regards the
couple at the center of the novel and, as in both novels and historiography,
the reason that they were spared is their great beauty.

As with *Rhodanthe and Dosikles* but unlike the other nonfictional
sources of witness literature, however, *Drosilla and Charikles* is able to
give voice to the individual fears of female captives, and Drosilla's lament
is reported in direct speech. The context of her speech, moreover, gives
voice to the emotions and concerns of the other women in similar situations whose words are either omitted or reported summary or indirect
speech. The subject of her speech is her love for Charikles—"allow me,
Charikles, to reciprocate the love of him who loves me" (Δὸς ἀντιφιλεῖν,
Χαρίκλεις, φιλοῦντά με) she says—but her speech is filled with anxiety,
loss, and fear, as would be expected given her circumstances.[237] Her main

[236] *D&C* 4.87, 90–93.
[237] *D&C* 5.34.

3 THE CARCERAL IMAGINARY IN BYZANTIUM: THE KOMNENIAN ... 211

concern is family separation, specifically from Charikles, and her lament emphasizes the limits of her agency, as a slave, of enacting her will: "as long as you in your heart of hearts do not want to love me, | I think I possess only half the life I desire" (σοῦ μὴ φιλεῖν θέλοντος ἐκ ψυχῆς μέσης, | δοκῶ ποθεινῆς ἥμισυ ζωῆς ἔχειν).[238]

At this point, Charikles begins to speak, and Eugenianos presents a conversation between two slaves in love who fear that, because of their position, they will be forced to marry others against their will. The grief they express, though perhaps expressed in the higher register of the novel than it may have been otherwise, nevertheless reflects the lived experience of many slaves. Charikles, for instance, speaks specifically to the trauma of family separation: "

> You [Zeus] pledged me to marriage with Drosilla,
> and now a savage old barbarian woman
> is trying to separate Charikles from her.
> You see the anguish which she brings, you see the sickness.

> Σύ μοι Δροσίλλας ἠγγυήσω τὸν γάμον·
> καὶ νῦν γυνὴ γραῦς βαρβαρόφρων ὠμόνους
> ζητεῖ διασπᾶν τῆσδε τὸν Χαρικλέα.
> Βλέπεις ἀνάγκην ἣν φέρει, βλέπεις νόσον.[239]

Eugenianos also suggests the possibility of a gendered response to these circumstances in the differing valences toward which the characters direct their grief. Charikles' grief is turned outward: he asks Zeus to

> slay Kratylos and Kleinias,
> yes and kill yourself too, Lady Chrysilla.
> In that way you would please your servant Charikles.

> Τὸν Κρατύλον φόνευε καὶ τὸν Κλεινίαν,
> ναὶ καὶ σὺ σαυτήν, ὦ Χρυσίλλα κυρία,
> οὕτω Χαρικλῆν ἡδυνεῖς σὸν οἰκέτην.[240]

---

[238] *D&C* 5.35–36.

[239] *D&C* 5.94–97.

[240] *D&C* 5.98–100.

212   A. J. GOLDWYN

Drosilla's grief, by contrast, is turned inward. Unlike Charikles, who dreams of the death of his captors, she dreams of her own death:

> Why did the sea's expanse not swallow me up?
> Why did the barbarian sword not slaughter me?
> Since you wish me to continue living unhappily,
> why did you not turn me to stone?"

> Τί μὴ θαλάσσης ὑπεδέξατο στόμα;
> Τί βάρβαρόν με μὴ κατέκτεινε ξίφος;
> Ἐπεὶ δέ με ζῆν δυστυχῶς θέλεις ἔτι,
> τί πρὸς λιθώδη μὴ μετατρέπεις φύσιν[241];

This conversation, then, represents another aspect of the slave experience, the conversation of two enslaved lovers on the cusp of their separation and forced marriage to others, and in it, the slaves wish for two different alternate pasts befitting their gender. The separation, however, does not occur as the lovers expect; rather, the remainder of Book 5 is a description of an Arab siege of the Parthian city in which they are captive. The Arabs, victorious in battle, "separate[e] the male captives from the women" (τοὺς δ' αἰχμαλώτους τῶν γυναικῶν χωρίσας)[242] and press them into a forced march to a third captivity. On the way, Drosilla is knocked off a wagon and falls into the sea far below.

This moment offers yet another glimpse into the experience of slaves that nonfictional accounts do not narrate. In the historiographical narratives of, for instance, Niketas Choniates, the forcible relocation of captive populations is a frequent and cursorily narrated occurrence.[243] Kaminiates, too, gives some more detail; he describes how his brother's wife was sold into slavery and her fate unknown during the forced relocation, but does not record his brother's response, and mentions only in passing the death of his own child under similar circumstances.[244] Thus, though the deaths of slaves in transport must have been a common occurrence, the constraints of nonfiction and the narratological choices of focalization (for Niketas, of narrating only from the perspective of elite politics and, for

[241] *D&C* 5.111–114.

[242] *D&C* 6.5.

[243] For which, see the beginning of Chapter 4, p. 231.

[244] Kam. *Ex. Thess.* 73.

3 THE CARCERAL IMAGINARY IN BYZANTIUM: THE KOMNENIAN ...   213

Kaminiates, only through his own experience) limit these authors' ability to narrate a scene like this.

Here, too, the genre of the novel allows the writer to both articulate the full extent of human suffering for his audience while also simultaneously protecting them from its harshest consequences. As a novel, its generic mandate requires both that the sufferings of the lovers be extreme but ultimately temporary: the audience can emote fully as though it were a death, but of course they know it can't be final. The couple must reunite for a happy ending. In this, of course, it differs radically from the actual experience of slaves, for whom the experience of family separation and death was more often than not permanent.

Nevertheless, insofar as Charikles believes at this moment in the narrative that Drosilla is truly dead, the lament he delivers has the emotional force of one slave lamenting the death of his also-enslaved beloved and shows the mental twists and turns that such a lament might take, its emotional ups and downs, a list of hopes and fears. Charikles laments Drosilla's presumptive death then laments his own fate as a survivor, and his thoughts—like the citizens of Thessaloniki described by Kaminiates and Eustathios who hurled themselves from the roofs,[245] the African slaves who hurled themselves into the ocean,[246] or the Auschwitz inmates who ran into the electrified fences[247]—turn to suicide: "I have wanted either to look on Drosilla while she lives, | or not to look on myself when she is dead to me" (Ἦ καὶ Δροσίλλαν ζῶσαν ἤθελον βλέπειν | ἢ μηδ' ἐμαυτόν, τῆσδέ μοι νεκρουμένης).[248] His suicidal despair gives way to nostalgia for the life he has lost, "How fortunate I was a short time ago, maiden, | when you shared my good cheer" (Ὡς εὐτυχὴς ἦν καὶ πρὸ μικροῦ, παρθένε, | ἔχων σε συμπάσχουσαν εἰς εὐθυμίαν),[249] then slumps into disbelief and denial, "I am bewildered; I am astounded" (Ἐπαπορῶ· τὸ πρᾶγμα θαῦμά μοι φέρει), he says, that Drosilla could have died.[250] Lastly, he comes back to the present moment, lamenting his powerlessness to change this reality given his current circumstances: "[...] I cannot

---

[245] For which, see above, p. 153.

[246] For which, see Equiano (1999: 60).

[247] See, for instance, Améry (1980: 17).

[248] D&C 6.55–56.

[249] D&C 6.60–61.

[250] D&C 6.72.

214   A. J. GOLDWYN

run | to seek you out, maiden, laden as I am with chains" ([…] Οὐ δραμεῖν γὰρ ἰσχύω, | δεσμοῖς κρατηθείς, ψηλαφᾶν σε, παρθένε).[251] As an ethopoeia, Charikles' lament thus reflects the situation "what a slave would say who loses his enslaved beloved," and represents a kind of thought-experiment in sympathetic imagination.

This lament is overheard by Chagos, the leader of the conquering army, who asks him the formulaic question of identity, an echo of the question of Kleandros' question at the opening of the novel: "Who are you? Whence do you come? Why do you weep?" (Τίς; Πόθεν; Τί δακρύεις;)[252] Charikles' response, however, differs significantly from his response to Kleandros; to Chagos, he replies: "I was Kratylos' captive, | now I am your slave; my homeland is Phthia" (Αἰχμάλωτος Κρατύλῳ, | δοῦλος δὲ σὸς νῦν· ἡ πατρὶς δέ μοι Φθία).[253] Though he still refers to his homeland as Phthia, the names of his parents are replaced by those of his slave–master. His identity is now as slave, rather than as free person born to free people—at least in the context of a speech given to a slave–master. That is to say, Charikles' articulation of his own identity is highly dependent on to whom he is speaking: in a slave ship speaking to another slave, he finds consolation and community, and thus speaks at length of his identity as a free man. By contrast, when speaking in the context of Selektion to the man who has enslaved him, he subsumes that identity and foregrounds his position as slave. Chagos is so impressed by Charikles' speech that he sets them both free with one *mina* compensation for the death of Drosilla. As in the other instances of Selektion, the arbitrary decision of the sovereign determines life and death, freedom and slavery. In this instance, Chagos grants freedom to two slaves, when the aim of the expedition was to capture slaves in the first place, and he compensates them for the death of Drosilla, even though death and family separation were the inevitable consequences of slave raiding. Chagos takes the rest of the captives with him into slavery and, presumably, executes or lets die many along the way. The novel thus brings its audience to the cusp of the historical truth of the fate of many of the slaves, but ultimately chooses to follow the exceptional case—those slaves freed and allowed to return home—rather than following those slaves whose lives would be more typical—those who

[251] *D&C* 6.93–94.
[252] *D&C* 6.100.
[253] *D&C* 6.101–102.

3 THE CARCERAL IMAGINARY IN BYZANTIUM: THE KOMNENIAN ... 215

remained in slavery. The novel gives its audience a glimpse of the ultimate horror but, in the end, turns its narrative toward a happier conclusion. This narratological shift in focus thus renders in novelistic terms Levi's assertion that the survivor is not the true witness, since the true witness is dead.

The scene of the novel thus shifts to Drosilla, who it turns out is alive, and she is able to make her way to an inn where a dream told her she would find Charikles. However, before the two meet, Drosilla is approached by a wealthy nobleman, Kallidemos, who delivers a speech of just over 300 lines in which he expresses his undying love and desire to marry her.[254] By contrast, Drosilla, "who had been weeping since daybreak" (δακρύουσαν ὀρθρόθεν) is not given direct speech.[255] At last, however, Maryllis (the old woman who has taken her in) asks her the formulaic question that twice has been posed to Charikles and which he, in different ways, had responded at length: "Come, child, tell me; | where do you come from and who is your father and what is his city" (Δεῦρο, τέκνον, ἐξάγγελλέ μοι· | πόθεν τίνος σὺ καὶ πατὴρ τίς καὶ πόλις).[256] Like Rhodanthe, however, Drosilla is only allowed to begin what would no doubt otherwise be a long answer before she is interrupted: "Since you want to learn, mother, from me, the foreigner | about what happened to me and to Charikles" (Ἐπεὶ μαθεῖν ζητεῖς με, μῆτερ, τὴν ξένην | τὰ κατ' ἐμαυτὴν καὶ τὰ τοῦ Χαρικλέος) she begins, before Kleandros interrupts her with the news that Charikles is alive and nearby.[257] This question and the beginnings of this answer have elsewhere opened up extended autobiographical narratives that reveal the way characters consider their past in relation to their present and how they understand an evolving sense of self in light of changes in social circumstances, not only in *Drosilla and Charikles*, but also in *Rhodanthe and Dosikles*; in this instance, however, just as Drosilla is about to articulate her own sense of self, she is interrupted; she says nothing more, thus representing once again the problem of female narrativity, agency, and individuality not just within nonfictional histories and witness accounts, but in fictional accounts as well.

[254] *D&C* 6.332–643.

[255] *D&C* 7.13.

[256] *D&C* 7.14–15.

[257] *D&C* 7.25–26.

216   A. J. GOLDWYN

Indeed, it is perhaps telling as regards the gendered dynamic of slave narratives and narrators that shortly after their reunion, Maryllis ignores Drosilla entirely, turning her instead to Charikles and saying:

> since you have come opportunely, child, it is now your opportunity to tell us
> how the two of you came to your union,
> what is your homeland, and what the origins of your passion.

> ὡς εὖ μὲν ἦλθες, τέκνον, εὖ δὲ καὶ λέγοις
> ὅπως μὲν εἰς σύμπνοιαν ἤλθετον μίαν,
> ποία δὲ πατρὶς καὶ τὰ τοῦ πόθου πόθεν.[258]

It is significant in this regard that Maryllis asks Drosilla to tell her story when she is alone with her, but once Charikles returns, the narratorial authority transfers to Charikles. Indeed, Maryllis admits as much: "The maiden was starting to tell me | and was about to explain all this | yes, and to recount it all in sequence, | before you arrived at the house" (Ἔμελλε πάντως τοῦ λέγειν ἀπηργμένη | ἡ παρθένος μοι ταῦτα διεξιέναι, | ναὶ καὶ καθ' εἱρμὸν πάντα τετρανωκέναι | πρὸ τοῦ σὲ τὸ στέγασμα κατειληφέναι).[259] Thus, the first time, Drosilla was prevented from speaking because she was interrupted; the second time, when there are no more interruptions, however, she is not allowed to resume her narrative, but her agency and voice in telling her own story are transferred to Charikles.

This narrative silencing continues, as Maryllis asks "What is it that grieves Drosilla still, or what is that troubles her, now that you, Charikles, have arrived?" (Τί γὰρ τὸ λυποῦν τὴν Δροσίλλαν εἰσέτι | ἢ τὸ θλίβον τί, σοῦ, Χαρίκλεις, ἰγμένου;)[260] Despite the fact that Drosilla is still standing there, she is not given the chance to narrate her own sorrows; this falls to Charikles, who begins in the way typical of slave narratives: "Know then that our homeland is Phthia, | my mother is Krystale and my father Phrator, | Drosilla's parents are Myrtion and Hedypnoe" (Εὖ δ' ἴσθι· πατρίς ἐστιν ἡμῶν ἡ Φθία· | μήτηρ ἐμοὶ μὲν Κρυστάλη, πατὴρ Φράτωρ, |

---

[258] *D&C* 7.90–92, 96–99.
[259] *D&C* 7.96–99.
[260] *D&C* 7.109–110.

τῇ δὲ Δροσίλλᾳ Μυρτίων, Ἡδυπνόη).[261] Charikles here gives the foundational statement of identity—parentage and place of birth—not just for himself, but also for Drosilla.

3.7 HYSMINE AND HYSMINIAS: THE SYMPOSIUM AND THE SLAVE SHIP

Many of the same themes initiated in *Rhodanthe and Dosikles* and reconfigured in *Drosilla and Charikles* also appear in Eumathios Makrembolites' *Hysmine and Hysminias*: the lovers meet and fall in love in a garden, a representation not just of their wealth, harmony, and freedom, but also a representation of their inclusion in a broader social and political order. The lovers are then separated by a storm, leading to parallel narratives of slavery before their eventual reunion and marriage. In this, then, *Hysmine and Hysminias* shares many of the same features that define it as a fictional slave novel, and thus has points of comparison with other fictional slave narratives like *Rhodanthe and Dosikles* and *Drosilla and Charikles* with other nonfictional slave narratives like John Kaminiates' and Eustathios of Thessaloniki's accounts of their experiences in Thessaloniki.

Indeed, upon first glance, *Hysmine and Hysminias* seems to have more in common with the *Capture of Thessaloniki* than with *Rhodanthe and Dosikles*. Like the former but unlike the latter, *Hysmine and Hysminias* is in prose (*Rhodanthe and Dosikles* is in twelve-syllable verse); the narrative is told in the first person, and has a specific addressee—Hysminias refers in the vocative to "my handsome Charidoux" (κάλλιστέ μοι Χαρίδουξ) a figure who, like Kaminiates' addressee Gregory of Cappadocia, is an otherwise unknown figure whose identity has been guessed at but not definitively determined.[262] It is possible that Charidoux is an actual person; it is equally possible that he is a narrative fiction whose textual presence echoes the conventions of the slave narrative as a dialogic genre.

Similarly, where *Rhodanthe and Dosikles* begins with the barbarian sack of Rhodes and the enslavement of the protagonists, *Hysmine and Hysminias* begins like the *Capture of Thessaloniki* with an almost utopian description of the city: "The city of Eurykomis is excellent in many

---

[261] *D&C* 7.133–135.

[262] *H&H* 1.2.1, for Charidoux, see Jeffreys (2014: 178, n. 4), Alexiou (2002: 115).

218   A. J. GOLDWYN

respects, not only because it is garlanded by the sea and watered by rivers and luxuriates in meadows and flourishes with bounteous food, but also because of its piety to the gods and even more than golden Athens it is entirely given over to altars, sacrifices and offerings to the gods" (Πόλις Εὐρύκωμις καὶ τἆλλα μὲν ἀγαθή, ὅτι καὶ θαλάσσῃ στεφανοῦται καὶ ποταμοῖς καταρρεῖται καὶ λειμῶσι κομᾷ καὶ τρυφαῖς εὐθηνεῖται παντοδαπαῖς, τὰ δ' εἰς θεοὺς εὐσεβής, καὶ ὑπὲρ τὰς χρυσᾶς Ἀθήνας ὅλη βωμός, ὅληθῦμα θεοῖς καὶ ἀνάθημα).[263] The opening of the novel thus establishes that, though *Hysmine and Hysminias* is set in an undifferentiated but clearly pagan past (as evidenced by sacrificial altars to gods plural), it exists in a recognizably real world: it compares favorably to Athens, a historical city in a world of otherwise imaginary ones. Indeed, in this comparison, Makrembolites seems to be following the advice of Menander Rhetor, who urges comparison of topographical features such as seas and rivers and agriculturally rich meadows as well as cultural characteristics such as piety and developed architecture for the practice of religion.[264] Perhaps more intriguingly, the exact nature of the comparison also evokes John Kaminiates' Thessaloniki, as both that city and Eurykomis are known for the same thing: their piety (εὐσεβής). Indeed, Eurykomis and Thessaloniki share close parallels at the linguistic level: John Kaminiates writes that the city is "great and wide" (μεγάλη τε καὶ εὐρεῖα) the very term encoded in Eurykomis' name: Εὐρύ—(wide) and—κωμις (village).[265] Hysminias then goes to Aulikomis, where he provides a series of extended ekphraseis on the gardens that create the same kind of idyllic sense of harmony and balance that Kaminiates provides in his description of Thessaloniki.

Indeed, unlike *Rhodanthe and Dosikles*, the barbarian raid that results in the enslavement of the protagonists does not occur at the outset of the novel, but rather occurs in Book 8, when Hysminias is dragged off by "an incalculable host of Ethiopians" (πλῆθος οὐκ εὐαρίθμητον Αἰθιόπων).[266] Though Hysmine and Hysminias had already been separated (Hysmine is thrown overboard to quell a storm in Book 7), the scene in the harbor and on the seashore features many of the same elements as seen in the *Capture*

---

[263] *H&H* 1.1.1.

[264] For which, see Chapter 2, p. 86.

[265] Kam. *Ex. Thess.* 4.1. I am not suggesting that Eurykomis is modeled on Thessaloniki, only that the conventional description of the prosperous city has certain characteristics.

[266] *H&H* 8.1.1.

3   THE CARCERAL IMAGINARY IN BYZANTIUM: THE KOMNENIAN ...   219

of Thessaloniki and *Rhodanthe and Dosikles*. Once taken on board, the prisoners go through Selektion: "All the men, all the youths, all the maidens and women they stripped of their tunics and they were uncovered right down to their private parts and had their whole body naked" (τούτων δ' ὅσον ἐν ἀνδράσιν, ὅσον ἐν νεανίσκοις, ὅσον ἐν παρθένοις καὶ γυναιξίν, ἀπεδύετο τὸν χιτῶνα καὶ ἦν ἀπερικάλυπτον καὶ μέχρις αἰδοῦς καὶ γύμνωσιν καθ' ὅλου φέρον τοῦ σώματος).[267] After the conventional stripping of the clothing of the prisoners, the prisoners are separated by sex: "The youths and men were received by the trireme's hold but the barbarians' immorality and licentiousness was reserved for the women, while the maidens, by what barbarian law I do not know, were clad in a tattered tunic and no presumptuous hand was laid on them nor was anything barbaric or shameful done to them" (Ὁ μὲν οὖν δὴ πυθμὴν τῆς τριήρους τοὺς νεανίσκους καὶ τοὺς ἄνδρας ἐδέχετο, τὰς δέ γε γυναῖκας αἰσχύνη καὶ βαρβαρική τις ἀσέλγεια· παρθένοις γὰρ οὐκ οἶδ' ὅπως ἢ τίνι νόμῳ βαρβαρικῷ καὶ χιτὼν διερρωγώς τις ἐπεδιδύσκετο καὶ χεὶρ αὐθάδης οὐκ ἐπετίθετο οὔτε τι βαρβαρικὸν ἐπὶ ταύταις αἰσχρῶς κατεπράττετο).[268] Thus, men and women are separated, with men in the hold of the ship, and virgins separated from the other women, who are then subject to mass rape. The sovereign decision is then enacted upon the male prisoners, with "the youths (there were few of them) to the oars" (τοὺς μὲν νεανίσκους [ὀλίγοι δ' οὗτοι] ταῖς κώπαις) that is, placed in forced labor, while "those somewhat older (woe to the barbarians' pitiless souls) became fodder for the sword" (ὅσοι δ' ὑπερβεβήκασι τούτους [βαβαὶ τῆς τῶν βαρβάρων ἀμειλίκτου ψυχῆς] ξίφους γεγόνασι παρανάλωμα) and "the women lay shamefully with the barbarians, and the trireme became a brothel" (αἱ δέ γε γυναῖκες αἰσχρῶς τοῖς βαρβάροις συνανεκλίθησαν· καὶ ἦν ἡ τριήρης πανδοχεῖον).[269] Indeed, the emphasis on sexual violence and sex slavery continues even into the slave markets; "Concerning the women and us young men who were captives there was little discussion among the inhabitants of Artykomis – or rather, none; their entire attention was devoted to the acquisition of the maidens" (Καὶ γυναικῶν μὲν καὶ νεανίσκων αἰχμαλώτων ἡμῶν ὀλίγος τοῖς ἐξ Ἀρτυκώμιδος λόγος ἢ μᾶλλον οὐδείς, τὸ πᾶν δ' ἐκεχήνει περὶ τὴν τῶν

---

[267] *H&H* 8.3.1.

[268] *H&H* 8.3.2–3.

[269] *H&H* 8.4.3.

220 A. J. GOLDWYN

παρθένων κτῆσιν).[270] The principle aim of the raids was the capture of beautiful women in sex slavery.

Makrembolites describes this scene as "a symposium of blood" (συμπόσιον αἵματος) thus using metaphor to underscore the centrality of the symposium as the institutional marker of *bios* for free people and, in this case, its inverse as the marker of their new exposure to bare life under the new sovereign.[271] The loot—"everything made of silver, gold, bronze and iron and all the clothing" (Ὅσον μὲν οὖν ἐν ἀργύρῳ καὶ χρυσῷ καὶ χαλκῷ καὶσιδήρῳ καὶ χιτωνίσκοις)—is then sold on land, though what Hysmine calls "the loot that consisted of us human beings" (τὸ δ' ὅσον τῆς λείας ἐν ἀνθρώποις) remained in the hold of the ship.[272]

The barbarian captors are then themselves conquered by a different group of Greeks, and Hysminias is sold to a different mistress who asks him to tell her his life story: "Who are you? Where are you from? What is your country and who are your parents?" (τίς πόθεν εἷς ἀνδρῶν, πόθι τοι πόλις ἠδὲ τοκῆες;)[273] At first, Hysminias tries to resist telling his story, noting that "I am your slave" (Ἐγὼ δ' ἀλλ' ὦ δέσποινα, δοῦλος σός) a statement of identity-negation that parallels Dosikles' initial refusal to tell his story to Kratandros in *Rhodanthe and Dosikles*. In that novel, when Dosikles spoke to his fellow slave and companion Kratandros, he anticipated feeling relief at the telling. In *Hysmine and Hysminias*, however, when the protagonist is asked for his life story, the protagonist intuits that she does not want to hear it for his benefit, but for her own. Thus, where elsewhere, slaves had spoken movingly and at length to other slaves (Dosikles to Kratandros, Charikles to Kleandros, John Kaminiates to Gregory of Cappadocia), Hysminias replies: "when you ask to know more you are asking for a whole play, a complete tragedy" (τὰ δ' ἄλλα ζητοῦσαμαθεῖν ὅλον δρᾶμα ζητεῖς καὶ ὅλον τραγῴδημα), suggesting that the story holds only entertainment value for her.[274] Because of the difference in their social circumstances, the slave owner cannot identify with him

---

[270] *H&H* 8.7.1.

[271] *H&H* 8.4.3.

[272] *H&H* 8.6.3.

[273] *H&H* 8.11.2. Jeffreys notes that this is "a Homeric formula" with references to places in the *Odyssey* where the question is posed, but it also has its roots in the tradition of monody and lament, for which, see Goldwyn (2014: 97).

[274] *H&H* 8.11.2.

3 THE CARCERAL IMAGINARY IN BYZANTIUM: THE KOMNENIAN ... 221

on a human level as his fellow slaves can; the slave's narrative can only be a source of entertainment for slavers, as watching a play. Recognizing this, he then adds "I am the exemplification of Fate, a ghost from the underworld, a plaything of the gods" (Παράδειγμα Τύχης ἐγώ, νερτέρων σκιά, δαιμόνων παίγνιον) all terms by which he articulates his own dehumanization and lack of agency by denying himself a connection to his own past.[275] His masters insist, however, revealing explicitly their true interest in hearing from him: "It is the time for a meal; let us take our places for dinner and at the table, and in the midst of eating let us give some time to our slave's story" ("καιρὸς ἀρίστου" φησίν, "ἀνακλιθῶμεν ἐπὶ τὸ δεῖπνον, καὶ περὶ τὴν τράπεζαν καὶ μέσας τροφὰς τῇ γλώσσῃ τοῦ δούλου καιρὸν χαρισώμεθα").[276] His sufferings are their dinner entertainment.[277]

Nevertheless, when he finally does speak, he begins with the conventional narrative opening: "My home city is Eurykomis, my father Themisteus and my mother Dianteia; whether they are prosperous, whether they hold the first rank among the inhabitants of Eurykomis, is not for me to say. [...] I came as herald to Aulikomis" (Ἐμοὶ πατρὶς πόλις Εὐρύκωμις, πατὴρ Θεμιστεὺς καὶ μήτηρ Διάντεια· εἰ δ᾽ εὐτυχοῦντες, εἰ τὰ πρῶτα φέροντες τῶν ἐν Εὐρυκώμιδι, οὐκ ἐμόν ἐστι λέγειν. [...] κήρυξ ἧκον εἰς Αὐλικώμιδα).[278] The opening of his narrative thus establishes his inclusion within the social, political, and economic institutions of the city: he has a family, they are wealthy, they hold political rank, as does he. This is a picture of *bios*, which then, in the second part of his narrative, shifts—"What happened next?" (Τὰ δ᾽ ἐφεξῆς ὁποῖα;)[279]—to his exclusion from these same institutions and his journey toward bare life, *zoē*: his fiancée is "torn pitiably from my hands" (Ἡ δέ μου τῶν χειρῶν ἐλεεινῶς ἐκσπασθεῖσα) marking his separation from his family, and he is taken captive, "a slave instead of a herald" (τρίδουλος ἀντὶ κήρυκος) and thus excluded from the political protection afforded him by his economic status and political rank.[280]

---

[275] *H&H* 8.11.2.

[276] *H&H* 8.11.4.

[277] Nilsson (2017: 307): "Not only does this have no effect, but his sad story does not seem to raise compassion but rather offer a sort of entertainment (a drama, a tragedy).".

[278] *H&H* 8.13.1.

[279] *H&H* 8.13.3.

[280] *H&H* 8.13.4.

222 A. J. GOLDWYN

As in the case of Rhodanthe, the response of his new masters demonstrates the way that dialogical autobiographical narration as a means for building identity relies on the power dynamics of narrator and audience.[281] Unlike the fellow slaves Kratandros and Dosikles, who find solace in telling their stories to one another, Hysminias, in telling his story to his masters, only reaffirms the powerlessness of his new position. After hearing Hysminias' story, his master erases each aspect of Hysminias' identity: "If your country is illustrious and your lineage brilliant and your home luxurious, now you have none of those things: you are a slave, and you are our slave" (εἰ μέν σοι πατρὶς περιφανὴς καὶ γένος λαμπρὸν καὶ τὰ κατ' οἴκους πολυτελῆ, νῦν τούτων ἔχεις οὐδέν· δοῦλος γὰρ εἶ καὶ δοῦλος ἡμῶν·).[282] Thus, where Hysminias had spoken of his city Eurykomis, his parents, and his parent's wealth and stature, all aspects that individuate him and connect him through time to a world—and thus a political and personal identity—beyond his own immediate circumstances, his master separates him from each of these. "You have none of these things," his master says, erasing his past, and "you are a slave" (νῦν τούτων ἔχεις οὐδέν) he says, emphasizing his existence in the present. Having severed Hysminias from his origins, the new master then attempts to remove from Hysminias' narrative its central plot motif: "If you exchanged chastity and virginity for Aphrodite and Eros, the virgins' garland for the rose garland of passion, have nothing more to do with this, but cultivate chastity and love sobriety" (εἰ δὲ καὶ σωφροσύνης καὶ παρθενίας Ἀφροδίτην ἀντηλλάξω καὶ Ἔρωτα, εἰ δὲ καί, στεφάνων <ἐκ> δάφνης παρθενικῶν στέφανον ἐκ ῥόδων ἐρωτικόν, μὴ σύ γε τὸ ἀπὸ τοῦδε· ἀλλὰ κτῆσαι τὸ σῶφρον καὶ τὸ φιλόσωφρον ἀγάπησον).[283] Again, the master tells the new slave to reject what had come before and accept the new circumstances: whereas once he had the privilege as a free man to pursue his amorous desires, he now has no individual agency of his own. His desires are no longer his own but are those of his master. Commensurate with this is the threat of physical violence, as the master concludes his speech, saying that if Hysminias

---

[281] Nilsson also recognizes the significance of the power disparity between teller and listener in these narratives, noting that "the hero-narrator [Hysmine] has no equal with whom to share his misfortunes, but tells his story only to characters of superior power: first to his new master and mistress, then to Rhodope, the mistress of Hysmine" (2017: 305).

[282] H&H 8.14.3–4.

[283] H&H 8.14.4.

3 THE CARCERAL IMAGINARY IN BYZANTIUM: THE KOMNENIAN ... 223

does attempt to exert his own agency and subjectivity by pursuing his own will and desire, he will "learn chastity the hard way and find the master's hand a teacher" (ἵνα μὴ τὴν σωφροσύνην ἐξ ἔργων μάθῃς αὐτῶν καὶ χεῖρα δεσπότου κτήσῃ διδάσκαλον.)[284] Thus, among their fellow slaves, Dosikles and Kratandros and Charikles and Kleandros find solace and reaffirmation of their histories, emotional lives, and shared humanity. Hysminias, by contrast, though also a slave telling his story, is further dehumanized by his master, with the threat of violence lingering over any attempt to exert his own individuality. Indeed, such is the contrast between the two kinds of audiences that where Kratandros hears Dosikles and devotes himself to helping him achieve his (re)union with Rhodanthe and Kleandros similarly binds himself to Charikles, Hysminias' owners fulfill the witness' great fear in narrating their stories, namely that they will not be believed, and indeed, Hysminias' mistress later says: "This one has a tall tale about having been a herald, and boasts about his family and country, and goes on endlessly about all sorts of other marvels" (ὁ δὲ καὶ κῆρυξ γεγονέναι τερατολογεῖ καὶ γένος καὶ πατρίδα λαμπρολογεῖ καὶ ἄλλ' ἄττα πολλὰ καταγλωσσαλγεῖ).[285]

In this light, Hysminias' ensuing narration after his master's speech takes on new significance: "I remained silent and kept my eyes on the ground, all full of tears" (ἐγὼ δ' ἐσίγων καὶ τοὺς ὀφθαλμοὺς εἶχον ὁρῶντας εἰς γῆν καὶ ὅλους δακρύων μεστούς) he says, demonstrating outward subservience to his master's will.[286] And yet, despite this outward appearance, Hysminias articulates an oppositional interiority that reaffirms the essential aspects of his identity: "the meal came to an end and I, Hysminias, the herald of the Diasia" (καὶ ὁ τῶν Διασίων κῆρυξ Ὑσμινίας ἐγώ) he says, asserting at the climactic end of the clause ἐγώ: the subjective "I" that is so essential to the slave identity, his name, and his official title.[287] He then lists the important moments of his past, such as his journey from Eurykomis to Aulikomis as herald, and contrasts his former condition with the present. I, he says

---

[284] *H&H* 8.15.4.

[285] *H&H* 8.20.3.

[286] *H&H* 8.15.1.

[287] *H&H* 8.15.1.

224 A. J. GOLDWYN

who had sat at Sosthenes' brilliant banquet, now sat at a slave's table with
my band of fellow slaves, and perform a slave's tasks, and am completely
a slave, taking on a servile demeanour and functioning as a slave, quite
stripped, O Zeus and the gods, of my herald's rank and that of a free man.

ὁ πολυτελῶς ἐπὶ τῆς τοῦ Σωσθένους λαμπρᾶς τραπέζης ἀνακλιθείς, ἐπὶ
δουλικῆς τραπέζης νῦν ἀνακέκλιμαι σὺν ὁμοδούλων χορῷ καὶ τὰ τῶν δούλων
ὑπηρετῶ καὶ ὅλος δοῦλός εἰμι καὶ ὅλην δουλείαν ἐνδέδυμαι καὶ ὅλην
δουλοπρέπειαν ὑποκρίνομαι, ὅλον ἀποδυθείς, ὦ Ζεῦ καὶ θεοί, τὸ κηρύκειον
καὶ ὅλον τὸ ἐλεύθερον.[288]

Hysminias thus again emphasizes the contrast between the symposium as
the locus of *bios* and slavery as the locus of *zoē* and bare life—he repeats
the word slavery five times in the course of the sentence, contrasting it
with the final "freedom" (ἐλεύθερον). Perhaps as important as his refusal
to relinquish his past is his refusal to abandon the animating force driving
his hopes for the future: "not even in the midst of these terrible circumstances did I allow myself to forget Hysmine, my maiden" (ἀλλ᾽ οὐδ᾽
ἐν μέσοις οὕτω δεινοῖς Ὑσμίνης λήθην παρθένου φίλης ἐμῆς ἔπαθον).[289]
Thus, though he adopts the exteriority of slavery to navigate his present,
his interiority remains rooted in his own identity as regards both past
(his city, his parents) and future (his hoped-for reunion with Hysmine).
Hysminias' determination to retain his own identity, will, and desires thus
also represents the slave narrative as an act of resistance to the dehumanizing power of slavery that his master sought to enact on his body ("learn
the hard way and find the master's hand a teacher") and on his mind
(about his past, he says, "you have none of those things" and about his
future, "have nothing more to do with" his amatory desires").

Hysminias, however, learns to navigate between the external circumstances of his slavery and his own interiority as a subject with individual
desires and desires. Indeed, he describes how he manages this dichotomy,
dividing himself between one form of servile exteriority and resisting
interiority:

I mourned, but it was a surreptitious mourning; I wept, and I concealed
my eyes from my masters. I repressed my soul, my voice, my tongue and

[288] *H&H* 8.15.2.
[289] *H&H* 8.15.3.

3 THE CARCERAL IMAGINARY IN BYZANTIUM: THE KOMNENIAN ...

my tears. The herald who had become a slave held piteous discourse, I held up to my mind Eurykomis, Aulikomis, the herald's wand, Sosthenes' garden, the well within the garden, the birds on it, the golden eagle, Hysmine pouring out the wine, teasing me with passion, playing with my feet, playing with the cups and everything else that we did in our sport (alas for those passionate delights in my dreams); and above all else I whispered softly, "Hysmine, my beloved."

Ἐθρήνουν, ἀλλὰ τὸν θρῆνον ὑπέκλεπτον· ἐδάκρυον, καὶ τοὺς ὀφθαλμοὺς ὑπεκρυπτόμην τῶν δεσποτῶν· τὴν ψυχὴν εἶχον καὶ φωνὴν καὶ γλῶσσαν καὶ δάκρυα. Δοῦλος ὁ κῆρυξ ἐλεεινολογούμενος ὅλην ἀνεπλαττόμην τῷ νῷ τὴν Εὐρύκωμιν, τὴν Αὐλίκωμιν, τὸ κηρύκειον, τὸν τοῦ Σωσθένους κῆπον, τὸ περὶ τὸν κῆπον φρέαρ, τὰ παρὰ τούτῳ πτηνά, τὸν κατάχρυσον ἀετόν, τὴν Ὑσμίνην κιρνῶσαν, ἐρωτικῶς μοι προσπαίζουσαν, τοῖς ποσί μου συμπαίζουσαν, ταῖς κύλιξι καταπαίζουσαν, καὶ τἆλλ' ὁπόσα (βαβαὶ τῶν ὡς ἐν ὀνείροις ἐρωτικῶν ἡδονῶν) κατεπαίζομεν· καὶ ἐπὶ πᾶσι τούτοις "Ὑσμίνη μοι φίλη" λεπτὸν ἐψιθύριζον.[290]

The external and the internal are compared through opposite pairs: "I wept," he says, but "surreptitiously"; he cries, he says, but hides his tears. Behind the external appearance of servile slavery, Hysminias conceals a rich interiority of memories and emotions, and his continued guarding of this interiority is indeed an act of resistance against the desubjectification of his position as an enslaved person.

Indeed, later in the novel, when Hysminias is wooed against his will by Rhodope, when she asks him his name, he replies:

My lady, the gods have removed even this; they have not spared even my name, but when they made me a slave instead of being a free man and replaced the honey of freedom with the bitterness of slavery and brought darkness in place of light, they also replaced my Hellenic name with a barbarian one, and called me Artakes instead of Hysminias.[291]

Deep into his period as a slave, Hysminias reveals another aspect of his desubjectification: he has lost his name and had it replaced with a new one, thus, as he acknowledges, stripping him not just of a name but of

[290] *H&H* 8.16.1.
[291] *H&H* 9.14.4–5.

226 A. J. GOLDWYN

his identity as a free man: "So now I am a slave entirely, both in name and in deed."[292] And, indeed, it is perhaps telling in this regard that he emphasizes his new identity in the ensuing narrative by closely associating himself (ἐγώ) and his positionality (δοῦλος): at 9.16.1 (ὁ δοῦλος ἐγώ), 10.6.4 (ἐγὼ δ' ὁ δοῦλος), and 10.7.2 (δοῦλος Ὑσμινίας ἐγώ).

In light of the shifting positionality of the central couple, then, the intertwined relationship between the slave narrative and the love narrative takes on a new dynamic. Read as romantic narratives, the slave narrative embedded within it is just one more example of the difficulties the lovers have to overcome to be together. Read primarily as a slave narrative with a romance plotline embedded within it, however, the difficulties of the lovers take on a new meaning: controlling the slave's sexual desires is the principal way in which the narrative demonstrates the slave's loss of agency. They are no longer able to manifest their will in the world in the most important and intimate way available to a free person, by choosing whom to love and being with that person. Hysmine and Hysminias' refusal to accede to their masters' wishes for whom they should love becomes the central way in which they maintain a sense of ontological freedom despite physical bondage. Hysmine, for instance, emphasizes this distinction between exterior and interior when she tells Hysminias that "even if physically I am a slave, my soul's freedom is untrammeled."[293] For Hysminias, too, love is the central aspect of his own identity and individuality that connects him to his life as a free man: "I would pray to die a slave with Hysmine rather than be free and immortal with Rhodope."[294] The chance freeing of Hysmine and Hysminias at the altar of Apollo, therefore, leads inevitably to their marriage, which comes to signify not only the completion of the marriage plot element of the novel but also, in that they can again make their own choices in whom to love and are able to manifest their desires into reality, mark them again as free, and thus also brings to an end the slave narrative.

[292] H&H 9.14.5.
[293] H&H 10.16.5.
[294] H&H 10.17.1.

3 THE CARCERAL IMAGINARY IN BYZANTIUM: THE KOMNENIAN ...

BIBLIOGRAPHY

Adorno, Theodore. 1983. *Prisms*, trans. Nicholsen, Samuel and Sherry Weber. Cambridge, MA: MIT Press.

Agamben, Giorgio. 2017. *The Omnibus Homo Sacer*. Palo Alto: Stanford University Press.

Alexander, Michelle. 2010. *The New Jim Crow: Mass Incarceration in the Age of Colorblindedness*. New York: The New Press.

Alexander, Patrick Elliot. 2018. *From Slave Ship to Supermax: Mass Incarceration, Prisoner Abuse, and the New Neo-Slave Novel*. Philadelphia: Temple University Press.

Alexiou, Margaret. 2002. *After Antiquity: Greek Language, Myth, and Metaphor*. Ithaca: Cornell University Press.

Améry, Jean. 1980. *At the Mind's Limits: Contemplations by a Survivor on Auschwitz and Its Realities*, trans. Sidney Rosenfeld and Stanley Rosenfeld. Bloomington: Indiana University Press.

Beaton, Roderick. 1996. *The Medieval Greek Romance*, 2nd ed. London and New York: Routledge.

Bourbouhakis, Emmanuel. 2009. Exchanging the Devices of Ares for the Delights of the Erotes. In *Plotting with Eros: Essays on the Poetics of Love and the Erotics of Reading*, ed. Ingela Nilsson, 213–234. Copenhagen: Museum Tusculanum Press.

Budick, Emily Miller. 2015. *The Subject of Holocaust Fiction*. Bloomington: Indiana University Press.

Butler, Judith. 2005. *Giving an Account of Oneself*. New York: Fordham University Press.

Childs, Dennis. 2015. *Slaves of the State: Black Incarceration from the Chain Gang to the Penitentiary*. Minneapolis: University of Minnesota Press.

Cohn, Dorrit. 1978. *Transparent Minds: Narrative Modes for Presenting Consciousness in Fiction*. Princeton: Princeton University Press.

Equiano, Olaudah. 1999. The Interesting Narrative of the Life of Olaudah Equiano, or Gustavus Vassa, the African". In *I Was Born a Slave: An Anthology of Classic Slave Narratives*, vol. 1, ed. Yuval Taylor and Charles Johnson, 29–179. Chicago: Lawrence Hill Books.

Fletcher, Alana. 2016. Transforming Subjectivity: *Se questo è un uomo* in Translation and Adaptation. In *Translating Holocaust Literature*, ed. Peter Arnds, 33–44. Gottingen: V&R Press.

Gaca, Kathy. 2010. The Andrapodizing of War Captives in Greek Historical Memory. *Transactions of the American Philological Society* 140 (1): 117–161.

Goldwyn, Adam J. 2014. "'I come from a cursed land and from the depths of darkness': Life after death in Greek laments about the fall of Constantinople." In *Wanted Byzantium: The Desire for a Lost Empire*, ed. Ingela Nilsson and Paul Stephenson, 93–108. Uppsala: Studia Byzantina Upsaliensia.

228 A. J. GOLDWYN

Goldwyn, Adam. 2015. John Malalas and the Origins of the Allegorical and Novelistic Traditions of the Trojan War in Byzantium. *Troianalexandrina* 15: 23–49.

———. 2018. *Byzantine Ecocriticism: Women, Nature, and Power in the Medieval Greek Romance*. New York: Palgrave MacMillan.

Goldwyn, Adam, and Ingela Nilsson. 2019. "Notes on the Late Byzantine Romances and Their Editions". In *Reading the Late Byzantine Romance: A Handbook*, ed. Adam Goldwyn and Ingela Nilsson, xiii–xix. Cambridge: Cambridge University Press.

Grass, Sean. 2003. *The Self in the Cell: Narrating the Victorian Prisoner*. New York: Routledge.

Hartman, Geoffrey. 2004. *The Struggle Against Inauthenticity*. New York: St. Martin's.

Haynes, Katharine. 2003. *Fashioning the Feminine in the Greek Novel*. London: Routledge.

Holton, David. 1991. Romance. In *Literature and Society in Renaissance Crete*, ed. David Holton, 205–238. Cambridge: Cambridge University Press.

Jeffreys, Elizabeth. 2014. *Four Bryznatine Novels*. Liverpool: Liverpool University Press.

Jouanno, Corinne. 2006. Women in Byzantine Novels of the Twelfth Century: An Interplay Between Norm and Fantasy. In *Byzantine Women: Varieties of Experience, 800–1200*, ed. Lynda Garland, 141–162. Aldershot: Ashgate.

Lambert, Raphaël. 2019. *Narrating the Slave Trade, Theorizing Community*. Leiden: Brill.

Lang, Berel. 2003. *Act and Idea in the Nazi Genocide*. Syracuse: Syracuse University Press.

Levi, Primo. 1959. *If This Is a Man*, trans. Stuart Woolf. New York: Orion Press.

———. 1989. *Se questo è un uomo*. Torino: Einaudi.

Levine, Michael. 2006. *The Belated Witness: Literature, Testimony, and the Question of Holocaust Survival*. Palo Alto: Stanford University Press.

Lilie, Ralph-Johannes. 2014. Reality and Invention: Reflections on Byzantine Historiography". *Dumbarton Oaks Papers* 68: 157–210.

Melville-Jones, John. 1988. "Appendix 1: Eustathios on the Writing of History." In *The Capture of Thessaloniki, Eustathios of Thessaloniki*, 230–234. Canberra: Byzantina Australiensia.

Messis, Charis. 2006. "La mémoire du 'je' souffrant. Construire et écrire la mémoire personnelle dans les récits de captivité." In *L'écriture de la mémoire. La littérarité de l'historiographie*, ed. Paolo Odorico, Panagiotis Agapitos, and Martin Hinterberger, 107–146. Paris: Centre d'études byzantines, néo-helléniques et sud-est européennes.

Nilsson, Ingela. 2001. *Erotic Pathos, Rhetorical Pleasure: Narrative Technique and Mimesis in Eumathios' Makrembolites' Hysminie & Hysminias*. Uppsala: Studia Byzantine Upsaliensa.

———. 2004. From Homer to Hermoniakos: Some considerations of Troy matter in Byzantine Literature. *Troianalexandrina* 4: 9–34.

———. 2014. *Raconter Byzance: La Littérature au XIIe siècle*. Paris: Les Belles Lettres.

———. 2017. Comforting Tears and Suggestive Smiles: To Laugh and Cry in the Komnenian Novel. In *Greek Laughter and Tears: Antiquity and After*, ed. Margaret Alexiou and Douglas Cairns, 291–311. Edinburgh: Edinburgh University Press.

Papadogiannakis, Ioannis. 2017. Lamenting for the Fall of Jerusalem in the Seventh Century CE. In *Greek Laughter and Tears: Antiquity and After*, ed. Margaret Alexiou and Douglas Cairns, 187–198. Edinburgh: Edinburgh University Press.

Reardon, B.P. 2008. *Collected Ancient Greek Novels*. Oakland: University of California Press.

Rediker, Martin. 2007. *The Slave Ship: A Human History*. New York: Viking Press.

Roilos, Panagiotis. 2005. *Amphoteroglossia: A Poetics of the Twelfth-Century Medieval Greek Novel*. Cambridge, MA: Harvard University Press.

Smith, Valerie. 2012. *Toni Morrison: Writing the Moral Imagination*. London: Wiley-Blackwell.

Sullivan, Denis. 2000. *Siegecraft: Two Tenth-Century Instructional Manuals by 'Heron of Byzantium*. Washington, DC: Dumbarton Oaks Research Collection and Library.

Trezise, Thomas. 2013. *Witnessing Witnessing: On the Reception of Holocaust Survivor Testimony*. New York: Fordham University Press.

Vice, Sue. 2000. *Holocaust Fiction*. London: Routledge.

White, Hayden. 2004. Figuring Realism in Witness Literature. *parallax* 10 (1): 113–124.

Young, James Edward. 1988. *Writing and Rewriting the Holocaust: Narrative and the Consequences of Interpretation*. Bloomington: Indiana University Press.

Youngquist, Paul. 2011. The Mothership Connection. *Cultural Critique* 77: 1–23.

CHAPTER 4

The Refugee as Historian: Niketas Choniates and the Capture of Constantinople

4.1 NIKETAS AS HISTORIAN AND THE CAMPAIGN OF JOHN II KOMNENOS

Shortly after he ascended the throne, the emperor John II Komnenos, according to the historian Niketas Choniates, "seeing that the Turks were violating their treaties with his father, in great numbers overrunning the cities throughout Phrygia and along the Maeander" (Ὁ δὲ βασιλεὺς τοὺς Πέρσας ὁρῶν παρ' οὐδὲν θεμένους τὰς πρὸς τὸν ἑαυτοῦ πατέρα ξυνθήκας καὶ παμπληθεὶ τῶν πόλεων καταθέοντας, ὁπόσαι περὶ Φρυγίαν καὶ ποταμὸν τὸν Μαίανδρον ἵδρυνται), decided to march against them.[1] This is the first description of city-sacking in Niketas' *History* (χρονικὴ διήγησις), which covers the period from John's accession in 1118 to 1205/6/7 (depending on the manuscript), the aftermath of the Crusader Sack of Constantinople.[2] In Constantinople, this period was one of the most fertile for artistic, scholarly, and cultural production. It was also, increasingly as the century wore on, one of the catastrophic

[1] Chon. *Hist.* 12.

[2] For the most recent and perhaps definitive studies of the manuscript tradition, see Simpson (2013a: 68–127), a revision of Simpson (2006), much of which builds on the information in the introduction of Van Dieten's critical edition. For Choniates' life, see Simpson (2013a: 11–23). The manuscripts and biographical information are also covered in much abbreviated form in Neville (2018: 219–225).

© The Author(s), under exclusive license to Springer Nature Switzerland AG 2021
A. J. Goldwyn, *Witness Literature in Byzantium*,
New Approaches to Byzantine History and Culture,
https://doi.org/10.1007/978-3-030-78857-5_4

232 A. J. GOLDWYN

violence for the average citizens of the empire and its environs. Indeed, reading the narrative of the campaigns and counter-campaigns of John and his enemies with which Niketas opens his *History* demonstrates just how much human suffering is contained in the word translated here as "overrun": καταθέοντας. Niketas' *History* contains countless references to city-sacking—countless because the conquest of cities was so frequent that Niketas, as in the sentence above, simply lumps them all in together, eliding the sacking of multiple cities and the deaths and traumas of innumerable people. Like most Byzantine historiography, Niketas' account is centered around the small circle of powerful figures at the center of imperial high politics, set against the backdrop of the great mass of ordinary people. And yet, in one remarkable narrative sequence during the 1204 Sack of Constantinople, Niketas' narrative shifts dramatically to focus on one otherwise unremarkable refugee family whose experience is substantially like the thousands of other casualties and refugees over whom he passes in silence elsewhere in the *History*. This makes sense, however, since that family was none other than Niketas' own, and the refugee at the center of that narrative is none other than Niketas himself. In this, his narrative forms a kind of hybrid: historiography proper, modeled on older and earlier Byzantine sources on the one hand,[3] and the more recent genres of witness literature and the Komnenian novels on the other, with the form of the narrative shaped in large part by the author's relation to the events he describes.

Niketas explicitly identifies this in his prefatory remarks as one aspect of his principles of selection: "This history will touch only briefly upon the reign of John, who succeeded Alexios to the throne, but will not dwell long thereon as it will on succeeding events. Since I was not an eyewitness of that which I have recorded, I could not describe these events extensively" (ἐν κεφαλαιώδεσι δ' ἐπιτομαῖς τὰ κατὰ τὸν αὐτοκράτορα Ἰωάννην τὸ ἱστορεῖν διηγήσεται, ὃς Ἀλεξίῳ διάδοχος γεγένηται τῆς ἀρχῆς, οὐδ' ἐμβραδυνεῖ ταῖς κατ' αὐτὸν ἀφηγήσεσιν, ὥσπερ ἐν τοῖς ἐφεξῆς ἐργάσεται λόγοις, οἷα καὶ ἡμῶν μὴ τὰ τοῖς ὀφθαλμοῖς ἐπὶ τῷδε παρειλημμένα συγγραφομένων κἀντεῦθεν μηδ' ἐπιτάδην ἐχόντων ταῦτα διεξιέναι).[4] The narration of the past, Niketas suggests, depends upon the

---

[3] For which, see Urbainczyk (2018: 59–80) and Simpson (2013a).

[4] Chon. *Hist.* 4.

author's positionality: that to which he is eyewitness will be treated differently than that which he himself observed and experienced; the closer in time and space the events are to him, the more detailed narration they merit. This distinction between the witness and the historian is particularly significant for examining Niketas' *History*, which is not a single unified work, but rather the result of what Alicia Simpson calls an "elaborate 'editorial' procedure which spanned decades and was influenced, if not defined, by the circumstances and purpose of the author at each distinctive phase of the composition."[5] By "circumstances and purpose," Simpson means the dramatic change in fortune that marked Niketas' life and, consequently, his vision of the past and his narration of that vision.

Simpson traces three main families of manuscripts: (b)revior, (a)uctior, and LO. b "is an older and shorter version of the text" much of which was written, Simpson demonstrates, before the fall of Constantinople (1-535/2).[6] During this period, Niketas held the post of logothetes ton sekreton, which "theoretically speaking [...] placed Niketas in charge of the entire civil service and situated him at the head of the senate."[7] Niketas had at least two residences, including one that he describes as "incomparable in beauty and immense in size" (ἄμαχος τῷ κάλλει καὶ τῷ μεγέθει μέγιστος).[8] LO and what she calls "b-after 1204," by contrast, were written in the immediate aftermath of the conquest of the city, which turned Niketas into a refugee. Finally, the a manuscript, which Simpson speculates was written between 1215 and the author's probable death in 1217,[9] represents the author's attempt, at the end of his life, to perform a fundamental revision from beginning to end. This revision was driven in large part by the author's own experience as a victim of conquest and his subsequent decade and a half living as "an impoverished and embittered

---

[5] Simpson (2013a: 68). A near-verbatim version of the piece was published as Simpson (2006).

[6] Simpson (2013a: 70). For a more detailed summary, see Simpson (2004: 32): "The original Niketastext has five distinct phases of composition: 1) 1-535/2 original version of b; 2) 1-535/2 b + 535/3-582/46 LO; 3) 1-535/2 b + 535/3-583/36 + 585/58-646/64 + 647, 1-655/65 from LO from 535/3-655/65 provisionally revised; 4) 1-535/2 b + 535/3-614/7-10 b revised; 5) 1-646 version a".

[7] Simpson (2004: 20); see n. 40 for a detailed bibliography discussing the particulars of the position.

[8] Chon. *Hist.* 587, for which, see Simpson (2004: 20; 2013a: 278).

[9] Simpson (2004: 63).

234   A. J. GOLDWYN

refugee, excluded from an active role in the political affairs of the Empire of Nicaea and writing in the aftermath of 1204," a far cry from his former life at the center of elite politics and wealth.[10]

Indeed, Simpson notes how b-before 1204 introduces its author with the full range of his impressive titles: τοῦ λογοθέτου τῶν σεκρέτων καὶ ἐπὶ τῶν κρίσεων, γεγονόντος δὲ καὶ ἐφόρου καὶ κριτοῦ τοῦ βήλου, γενικοῦ καὶ προκαθημένου τοῦ κοιτῶνος Νικήτα τοῦ Χωνιάτου ἱστορία. In the a-text, however, there are no titles left: "the historical narration of mister Niketas Choniates" (χρονικὴ διήγησις τοῦ Χωνειάτου κῦρ Νικήτα), a mark of how radically different were the positions of the historical author and the self-presentation of the narrator in the text.[11]

Niketas uses a mode of ostensibly impersonal objective narrativity, what might be described as a historical mode, to describe the events that happened to other people, and a subjective and personal mode, that of the witness, to describe similar events when they happened to him. Examining the difference between these two modes of narration within the same work can elucidate the different rhetorical strategies that define both genres and, perhaps more importantly, how these rhetorical strategies and the positionality of the author relative to the events he describes conceal and reveal different aspects of the past.

Other than that they were overrun, for instance, Niketas tells us nothing more about the fate of the cities throughout Phrygia and along the Maeander, much less of the people who inhabited them. And yet, during the course of the campaign with which the work opens and throughout the *History* as a whole, Niketas narrates the costs and consequences of being conquered at various levels of detail and, taken together, such fragmentary accounts offer a comprehensive picture of the experience of being conquered. At the most general level, Niketas does not even name the cities throughout Phrygia and along the Maeander which were pillaged. Niketas' meticulous attention to detail where he wants suggests that he could have named these cities had he wanted to, but to his mind, they did not rise to the level of narratability. And yet, as the previous chapters have shown, witness literature can show us exactly what is entailed in the word "overrunning" at the level of the scene: the fate of the peoples in Phrygia and along the Maeander are no different than those of John

[10] Simpson (2004: 70).
[11] Simpson (2004: 37–38).

4 THE REFUGEE AS HISTORIAN: NIKETAS CHONIATES ...   235

Kaminiates, Eustathios of Thessaloniki, the fictional protagonists of the Komnenian novels, and even of Niketas himself.

For instance, in his account of John's defeat of the Patzinaks in 1123, Niketas writes: "The wagon folk fell by the thousands, and their palisaded camps were seized as plunder. The captives were beyond number" (κατὰ χιλιοστύας τοίνυν πίπτει τὸ ἁμαξόβιον καὶ διαρπάζονται χάρακες· τὸ δὲ συλληφθὲν δορυάλωτον καὶ ἀριθμοῦ κρεῖττον ὁρᾶται).[12] Thus, included in this description is the seizing of plunder as well as the taking of captives, two elements that reappear time and time again in the *History* and the experience of which was dealt with at length in Eustathios' and Kaminiates' accounts. In 1123, John set out against the Serbs, here called Tribaloi, "And carrying away from there plunder beyond measure and heaping countless spoils upon the army, he transferred the captive part of the population to the East" (καὶ λείαν ἐκεῖθεν ἐλάσας οὐ σταθμητὴν καὶ πλείστων ὠφελειῶν ἐμπλήσας τὸ στράτευμα ἐς τὴν ἕω διαβιβάζει τὸ τοῦ πλήθους αἰχμάλωτον).[13] This account builds on the capture of plunder and the taking of captives, though here Niketas offers the added detail that the captive populations were sent into exile, forcibly resettled far from their homelands. But much human suffering is condensed in these clauses; again, Kaminiates' and Eustathios' accounts hover like a shadow over Niketas' narrative—implicitly in the case of the former and explicitly in the case of the latter—allowing a ground-level view of the events that Niketas surveys, so to speak, from the air.

Thus, when Niketas speaks of "carrying away from there plunder beyond measure," Eustathios' account shows exactly what that looked like when he describes the Latins torturing the homeowners to find their hidden valuables.[14] When Niketas writes of "transfer[ring] the captive population, he elides the heart-wrenching scenes Kaminiates describes in the harbor of Thessaloniki and on the slave ships themselves.[15]

Even the events leading up to the battle itself suggest the differences between the aims and methods of these two narrative modes. On the one hand, Niketas depicts the strategic maneuvering of the Byzantine elites: "The emperor, first resorting to a stratagem, dispatched

---

[12] Chon. *Hist.* 16.

[13] Chon. *Hist.* 16.

[14] Eust. *capta Thess.* 132, for which, see above, p. 22.

[15] Kam. *ex. Thess.* 35–36 and elsewhere.

236   A. J. GOLDWYN

Patzinak-speaking envoys to attempt to persuade the enemy to come to terms" (Τὰ μὲν οὖν πρῶτα στρατηγικῇ μεθόδῳ χρώμενος ὁ βασιλεὺς δι'ἀποστολῆς ὁμογλώττων τοῦ τῶν Σκυθῶν ἀποπειρᾶται στρατεύματος, εἴ πως ἐς ὁμολογίας ξυμβαῖεν).[16] While he narrates the response of the Patzinak leaders, he is silent on the actual contents of their discussion, noting only that "Those chiefs he won over were greeted with every kindness" (ἐφελκυσάμενος οὖν τόνδε τὸν τρόπον τινὰς τῶν παρ' αὐτοῖς τὰ πρῶτα φερόντων πᾶσαν φιλοφροσύνην ἐπ' αὐτοῖς ἐπιδείκνυται).[17] John Kaminiates, on the other hand, depicts these events from the perspective of those about to be attacked, and his account shows little interest in political and military machinations; rather, he is concerned with the affective states of those in the city: he notes their fear, anxiety, and inability to determine clear information upon the arrival of enemy emissaries:

> It was precisely at this juncture that a messenger from the ruler of the Roman world, the most pious Leo, arrived post haste with new of the approach of the barbarians [...] Once these dreadful tidings had been received, confused and panic-stricken rumours were rife throughout the city. But though, at first, the unaccustomed and terrifying character of the event filled our ears with consternation, we nevertheless resolved to ensure our own safety [...] each man's mind was weighed down by all the usual anxieties aroused by military inexperience.

> ἐν τούτοις γὰρ ὄντων ἡμῶν ἦκέτις ταχυδρόμος ἄγγελος ἀπὸ τοῦ κρατοῦντος τὰ τῶν Ῥωμαίων σκῆπτρα, Λέοντος τοῦ φιλευσεβοῦς ἄνακτος, τὴν ἔφοδον τῶν βαρβάρων [...] ταύτης οὖν ἀγγελθείσης τῆς πονηρᾶς ἀγγελίας, θροῦς μὲν ἐγένετο κατὰ πᾶσαν τὴν πόλιν καὶ φόβος καὶ τάραχος, ἀσυνήθους πράγματος καὶ φοβεροῦ ταῖς ἀκοαῖς ἡμῶν ἐν ἀρχαῖς προσπεσόντος, ἐβουλευσάμεθα δ' ὅμως τὴν οἰκείαν περιποιήσασθαι σωτηρίαν [...] πλὴν ἔκαμνε μὲν ὁ λογισμὸς ἑκάστου καὶ ταῖς ἄλλαις μερίμναις τῆς ἀπειρίας τοῦ μάχεσθαι.[18]

Where Niketas focuses on high politics, Kaminiates focuses on the psychological interiority of the common inhabitants of the city, two different perspectives that represent the authors' differing positionality with regard

---

[16] Chon. *Hist.* 14. Slightly modified from Magoulias, who renders "εἴ πως ἐς ὁμολογίας ξυμβαῖεν" as "agree to withdraw" rather than "to come to terms."

[17] Chon. *Hist.* 14.

[18] Kam. *ex. Thess.* 16.2–4.

4 THE REFUGEE AS HISTORIAN: NIKETAS CHONIATES ...   237

to the events. For Niketas, whose interest at this point is imperial decision-making and military tactics, the actual impact of the negotiations on the inhabitants is irrelevant. Kaminiates, by contrast, shows how each twist and turn in the negotiations has a significant emotional cost for those most directly affected by them; he records their various shifts in hope and despair, determination and resignation, fear and resolve.

These same narrative consequences are evident in the narration of the actual engagement. Niketas writes:

> John gathered the Roman forces, equipping them with the best arms possible, and marched against them. [...] Setting out from the region of Beroē (where they were encamped), John engaged the Patzinaks in combat in the morning twilight, and there ensued one of the most frightful and terrifying battles ever fought.

> ἔξεισι κατ' αὐτῶν τὰς Ῥωμαϊκὰς ἀθροίσας δυνάμεις καὶ ὡς ἐνῆν ὁπλισάμενος γενναιότατα. [...] Ἄρας τοίνυν ἐκ τῶν τῆς Βερόης μερῶν (ἐκεῖσε γὰρ ἐστρατοπεδεύετο) κνεφαῖος τοῖς Σκύθαις συρρήγνυται. γίνεται τοίνυν φρικαλέα τις συμβολὴ καὶ καταπληκτικωτέρα τῶν πώποτε μάχη συνίσταται.[19]

Niketas here drastically compresses the amount of narrative space allotted to the march from the Byzantine camp to where the battle took place, thus also requiring him to omit the experiences of the Patzinaks to the passage of time during these last moments.

In this regard, too, the contrast with Kaminiates is illustrative. Over the course of several pages, Kaminiates describes the vicissitudes of fear and hope experienced by the citizens of Thessaloniki between the time the Abbasids set out against them and the time they arrive. The citizens of Thessaloniki are relieved by the arrival of a Byzantine military officer, Petronas, who begins to fortify the city; "but just when the fence designed to cross the seabed had reached a point somewhere around the middle of the threatened area and our fears were beginning to evaporate, along came another envoy" (Ἤδη γὰρ περὶ τὰ μέσα που τοῦ κινδυνώδους τόπου πεφθακότος τοῦ τοιούτου διαποντίου φραγμοῦ καὶ πᾶσαν ἡμῶν ὑπόνοιαν ἐπίφοβον καὶ πονηρὰν ὑποτέμνοντος, ἦκέ τις ἕτερος).[20] This Leo relieves Petronas of duty and begins a new defensive scheme, and "a strong

---

[19] Chon. *Hist.* 14.

[20] Kam. *ex. Thess.* 18.1.

238 A. J. GOLDWYN

sense of impending disaster was clearly conveyed to us citizens" (τοσοῦτον ἐφαίνετο τὸ λεῖπον τοῖς πολίταις ἡμῖν παντὸς κινδύνου καθυπεμφαῖνον ὑπόνοιαν).[21] Their hopes are restored by the arrival of yet another leader, Niketas, who ultimately betrays the Thessalonians, and "thus we were deceived in the hopes which we had entertained of our Sklavene allies. [...] Our complete inexperience of warfare and lack of previous training made the enemy attack an object of limitless fear and trepidation" (Οὕτω δὲ τῆς ἀπὸ τῶν συμμάχων Σκλαβήνων ἀποβουκοληθέντες ἐλπίδος [...] τὸ μηδεμίαν πεῖραν πολέμου ἐνυπάρχειν ἡμῖν μηδὲ προαποκειμένην ἔχειν τὴν περὶ τούτου μελέτην φοβεράν τινα καὶ ἐκπλήξεως γέμουσαν τὴν ἔφοδον αὐτῶν ἐνεποίει).[22] All of this and more takes place during the brief period of time between when the Thessalonians first hear the messenger's report of the Abbasid fleet and the day the fleet actually arrives. Of the emotions and feelings of the men and women (if there were any, since it was a raiding army) in the Patzinak camp, Niketas is silent, just as he is silent about the anticipatory dread of the men and women "throughout Phrygia and along the Maeander" and all the other people killed, enslaved, or exiled during the course of John's campaign. While these events may not matter to the historian, who is interested in the broadest temporal and geographic encapsulation of Byzantine history, they are of the utmost importance to the actual people who participated in these events—indeed, as irrelevant as the life of a John Kaminiates is to a Niketas Choniates, just as irrelevant is the broad scope of Byzantine history to the average citizen awaiting the impending arrival of an enemy army. Thus, though he calls it "one of the most frightful and terrifying battles ever fought," Niketas' minimal apportionment of narrative space to the Battle of Beroia is perhaps a better marker of its broader significance to Niketas' conception of Byzantine history. Kaminiates, by contrast, has less emphasis on the broader political stakes, instead focusing on an affective vocabulary of fear and hope.

As if to emphasize his indifference to human life, shortly after his description of the conquest of the Tribaloi, Niketas describes the counterattacks of the Hungarians, who "crossed the Istros and sacked Braničevo, where they tore down the walls, whose stones they transported to Zevgminon. They also plundered Sardica" (τὸν Ἴστρον διαβάντες οἱ Οὖννοι

---

[21] Kam. *ex. Thess.* 18.5.
[22] Kam. *ex. Thess.* 21.1. Translation slightly modified.

4 THE REFUGEE AS HISTORIAN: NIKETAS CHONIATES ... 239

τήν τε Βρανίτζοβαν ἐξεπόρθησαν, κατερείψαντες τὰ τείχη καὶ τοὺς λίθους μετενεγκάμενοι εἰς τὸ Ζεύγμινον, καὶ τὴν Σαρδικὴν ἐληΐσαντο).[23] This account of the conquest of these cities offers no details into the actual experience of those who lived there; indeed, the (narrated) fate of the building stones is more important than the (unnarrated) fate of the people. By contrast, Niketas' account of John's 1135 conquest of Gangra offers a closer look at what he elides with such generalities. He describes how,

> resorting to siege tactics because the wall appeared vulnerable, they [the Byzantines] kept up a constant barrage of missiles. But John was unable to make any progress because the ramparts were sturdy and the defenders put up such fierce resistance, so he ordered the stone missiles be directed away from the walls and hurled instead against the houses which could be seen from the hilltops. [... D]ischarging round and light stones which seemed to be flying rather than being shot from engines of war, [they] shattered the houses; the inhabitants within fell to their knees and were killed by the caving-in of the roofs. As a result it was no longer safe to walk the streets nor to remain indoors.

> εἶτα τειχομαχίαις χρησάμενος, ἧπερ ἦν ἐπίμαχος ὁ περίβολος, συνεχῶς ἔτυπτετοῦτον. μὴ προχωροῦντος δὲ τοῦ ἔργου διὰ τὴν τῶν ἐπάλξεων ὀχυρότητακαὶ τὸ ἐπὶ πολὺ ἐκθύμως ὑπέχειν τοὺς ἐναντίους, βάλλειν τὰ τείχη παρεὶς κατὰ τῶν οἰκιῶν ἐγνώκει διασφενδονᾶν τοὺς λίθους, προφαινομένων ἐκτῶν ἔξωθεν κολωνῶν [. ...] οἱ γοῦν ἐπὶ τῶν μηχανῶν λίθους στρογγύλους καὶ κούφους διὰ τὸ εὐσύνοπτον ἐς ὅτι πορρωτάτω διαφιέντες, ὡς δοκεῖν ἵπτασθαι τούτους, οὐκ ἀπὸ μηχανημάτων προΐεσθαι, τοὺς δόμους κατέσειον· οἱ δ' ἐπὶ γόνυ κλινόμενοι καὶ τοὺς ὀρόφους διαλυόμενοι τὸ ἐνοικοῦν πλῆθος ἀπώλλυον, ὡς ἐντεῦθεν εἶναι καὶ τὴν ἐν ταῖς ἀμφόδοις ἐπισφαλῆ πάροδον καὶ τὸ ἔνδον ἡσυχῇ καθῆσθαι πάντη ἀσύμφορον.[24]

These are the kinds of experiences common to the men and women who were victims of Byzantine sieges, and those who were in cities that were plundered, but this image of cowering defenseless citizens dying in their own homes adds a new dimension to the horrors of the kind of warfare that is common-place in the *History*. After his victory, John expels "the Turkish hordes" (τὸ πολὺ τῶν Περσῶν) living in Gangra and then departs,

---

[23] Chon. *Hist.* 17.
[24] Chon. *Hist.* 20.

240 A. J. GOLDWYN

only to have the Turks counter-attack and "starve the city into submission" (λιμῷ παρεστήσατο).[25] Again, Niketas mentions starvation only in passing; it is left to John Kaminiates and Eustathios of Thessaloniki to actually describe what that means: the physical trauma of hunger pangs; the psychological trauma of eating food mixed with excrement; the particular ways in which food distribution varied among the different economic, social, and ethnic groups within a besieged city; and the other associated horrors they describe. These difficulties only become part of Niketas' own narrative when they happen to him.

One of the few examples in which Niketas offers an anecdote about the unique manifestation of the general plight of victims of conquest occurs during the 1165 Sack of Zevgminon:

> One of the inhabitants of this city, not a man of the rabble and vulgar mob but a rich and eminent nobleman, took pride in possessing a wife who was both graceful and very shapely. Seeing her being dragged away to be violated by one of the Roman soldiers and unable to protect her from being tyrannized, or to repel force by force and turn aside this iniquitous carnal passion, he resolved on an action that was more noble than daring and unlawful, but suited to the present fateful circumstances: he thrust his sword, which he carried with him, through the entrails of his beloved. Thus the irrational desire of the lawless lover who lusted madly after the woman was extinguished, since the cause was no more; and this truly wretched woman, who had been so passionately desired, was deprived of the gladdening light of life.

> εἷς δὲ τῶν οἰκητόρων ἐκείνης τῆς πόλεως, καὶ οὗτος οὐ τῶν συγκλύδων καὶ τῶν συρφάκων ἀλλὰ τῶν πλούτῳ λαμπρῶν καὶ γένει ἐπισήμῳ διαπρεπῶν, ἀστεῖον τὸ εἶδος ηὔχει γύναιον καὶ σφόδρα καλὸν τὴνμορφήν. ὁρῶν δὲ παρά του τῶν Ῥωμαίων εἰς ὕβριν ἑλκόμενον καὶ μὴ ἔχων ἐπαμῦναι τυραννουμένῳ ἢ βίᾳ τὴν βίαν ὠθῆσαι καὶ στῆσαι τὸνἄδικον ἐκεῖνον ἔρωτα βουλεύεται βουλὴν οὐχ ἥκιστα γενναίαν ἢ τολμηρὰν καὶ ἀθέμιτον καὶ τῷ τῆς τύχης ἐνεστῶτι κατάλληλον· διελαύνει τῶν σπλάγχνων τῆς φιλτάτης ὃν ἔφερεν ἀκινάκην. οὐκοῦν ὁ μὲν τῇ γυναικὶ ἐπιμαινόμενος ἄθεσμος ἐκεῖνος ἐραστὴς τὴν ἄλογον ἐμάρανεν ἔφεσιν οὐκέτι ὄντος τοῦ ὑπεκκαύματος, τὴν δὲ σχετλίαν τῷ ὄντι ἐρωμένην τὸ ἦμαρ ἔλιπε τὸ εὐφρόσυνον.[26]

---

[25] Chon. *Hist.* 21.
[26] Chon. *Hist.* 134–135.

4 THE REFUGEE AS HISTORIAN: NIKETAS CHONIATES ... 241

In the entirety of the *History* before the account of the Sack of Constantinople, this is the only moment in which Niketas takes a granular enough look at the experience of an ordinary civilian woman; indeed, the intimacy of the moment stands in sharp contrast to the perfunctory, almost formulaic ways in which Niketas describes the large groups of people captured, killed, or exiled during the campaigns he describes. And yet, it is significant in this regard that the only individuated woman remains unnamed (as does her husband) and she is only individuated because of the unique conclusion (her husband kills her) of her very common impending fate (rape by conquering soldiers). Theresa Urbainczyk sees this as part of Niketas' broader diminishment of women in the *History* ("For Niketas then women are there to be admired for their beauty and their virtue, not to be actors in the historical drama"),[27] and she also rightly compares this episode to Niketas' own experience fleeing Constantinople when he turns back and saves a girl from a similar fate.[28] While Urbainczyk is right to note that this scene is consistent with Niketas' treatment of women throughout the *History*, it is also consistent with his general indifference toward civilian suffering in warfare generally. It also, moreover, demonstrates the importance of considering the Komnenian novels as models and comparators for historiographical texts. As in the novels, women's narratives are only foregrounded insofar as they bear on their sexuality: just as the Charkiles and Dosikles fear the rape of their beloveds, so too does this husband fear the rape of his wife. And yet, as works of imaginative fiction, the novels give a glimpse into the experiences of the women themselves: both Rhodanthe and Drosilla are given some amount of direct discourse to speak their own laments and articulate their own fears. The reverse, however, is also true. The generic requirement of novels to have a happy ending with the central couple married and reunited with their families means that the authors of the novels were unable to narrate lovers' deaths. Historiography, having no such constraints, narrates the death of this woman, and thus this episode shows what the novels cannot. Novels can narrate individual experience but not the individual experience of death; history can narrate death, but not individual experience.

---

[27] Urbainczyk (2018: 40).

[28] For which, see below, pp. 232 and 267.

Both the frequency with which such episodes of city-sacking are narrated and the generality of such descriptions reveal the ideology and sympathies which underlie Niketas' historiographical principles of selection: he is concerned with the military and political consequences of war and the experiences of its elites and is ultimately indifferent to the experiences of those whose lives are affected by these political and military decisions. As can be seen from these various iterations, moreover, each instance of city-sacking is narrated at various levels of detail. With the exception of the climactic sack of Constantinople in 1204, however, what unites these episodes is the level of generality with which Niketas narrates them: in collating just a few of the instances of city-sacking that occur in the opening section of the work, a holistic picture comes into view of what the word "overrun" actually means: starvation and destruction during the siege, looting, captivity and exile after the conquest, with the particular horror of sexual violence against women. Though Niketas often narrates the actions of individual soldiers and, especially, military and political leaders, he never describes the plights of any specific, named, individuated people from among the masses whose lives are ended or upended by the ceaseless tide of city-sacking he describes. Where the rhetoric of witnesses like John Kaminiates is filled with affective vocabulary, Niketas' own positionality allows him to retain a rhetorical indifference to these aspects of the events he describes.

4.2   The Historian and the Witness: Niketas and Eustathios on the Sack of Thessaloniki

The difference between the way a historian treats an iteration of conquest and the way a witness does can be seen in the parallel treatment of the same event by writers who embody each of these different positionalities. Niketas' description of the 1185 sack of Thessaloniki by the Normans, on the one hand, and Eustathios' eyewitness account on the other, demonstrate these two poles. Since Niketas explicitly cites Eustathios as his source for these events, moreover, they can also show how the historian adapts witness testimony into a different generic framework by stripping

4 THE REFUGEE AS HISTORIAN: NIKETAS CHONIATES ...   243

away the personal elements of the narrative.[29] Indeed, it seems as though Eustathios himself understood how these two differing modes of narration would produce, in the terms of the historian, different accounts of the same historical event or, in the terms of the narratologist, different stories from the same fabula. When the Latins enter the city and begin their campaign of plunder and killing, Eustathios writes:

> In such a situation a man 'unstuck' and 'unstabbed' should have viewed the battle from some point on high and should have taken note of the events while 'the god warded off the force of the darts;' for a man who was entangled in this disaster, and whose attention was for the most part concentrated on his own affairs, would not have been able to describe the whole of it with exactness, but only certain incidents of which he had knowledge and in which he was involved in one way or another.

> Καὶ ἐχρῆν μὲν ἐν τούτοις ἄβλητόν τινα καὶ ἀνούτατον ἐκ μετεώρου ποθὲν τὴν μάχην σκέπτεσθαι καὶ παρασημαίνεσθαι, τοῦ Θεοῦ βελέων ἀπερύκοντος ἐρωήν· ἄνθρωπος γάρ, ἐνδεθεὶς τοιούτῳ κακῷ καὶ πρὸς ἑαυτῷ τὰ μάλιστα τὸν νοῦν ἔχων, οὐκ ἂν σχοίη ἀκριβῶς τὸ πᾶν συγγράψασθαι, πλὴν εἰς ὅσον τὰ καίρια, ὧν τε ἔμαθε καὶ οἷς αὐτὸς πολυτρόπως ἐπέστησεν.[30]

Eustathios thus makes the claim for two different perspectives: that of the historian, who is able to produce "from on high" (ἐκ μετεώρου ποθὲν) a more synoptic and comprehensive view of the events, and that of the eyewitness—the "man who was entangled in this disaster" (ἄνθρωπος γάρ, ἐνδεθεὶς τοιούτῳ κακῷ). But Eustathios also signals the different epistemological foundations of these two kinds of people: he does not suggest that one has a better knowledge of the truth, only that they each can see different aspects more clearly. The eyewitness, he writes, "would not have been able to describe the whole of it with exactness" (οὐκ ἂν σχοίη ἀκριβῶς τὸ πᾶν συγγράψασθαι) thus implying that the man who stands at some distance from the event—the historian, perhaps—could. But within this, he does carve out a special sphere of knowledge for the eyewitness; if Eustathios won't allow that the eyewitness can see the whole of the

---

[29] Chon. *Hist.* 307. For a discussion of the influence of Eustathios on Niketas, see Simpson (2013b: 225–229), who focuses largely on the depiction of the historical information and presentation of emperors (and Andronikos in particular) rather than the account of the sack of Thessaloniki.

[30] Eust. *capta Thess.* 106.

244   A. J. GOLDWYN

event, he does explicitly allow its opposite: he can see with exactness "only certain incidents of which he had knowledge and in which he was involved in one way or another" (πλὴν εἰς ὅσον τὰ καίρια, ὧν τε ἔμαθε καὶ οἷς αὐτὸς πολυτρόπως ἐπέστησεν). Thus, if the eyewitness cannot see everything, he nevertheless has a privileged view of certain aspects—those he experienced—to which the viewer from on high has no access. The differing stories within the same fabula that Niketas and Eustathios thus produce are not, therefore, in competition with one another as regards objective facts but are in a complementary and productive tension at the levels through which the primary narrator-focalizer conveys his vision of the events to their respective audiences.

This tension is present from the very moments after the city falls. Niketas writes that

> the city capitulated after putting up a brief resistance. The evils which ensued were another succession of Trojan woes surpassing even the calamitous events of tragedy, for every house was robbed of its contents, no dwelling was spared, no passageway was free of despoilers, no hiding place was long hidden. No piteous creature was shown any pity; neither was any heed paid to the entreaty, but the sword passed through all things, and the death-dealing wound ended all wrath.

> ἐπ' ὀλίγον ἀντισχοῦσα τοῖς ἐχθροῖς ὑπέκυψε. Τὰ δ' ἐπὶ τούτοις γεγενημένα ἄλλη τίς ἐστιν Ἰλιὰς καὶ τραγικὰς ὑπερβαίνουσι συμφοράς· ἅπας γὰρ οἶκος τῶν ἐνόντων ἠρήμωτο, οὐδ' ἦν οἰκία τις σώζουσα, οὐ στενωπὸς τῶν ἀναιρούντων λυτρούμενος, οὐ κατάδυσις ἐπὶ πολὺ ἀποκρύπτουσα. ἀλλ' οὐδὲ σχῆμα ἠλεεῖτο ἐλεεινόν, οὐδ' ἐδυσωπεῖτο δυσώπησις, ἀλλὰ διὰ πάντων ἐχώρει τὸ ξίφος καὶ θυμοῦ λῆξις ἦν ἡ ἀπάγουσα τοῦ βίου πληγή.[31]

Within the context of the *History*, this is a fairly conventional if somewhat more elaborate description. As presented, however, it offers a vision of city-sacking in which no particular individual actually perceives, or, in narratological terms, without an embodied primary narrator-focalizer. In this, it contrasts with Eustathios' narrative, which emphasizes the phenomenological aspects of the conquest focalized through his perceptions, feelings, and experience. After the fall of the city, for instance, Eustathios notes that "It was not easy to recognise among them even

---

[31] Chon. *Hist.* 299.

4 THE REFUGEE AS HISTORIAN: NIKETAS CHONIATES … 245

a dear friend" (Ἦν οὖν ἔργον γνωρίσαι καὶ τὸν πάνυεν τούτοις φίλτατον); "one could go into the churches and observe" (Ἰτέον ἐπὶ τὰς ἐκκλησίας καὶ θεωρητέον τοὺς τοιούτους); "One could also survey the food which each person ate, and see there was nothing to be got" (Σκοπητέον καὶ τὰς ἑκάστων τροφὰς καὶ γνωστέον ὡς ἐκ τῶν συμφυλετῶν μὲν οὐκ ἦν).[32] All of these expressions foreground the visual and experiential nature of the narration using focalizing words of perception (γνωρίσαι, θεωρητέον, σκοπητέον, γνωστέον).

Where Niketas has the city fall in a sentence, Eustathios describes it at length through rich sensory images: "That day was no longer a day in its appearance, but rather it resembled night, and it seemed to suffer and to bear a gloomy appearance because of the things which it saw" (Καὶ ἦν ἰδεῖν τὴν ἡμέραν τότε οὐκέθ' ἡμέραν, ἀλλὰ νυκτὶ ἐοικυῖαν καὶ οἷον παθαινομένην καὶ σκυθρωπάζουσαν ἐφ' οἷς ἑώρα) he writes.[33] The use of perceptual comparative figures—"in its appearance," ἰδεῖν; "resembled night" (νυκτὶ ἐοικυῖαν), "the things it saw" (οἷς ἑώρα)—is also significant in this regard, since Eustathios uses visual language to convey a subjectively truthful sense of the experience of being there rather than just, as Niketas, the seemingly objective truth that the city fell.[34]

In this, Eustathios seems to be following the plan originally laid out in his introduction; while he concedes that the eyewitness "would not add ornaments to his language" (καλλύνειν τοὺς λόγους) he does allow for the possibility that "he will make use of other narrative techniques with restraint" (τὰ ἄλλα δὲ συγγραφικὰ εἴδη σωφρόνως μεταχειριεῖται).[35] For Eustathios, the use of what he calls "a suitably elevated rhetoric" (μεγαλείως ἀφηγεῖσθαι) can allow for different kinds of narrative strategies: "Our account will sometimes be written simply when this is appropriate, and at other times in a more polished manner" (καὶ πῆ μὲν ἀφελῶς, ὡς ἐχρῆν, πῆ δὲ καὶ γλαφυρώτερον).[36] Thus, Eustathios allows for the use of figurative language when it is appropriate.

[32] Eust. *capta Thess.* 124.

[33] Eust. *capta Thess.* 104.

[34] Eust. *capta Thess.* 104.47, for which, see above p. 1.

[35] Eust. *capta Thess.* 2.26–28. Perhaps more literally "would not beautify his language," a sentiment shared among other writers of historical trauma; Aharon Appelfeld, for instance, wrote that "any embellishment or sweetening was jarring" in Holocaust narratives (Appelfeld 1988: 89).

[36] Eust. *capta Thess.* 4.

246   A. J. GOLDWYN

Though he doesn't mention under what circumstances he thinks such rhetoric should be used, the passages in which he uses an elevated style demonstrate his principles of composition in this way, as can be seen from the passage in which he describes the moment of the city's fall. Eustathios continues in this same style:

> A thick mist spread over it, like a cloud of dust raised up by a whirlwind or by the hooves of animals in their limitless multitude, so that one might say that the sun was ashamed to shine because the flashing of the weapons outshone it.

> Ὁμίχλη γὰρ αὐτὴν βαθεῖα ἐπάχυνεν, ὡσεὶ καὶ ἐκ κονιορτοῦ, ὃν ἢ τυφὼς αἴρει ἢ πόδες ζῴων, ἅπερ ἀριθμὸς μετρεῖ ἀπειροπληθής, ὡς εἶναι εἰπεῖν ὀκνεῖν λάμπειν τὸν ἥλιον οἷς αἱ τῶν ὅπλων ὑπερηύγαζον αὐτὸν λαμπρότητες.[37]

Eustathios here offers two similes, comparing the thick mist to a cloud raised up by a whirlwind or by running animals. In each of these cases, as in the previous example, Eustathios uses figurative language to try and help his audience, who not only was not in Thessaloniki at the time but also has likely never experienced anything like being in a conquered city at all, visualize and understand an unfamiliar thing through comparison with a familiar one with which it shares certain features (in this case, the dark sky and mist). Eustathios' use of the conditional "one might say" (ὡς εἶναι εἰπεῖν) here serves a similar purpose: since the audience cannot understand the experience being described, Eustathios attempts to rephrase it in a way, which may be familiar to his audience.

He continues with this strategy in the next sentence:

> It might also be said, as a parody of the ancient Muse, that the city like a ship 'travelled over the sea for eighteen days' and then 'on the nineteenth there appeared the shadowy mountains' by which the sun of our life was blocked off as they cast a black shadow covering us, as the psalmists says.

> παρῳδῆσαι δὲ καὶ ἐκ παλαιᾶς Μούσης «ὀκτωκαίδεκα μὲν πλέεν ἤματα ποντοπορεύον» τὸ τῆς πόλεως σκάφος, «ἐννεακαιδεκάτῃ δ' ἐφάνη οὔρεα

---

[37] Eust. *capta Thess.* 104.

4 THE REFUGEE AS HISTORIAN: NIKETAS CHONIATES ... 247

σκιόεντα», δι' ὧν ὁ τῆς ζωῆς ἡμῖν ἥλιος ἀποτειχιζόμενος ἐμέλαινε σκιὰν ἐπικαλύψουσαν ἡμᾶς ψαλμικῶς.[38]

Here, too, Eustathios uses another rhetorical technique to try and help the audience imagine a phenomenon so far outside the realm of their own lived experience. Whereas previously he used figurative language and indirect discourse, here he uses citations of other familiar literary sources with the goal of creating in his readers the same emotional response to his narrative as they felt in those. Eustathios' frequent allusions to Homer thus offer the *Iliad* and the *Odyssey* as familiar literary prisms of falling cities through which the members of his audience, who were not present at the fall Thessaloniki, could understand the event. This seems to have been an effective method, for tit is also through the Homeric intertext that Niketas understands these events himself when he writes that "the evils which ensued were another succession of Trojan woes."[39]

Nor does Eustathios make only a visual appeal; in describing those initial moments, he writes: "The shouting of a little while before, the cries of the battle and the din which it causes, were no longer heard; rather, to adapt the words of the psalm, there was no shouting in their number. You would have seen the air empty of birds" (Οἱ δὲ χθὲς καὶ πρῴην ἀλαλαγμοὶ καὶ αἱ κατὰ πόλεμον βοαὶ καὶ ὁ ἐντεῦθεν θροῦς οὐκέτ' ἦσαν, ἀλλ' ἀντιστρέψαντα τὸ ψαλμικόν, οὐκ ἦν ἀλαλαγμὸς ἐν τοῖς ἡμῶν πλήθεσιν. Εἶδες δ' ἂν καὶ ὀρνέων πετομένων κενὸν τὸν ἀέρα).[40] The auditory and visual contrasts—the shouting of the previous day, the silence of today; the sight of birds yesterday and the absence of birds today—create an affective atmosphere of ominous foreboding that grounds the audience in the experiential sensory phenomena he experienced augmented by focalizers of perception such as "were no longer heard" (θροῦς οὐκέτ' ἦσαν) and "you would have seen" (Εἶδες δ' ἂν).

Eustathios closes this section by writing "so much for this addition to our account of events, which should not be considered superfluous" (καὶ τοιοῦτον μὲν καὶ τοῦτο, παραρριφὲν οὐ περιττῶς εἰς συγγραφήν).[41] The preceding passage is not the stuff of history proper, and so Eustathios feels

---

[38] Eust. *capta Thess.* 104.

[39] Chon. *Hist.* 165.

[40] Eust. *capta Thess.* 104.

[41] Eust. *capta Thess.* 104.

248   A. J. GOLDWYN

the need to justify its presence in his narrative, but he also clarifies that it περιττῶς εἰς συγγραφήν, which Melville-Jones translates as "should not be considered superfluous" but, given the emphasis he places on συγγραφή as marking the work as an eyewitness account distinct from history, is perhaps better understood as signifying that the use of metaphors and sensory language should not be considered strange or unusual (περιττῶς) in witness literature (εἰς συγγραφήν).

As this passage contains no historical material—indeed, Niketas does not include any mention of these aspects of the city during its fall—its function cannot be the transmission of factual information. Rather, it is not superfluous, that is to say, it is necessary and essential to the narrative because it attempts to convey experience, what the events looked like, and how the emotional content of those events affected how those who lived through them perceived the world. Eustathios' use of comparative verbs, similes, and quotations from religious and classical literature convey the experience of conquest in a way that Niketas' narrative cannot.

The different narrative modes of history and testimony are perhaps most clearly visible in Niketas' and Eustathios' treatment of the biopolitical aspects of conquest. This is borne out in the differing ways in which Niketas, standing in here for the man who viewed the events from on high, and Eustathios, who was entangled in them himself, narrate the sack of Thessaloniki. When the Latins enter the city, for instance, Niketas offers a familiar description at the general level: "Bursting in upon the sanctuaries with weapons in hand, the enemy slew whoever was in the way, and as sacrificial victims mercilessly slaughtered whomever they seized" (κἂν τοῖς ἱεροῖς γὰρ μεθ' ὅπλων ἐπεισπηδῶντες οἱ ἐναντίοι τὸν ἐν ποσὶν ἀνῄρουν ἀεὶ καὶ ὡς θύματα τοὺς καταλαμβανομένους ἀνηλεῶς ἐκεράϊζον).[42] This is a standard kind of conventional narrative of city-sacking in Niketas' *History*. But this narration at the general level and the inclusion of standard scenes necessarily results in the omission of the variety of individual experiences. Thus while Niketas subsequently writes that "futile was the flight of many to the temples" (κενὴ δὲ καὶ ἡ κατὰ τοὺς ἱεροὺς νεὼς συνδρομὴ τῶν πολλῶν ἐδείκνυτο), he is silent about what happens to those who were not in that many, including Eustathios. Niketas, narrating about a mass of people, cannot distinguish them individually. Eustathios, by contrast, cannot narrate about the mass of people, but shows an aspect of the event

[42] Chon. *Hist.* 299.

4 THE REFUGEE AS HISTORIAN: NIKETAS CHONIATES ...   249

that Niketas can't: "We ourself had given up hope of holding the acropolis" (Ἡμεῖς οὖν τῆς μὲν ἀκροπόλεως ἀπογνόντες) he writes, adding the articulation of the emotional experience that is so central to the experience of the masses of people Niketas describes. Further, Eustathios writes that they had given up this hope "because its water supply had, as it were, gone voyaging with our commander" (διὰ τὴν τοῦ ἐκεῖσε ὕδατος ἐκδημίαν, ἧς ὁδηγὸς ὁ στρατηγὸς γέγονε).[43] Not only does Eustathios tell us that he had lost hope, he also describes why—the lack of water—and in terms that reveal the feelings of betrayal and anger he experienced. Niketas is unable or unwilling to describe why the people fled, what on the ground knowledge they had to inform their decisions, and how their own emotions could shape those decision-making processes.

Perhaps as importantly from the narratological standpoint, Eustathios was not among Niketas' "of the many" (τῶν πολλῶν) who fled to the temples: "We rejected the thought of taking refuge in the holy tomb of the Myrobletes or in an of the other churches, for we could not fail to see that when all the fugitives rushed into them, many would be swept to their deaths in the crush or would suffocate there" (μερίμνης δὲ θέμενοι ἔξω καὶ τὴν εἰς τὸν ἅγιον τάφον τοῦ Μυροβλήτου καταφυγήν, ἔτι δὲ καὶ τὴν εἰς ἑτέρους θείους ναούς, οὐ γὰρ δήπουθεν ἐλάνθανεν ἡμᾶς ὡς, πάντων τῶν φευγόντων ἐν τοῖς τοιούτοις ῥυϊσκομένων, πολλοὶ παρασυρήσονται τοῦ ζῆν ὠθισμοῖς καὶ τοῖς ἐντεῦθεν πνιγμοῖς).[44] Eustathios is able to narrate the observable reality of the moment, to articulate the emotions that informed his decisions. Yet, as he is limited to narrating only what he himself experienced and observed, cannot encompass the entirety of the scene.

Eustathios' narrative, by contrast, follows in great detail the author's own voyage through the city, again emphasizing the sensory and affective aspects of the experience that Niketas elides under "the sword passed through all things, and the death-dealing wound ended all wrath." As he navigates his way through the city, "we observed and suffered innumerable evils which it is a wonder that we survived" (καὶ πολλὰ καὶ μυρία κακὰ καὶ τεθεαμένοι καὶ πεπονθότες, ἐφ᾽ οἷς θαυμαπερίεισιν ἡμᾶς ὅπως

---

[43] Eust. *capta Thess.* 106.

[44] Eust. *capta Thess.* 106.

250 A. J. GOLDWYN

ἀντέσχομεν),[45] with again the emphasis on the visual: "we observed" (τεθεαμένοι).[46]

Other aspects of the biopolitics of conquest similarly demonstrate the difference between the two authors' narratives as a result of their positionality. Niketas writes that during the eight days of the occupation, the Latins

> appropriated the dwellings expelling their masters and depriving them of the treasures stored within, and they also removed their clothing, not even refraining from taking their last undergarments, which conceal what nature has commanded to be covered as unseemly. Nor did they dispense to the masters any morsel of the fruits of their labors into which they had entered, and they made merry all day long. Those who had gathered in the dainties of cuttlefish were left to wander about hungry in the streets, barefoot and without tunic.

> γὰρ οἰκιῶν μόνον τοὺς δεσπότας ἐξήλασαν κα ἰτῶν κειμηλιουμένων ἐντὸς ἀπεστέρησαν αὐτοὶ ταῦτα ἰδιωσάμενοι, ἀλλὰ καὶ τὰ ἱμάτια προσαφείλοντο μηδὲ τῶν ἐσχάτων ὑποδυτῶν ἀποσχόμενοι τῶν κρυπτόντων, ἃ ἡ φύσις ὡς ἀσχήμονα καλύπτειν ἐπέταξε, μήτε μὴν τρύφους τοῖς δεσπόταις μεταδιδόντες, ὧν αὐτοί περ εἰς τοὺς κόπους εἰσεληλύθεσαν, ἀλλ᾽ οἴκοι μὲν οἱ ἀλλότριοι καθήμενοι κατεσπάθων τὰ ἐνόντα καὶ ὁσημέραι ἐκώμαζον, τοὺς δὲ συγκεκομικότας εἰς τὰς σηπίας εἴων ἐπὶ τῶν τριόδων πλάζεσθαι νήστιδας, χαμαιεύνας, γυμνόποδας καὶ ἀχίτωνας.[47]

Niketas' focus again on the essentials of life—food, clothing, shoes— reveals none of the individual experience of the Thessalonians who suffered in this way. This is true, too, of his similar description of the men and women of Thessaloniki; the Latins laughed, he writes,

> whenever someone emaciated from hunger passed by with swollen abdomen, sallow and corpselike from feasting on vegetables and banqueting only on bunches of grapes gathered in fear from nearby vineyards. Thus did they take pity on those who wore tattered garments an covered those parts of the body which needs to be hidden with rush mats.

---

[45] Eust. *capta Thess.* 106.
[46] Eust. *capta Thess.* 106.
[47] Chon. *Hist.* 302.

4 THE REFUGEE AS HISTORIAN: NIKETAS CHONIATES ... 251

ἡνίκα ἄν τις παρῄει ἐκτεταριχευμένος ἀπαστίᾳ, ᾠδηκὼς τὴν γαστέρα, τὴν ὄψιν ὕπωχρος καὶ νεκρώδης ἐκ τοῦ λαχάνοις ἐνευωχεῖσθαι καὶ μόνοις ἐνεορτάζειν βότρυσιν ἐκ τῶν ἐκεῖ που ἀμπελώνων σὺν δέει συλλεγομένοις. οὕτω δ' ᾤκτειρον τοὺς διερρωγόσι περιβλήμασι κεχρημένους καὶ περιστέλλοντας ψιάθῳ κρύπτειν χρεὼν μέρη τοῦ σώματος καὶ ταῖς τῶν σχοίνων ἐκφύσεσιν εἰς πλέγμα συνεστραμμέναις τὴν κεφαλὴν συσκιάζοντας.[48]

Eustathios' description, by contrast, focuses on the individual. In his long description of the clothing woes of the Thessalonians, for instance, they did not, as a whole, wear rush mats; rather, according to Eustathios, "One man bored holes in a rush mat and tied it in front of himself to hide his shame" (Ἐτρύπησέ τις ψίαθον καὶ περιβαλόμενος ἔκρυπτε μόγις τὴν προσθίαν αἰσχύνην).[49] From this man, Niketas generalizes to the citizens as a whole, using the example of one man as a representative of many different kinds of people. But for Eustathios, the rush mat covering was the solution of one man to the particular situation in which he found himself; others use different methods.

Indeed, perhaps the defining feature of the distinction between these two modes of narrative is just this very level of detail. When observing from a distance, the historian can see the whole scope of events, the masses of people, but he cannot give the texture or detail that gives the reading of witness testimony its emotional force. This is evident in a similar scene narrated by both Niketas and Eustathios where, again, Eustathios narrates one individual iteration of an event in great detail and Niketas expands that incident to a general condition affecting the whole population. Niketas writes:

> These utterly shameless buffoons, having no fear of God whatsoever, would bend over and pull up their garments, baring their buttocks and all that men keep covered; turning their anus on the poor wretches, close upon their food, the fools would break wind louder than a polecat. Sometimes they discharged the urine in their bellies through the spouts of their groins and contaminated the cooked food, even urinating in the faces of some, or they would urinate in the wells and then draw up the water and drink it. The very same vessel served them as chamber pot and wine cup; without having been cleansed first, it received the much-desired win and water and also held the excreta pouring out of the body's nozzle.

[48] Chon. *Hist.* 304.
[49] Eust. *capta Thess.* 122.

252 A. J. GOLDWYN

οἱ δ᾽ ἀναιδείας πληρέστατοι καὶ γελοιασταὶ καὶ τὸ θεῖον δεδιότες μηδ᾽
ὁπωσοῦν κατακύπτοντες ἐς ἱκανὸν καὶ τὰς πυγὰς καὶ ὅσα περιστέλλουσιν
ἄνθρωποι τῇ ἀνελκύσει τῶν ἐσθήτων ἀπογυμνοῦντες τὸνπρωκτὸν ἐς αὐτοὺς
ἔτρεπον καὶ τῶν σιτίων γινόμενοι ἔγγιστα ἀπέπερδον δριμύτερον γαλῆς οἱ
ἀβέλτεροι. ἔστι δ᾽ ὅτε καὶ τὰ τῆς γαστρὸς λύματαώς διὰ σίφωνος τῆς ἕδρας
ἀκοντίζοντες ἔχραινον τὰ ὄψα καὶ κατὰ τῶνπροσώπων ἐνίους ἐμόλυνον.
ἐνούρουν τε τοῖς φρέασι καὶ ἐξ αὐτῶν ἐσέπειτα τὸ ποτὸν ἀνιμώμενοι
προσεφέροντο. καὶ τὸ αὐτὸ παρ᾽ αὐτοῖς ποτήριον ὡς ἀμὶς καὶ οἰνοχόη πρὸς
ἄμφω ἦν ἐπιτήδειον· μὴ πρότερον βαπτιζόμενον τόν τε καταποθησόμενον
οἶνον καὶ τὸ ὕδωρ εἰσεδέχετο καὶ ἔστεγεν ὁμοίως τὸ ἐκ τοῦ σωματικοῦ
κρουνοῦ ἀποχεόμενον περίττωμα.[50]

This is drawn from a passage in which Eustathios recounts a particular
dinner he had at which the Latins behaved particularly savagely:

For we were sitting in a group of beggarly fellow-diners, with our cakes
of bran set before as victuals, when the boorish creatures [...] approached
us, then turned around and bared their rumps to us, crouching to void
themselves and aiming so as to deposit before us the overflow of their
bowels, which were streaming with liquid from the diarrhea produced by
the grapes they had eaten. Such was the way in which they behaved, and
my companions, [...] were nauseated, as might be expected.

Ἐκαθήμεθα μὲν γὰρ ὁμιλαδὸν οἱ πτωχοὶ σύσσιτοι, τοὺς πιτυρίας
προβεβλημένοι πρὸς τροφήν, οἱ δὲ ἀπαίδευτοι [...] ἐγγίσαντες, εἶτα
στραφέντες καὶ τὰ περὶ τὴν ἕδραν γυμνώσαντες καὶ εἰς ἔκκρισιν ὑφιζήσαντες
κατεστοχάζοντο ἐξ ἐναντίας ἡμῶν ἀποκοντοῦν τὰ περιττὰ τῆς γαστρός,
ῥυϊσκόμενα καθ᾽ ὕδωρ διὰ τὰς ὀχετηγοὺς σταφυλάς. Καὶ ἐποίουν οὕτω. Καὶ
οἱ μὲν μεθ᾽ ἡμῶν βδελυττόμενοι, ὡς ἔδει.[51]

What for Eustathios was a specific instance becomes for Niketas a
generalizable occurrence.

These different narrative techniques also reveal the different aspects
of the past that are revealed or concealed by these different forms of
narration. For Niketas, the scene is one more example of the traumas
of conquest. For Eustathios, by contrast, the scene has a more nuanced
significance. While it is certainly evidence of the degradation of the

---

[50] Chon. *Hist.* 305.

[51] Eust. *capta Thess.* 110–112. The passage is discussed in Nilsson (2013: 15–17).

4 THE REFUGEE AS HISTORIAN: NIKETAS CHONIATES ... 253

conquered Greeks, Eustathios' detailed narrative of the event offers some insight into the psychological and emotional contexts meaning that would move Eustathios to include this particular event from among all the possible events he witnessed into the narrative. Ingela Nilsson argues that the Byzantine garden "was a place for reflection and beauty, but also a place of order, harmony, and safety,"[52] and thus, from the perspective of biopolitics, the paradigmatic place of *bios* in the Byzantine tradition.[53] By defecating on the table, the Latins demonstrate to the Greeks their degraded proximity to *zoē*: the appropriate localization and sanitary care of feces is a foundational distinction between the civilized human and the animal. The rumor of bread mixed with feces, alluded to earlier, is here realized in a manifestly more vivid form. But, for Eusathios, the incident also marks one small—but, given the significance of the garden in general and the church garden in particular[54]—moment of Greek resistance to their desubjectification. Eustathios notes that his companions "were ready to burst with rage and were inflamed with desire to drive them away ignominiously, [...] But we restrained them from doing so, because in our judgement those who roll in the mire with sinners may expect to acquire the same odours" (διερρήγνυντο θυμῷ καὶ κατηκονῶντο ἀτίμως ἀπαγαγεῖν τούς, [...] ἡμεῖς δὲ ἐπείχομεν τοῦ ἔργου, κρίνοντες ὡς οἱ ἁμαρτιῶν βορβόροις ἐγκαλινδούμενοι καὶ τοιούτων ἀποβαίνουσιν ὀδμῶν ἄξιοι).[55] Eustathios offers in this scene an example of how the Greeks maintained their identity and values in these dire circumstances. Even in conquest, the Greeks remain civilized, insisting on their own *bios*; the Latins, however, despite their superior military and political position in the city, despite the utter impunity with which they act, nevertheless remain in a state of *zoē*. Eustathios' explicit moral—that "those who roll in the mire with sinners may expect to acquire the same odours"—is lost, as is the higher meaning of this scene beyond, as in Niketas' account, one more instance of degradation among many.

---

[52] Nilsson (2013: 18).

[53] For the contrast between *bios* and *zoē* as parallel to the symposium/slavery, see p. 183.

[54] Nilsson notes that the scene may also evoke the Eucharist, "as the Archbishop and his men sit down to have bread and wine in the garden" (2013: 17 n.6).

[55] Eust. *capta Thess.* 112.

254   A. J. GOLDWYN

4.3   Niketas as Witness
and the Sack of Constantinople

Eustathios begins his preface to the *Capture of Thessaloniki* by asserting that "the capture of a city is generally reported in the same manner, whether it is recorded by a historian or an eyewitness. But no narrator will necessarily deal with everything that has occurred, and the events which are selected will not be treated in the same way by both kinds of writers" (Πόλεων ἁλώσεις ἱστορούμεναι εἴτε συγγραφόμεναι μεθόδοις διοικοῦνται ὡς τὰ πολλὰ ταῖς αὐταῖς. Οὔτε δὲ ἁπάσας τὰς ἐπιβαλλούσας ἠναγκασμένως ὁ γράφων διαχειρίσεται, οὐδὲ μὴν τὰς ἀμφοτέρωθι χρηστὰς ὡσαύτως διοικονομήσεται).[56] Eustathios' distinction between the eyewitness and the historian is a narratologial one. Eustathios acknowledges that principles of selection must be at work in the creation of such a story, since everything cannot be narrated. Thus, the fabula of the historian's account and the witness's account is the same, but the story they create from those events will be different. Not only will different scenes be narrated or omitted from these two kinds of events, but they will also narrate them in a different way. This distinction marks Niketas' *History* as well. On April 11, 1204, the Crusaders penetrated the walls of Constantinople and prepared to plunder the city. From this moment on, Niketas' life changed dramatically: he went from being one of the most powerful men in the empire to being one among innumerable refugees. This sudden and dramatic trauma affected him on a number of levels: personally, in addition to many of his friends dying, he lost numerous powerful patrons; politically, he lost the sovereign protection of the centralized Byzantine state and his own position; economically, he was thrust from a life of abundance to one of penury; and geographically, he was forced to flee Constantinople and find refuge first in Selymbria, then back in Latin-occupied Constantinople and finally in Nicaea. These events influenced both the content and the form of his work: no longer historian, his narrative adopts the positionality of the witness.

Perhaps most significantly, he revised the entirety of his narrative before 1204. This revision is important for considering how affect informs the seemingly dispassionate genre of history writing. Simpson has described at length how his view of history and his narration of the past was deeply influenced by his deepening despair at the end of his life; she

---

[56] Eust. *capta Thess.* 3.

4 THE REFUGEE AS HISTORIAN: NIKETAS CHONIATES ...   255

describes how "the author's intrusion into the narrative is most evident in this [a] version, as Niketas assumes the role of a grave chastiser of his contemporaries' evils; denouncing and censuring his compatriots, whether emperors, churchmen or laymen, in an emotionally charged and ultimately personal evaluation of an entire era of Byzantine history."[57] His revisions to the narrative set out in b, moreover, "take[] the form of an authorial commentary on the historical action. It is characterised by continuous foreboding, lamentations, personal outbursts at regular intervals and a tendency to moralise. These types of interventions are primarily found in the second half of the text (post 1180) [. ...] In these cases, the demoralizing influence of 1204, as well as the historian's continual attempts to argue cause and effect to explain the calamity, is clearly apparent."[58] Indeed, as significant as what he added are what he had initially suppressed: "The bulk of his account centres on foreign affairs, usually wars. While this could have been where our historian's interests lay, the fact that detrimental information concerning the internal policies and private lives of the emperors is underlined in version a, leads us to believe that it was intentionally suppressed in b, so as not to stain the Komnenian image."[59] Thus, Niketas' principles of selection are revealed to have as much to do with his own positionality as the events themselves.[60]

However, as much as Niketas may have revised his view of the events of the previous century in light of his new circumstances, he also radically changed the way he wrote about the present: "Following the events of 1204, and despite the difficult circumstances of exile, Niketas wrote a supplement to the *History* that narrates the events of the Fourth Crusade and its aftermath (the b-text from 535.3 through 614.10) during his sojourn in Selymbria (April 1204–June 1206) and Constantinople [...] This is a work of a more personal nature, with Niketas taking on the role of the protagonist and relating in detail his own sufferings."[61] Indeed,

---

[57] Simpson (2004: 62).

[58] Simpson (2004: 71).

[59] Simpson (2004: 93).

[60] See, for instance, Simpson on Niketas' organization and depiction of imperial biographies: "But they were not chosen at random; the historian's own process of selection and emphasis introduces, whether implicitly or explicitly, a strong element of interpretation" (Simpson 2004: 94).

[61] Simpson (2004: 72).

256 A. J. GOLDWYN

he signals the impending disaster in terms that evoke Eustathios' description of the fall of Thessaloniki: "To continue with the remaining portions of my narrative, the day waned and night came on" (Καὶ ἵνα τῷ λόγῳ προβιβάσω τὸ λεῖπον, κέκλικεν ἡ ἡμέρα καὶ ἡ νὺξ προύκοπτε).[62] As with other writers of witness literature, Niketas indicates the ensuing disaster with the coming of night. Here, too, the authorial voice begins to intrude into the narrative as well: "What then should I recount first and what last of those things dared at that time by these murderous men?" (Τί δ' ἂν πρῶτον, τί δ' ἔπειτα, τί δ' ὑστάτιον καταλέξαιμι τῶν τηνικαῦτα τολμωμένων παρὰ τῶν παλαμναίων ἐκείνων ἀνδρῶν).[63] While Magoulias rightly notes that this expression is part of Niketas' broader use of the Homeric epics as intertext (the line is taken from *Od.* 9.14),[64] it also evokes the rhetoric of witness, as when Kaminiates asks a similar question with similar words: "But which of these things shall I relate first? Which incident shall I single out as having a better claim on one's sympathy?" (ἀλλὰ ποῖον τούτων πρῶτον ἐξείπω; ποῖον δὲ κατ' ἀξίαν ἐλεεινότερον κρινῶ;).[65] Like Kaminiates, Niketas makes explicit that his narrative must be only partial, and that he is making decisions of narratological order, inclusion, and omission, and that these decisions are shaped by his own positionality and narrative aims.

So, too, are his narrative decisions influenced by his emotions and thus interpretable within the framework of affective narratology. Perhaps the clearest examples of this comes from his own explicit admissions, at 535, when Niketas transitions to his discussion of the Fourth Crusade. At this moment, the historical narrative pauses, and the voice of the historian himself intrudes to reflect on his thoughts and emotions during the process of writing his history:

Up to now, the course of our history has been smooth and easily traversed, but from this point on I do not know how to continue. What judgment is reasonable for him who must relate in detail the common calamities which this queen of cities endured during the reign of the terrestrial angels I would that I might worthily and fully recount the most oppressive and grievous of all evils. But, since this is impossible, I shall abbreviate

---

[62] Chon. *Hist.* 571.

[63] Chon. *Hist.* 573.

[64] Magoulias 406, n.1520.

[65] Kam. *ex. Thess.* 60.4.

4 THE REFUGEE AS HISTORIAN: NIKETAS CHONIATES ... 257

the narration in the hope that it will be of greater profit to posterity because moderation has been exercised in reporting the sufferings, thereby mitigating excessive grief.

Ἀλλὰ μέχρι μὲν δὴ τούτων εὔδρομος ἡμῖν ὁ λόγος καὶ διὰ λείας φέρων ὁδοῦ, τὸ δ' ἐντεῦθεν οὐκ οἶδ' ὅπως τῷ λόγῳ χρήσομαι. τίνα γὰρ ἂν γνώμην ἔχειν εἰκὸς τὸν τὰς κοινὰς διεξιέναι μέλλοντα συμφοράς, ὧν ἡ τῶν πόλεων αὕτη πεπείραται βασιλὶς τῶν γηΐνων ἀγγέλων βασιλευόντων; ἐβουλόμην μὲν οἷός τε εἶναι διεξελθεῖν ἀξίως τῷ λόγῳ τὰ πάντων τῶν κακῶν ἀχθεινότατά τε καὶ χαλεπώτατα· ἐπεὶ δὲ τοῦτο ἀδύνατον, ἐν ἐπιτόμῳ καὶ δὴ ποιήσομαι τὴν ἀφήγησιν, κερδαλεωτέραν ἐσομένην δήπου τοῖς ὀψιγόνοις διὰ τὴν τῶν ἀλγεινῶν ἀκουσμάτων μετρίασιν καὶ τὴν ἐντεῦθεν τῆς πλείονος λύπης ὑφαίρεσιν.[66]

Niketas acknowledges the relationship between historical narration and emotion: to "mitigate excessive grief" (τῆς πλείονος λύπης ὑφαίρεσιν), he will "abbreviate the narration" (ἐν ἐπιτόμῳ καὶ δὴ ποιήσομαι τὴν ἀφήγησιν). In this, he echoes the similar sentiment of John Kaminiates, who writes that "up to the present point in my narrative I have been somehow carried along by the force of my words" (μέχρι γὰρ τοῦδε τοῦ διηγήματος οὐκ οἶδ' ὅπως τῇ ῥύμῃ τοῦ λόγου συναπαχθείς) but now finds himself at a loss: "I do not know what is to become of me, what direction I am to take in my narrative or which to omit" (οὐκ οἶδα τίς γένωμαι ἢ ποῖ τῷ λόγῳ χωρήσω, ποῖον δὲ παραλείπω).[67] Similar issues of order and patterning, of inclusion and omission, are shaped by the narrator's emotions. Similar, too, are the authors' recognition of the limits of what is possible to narrate. Just as Kaminiates settles on the narration of the "essential detail" as a solution for the impossibility of complete narration, so does Niketas wish that "I might worthily and fully recount the most oppressive and grievous of all evils" (διεξελθεῖν ἀξίως τῷ λόγῳ τὰ πάντων τῶν κακῶν ἀχθεινότατά τε καὶ χαλεπώτατα), but, given that this is "impossible" (ἀδύνατον), he settles for an abbreviated form (ἐπιτόμῳ). Niketas shapes the narrative of trauma and calamity conscious of the emotional toll of the narrative.

At 646, moreover, Niketas reflects on the way the autobiographical elements of his narrative are shaped by his personal suffering: "we chose

---

[66] Chon. *Hist.* 535.

[67] Kam. *ex. Thess.* 10.6.

258   A. J. GOLDWYN

to reside, as though we were captives, in Nicaea on Lake Askania, the chief city of the province of Bithynia, and huddled about the churches where we were looked down upon as aliens" (ἐξ ὅτου τὴν παρ᾿ Ἀσκανίᾳ λίμνῃ τῆς Βιθυνῶν ἐπαρχίας προεδρεύουσαν Νίκαιαν παροικεῖν εἱλόμεθα ὡς αἰχμάλωτοι, καὶ παρὰ τοῖς αὐτοῖς συνιόντες τεμένεσιν ἀσυναφεῖς τἆλλα καθεωράμεθα).[68] This more or less objective information fits in with the autobiographical element of the narrative, creating the potential for a subsequent narrative of his life as a refugee beyond the events surrounding his escape. Niketas, however, decides not to continue in this way: "But what need is there for me to trouble my history with such accounts, to depict all that had happened to the Romans as a cup of unmingled wine or a wine cup filled with the wine's dregs? Let the narrative take us back once again to the turning post so that we may continue with our history" (Ἀλλὰ τί μοι καὶ τῷ τὴν ἱστορίαν παρακινεῖν ταῖς τοιαῖσδε τῶν διηγήσεων καὶ παριστᾶν ἐντεῦθεν ὡς ἀκράτου ποτηρίου καὶ τρυγοφόρου κύλικος τὰ τῶν Ῥωμαίων ἀπαξάπαντα προσδεᾶ; περὶ τὴν νύσσαν τοίνυν τὸ λέγειν αὖθις ἐπαναγέσθω καὶ τῶν προκειμένων ἐχέσθωμοι).[69] Faced with the prospect of narrating further personal trauma, Niketas decides that there is no more need for further description, and therefore shifts the focus of the narrative away from his own plight as a refugee toward the high imperial politics of the war of Emperor Henry against the Cumans and Vlachs.

This awareness of the relationship between emotion and narration is manifested in other places as well. In b-after 1204, for instance, he describes the sack of Adrianople and begins to write about its aftermath: "The rest [of the army] went to Adrianople on foot; there they attacked the camp and thus attempted to take it by force" (ἡ δὲ λοιπὴ ἐς τὴν Ἀδριανοῦ παρὰ πόδας ἰοῦσα ἐκεῖσέ πη βάλλει στρατήγιον καὶ ταυτηνὶ πειρᾶται κατὰ κράτος ἑλεῖν).[70] At this point, however, he interrupts the narrative, adding: "But because I have grown tired of narrating the misfortunes that befell my own people, and since I am already completely immersed in preparing for my transfer to the east, hence I will desist from the narrative and put an end to the vertigo of evils" (ἀλλ᾿ ἐπεὶ ἀπείρηκα τὰς τῶν οἰκείων συμφορὰς συγγραφόμενος, ἤδη δὲ καὶ τῆς ἐς ἕω μεταβάσεως ἅπας γίνομαι, ἐνταῦθα τοῦ λέγειν σχάσας τοῦ τῶν κακῶν ἰλίγγου

[68] Chon. *Hist*. 645.

[69] Chon. *Hist*. 645.

[70] Chon. *Hist*. b 614.7–10; translation my own.

4 THE REFUGEE AS HISTORIAN: NIKETAS CHONIATES ... 259

πεπαύσομαι).[71] For Simpson, this becomes a crucial piece of evidence for the dating of the text: "This clearly indicates that Niketas abandoned the *History* when preparing his move to Nicaea (end of 1206/beginning of 1207) in order to enter into the service of the new Byzantine government in exile."[72] From the perspective of affective narratology, however, the passage demonstrates how Niketas' personal circumstances as a newly impoverished refugee struggling to make a living affect the writing of history: the subsequent events at Adrianople are not omitted for any reason having to do with the historical significance of the events themselves, but rather because of the emotional state of the author. The inclusion or exclusion of historical events is not determined by principles of selection relating to the narrating of history; rather the principles of selection are far more subjective and experiential. As regards emotion, they cause him distress, and so he omits them. As regards experience, the narrative is shaped by his material and geographic circumstances: he had to move, and therefore did not have time to write. Perhaps as importantly, in his subsequent revision of the text, he removes both of the above sentences; the effect on the narrative itself remains the same—the events in Adrianople remain unnarrated—but the reason for their omission—the author's affective state of grief and the pressures of relocation—has been edited out, thus suggesting both the explicit and implicit influence of emotion and positionality on historical writing.

A similar statement occurs at the opening of Book 10, which begins the continuation of the narrative found in the manuscripts LO, V, and Z.[73] This section, "conventionally entitled *De Signis* or *De Statuis*," was composed in 1207 during Niketas' time as a refugee first in Selymbia and then in Nicaea.[74] Simpson speculates that Niketas "never intended *De Statuis* to be included in the larger work" and that it "seems to have been incorporated into the *Historia* proper after the author's death."[75] In LO, the narrative begins with the author's declaration of his principles of selection in organizing the narrative the way he does: "So that our sorrows should not become more acute by protracting our history,

[71] Chon. *Hist.* b 614.7–10 as translated in Simpson (2013a: 73).

[72] Simpson (2013a: 73).

[73] Simpson (2004: 312).

[74] Simpson (2013a: 75).

[75] Simpson (2004: 60); see also Simpson (2006: 217; 2013a: 76), n.24.

260 A. J. GOLDWYN

we shall pass on from the former to a brief account of the latter" ("Ἵνα δὲ μὴ μακροτέρᾳ τῇ ἱστορίᾳ χρώμενοι πολυπλοκωτέρας ἐντεῦθεν τὰς λύπας κτώμεθα, ταυτὶ μὲν παρήσομεν, ἐκεῖνα δ' ἐν ἐπιτομῇτῷ λόγῳ δώσομεν).[76] Thus, for this section of the work, Niketas explicitly links the narrative to his emotions: the longer he narrates, the sadder he becomes. As a result, he decides to narrate briefly. This is significant again not only for what it says about the influence of the author's emotion on the construction of this particular section of the work but also for those other passages where affect may play a role even when there is no explicitly authorial intervention connecting emotions and narrativity. Indeed, this passage is particularly germane in this regard, since two of the manuscripts— L and O—begin with this statement, while two other manuscripts—Z and V—omit the authorial intervention and begin immediately with the same narrative. This example, as the previous one, demonstrates how the emotional state of the historian affects the narrative itself, and, also like the previous example, this passage demonstrates that this principle is at work whether the author says so or not. In alternately making such claims and then editing them out while not changing the narrative itself, Niketas reveals the visible and invisible ways in which emotion affects narrative.

In line with his new position, the narrative voice shifts as well, sharing more similarities with Kaminiates' and Eustathios' descriptions of the fall of Thessaloniki than with Niketas' earlier descriptions of the campaign of John II Komnenos. He adopts, for instance, the conventions of Gigliotti's "sensory witness" to implicitly reveal his principles of selection. Describing the desecration of holy objects, Niketas writes "The thing so horrible to hear about was to see the Divine Body and Blood of Christ poured out and thrown to the ground!" (τὸ δὲ φρικῶδες καὶ ἀκουόμενον, ἦν ὁρᾶν τὸ θεῖον αἷμα καὶσῶμα Χριστοῦ κατὰ γῆς χεόμενον καὶ ῥιπτόμενον) which thus allows the reader to follow the witness's own auditory and visual focalization.[77] Similarly, a few lines later, he writes that "the report of the impious acts perpetrated in the Great Church are unwelcome to the ears" (Τὰ δ' ἐπὶ Νεὼ τοῦ Μεγίστου ἠσεβημένα οὐδ' ἀκοαῖς εἰσιν

---

[76] Chon. *Hist.* 647.

[77] Chon. *Hist.* 573. I have adapted the translation because Magoulias seems to have missed the double sensory nature of the sentence, omitting ἀκουόμενον, thus instead rendering the sentence "How horrible it was to see...".

4 THE REFUGEE AS HISTORIAN: NIKETAS CHONIATES ... 261

εὐπαράδεκτα.)[78] thus offering an auditory focalizing complement to the visual.

Indeed, alongside the visual element of the Latins smashing up and carrying off the precious objects from the church, loading the pack animals with loot and other visual elements, Niketas describes how "a certain silly woman [...] sat upon the synthronon and intoned a song, and then whirled about and kicked up her heels in a dance" (ἀλλὰ καὶ γυναικάριον [...] ἐπὶ τοῦ συνθρόνου καθῖσαν κεκλασμένον ἀφῆκε μέλος καὶ πολλάκις περιδινηθὲν εἰς ὄρχησιν τὼ πόδε παρενεσάλευσε) thus combining the visual and auditory into one scene of destruction.[79]

Niketas' depiction then moves on to the conventional description of serial rape: "Did these mad men, raging thus against the sacred, spared pious matrons and girls of marriageable age or those maidens who, who, having chosen a life of chastity, were consecrated to God?" (πάνυ δ' ἂν ἐφείσαντο γυναικῶν εὐλαβῶν καὶ κορίων ἐπιγάμων ἢ τῶν θεῷ ἀνακειμένων καὶ παρθενεύειν ἑλομένων οἱ κατὰ τῶν θείων οὕτω λυττήσαντες).[80] This description of rape is also rendered in the terms of sensory witness, including both auditory aspects, "There were lamentations and cries of woe and weeping in the narrow ways, wailing at the crossroads, moaning in the temples, outcries of men, screams of women" (ἐν στενωποῖς θρῆνοι καὶ οὐαὶ καὶ κλαυθμοί, ἐν τριόδοις ὀδυρμοί, ἐν ναοῖς ὀλοφυρμοί, ἀνδρῶν οἰμωγαί, γυναικῶν ὀλολυγαί) and visual elements, "the taking of captives, and the dragging about, tearing in pieces, and raping of bodies heretofore sound and whole. They who were bashful of their sex were led about naked, they who were venerable in their old age uttered plaintive cries, and the wealthy were despoiled of their riches" (ἑλκυσμοί, ἀνδραποδισμοί, διασπασμοὶ καὶ βιασμοὶ σωμάτων συναφῶν πρότερον. οἱ τῷ γένει σεμνοὶ γυμνοὶ περιήεσαν, οἱ τῷ γήρᾳ γεραροὶ γοεροί, οἱ πλούσιοι ἀνούσιοι).[81] In this, it contrasts with his previous descriptions of similar scenes as, for instance, the unnamed wife of the Hungarian nobleman and (presumably) the many other women who were raped (or spared from rape by death), none of whom is reported by Niketas to have made a sound during the conquest of Zevgminon. Thus, from the moment when the Latins breach

---

[78] Chon. *Hist.* 573.
[79] Chon. *Hist.* 574.
[80] Chon. *Hist.* 574.
[81] Chon. *Hist.* 574–575.

262   A. J. GOLDWYN

the gate, Niketas goes from being a disinterested observer to being an active participant in the events he is describing, and this shift in positionality is accompanied by a commensurate shift in tone and rhetoric. As the primary narrator-focalizer, his description is filled with the things he himself experienced, and this is reflected in the increased reference to the things he himself saw and heard. In this, the narrative of the fall of Constantinople differs from all the previous accounts of conquest at the level of narrative and focalization.

This section also differs from the previous ones in showing not just the exterior auditory and visual impressions of conquest on the primary narrator-focalizer, but his interiority as well. Niketas delivers two laments for the fall of the city, and they differ in two significant ways as regards their presentation in the text. The second one is explicitly direct discourse addressed to the walls of the city: "'If for those things you were erected,' I said" ("εἰ γὰρ ὧν ἕνεκα ἔκτισθε" εἶπον), it begins, and Niketas as narrator interrupts Niketas as speaker to again emphasize the oral delivery of the speech: "'O imperial City,' I cried out" ("καὶ σὺ δὲ ὦ πόλις" ἔφην "βασίλεια").[82] The lament concludes with the narrator's admission that his was but one of numerous such laments said out loud by the refugees streaming out of the city: "Emptying out the vexations overflowing from our souls in this fashion, we went forth weeping and casting lamentations like seeds" (Ταῦτ' ἐξ ὑπεράντλου ταῖς ἀχθηδόσι ψυχῆς κενώσαντες πορευόμενοι ἐπορευόμεθα, κλαίοντες καὶ βάλλοντες τοὺς θρήνους ὡς σπέρματα).[83] The repetition of εἶπον and ἔφην indicates the orality of the lament, while the sentence after the conclusion of the lament indicates that Niketas has prioritized the lament of the primary narrator-focalizer as one representative lament among many other similar laments delivered by the refugees: many refugees were speaking, but he prioritizes his own voice over the others.

The marked orality of the second lament is all the more striking because it emphasizes the unspoken nature of the first longer lament, which, though carefully constructed along the rhetorical regulations of the lament as genre, nevertheless reads as an interior monologue. And, while the second lament is spoken by Niketas the refugee in the moment of his flight, the first lament is not delivered by Niketas the protagonist,

---

[82] Chon. *Hist.* 591.

[83] Chon. *Hist.* 593.

but Niketas the narrator; that is, it is an authorial interruption which is spoken from the perspective of the survivor of the traumatic episode in which it is embedded. In this, it is unique among laments not just in the *History*, which features no other interior (or, even spoken) monologues of refugees from fallen cities, but in Byzantine historiography and witness literature writ large. A close reading of the first lament, however, reveals the double failure at the heart of Niketas' attempt to narrate trauma. While Niketas' vast repertoire of allusions to other sources in the *History* has long been recognized, the first lament appears nearly as a cento of (principally) biblical but also Homeric and other classical sources, a marked stylistic departure from the style of the rest of the work.

In some sense, then, Niketas outsources the narration of the trauma to other voices, a rhetorical move that renders literal the otherwise seemingly performative utterance that he offers partway through the lament: "But now even my power of speech fails me, like a body which, united to the soul as her attendant, succumbs and dies together with thee, O nurturer of the word!" (Ἀλλ' ἤδη μοι καὶ τὸ λέγειν αὐτὸ ἐπιλέλοιπεν, ὅσα καὶ σῶμα συμφυὲς ψυχῇ καὶ ὁμόστολον τῇ τοῦ λόγου σοι τροφῷ συναπιόν τε καὶ συνθανόν).[84] Niketas thus acknowledges his own inability to narrate these events himself and, as importantly, the impropriety of history as a genre for narrating the events he is describing: "One ought to dedicate to thee copious lamentations with muted tears and stifled groaning and refrain from continuing the sequence of this history" (κωφοῖς τοίνυν δάκρυσι καὶ στεναγμοῖς ἀλαλήτοις τὰ πολλὰ τῶν θρηνημάτων ἀφοσιωτέον σοι καὶ τοῦ περαιτέρω ἀφεκτέον τῆς ἱστορίας εἱρμοῦ).[85] A reading of these lines from the perspective of affective narratology suggests that Niketas is struggling with two competing demands: on the one hand, what he should do—lament his traumatic experience—and, on the other, what the genre demands—continue the historical narrative—and yet, to him, these two genres or modes of narration seem incompatible.

At the heart of the tension between them is the different perspectives they offer on the events themselves: "How then can I devote the very best thing and the most beautiful invention of the Hellenes – history – to the recounting of barbarian deeds against Hellenes?" (πῶς ἂν ἔγωγε εἴην τὸ βέλτιστον χρῆμα, τὴν ἱστορίαν, καὶ κάλλιστον εὕρημα τῶν Ἑλλήνων

---

[84] Chon. *Hist.* 579.
[85] Chon. *Hist.* 579–580.

264 A. J. GOLDWYN

βαρβαρικαῖς καθ' Ἑλλήνων πράξεσι χαριζόμενος); he asks.[86] For Niketas' then, the subject matter of his narration—the Latin conquest of the city—is at odds with the form—history—and the reason for this is the function of the genre: it memorializes events which he wishes he to be forgotten: "But let these, like, the incendiary of the temple of Artemis in Ephesos, be gone out of sight and hearing, not even meriting a greeting from us until the iniquity as passed away and God be entreated concerning his servants" (Ἀλλ' οὗτοι μὲν κατὰ τὸν ἐμπρήσαντα τὸν ἐν Ἐφέσῳ ναὸν τῆς Ἀρτέμιδος οἰχέσθωσαν ἄϊστοί τε καὶ ἄπυστοι, μηδὲ προσρήματος γοῦντινος ὑφ' ἡμῶν ἀξιούμενοι, ἕως οὗ παρέλθῃ ἡ ἀνομία κἀπὶ τοῖς δούλοις αὐτοῦ τὸ θεῖον παρακληθήσεται).[87] Indeed, Niketas himself seems to recognize the paradox: he asks that these events be forgotten, even as he himself is the one who bears witness to them for posterity.

Though the references to Homer, the Bible, Plutarch, and other Classical sources are explicit, Niketas' use of previous examples of witness literature remains more subtle and implicit. Thus, for instance, his description of the events of April 13 echoes Kaminiates and Eustathios without mentioning them by name: "The despoilers took up quarters in the houses spread out in all directions, seized everything inside as plunder, and interrogated their owners as to the whereabouts of their hidden treasures, beating some, holding gentle converse with many, and using threats against all" (οἱ σκυλευταὶταῖς ὁπηοῦν οἰκίαις ἐναυλισάμενοι τά τε ἔνδον διήρπαζον καὶ περὶ τῶν ἀφανῶν τοὺς δεσπότας ἀνέκρινον, πληγὰς ἐντείνοντες ἐνίοις, πολλοῖς δὲ καὶ προσηνῶς συγγινόμενοι, ταῖς δ' ἀπειλαῖς ἐπὶ πᾶσι χρώμενοι).[88] In this, Niketas shares with Eustathios and Kaminiates (and Elie Wiesel) the hiding of goods and the beatings and torture in order to find the plunder.[89]

Indeed, Niketas describes the departure of the Constantinopolitan refugees in similar terms as Eustathios and Kaminiates: "Gathered into groups, they went forth wrapped in tatters, wasted away from fasting, ashen in complexion, their visages corpse-like, and their eyes bloodshot, shedding more blood than tears" (κατὰ συμμορίας τοίνυν ἀγειρόμενοι ἐξῄεσαν, ῥακίοις ἐσπειραμένοι, ἀπαστίᾳ ἐκτετηγμένοι, τὸν χρῶτα τραπέντες,

---

[86] Chon. *Hist.* 580.

[87] Chon. *Hist.* 580.

[88] Chon. *Hist.* 586.

[89] For which, see above (22).

νεκρώδεις τὰς ὄψεις καὶ ὕφαιμοι τοὺς ὀφθαλμούς). The fleeing Constanti-nopolitans, suffering from hunger and thirst, pale and dressed in rags like the Thessalonians of Eustathios' *Capture*, stream out of the city before Niketas' eyes.

4.4 NIKETAS AS NOVELIST AND HERO OF THE NOVEL

Among the scenes of devastation in the early aftermath of the city's conquest, Niketas notes: "My own situation in the course of events was as follows" (Ἵνα δὲ καὶ τὰ κατ' ἐμὲ συνείρω τῇ ἱστορίᾳ) thus merging the primary narrator-focalizer and the main protagonist. This merging is at the heart of what witness literature is: the detailing of individual expe-rience within the context of actual historical events, the merging of the account of the individual with the account of those on whose behalf the individual is narrating. In this, it echoes the similar transitional passages in Eustathios (106.13) and Kaminiates (42.2) in which the authors tran-sition from the scenes of general devastation to the first-person narratives of their own experience against the background of the broader catas-trophe. In that the ensuing narration shares more with Kaminiates and Eustathios than with Niketas' previous narrative style, this passage repre-sents a remarkable shift in narrative strategy for Niketas—shifting from third person to first person and from the general to the specific—and in narrative values—away from a narrative that values high politics and great men at the expense of the ordinary victims of conquest and toward a narrative that values the lives of individual refugees over those of great men. Indeed, this shift calls into question the very categorization of the *History* if it is to be spoken of as a unified work legible within a specific or single generic framework. Jonathan Harris notes, for instance, that "it therefore seems clear enough that in the eyes of Nicetas Choniates [sic], and those who wrote in the same genre, the emperor was the central concern of the historian."[90] And yet, at this crucial moment in Byzantine history, the emperor does not figure at all into the narrative. Rather, it focuses on the plight of a single rather ordinary citizen of the falling city,

[90] Harris (2000: 31).

266   A. J. GOLDWYN

thus challenging the notion of the work as historiography and placing it within the generic concerns of the Komnenian novel.[91]

Emplotting his flight from falling Constantinople within a novelistic framework would be in line with Niketas' method for narrating certain elements of his history; as Emmanuel Bourbouhakis has demonstrated, the Komnenian novels formed the basis of how Niketas presented one of the central figures of the *History*, Andronikos Komnenos. The narrative of the rise and fall of the last of the Komnenian emperors

> is where literary style, or form, meets historical content, as the historian shapes the story to meet the demands of rhetorically charged narrative drama. The manner of the telling in this case [...] would be virtually indistinguishable from a fiction [... and] appropriate and even necessary for the telling of the 'romantic' or 'erotic' tales involving love, lust, and daring escapes. There is, I would argue, nothing in his account of Andronikos' erotic exploits to distinguish them from the accounts in the erotic novels of Antiquity or Byzantium, except, of course, that they purport to be true, *history* in fact, and a good deal more extravagant.[92]

Like the three extant Komnenian novels, a barbarian raid and the subsequent conquest of the narrator's city overturn the narrator's previous life of wealth and power (though in *Drosilla and Charikles* the city itself is not conquered; the protagonists are captured beyond the walls). The narrator witnesses scenes of violence and destruction. As in the novelistic accounts, the great fear of the heroes of the novels is sexual violence perpetrated against young virgins. And indeed, as he is fleeing, Niketas pauses to note the ever-present fear of sexual violence as they fled: "still others [of the conquerors] looked with steadfast and fixed gaze upon those women who were of extraordinary beauty with intent to seize them forthwith and ravish them" (οἱ δὲ καὶ γυναικῶν ταῖς κάλλει διαφερούσαις πεπηγόσι βλέμμασι μηδὲ ῥᾳδίως ἀποσπωμένοις ἐνατενίζοντες ὡς ἁρπάσοντες αὐτίκα καὶ βιασόμενοι)[93]; such was their fear that "we put them in the middle as though in a sheepfold and instructed the young girls to rub their faces

---

[91] For Niketas' appropriation of the rhetoric of the novel elsewhere in the *History*, see Nilsson (2014), for whom "Nicétas se montre un véritable romancier" in his descriptions of Manuel and Andronikos Komnenos (174).

[92] Bourbouhakis (2009: 228–229).

[93] Chon. *Hist.* 589.

4 THE REFUGEE AS HISTORIAN: NIKETAS CHONIATES ... 267

with mud to conceal the blush of their cheeks" (τὰς μὲν ὡς ἐν σηκῷ τῷ μέσῳ ἡμῶν ἀπειλήφειμεν, ταῖς δὲ νεάνισιν ἐπεσκήψαμεν ἐντρίψασθαι πηλῷ τὰ πρόσωπα ἀντίρροπα τῶν πρώην κομμώσεων καὶ τὸν πυρσὸν οὕτω κατασβέσαι τῶν παρειῶν).[94] Fear of sexual assault and of rape, particularly of virgins, is perhaps the greatest fear articulated in the Komnenian novels; here, Niketas details how fleeing men shielded women from that fate, thus offering a counterpoint to the scenes of women being captured in the novels.

Indeed, the narrative's affinity with the novels continues through the remainder of Niketas' description of his flight. Thus, it is within the generic confines of the novel that Niketas subsequently narrates:

> As we came to the Church of the Noble Martyr Mokios, a lecherous and unholy barbarian, like a wolf pursuing a lamb, snatched from our midst a fair-tressed maiden, the young daughter of a judge. Before this most piteous spectacle our entire company shouted out in alarm. The girl's father, afflicted by old age and sickness, stumbled, fell into a mud-hole, and lay on his side wailing and wallowing in the mire.

> Ὡς δὲ περὶ τὸν νεὼν ἥκομεν Μωκίου τοῦ καλλιμάρτυρος, ὑβριστὴς καὶ ἀνόσιος βάρβαρος ὡς ἀμνάδα λύκος ἐκ μέσων ἡμῶν ἀφαρπάζει κόρην εὐπλόκαμον, τινὸς τῶν ἐπὶ τῷ δικάζειν θυγάτριον. πρὸς τὴν οἰκτροτάτην τοίνυν ταυτηνὶ θέαν ἡ μὲν συνοδία πᾶσα διαθροηθέντες ἐξεβοήσαμεν, ὁ δὲ πατὴρ τῆς παιδὸς γήρᾳ καὶ νόσῳ τετρυχωμένος, τότε δὲ καὶ σφαλεὶς κατὰ τέλματος, ὀλοφυρόμενος καὶ τῷ πηλῷ φυρόμενος δόχμιος ἔκειτο.[95]

The kidnap and near rape of a beautiful young woman during the sacking of a city is the opening theme of both *Rhodanthe and Dosikles* and *Drosilla and Charikles*, and here Niketas opens up the same possibility for this young woman, whose male guardian, old and ill, now lies helplessly on the ground, covered in mud. As much as this moment dramatizes the helplessness of fathers to protect their children, it also opens up for other men the possibility of demonstrating great heroism. Thus, Niketas continues with the story: the girl's father, "turning to me in utter helplessness and calling me by name, he entreated that I do everything possible to free his daughter" (ὡς εἰς συκίνην ἐπικουρίαν ἀφορῶν συχνάκις ἐμέ,

---

[94] Chon. *Hist*. 589.
[95] Chon. *Hist*. 590.

268   A. J. GOLDWYN

καὶ πρὸς ὄνομα δεόμενος συνάρασθαί οἱ τὰ δυνατὰ πρὸς τὴν τῆς παιδὸς ἀπόλυσιν).[96] Niketas is thus called to a heroic task: to help the helpless father and save the girl from almost certain rape and sex slavery. Like a hero of the novel, he bravely accepts:

> I immediately turned back and set out after the abductor, following his tracks; in tears I cried out against the abduction, and with gestures of supplication I prevailed upon those passing troops who were not wholly ignorant of our language to come to my aid, and I even held onto some with my hand.

> ἐπιστραφεὶς οὖν αὐτίκα μάλα, ὡς εἶχον, κατ' ἴχνια τοῦ ἅρπαγος ἔβαινον, μετὰ δακρύων τὴν βίαν ἐπιβοώμενος καὶ σχήμασιν ἱλασίμοις εἰς ἀρωγὴν ἐπισπώμενος τοὺς μὴ πάντη ἀμαθεῖς τῆς ἡμετέρας φωνῆς ἐκ τοῦ στρατεύματος παριόντας, ἔστι δ' ὧν καὶ χειρὸς ἁπτόμενος.[97]

Niketas, alone in a sea of enemies, convinces a group of Latins to help him and, together, they find the man who had dragged off the girl. He then gives a moving speech, appealing both to their emotions as husbands and as fathers of "beloved children" (τῶν φίλων ὑμῖν τέκνων)[98] and to the law itself:

> You have decreed and have sworn the most awesome oaths to refrain from intercourse with, and, if possible, from even casting an adulterous eye on, married women, maidens who have never known any man, and nuns consecrated to God.

> ὑμεῖς μὲν γὰρ γυναιξὶ ταῖς ὑπὸ ζυγὸν καὶ ταῖς ὅλως ἀπειράτοις ἀνδρὸς καί γε ἔτι ταῖς ἀποθριξαμέναις θεῷ μηδὲ μοιχικοῦ μέχρι βλέμματος, εἰ δυνατόν, συνελθεῖν ἐθεσπίσατε καὶ ὅρκοις τὰ περὶ τούτων φρικώδεσι διειλήφατε.

Women here are divided into two categories: women who cannot be raped (virgins, nuns, married women) and women who can (unmarried women who have had sex but perhaps also widows and divorcées). In this, the distinctions the barbarians make between different kinds of women and

[96] Chon. *Hist.* 590.
[97] Chon. *Hist.* 590.
[98] Chon. *Hist.* 590.

4 THE REFUGEE AS HISTORIAN: NIKETAS CHONIATES ... 269

the behaviors appropriate toward each also echo similar such discussions in the novels as, for instance, the virginity test at the spring of Artemis, which makes an organized spectacle out of these kinds of decisions[99] or in the hold of the pirate ship, where women are raped but virgins spared.[100] While these arguments are convincing to those who accompany him, it is only the threat of force that compels the kidnapper to relinquish the girl. Niketas then successfully returns with the girl, bringing the episode to its conclusion: "The father rejoiced at the sight of his daughter, shedding tears as libations to God for having saved her from this union without marriage crowns and bridal songs. Then he rose to his feet and continued on the way with us" (περιχαρὴς οὖν ἐπὶ τῇ θέᾳ τῆς παιδὸς φανεὶς ὁ πατὴρ καὶ σπείσας θεῷ δάκρυα ἐπὶ τοῖς ἀστεφανώτοις ἐκείνοις καὶ ἀνυμεναίοις νυμφεύμασιν ἀναστὰς αὖθις σὺν ἡμῖν ἐπορεύετο).[101] Thus, Niketas presents a kind of novel in miniature, with himself as the hero: a young woman is in danger of being raped, and Niketas saves her from that fate.

Stephanos Efthymiades sees this episode as evidence that Niketas "was both a courageous man and concerned with real life. In 1204, nearing the age of fifty, i.e. at an old age, he defended a young girl in Constantinople who fell helpless in the hands of the Crusaders."[102] Indeed, the scene is certainly evidence that Niketas showed great personal bravery under difficult circumstances, but, in light of the narrative arc of the complete extant novels, it also reveals a culturally constructed script of what Niketas understood to be heroic within the context of a falling city. Despite his holding significant political posts throughout his life, the time he saved a young girl from being raped is the deed he himself considers most worth remembering from the entirety of his life, since it is the only one he actually records—the only personal anecdote he tells is about the time that he, like a hero of a novel, preserved the virginity of a damsel in distress. Indeed, Efthymiades implicitly considers Niketas' work within the conventions of narrative fiction when he cites T.S. Eliot's famous dictum in his 1923 review of James Joyce's *Ulysses*: "Writing this kind of history was for Choniates 'a way of controlling, of ordering, of giving a shape and a significance to the immense panorama of futility and anarchy

---

[99] *H&H*. 11.16–18.

[100] *H&H*. 8.3.2–3.

[101] Chon. *Hist*. 591.

[102] Efthymiades (2009: 35–36).

270 A. J. GOLDWYN

which is contemporary history.'"[103] And yet, it is significant in this regard that Eliot was not writing about nonfiction or historiography at all, but a novel. As an educated man in Constantinople living in the period in the generation after the composition of the novels, it is likely that Niketas himself was familiar with them, and that they influenced his narrative style and structure as well. And yet, unlike the epic, encomiastic, and other generic influences on the *History*, the presence of novelistic elements in Niketas' narrative has not yet been suggested, much less explored in depth.[104]

Thus, referring again to Hayden White's definition in "Figuring Realism" that the "meaning [of witness testimony] resides in large measure in the extent to which it copies the plot-structure of a poetic fiction," a new side of Niketas' text emerges.[105] If actual historical events inform the substructure of the Komnenian novels, then the conventions of the novel can also be considered one of the intertexts (along with Homer, Attic tragedy, the Bible, and other ancient sacred and classical sources) through which Niketas understood how to interpret his own experience. Like Levi, for whom "to kill and to die seemed extraneous literary things to me" (e uccidere e morire mi parevano cose estranee e letterarie),[106] Niketas understands and narrates his lived experience through literature. Thus, when he considers how to narrate his own actions, he chooses that event which seems ultimately most heroic within the narrative conventions that inform his interpretation of the events he experienced: saving a virgin from rape is the heroic act *par excellence* of the hero of the novel and thus merits narration within the conventional novelistic type scene of the flight from the fallen city.

Indeed, as scholars of Holocaust fiction have long noted, historiography and narrative fiction share numerous rhetorical strategies despite their seemingly oppositional epistemological foundations. This is perhaps even more true for ancient and medieval historiography than for histories

---

[103] Efthymiades (2009: 45), paraphrasing Eliot (1975), who describes Joyce's use of myth in *Ulysses* as "a way of cotrolling, of orrdering, of giving a shape and a significance to the immense panorama of futility and anarchy which is contemporary history" (178).

[104] Efthymiades points to the potential of such an investigation of Niketas as novelist in, for instance, his comparison of him to Victor Hugo and Alexandros Papadiamantis, but concludes by confirming his place within the genre of history (2009: 54).

[105] White (2004: 117).

[106] Levi (1959: 169; 1989: 231).

4 THE REFUGEE AS HISTORIAN: NIKETAS CHONIATES ... 271

of the Holocaust, since the older texts were bound by different perspectives on historical fidelity. Writing about how "Niketas moulded such scenes so as to fit his purpose," Simpson suggests "that entire episodes of this sort may have been simply invented by the historian. This is not because Niketas was a 'bad' historian who did not care for the truth; but because he, along with his contemporaries, conceived history in a very different way than we do."[107]

In considering how Niketas molded his narrative, moreover, it is as important to consider what he did not narrate as much as what he did, since the narrative of his flight from the city did not begin with the story of the rescue of the maiden, but with the different if equally desperate plight of another woman: Niketas' own wife: "It was a stormy and wintry day, and my wife was approaching the throes of childbirth" (καὶ χειμών, ἐπὶ δὲ καὶ πρὸς ὠδῖσιν ἔτι ἡμῶν ἡ σύζυγος).[108] Of his wife's experiences, what she said, what she did, what happened to her during and after the flight, he says nothing more. To leave his pregnant wife and other children to defend a captured young girl was certainly courageous, but, considered from a narratological perspective, the decision to include this scene must be explicable within Niketas' unstated principles of selection. Returning to the narratological distinctions of story and fabula, why, of all the possible events that happened to him during the sack of the city, during his flight from it, during the several days he hid in the house of his Venetian friend, and in the weeks and months after, does he narrate this event at such a level of detail? The narrative substructure of the novel and its influence on narrative descriptions of city conquest determine how the disparate elements of a fabula are molded into a single story. This distinction can be seen in particular in the two possible narratives of women's experiences that Niketas proposes in the scene of his flight from the city: that of his wife, and that of the kidnapped girl. Conquered women's experiences in the Komnenian novels are limited to similarly perfunctory statements about the hardships of women and their separation from their children; the only time their experiences are described in detail is when they are a virgin in danger of sexual violence. Indeed, there may be no other reference even to pregnant women at all in Byzantine accounts of conquest, either fictional or nonfictional. In this way, Niketas'

---

[107] Simpson (2004: 233).

[108] Chon. *Hist.* 589.

brief narration of his own wife's experience in favor of the experience of a young virgin whom he gives no indication in the text of having met before follows the narrative logic of the novels: a man of the upper-class who is exiled or captured or exiled as a result of barbarian conquest, and who narrates his circumstances in the first person and in the mode of lament and monody. Further, the novels foreground the personal danger of the hero as he attempts to rescue the damsel in distress whose virginity must be preserved.

John Kaminiates, too, describes at length his flight through the streets of Thessaloniki with his father, brother, and male cousins, with only passing reference to his own wife and daughters, though he does mention their suffering and those of his other female relatives (such as the sister-in-law sold into slavery) in passing. Leonora Neville argues in reference to John Kaminiates' description of his wife and daughter that "the ancient Greek injunction that simply mentioning women in public dishonoured them was well known and apparently in force in Byzantine culture" and that thus "John would have wanted to keep them out of any public discourse."[109] She argues that he chose a narrative strategy that allowed him "to record a history for posterity that did not air his personal familial woes in a public forum."[110] This suggestion, when examined in light of Kaminiates' work, may well also explain his reticence to describe his own family, but becomes harder to sustain when seen within the broader context of Byzantine witness literature as a whole, for it is not just John Kaminiates whose work minimizes the traumas of his female relatives, but Niketas' as well. Indeed, the Komnenian novels not only programmatically prioritize the voices of men over women, they only give voice to women's experiences insofar as they relate to their virginity and the threats to it.

What separates Niketas' "novel" from the Komnenian novels, however, is the sense of history. The narrative that emerges from Niketas' post-1204 revisions to the text is one of the decline and fall of the Byzantine Empire from its high-point under the leadership of John II Komnenos to its collapse under the squabbling emperors of the late twelfth and early thirteenth centuries. The novelistic section of his work is grounded in a broader historical context; the conquest of Constantinople and his

---

[109] Neville (2019: 68).

[110] Neville (2019: 68).

4 THE REFUGEE AS HISTORIAN: NIKETAS CHONIATES ...   273

becoming a refugee, though narratologically and rhetorically similar to the novels, thus has a very different literary function. It is the climactic scene of a century's worth of historical material that preceded it. In this, it shares some similarities with Eustathios of Thessaloniki, embedding, as it does, witness testimony in history. On the other side, the Komnenian novels (and, to a lesser extent, John Kaminiates' letter) exist in a world without historical context. Niketas spends many pages on the geopolitical situation that resulted in the Crusaders appearing at the gates of Constantinople.

Rhodanthe and Dosikles and *Drosilla and Charikles*, by contrast, present a narrative without even the slightest hint of context. The former begins with evening falling "when a trireme from the pirate fleet [...] put in to the harbour of Rhodes" (ναῦς τριήρης ληστρικῆς ναυαρχίας [...] ἐλλιμενίζει τῆς Ῥόδου τῷ λιμένι).[111] Prodromos is completely disinterested in answering seemingly obvious questions that are the more pressing concern of the historian: where did the fleet come from? What broader geopolitical context allowed a pirate fleet to descend upon the city? Why were the Rhodians not prepared? What economic, political, or military circumstances set this course of events in motion? In the opening of *Drosilla and Charikles*, too, "Parthians attacked the city of Barzon" (Πάρθοι παρεμπίπτουσι Βάρζῳ τῇ πόλει).[112] Eugenianos offers no more historical or political context to the inciting event of his novel than does Prodromos. In some sense, this makes sense with regard to the positionality of the characters. Unlike Niketas or Eustathios, high-ranking (lay and church) officials (in Constantinople) and Thessaloniki with direct access to the emperor and other elite decision-makers, the characters in the novels, living on the margins of the empire (or whatever broader government existed in the storyworlds in which the novels are set) and far from the centers of decision-making power, would themselves have had limited access to the broader geopolitical situation. All they would know is what they see on the horizon—pirate ships—without any understanding of the deep history that would have brought them there. Their suffering exists within the immediacy of the moment; Niketas' suffering, by contrast, is deepened by what he perceives to be a century's worth of decline that forebodes what comes to him to seem as an almost inevitable disaster.

[111] *R&D.* 1.5, 7.
[112] *D&C.* 1.6.

274   A. J. GOLDWYN

In his *History*, which covers the century during which the novels were written, Niketas mentions in passing the various kinds of pirate raids that form some of the central plot elements of the three complete extant Komnenian novels. His description of the raids led by the Genoese captain Gafforio can show again the kind of narrative gap in the nonfictional record which the fictional novels fill in. Gafforio, Niketas writes, "constructed biremes and triremes and fenced himself about with roundships. With these he plundered the coastal cities and the islands which rise up in the Aegean Sea" (νῆας δικρότους καὶ τρικρότους πηξάμενος καὶ πλοίοις στρογγύλοις φραξάμενος τὰς παραθαλαττίους ἔκειρε πόλεις καὶ τὰς νήσους ἐπιὼν ἐτίθει κακῶς, αἳ κατὰ τὸ Αἰγαῖον ἀνίσχουσι πέλαγος).[113] For Niketas, the raids of Gafforio are valuable as a historical phenomenon, which exemplify the increasingly unstable condition of the Byzantine navy and the geopolitical and strategic effects of these military and political considerations.[114] This political concern in the narrative comes at the cost of a concern with the plight of the individual people whose lives were ended and upended. Neither Niketas nor the other Byzantine historians show what the novelists do. The novels show the full depths of the wide swathe of humanity at a more granular narrative level. Slaves are differentiated from one another—some are old, some are young, men and women alike, of different professions and social classes. The novels humanize the slaves, showing their family lives before they were enslaved, showing the responses of grieving families who think their loved ones are dead, showing their joy when their loved ones are recovered. The novelists, moreover, attempt to imagine the slaves' interiority: the solace they find in the communal slave spaces they develop, their attempts to preserve their identity against the self-erasing social position of slavery through the telling of autobiography, their assumption of the role of both witness and witness to the witness (or supplementary witness), their attempts at suicide, their attempts to hold onto hope (particularly as regards the recovery of their beloveds). Though fictional, the novels offer access to a kind of truth that historiography is unable to probe—experiential, affective, subjective. Thus, when Niketas experienced a kind of horror that was

[113] Chon. *Hist.* 482.

[114] In the introduction to his translation, for instance, Henry Magoulias notes that "one of the chief causes of the fall of the empire was the deterioration of the Byzantine navy. The Byzantines lost control of the seas to the Italians, especially the Venetians, and thus they were no longer in command of their own destiny" (Magoulias 1984: xxv).

beyond the possible, with no recourse for how to narrate it, he may have understood his experience—and written about it—through the frame of the closest analog available in Byzantine literary culture: the novel. The fictional and the nonfictional, the novel and the history offer complementary portraits of the experiential, affective, and emotional context of human suffering in Byzantium.

BIBLIOGRAPHY

Appelfeld, Aharon. 1988. After the Holocaust. In *Writing and the Holocaust*, ed. Berel Lang, 83–93. New York: Holmes and Meier.

Bourbouhakis, Emmanuel. 2009. Exchanging the Devices of Ares for the Delights of the Erotes. In *Plotting with Eros: Essays on the Poetics of Love and the Erotics of Reading*, ed. Ingela Nilsson, 213–234. Copenhagen: Museum Tusculanum Press.

Efthymiades, Stephanos. 2009. Niketas Choniates: The Writer. In *Niketas Choniates: A Historian and a Writer*, eds. Alicia Simpson and Stephanos Efthymiades, 35–58. Geneva: Pomme d'Or.

Eliot, T. S. 1975. Ulysses, Order, and Myth. In *Selected Prose of T. S. Eliot*, ed. Frank Kermode, 175–178. San Diego: Harcourt.

Harris, Jonathan. 2000. Distortion, Divine Providence and Genre in Nicetas Choniates's Account of the Collapse of Byzantium 1180–1204. *Journal of Medieval History* 26 (1): 19–31.

Levi, Primo. 1959. *If This Is a Man*, trans. Stuart Woolf. New York: Orion Press.

———. 1989. *Se questo è un uomo*. Einaudi: Torino.

Magoulias, Harry. 1984. Introduction. In *Niketas Choniates, O City of Byzantium, Annals of Niketas Choniates*, ix-xxviii. Detroit: Wayne State University Press.

Neville, Leonora. 2018. *Guide to Byzantine Historical Writing*. Cambridge: Cambridge University Press.

———. 2019. Pity and Lamentation in the Authorial Personae of John Kaminiates and Anna Komnene. In *Emotions and Gender in Byzantine Culture*, ed. Stavroula Constantinou and Mati Meyer, 65–92. New York: Palgrave Macmillan.

Nilsson, Ingela. 2013. Nature Controlled by Artistry: The Poetics of the Literary Garden in Byzantium. In *Byzantine Gardens and Beyond*, ed. H. Bodin and R. Hedlund, 14–29. Uppsala: Acta Universitatis Upsaliensis.

Nilsson, Ingela. 2014. *Raconter Byzance: la littérature au XIIe siècle*. Paris: Les Belles Lettres.

Simpson, Alicia. 2004. *Studies in the Composition of the Historia*. PhD, Kings College London.

———. 2006. Before and After 1204: The Versions of Niketas Choniates' 'Historia.' *Dumbarton Oaks Papers* 60: 189–221.

———. 2013a. *Niketas Choniates: A Historiographical Study.* Oxford: Oxford University Press.

———. 2013b. From the Workshop of Niketas Choniates: The Authority of Tradition and Literary Mimesis. In *Authority in Byzantium*, ed. Pamela Armstrong, 259–268. London: Routledge.

Urbainczyk, Theresa. 2018. *Writing About Byzantium: The History of Niketas Choniates.* New York: Routledge.

White, Hayden. 2004. Figuring Realism in Witness Literature. *Parallax* 10 (1): 113–124.

CHAPTER 5

Pleasure, Pain, Perversity: Reading Byzantine Witness Literature After Auschwitz

In his preface to the *History*, Niketas Choniates writes: "Let no one be so mad as to believe that there is anything more pleasurable than history" (μὴ οὕτω μανείη τις ὡς ἥδιον ἡγεῖσθαί τι ἕτερον ἱστορίας).[1] Such a statement would have seemed true to Niketas at the time he wrote it, when he lived a life of wealth and privilege at the center of elite politics and culture. During this period, Niketas was writing about people other than himself, people who had either lived and died in the past or lived and died far away or, to use Eustathios' formulation about the historian, "since he is speaking without having suffered, he can choose his words to please the listener" (οἷα ἔξω πάθους λαλῶν, πολλὰ διαθήσεται πρὸς χάριν ἀκοῆς).[2] For the writer who has not suffered or is writing only about the suffering of others, pleasure seems a common if problematic response to narrative, especially narratives of trauma. The events of 1204, however, altered the course of Niketas' life in devastating ways; no longer "speaking without having suffered" (ἔξω πάθους λαλῶν) he was, to use Eustathios' definition of the historian as witness, "himself part of these

[1] Chon. *Hist.* 2.

[2] Eust. *capta Thess.* 3. I have amended ἔξω πάθους λαλῶν from Melville-Jones' "speaking without having been affected" to emphasize the nature of Eustathios' appeal to personal suffering, as discussed previously, p. 55.

© The Author(s), under exclusive license to Springer Nature Switzerland AG 2021
A. J. Goldwyn, *Witness Literature in Byzantium*,
New Approaches to Byzantine History and Culture,
https://doi.org/10.1007/978-3-030-78857-5_5

277

278   A. J. GOLDWYN

pitiful events" (ἐν ἐλεεινοῖς ὄντα).[3] Niketas thus describes his change in positionality when he finally settled in Nicaea after a brief stay in Selymbria and Latin-occupied Constantinople:

> our change of residence did not thing to improve our circumstances; once again we are deluged by sorrow [. ...] We are nourished by a little bread and sometimes a measure of wine, we are surfeited with the calamities of our countrymen as well as of our own, and we are offered the joyless cup of affliction. Like a line stretching out into infinity, all that was oppressive, horrible, heartrending, soul-destroying, wholly devastating, and utterly desolating in full measure they [the Latins] brought to the Roman nation.

> Πλὴν οὐδὲν ἄμεινον τὰ τῆς τοπικῆς ταυτησὶ μεταβάσεως τοῖς καθ' ἡμᾶς εἰσήνεγκαν πράγμασιν, ἀλλ' ἐσμεν καὶ πάλιν ταῖς λύπαις ὑπέραντλοι. [...] καί τρεφόμεθα μέν ἄρτῳ βραχεῖ καί μετρητῷ ἐνίοτε οἴνῳ, κατακόρως δὲ τὰς τῶν φυλετῶν καὶ ἡμῶν αὐτῶν συμφορὰς ψωμιζόμεθα καὶ τὸν σκύφον τῶν θλίψεων ἀκέραστον χαρμονῇ προσφερόμεθα· κατὰ γάρ τινα γραμμὴν μηκιζομένην ἐς τὸ ἀπέραντον ὅσα ἀχθεινά, ὅσα δεινά, ὅσα καρδίας ἐλέπολις, ὅσα ψυχῆς δαπάνησις, ὅσα πανώλειά τε καὶ παντελὴς ἐξολόθρευσις τῷ των Ῥωμαίων ἔθνει σαφῶς.[4]

The physical, psychological, economic, and emotional difficulties of his own situation as he describes it are reflected in the emotional toll of his writing. This passage, moreover, indicates the difficulty in assessing the emotional state of an author, since this passage appears only in the LO manuscripts. Written sometime around 1207, these manuscripts represent the author's initial attempt to wrestle with his own plight and, as a new refugee, he is more attuned to the intensity of his suffering. However, he revised this passage out of his subsequent versions, hiding his emotions from future readers. For Niketas, then, the rhetoric of the suffering author is not an empty formula, but the vessel through which he can convey authentic emotions specific to his condition, and those emotions change over time and writing contexts.

This same process of emotion, writing, and revision can be seen in the composition of *Night*. Wiesel's first version, written in Yiddish and titled *And the World Remained Silent* (*Un di velt hot geshvign*), was significantly

---

[3] Eust. *capta Thess.* 4.
[4] Chon. *Hist.* LO 635.

5 PLEASURE, PAIN, PERVERSITY: READING BYZANTINE ... 279

longer and aimed at as near a comprehensive account of the author's experiences as he could muster. *Night*, by contrast, aims for a more selective and representational mode of discourse; many elements are omitted, and many of these elements reflect the different positionality of the witness himself. Wiesel "began to write (or at least to outline his memoir) not ten years after the events of the Holocaust but immediately upon liberation, as the first expression of his mental and physical recovery" and he completed it "on board a ship to Brazil" to be ready for publication in 1954, a few years before he conceived of the French version, which was published in 1958.[5] Naomi Seidman argues that these two texts, written by the same person but at different points in his life, mean that there are, in effect, "two survivors, then, a Yiddish and a French."[6] Each of these survivors is embodied by the same man, Elie Wiesel, but due to the difference in time between the two compositions, the change in the author's sense of himself and his past between the initial moment of his writing upon leaving the camp and his revision of that text almost ten years later resulted in two different narrators in the text. To speak of Elie Wiesel the writer of witness literature, then, is to speak of multiple primary narrators blended into a single text, with the later writer, in a sense, a witness to the witness who was his younger self.

A similar model of authorship marks Niketas' text. On the one hand, he excised the longer autobiographical section about his circumstances in Nicaea, but retained a passage just prior, describing himself as: "O wretched author that I am, to be the keeper of such evils, and now to grace with the written word the misfortunes of my family and countrymen!" (Ὡς δυστυχὴς ἐγὼ συγγραφεύς, οἵοις κακοῖς ἐταμιευόμην, οἵοις ἐμοῖς τε καὶ τῶν φυλετῶν δυσπραγήμασι τὸν λόγον χαρίζομαι.).[7] This later Niketas does not describe himself as taking pleasure in writing as did his younger self; rather, he is a "wretched author" (δυστυχὴς [...] συγγραφεύς) an explicit connection of the relationship between his personal emotional pain and his writing. Indeed, he goes one step further, asking "Who can bear to contemplate such trophies raised by the enemy?" (τίς γὰρ ἂν καὶ σχοίη ὅλως ὑπενεγκεῖν τοιαῦτα θεώμενος τρόπαια πρὸς τῶν

---

[5] Seidman (2006: 219).

[6] Seidman (2006: 223).

[7] Chon. *Hist.* 634.

280 A. J. GOLDWYN

πολεμίων ἀνεγειρόμενα).[8] In this, Niketas is speaking in general about those who were present at the fall of the city, but he is doubly traumatized: he has to witness it again in contemplation. The Niketas who began his narrative by claiming that those who did not find history pleasurable were mad now cannot "bear to contemplate" (ὑπενεγκεῖν τοιαῦτα θεώμενος) past events.

In asking how one can bear to contemplate trauma, moreover, Niketas also challenges the reading of the *History* for pleasure. Emmanuel Bourbouhakis opens his 2009 article on Niketas' use of the Komnenian novels as an intertext for the *History* with a broad claim about the relationship between reading, writing, and pleasure in the *History*: "Niketas is that rare thing among Byzantine writers: an author one may read (assuming one's Greek is up to it) for 'pleasure.' And yet you would not guess from many references to his text by scholars, historians in the main, that pleasure of any kind might have played some part – a very significant part, I think – in the composition of his work."[9] Bourbouhakis thus foregrounds two aspects of critical analysis: the emotional state of the author when writing, and the emotional state of the audience when reading/listening. Bourbouhakis, moreover, ascribes to the idea that both reader and writer felt pleasure, a term that is perhaps simpler when considering works of fiction but holds a central and complicated position in reading witness literature. For instance, the comparison of the manuscripts from before 1204 and after reveal that the episode on which Bourbouhakis most focuses and which he sees as the most novelistic is the way Niketas treats the life of Andronikos Komnenos. About a particular episode in which Andronikos escapes from prison in a cunning and daring fashion, Bourbouhakis writes that "the story is indeed remarkable, and Niketas relishes telling it, as I think we can assume his audience relished hearing or reading it."[10] While he may have relished writing it at the time, after 1204, when he was no longer logothete but merely the "wretched author," the pleasure he took in recalling that episode may have been significantly diminished. Those passages that were added after 1204 reflect a changed emotional response to the events described as part of Niketas' revised and more tragic view of the century as he shifted from Komnenian court propagandist before

[8] Chon. *Hist.* 634.

[9] Bourbouhakis (2009: 213).

[10] Bourbouhakis (2009: 228); the scene referenced is Chon. *Hist.* 106.87–107.32.

1204 to fierce critic of the pre-1204 regimes. In light of what Niketas himself writes about his own circumstances and emotional state while writing, it is perhaps less likely that Nikeas "relished" telling it.

Indeed, whether the writer is Niketas Choniates, Eustathios of Thessaloniki, or John Kaminiates, the authorial interruptions characterized by statements of the authors' emotional experience of writing or recollection are uniformly of pain. Due to the narrative constraints of the genre of limited-perspective nonfiction, however, the emotional state of the writers when recalling their traumas can only be glimpsed in those passing moments when the authors allow their emotions to break through the surface of the narrative and, as the example of Niketas' revision suggests, these moments are conditioned by a variety of authorial decisions to reveal or conceal their feelings. The novels, by contrast, as fundamentally dialogic, once again offer a mimetic if fictional depiction of the experience of survivors of trauma narrating their own traumatic experience. And, as in the case of their nonfictional witness counterparts, the emotional response of both narrators and listeners to witness testimony in the novels shows that the range of emotions exhibited is contingent upon the social and affective position of the addressee relative to the narrator and the content in which the testimony is offered.

In *Hysmine and Hysmnias*, for instance, after the central lovers have been redeemed from slavery and reunited with one another and their families, the priest who was the agent of their freedom asks Hysminias to tell his story, but Hysminias, like so many victims of trauma, hesitates. The priest, however, insists: "Do not shrink from telling us all your adventures from the very beginning to the very end" (μὴ φείσῃ λέγων τὰ καθ᾽ ὑμᾶς ἀρχῆς ἀπ᾽ ἄκρης καὶ μέχρις ἄκρης αὐτῆς τελευτῆς).[11] Hysminias again demurs, saying: "You kindle for me a bowl of fire and you open up an ant-heap of disasters" (Ὅλους ἀνάπτεις μοι κρατῆρας πυρὸς καὶ μυρμηκιάν μοι τραγῳδημάτων ἀναστομοῖς).[12] The priest, however, remains undaunted, telling Hysminias again: "Do not omit one detail, by Apollo, not one, by your freedom and the brilliant wedding that Apollo prepares for you" ("Ἀλλὰ μὴ φείσῃ μοι" φησὶ "πρὸς Ἀπόλλωνος μηδενός, πρὸς ἐλευθερίας αὐτῆς καὶ νυμφῶνος, ὅν σοι λαμπρὸν Ἀπόλλων ἐνυμφοστόλησεν") and again Hysminias refuses: "Pardon me, master, for

---

[11] *H&H.* 10.17.1.

[12] *H&H.* 10.17.1.

282 A. J. GOLDWYN

my soul is thrown into confusion out of modesty and my mind is totally bewildered" (Σύγγνωθι, δέσποτα· ὅλην γὰρ ἐξ αἰδοῦς κατατεθορυβημένος εἰμὶ τὴν ψυχὴν καὶ ὅλον τεταραγμένος τὸν νοῦν).[13] On the next day, the priest again asks, repeatedly and persistently (τὰ καθ' ἡμᾶς ἐζήτει καὶ πάλιν μαθεῖν καὶ ἦν ἀμεταθέτως ἐγκείμενος),[14] and Hysminias notes that "even though I was reluctant and hesitant, nevertheless unwillingly made ready to tell the tale; my voice failed and my tongue stuck – however, I began, with a faltering voice" (ἐγὼ δ' ἀλλὰ κᾶν ὤκνουν, κᾶν ἔφριττον, ἀλλ' ἄκων ἀπεδυσάμην πρὸς τὴν διήγησιν, καὶ ἡ φωνή μου ἐπέλειπε καὶ ἡ γλῶσσα ἐπείχετο· ἄρχομαι δ' ὅμως ὧδε λεπτῇ τῇ φωνῇ).[15] Despite a happy outcome to his narrative, Hysminas, the survivor, the freed slave, reunited with parents and beloved, struggles to articulate his experience and feels sorrow and anguish in doing so, something the priest, whose desire to know the story is greater than his desire to spare the storyteller, ignores.

Hysmine, too, experiences great anguish in narrating her story; when she is asked, at first "she was silent, she only wept" (Ἡ δ' ἐσίγα καὶ μόνον ἐδάκρυεν) and then, upon being further pressured, "She, drenched with perspiration and tears and with faltering tongue and breath catching at her voice, kept her eyes fixed intently on the ground" (Ἡ δὲ περιρρεομένη πυκνοῖς ἱδρῶσι καὶ δάκρυσι καὶ τῇ γλώσσῃ διαμαρτάνουσα καὶ τὴν φωνὴν παρακοπτομένη τῷ ἄσθματι καὶ ὅλους τοὺς ὀφθαλμοὺς ἀτενῶς τῇ γῇ) and begins to speak.[16] The recollection of traumatic events is another kind of trauma, one about which the survivors themselves do not wish to revisit and do so only at the great emotional cost to themselves.

Indeed, in asking with such insistence, the priest's actions echo those of people far worse: the slavers who demanded that Hysminias tell them his story while they held him in bondage. Also staged around a meal, Hysminias demurs several times from the slaver's demand that he "tell me all, hold nothing back" (Μὴ φείσῃ μηδενός, ἀλλὰ πάντ' ἐκκάλυπτε λέγων),[17] the same imperative of the priest. He tells how "I fixed my eyes on the ground which I bedewed completely with my tears" (τοὺς

[13] H&H. 10.17.2, 10.17.3.
[14] H&H. 11.2.1.
[15] H&H. 11.2.2.
[16] H&H. 11.12.3, 11.13.1.
[17] H&H. 8.11.3.

ὀφθαλμοὺς ἐπεπήγειν τῇ γῇ καὶ ὅλην τοῖς δάκρυσιν ἔβρεχον),[18] again fore-shadowing the language he uses to describe the difficulty of speaking to the priest (ὀφθαλμοὺς ἀτενῶς τῇ γῇ) and, when he tries to begin, "My voice failed me, my tongue was stuck, and tears flowed in rivers from my eyes" (Ἐμοῦ δ' ἐπέλιπεν ἡ φωνή, καὶ ἐπείχετο ἡ γλῶσσα, καί μου τῶν ὀφθαλμῶν κατὰ ποταμοὺς ἀπέρρει τὸ δάκρυον)[19]; again, the same language as with the priest (ἡ φωνή μου ἐπέλειπε καὶ ἡ γλῶσσα ἐπείχετο). As the priest, so too his mistress insists: "Look, now is the time for you to picture your circumstances for us in words" (Ἰδού σοι καιρὸς τῇ γλώσσῃ κατὰ μέρος ἡμῖν καταζωγραφῆσαι τὰ σά).[20] Again, Hysminias describes the trauma that accompanies traumatic narration: "I, at the mere recollection, let out a piteous groan from my heart, and shed many tears from my eyes saying, Be sparing with my misfortunes, masters, lest I make the banquet a misery and pour out for you bowls of grief" (Ἐγὼ δὲ καὶ μόνον ἐπιμνησθεὶς ἐλεεινὸν ἐβρυχησάμην ἐγκάρδιον, πολλὰ δὲ τῶν ὀφθαλμῶν κατέσταξα δάκρυα, "Φείσασθε," λέγων, "δεσπόται, δυστυχημάτων ἐμῶν, μὴ τὴν τράπεζανεὶς κοπετὸν μεταβάλω καὶ πένθους ὑμῖν κρατῆρα κεράσωμαι.”),[21] the "πένθους ὑμῖν κρατῆρα" echoing the κρατῆρας πυρὸς of his attempt to avoid speaking to the priest. Indeed, from Hysminias' perspective, there is perhaps little difference after all between the priest and the slavers: he refers to them both in the same way when they demand he speak: "Pardon, master" (σύγγνωθι, δέσποτα).[22] In both cases, Hysminias' mode of address acknowledges the power differential between himself and the one compelling him to speak. Despite the difference in intention between the priest and slave–master, both are insistent, oblivious to the pain their demands cause the survivors. Hysminias thus resists telling his tale to both the well-meaning priest and the cruel slave–master: knowing that his narrative is mere after-dinner entertainment for them, Hysminias' trauma of recollection is the same despite the differences in his circumstances. As represented by the close verbal parallels in the two scenes, the priest and the slave–master thus represent two

[18] *H&H.* 8.11.3.
[19] *H&H.* 8.11.3.
[20] *H&H.* 8.12.1.
[21] *H&H.* 8.12.2.
[22] *H&H.* 8.21.7, 10.17.9.

284   A. J. GOLDWYN

different but equally troubling ways of listening to witness literature for pleasure.

As Adorno noted, to write poetry after Auschwitz is barbaric because it is, in some sense, to "squeeze aesthetic pleasure out of artistic representation of the naked bodily pain of those who have been knocked down by rifle butts," and this is, in some sense, what both the priest and slave–masters are attempting to get from Hysmine and Hysminias by making them, against their will and at a great emotional cost, narrate their stories during the course of a meal.[23] Irving Howe, in considering Adorno's claim, argues "that the representation of a horrible event, especially if in drawing upon literary skills it achieves a certain graphic power, could serve to domesticate it, rendering it familiar and in some sense even tolerable, and thereby shearing away part of the horror. The comeliness of even the loosest literary forms is likely to soften the impact of what is being rendered, and in most renderings of imaginary situations we tacitly expect and welcome this."[24] Howe then asserts that reading such texts for pleasure can "carry[ ] a share of voyeuristic sadomasochism," which he calls "a sort of pained illicit pleasure."[25] Similarly, Brett Ashley Kaplan suggests that the "aesthetic pleasure" of Holocaust narratives constitutes an "unwanted beauty."[26] Sarah Donovan argues that "most theories of literary criticism maintain that at least part of the purpose of literature is the stimulation of pleasure" and that "while the source and the importance of this pleasure vary, the insistence on the pleasurable emotion seems universal."[27] For Donovan, however, as with other scholars of beauty and aesthetics in reading traumatic narratives, the impulse toward pleasure must nevertheless be balanced when reading Holocaust literature or witness testimony more broadly: "Such a word 'pleasure' in a book about genocide may seem grotesque," she writes.[28] Carolyn Dean suggests that, where the aim of witness literature

---

[23] As cited in Howe (2014: 280).

[24] Howe (2014: 281–282).

[25] Howe (2014: 282).

[26] Kaplan (2007: 1).

[27] Donovan (2017: 73).

[28] Donovan (2017: 73).

5 PLEASURE, PAIN, PERVERSITY: READING BYZANTINE ... 285

may be to create empathy, the "voyeuristic" or even "pornographic" pleasure that can be drawn from reading such narratives can actually result in a numbing effect.[29]

Nevertheless, reading for pleasure, as Bourbouhakis suggests for Niketas, is a common position for reading Byzantine witness literature. John Melville-Jones, for instance, writing about Eustathios' inclusion of "some personal elements" in his narrative argues that "we must be grateful for this, because we can enjoy certain passages, written with considerable feeling, which are memorable."[30] As regards *Hysmine and Hysminias*, Margaret Alexiou has argued that "it would be perverse to suggest that it is not a love story, enjoyed, as intended, by readers throughout centuries in numerous manuscripts, printed editions, and translations."[31] It may be perverse to suggest it is not a love story, but it may also be necessary. Indeed, Hysminias himself, at the end of the story, positions pleasure as but one response to the text:

> Whatever in mankind is most responsive to passion will appreciate all the charming passion in this story; whatever is chaste and virginal will respond to its restraint; whatever is more inclined to sympathy will pity our misfortunes, and so memory of us will be undying.

> Ὅσον μὲν οὖν ἐν ἀνθρώποις ἐρωτικώτερον, τῶν πολλῶν ἐρωτικῶν χαρίτων ἡμᾶς ἀποδέξεται, καὶ ὅσον παρθενικὸν καὶ σεμνότερον, τῆς σωφροσύνης πάλιν ἀγάσεται· ὅσον δὲ συμπαθέστερον, ἐλεήσει τῶν δυστυχημάτωνἡμᾶς, καὶ οὕτως ἡμῖν ἔσται τὰ τῆς μνήμης ἀθάνατα.[32]

Seeing the novel only as a love story and responding to its erotic elements is but one of three possible ways that its own primary narrator-focalizer suggests it could be read. *Hysmine and Hysminias* is not only a love story, it is also a slave narrative, with all the attendant horrors such positionality entails: the characters lose loved ones, see people raped and executed before their eyes, see friends and strangers sold into slavery, suffer extreme bodily trauma (to the extent, for instance, that Hysminas doesn't even recognize Hysmine when they meet again after their enslavement), endure

---

[29] Dean (2004: 24–25).

[30] Melville-Jones (2017: 302).

[31] Alexiou (2002: 119).

[32] *H&H*. 11.23.1.

286   A. J. GOLDWYN

forced marches and servile labor, suffer from suicidal ideation and despair. Hysminias allows his listeners to experience these aspects of the tale as well: one who is "more inclined to sympathy" (συμπαθέστερον) will feel "pity" (ἐλεήσει), two essential characteristics for reading witness literature, as demonstrated by Eustathios' and Kaminiates' appeals.

Again, the works of witness literature themselves, both fictional and nonfictional, offer counter-examples of listening to those offered by the slave–masters and the priest. The Foreword to *Night*, for instance, was written by François Mauriac, a Christian French writer, future Nobel laureate in literature, and supporter of the collaborationist Vichy Regime during the early part of the war who later joined the Resistance. In the Foreword, Mauriac describes how, when Wiesel, then unknown to him, came to interview him and that, despite his long history of suspicion around journalists, Wiesel "won me over from the first moment" (m'inspira dès l'abord une sympathie dont je ne dus guère me défendre longtemps) and that "our conversation very quickly became more personal" (nos propos prirent très vite un tour personnel).[33] What Marion Wiesel translates as "won me over," however, is, in Mauriac's original French, none other than the crucial word of witness: "sympathie." As a result of this feeling, Mauriac begins to bear witness to Wiesel: "Soon I was sharing with him memories from the time of the Occupation" (J'en vins à évoquer des souvenirs du temps de l'occupation), an example of the kind of reciprocal witnessing evidenced in the Komnenian novels and the letter of John Kaminiates, whereby the supplementary witness often first speaks of their own trauma before listening to that of the protagonist.[34] Mauriac then continues about that which he himself had not personally witnessed, but which still haunted him nonetheless: "I confided to my young visitor that nothing I had witnessed during that dark period had marked me as deeply as the image of cattle cars filled with Jewish children at the Austerlitz train station" (Je confiai à mon jeune visiteur qu'aucune vision de ces sombres années ne m'a marqué autant que ces wagons remplis d'enfants juifs, à la gare d'Austerlitz).[35] Mauriac's language is one of sympathy, affect, and mutual understanding: "I was sharing with him memories" (j'en vins à évoquer des souvenirs), he

---

[33] Wiesel (2006: np; 2007: 25).

[34] Wiesel (2006: np; 2007: 25).

[35] Wiesel (2006: np; 2007: 25–26).

5 PLEASURE, PAIN, PERVERSITY: READING BYZANTINE ...   287

says, and "I confided" (je confiai), expressions of trust. He is emotionally "marked" (m'a marqué) by the events. Due to these displays of sympathy, Wiesel opens up to him: "I was one of them" (Je suis l'un d'eux).[36] Mauriac then switches roles, no longer the one bearing witness, but the witness to the witness, and he describes his thought process and intentions upon hearing Wiesel's story:

> What answer was there to give my young interlocutor [...]? What did I say to him? Did I speak to him of that other Jew, this crucified brother who perhaps resembled him and whose cross conquered the world? Did I explain to him that what had been a stumbling block for *his* faith had become a cornerstone for *mine*?

> Que pouvais-je répondre à mon jeune interlocuteur [...]? Que lui ai-je dit? Lui ai-je parlé de cet Israélien, ce frère qui lui ressemblait peut-être, ce crucifié dont la croix a vaincu le monde? Lui ai-je affirmé que ce qui fut pour lui pierre d'achoppement est devenu pierre d'angle pour moi?[37]

Mauriac's thought process circles around what words he should use in his response: "what answer" (Que pouvais-je répondre), "what did I say" (Que lui ai-je dit), "Did I explain" (Lui ai-je affirmé)—and yet, Mauriac reveals in the end that he did not do any of these things: "That is what I should have said to the Jewish child. But all I could do was embrace him and weep" (Voilà ce que j'aurais dû dire à l'enfant jutf Mais je n'ai pu que l'embrasser en pleurant).[38] In the end, Mauriac suppresses his own voice, his own opinions, his own words, and instead, demonstrates his capacity to be witness to the witness through his own silence and sympathetic listening. Mauriac's subsequent actions demonstrate the historical importance of such witnesses, since Wiesel himself acknowledges that it was through "the tireless efforts of the great Catholic French writer and Nobel laureate François Mauriac" (des efforts inlassables du grand François Mauriac) that "after months and months of personal visits, letters, and telephone calls, he finally succeeded in getting it into print"

---

[36] Wiesel (2006: np; 2007: 26).

[37] Wiesel (2006: np; 2007: 30).

[38] Wiesel (2006: np; 2007: 30).

288 A. J. GOLDWYN

(après des mois et des mois, et des visites personnelles, il finit par le placer).[39]

In this way, Mauriac is a real-life version of the kind of witness to the witness found in Byzantine witness literature as well. For Charikles, for instance, the listener is Kleandros, who describes himself as "a fellow prisoner, a foreigner in the same prison" (συναιχμάλωτος, συμφυλακίτης ξένος), and who, instead of repeatedly insisting on hearing the story of suffering, "hastened to console his fellow prisoner" (παρηγορεῖν ἔσπευδε συμπεπονθότα).[40]

Indeed, when Charikles hesitates to speak first, Kleandros allows him without hesitation to defer to the next day, instead offering to tell his own story first. Kratandros serves a similar function to Dosikles; "we are fellow prisoners" (συμπεφυλακίσμεθα), he says, an expression of solidarity that thus encourages speaking and consolation.[41] John Kaminiates concludes his letter Gregory of Cappadocia by noting that "you showed sympathy and shared in our suffering by manifesting your concern to hear the full story of these events" (συμπαθήσας τότε καὶ ἐν τούτῳ κοινωνήσας ἡμῖν τοῦ πάθους ἐν τῷ περὶ πολλοῦ ποιήσασθαι μαθεῖν τὴν περὶ τούτων ἀκολουθίαν).[42] Across texts of witness literature, the prefix συμ/v—becomes between teller and audience a marker of identification,

> where identification means putting oneself in the place of another without leaving one's own, where it fosters an empathy tempered by the awareness of an irreducible difference, where it sustains the relation between listener and witness, identification remains in the service of reception, since it is in this relation that, putting themselves in the place of listeners, silenced victims become storytelling survivors (without ceasing to have been silenced victims), and in this relation, therefore, that memory finds the space or "extent" of its articulation.[43]

Unlike the priest and the slave–master, free people who do not share the experiences of the slaves and thus represent the model of listening for their own pleasure, the fellow slaves, having shared the experience or at

[39] Wiesel (2006: np; 2007: 14).
[40] D&C. 1.260, 262.
[41] R&D. 1.139–143.
[42] Kam. ex. Thess. 78.
[43] Trezise (2013: 30).

least identifying with it, represent a model of listening that can bring consolation—a different kind of pleasure—to both speaker and listener. In this way, the significance of figures like Gregory of Cappadocia and Charidoux transcends the historians' and philologists' attempts to identify them with actual historical figures. In her memoir *Still Alive: A Holocaust Girlhood Remembered* (*weiter leben. Eine Jugend*, originally published in 1992), the Holocaust child-survivor Ruth Klüger describes how she and her mother approached the first American GI they saw after their liberation: "Since I knew no English, I couldn't understand his answer, but his gesture was unmistakable. He put his hands over his ears and turned away. [...] Here was my first American, and he deliberately closed his ears" (Was er antwortete, verstand ich nicht, weil ich noch kein Englisch konnte, aber seine Gebärde war unmißverständlich: Er legte die Hände an beide Ohren und wandte sich ab. [...] Hier war mein erster Amerikaner, und der hielt sich die Ohren zu).[44] In the end, perhaps it does not matter who Gregory of Cappadocia and Charidoux were; perhaps what matters is that they did not put their hands over their ears: they listened, from beginning to end, and thus provide a model for readers embedded within the text itself. Indeed, while much theory surrounding witness literature focuses on the difficulty of speaking, Trezise argues that "unspeakable" in this context may be more accurately understood as "I don't want to listen," a position of emotional indifference as frequently shown by various characters in witness literature in Byzantium as its opposite.[45] Thus, as much as the witnesses struggle with articulating the trauma, equally central is the inability or refusal of the audience to look and see, both in the literal sense of looking away and in the more metaphorical sense of focusing on other aspects of the texts that therefore do not require an engagement with their more traumatic aspects.

Agamben describes what could be called the ethical consequences of the narratological considerations inherent in the desire to tell or not to tell, to look or not look; he describes how in an "English film shot in Bergen-Belsen immediately after the camp's liberation in 1945 [...] the camera lingers almost by accident on what seem to be living people, a group of prisoners crouched on the ground or wandering on foot like ghosts," thus capturing that category of people whom camp

---

[44] Klüger (1992: 188–189; 2001: 149).

[45] Trezise (2013: 225).

290   A. J. GOLDWYN

inmates called "Muselmänner."[46] These men are the most debased of those in the camps, who thus for Agamben represents the quintessential limit figure who obviates previous ideas of humanity. "The same cameraman," Agamben continues, "who had until then patiently lingered over naked bodies, over the terrible 'dolls' dismembered and stacked one on top of another, could not bear the sight of these half-living beings; he immediately began once again to show the cadavers."[47]

From this perspective, then, Kaminiates, in his insistence that Gregory read his account even despite Kaminiates' reticence to write it, demands that even one as elevated as Gregory (who stands in for all readers past, present, and future) not look away from the victims of trauma. Kaminiates demands this at least three times, saying that the sack of the city happened "so that future generations may learn through our example" (ἵν' ἔχωσι γνῶναι διὰ τοῦ καθ' ἡμᾶς ὑποδείγματος οἱ μετέπειτα)[48] calling the sack of the city "such events which have left us as a novel and solemn warning to the world" (δι' ὧν τῷ βίῳ καινόν τι καὶ φοβερὸν ὑπελείφθημεν ἄκουσμα)[49] saying that God had ordained these events "in order that we might through our own sufferings serve as an example to others of what we had failed to learn from theirs" (ἵν' ὅπερ ἄλλων πασχόντων ἡμεῖς οὐκ ἐδιδασκόμεθα, τοῦτο ἡμεῖς παθόντες ἄλλοις ὑπόδειγμα ποιησώμεθα)[50] and that he is telling this story "so as to provide a clear and unmistakable warning for the advice and enlightenment of future generations" (ὡς εἶναι τοῖς μετέπειτα νουθεσίας ὑπόθεσιν καὶ ἐναργοῦς διδασκαλίας παραίνεσιν).[51] And, through his use of paradigmatic examples—not least of which the

[46] Agamben (2017: 791). The ethics and efficacy of using images as testimonial truth, with discussion of this particular passage are discussed in Wilson (2012: 127–129). Colin Davis takes particular issue with what he perceives as Agamben's misprision of the significance of the Muselmann in Levi, eg. "For all his close reliance on Levi, Agamben misses precisely this point. He endeavours to describe the significance of the *Muselmann* and his centrality to the experience of the camps despite Levi's implicit warning that this would be to find meaning—and comfort—where there is none. And Agamben's failure to understand Levi's point that the general significance of the *Muselmann*'s testimony is not available leads him to misunderstand Levi's related point that survivors speak 'in their stead, by proxy'" (Davis 2018: 15).

[47] Agamben (2017: 795).

[48] Kam. *ex. Thess.* 12.3.

[49] Kam. *ex. Thess.* 13.5.

[50] Kam. *ex. Thess.* 15.4.

[51] Kam. *ex. Thess.* 16.1.

example of his own experience—Kaminiates demands an acknowledgment of the continued persistence of the humanity of the citizens of Thessaloniki, even the most degraded, even those held, like him, in slavery. He urges his readers not to look away.

In the introduction to the most recent edition of *Night*, Elie Wiesel writes:

> Sometimes I am asked if I know "the response to Auschwitz"; I answer that not only do I not know it, but that I don't even know if a tragedy of this magnitude *has* a response. What I do know is that there is "response" in responsibility. When we speak of this era of evil and darkness, so close and yet so distant, "responsibility" is the key word.

> Parfois l'on me demande si je connais «la réponse à Auschwitz»; je réponds que je ne la connais pas; je ne sais même pas si une tragédie de cette ampleur possède une réponse. Mais je sais qu'il y a «réponse» dans responsabilité. Lorsqu'on parle de cette époque de malédiction et de ténèbres, si proche et si lointaine, «responsabilité» est le mot clé.[52]

In the case of Holocaust testimony, this responsibility can no longer fall only on the tellers of the tales, since the tellers are increasingly no longer alive. In the case of Byzantine writers, this is exclusively so. Thomas Trezise characterizes this kind of witnessing in which "there is no face-to-face encounter with survivors but rather one that is mediated by a recording of some kind, so that we can at best, and largely unbeknownst to survivors themselves" a "trusteeship," in which the recipient of the witness testimony must "act as the trustees of their testimony by ensuring its continued reception."[53] For Trezise, moreover, the principle function of the trustee is not what he calls "whatever specific social, political, historical or other purposes this trusteeship may serve," that is, its value for the purposes of the reconstruction of the past, but rather, that "receiving testimony is first of all an ethical exigency that tests our ability to empathize."[54] In a very real sense, then, the writers of witness testimony have done all they can; they have left behind all they will ever be able to say on the subject of their own trauma. The responsibility is thus

[52] Wiesel (2006: 13; 2007: 23).

[53] Trezise (2013: 223).

[54] Trezise (2013: 223).

292 A. J. GOLDWYN

no longer with the victims themselves; it falls now to those entrusted with the preservation, interpretation, and transmission of their testimony, and their responsibility is twofold: in the negative sense, not to look away or cover their ears and, in the affirmative sense, to speak out. If witness literature is, as Primo Levi says, "discourse on behalf of others," then scholarship or any other form of writing about witness literature is itself also a form of witnessing. The obligation of the witness to the witness, then, is to listen, even when that listening brings no pleasure.

If the rhetoric of authorial suffering is understood as the representation of authentic emotion, then reading for pleasure becomes more ethically fraught, derived as it is from witnessing another's suffering. Indeed, Robert Eaglestone argues that a defining feature of "testimony" is that "it is not pleasurable to read."[55] Contemporary theorists of witness literature posit an alternate method, of responsibility or trusteeship, a method already encoded within the representations of witnessing within the Byzantine tradition. Each reader of Byzantine witness literature thus has the choice to listen like the δεσπότας, the slave–master, whose mode of listening is such that, in the words of Hysminias, the witness is "compelled by force to endure what should not be demanded" (τολμᾷ θ' ἃ μὴ χρὴ τῇ βίᾳ νικώμενον),[56] or to listen with, in the words of John Kaminiates, συμπαθεστάτῃ φιλίᾳ, most sympathetic friendship.[57]

BIBLIOGRAPHY

Agamben, Giorgio. 2017. *The Omnibus Homo Sacer*. Palo Alto: Stanford University Press.

Alexiou, Margaret. 2002. *After Antiquity: Greek Language, Myth, and Metaphor*. Ithaca: Cornell University Press.

Appelfeld, Aharon. 1988. After the Holocaust. In *Writing and the Holocaust*, ed. Berel Lang, 83–93. New York: Holmes and Meier.

Bourbouhakis, Emmanuel. 2009. Exchanging the Devices of Ares for the Delights of the Erotes. In *Plotting with Eros: Essays on the Poetics of Love and the Erotics of Reading*, ed. Ingela Nilsson, 213–234. Copenhagen: Museum Tusculanum Press.

---

[55] Eaglestone (2004: 39).

[56] *H&H*. 8.12.2.

[57] Kam. *ex. Thess.* 1.5.5.

Dean, Carolyn. 2004. *The Fragility of Empathy after the Holocaust*. Ithaca: Cornell University Press.

Donovan, Sarah. 2017. *Genocide Literature in Middle and Secondary Classroom: Rhetoric, Witnessing, and Social Action in a Time of Standards and Accountability*. London: Routledge.

Efthymiades, Stephanos. 2009. Niketas Choniates: The Writer. In *Niketas Choniates: A Historian and a Writer*, eds. Alicia Simpson and Stephanos Efthymiades, 35–58. Geneva: Pomme d'Or.

Eaglestone, Robert. 2004. *The Holocaust and the Postmodern*. Oxford: Oxford University Press.

Howe, Irving. 2014. *A Voice Still Heard: Selected Essays of Irving Howe*. New Haven: Yale University Press.

Kaplan, Brett Ashley. 2007. *Unwanted Beauty: Aesthetic Pleasure in Holocaust Representation*. Urbana: University of Illinois Press.

Klüger, Ruth. 1992. *Weiter leben: Eine Jugend*. Göttingen: Wallstein Verlag.

———. 2001. *Still Alive: A Holocaust Girlhood Remembered*. New York: The Feminist Press at the City University of New York.

Levi, Primo. 1959. *If This Is a Man*, trans. Stuart Woolf. New York: Orion Press.

———. 1989. *Se questo è un uomo*. Einaudi: Torino.

Melville-Jones, John. 2017. *Eustathios as a Source for Historical Information: Decoding Indirect Allusions in His Works. In Reading Eustathios of Thessaloniki*, eds. Pontani, Filipmaria et al., 299–308. Berlin: Degruyte.

Neville, Leonora. 2018. *Guide to Byzantine Historical Writing*. Cambridge: Cambridge University Press.

———. 2019. Pity and Lamentation in the Authorial Personae of John Kaminiates and Anna Komnene. In *Emotions and Gender in Byzantine Culture*, eds. Stavroula Constantinou and Mati Meyer, 65–92. New York: Palgrave Macmillan.

Nilsson, Ingela. 2013. Nature Controlled by Artistry: The Poetics of the Literary Garden in Byzantium. In *Byzantine Gardens and Beyond*, eds. Helena Bodin and Ragnar Hedlund, 14–29. Uppsala: Acta Universitatis Upsaliensis.

Simpson, Alicia. 2004. *Studies in the Composition of the Historia*. PhD, Kings College London.

———. 2006. Before and After 1204: The Versions of Niketas Choniates' 'Historia'. *Dumbarton Oaks Papers* 60: 189–221.

———. 2013a. *Niketas Choniates: A Historiographical Study*. Oxford: Oxford University Press.

———. 2013b. From the Workshop of Niketas Choniates: The Authority of Tradition and Literary Mimesis. In *Authority in Byzantium*, ed. Pamela Armstrong, 259–268. London: Routledge.

Seidman, Naomi. 2006. Faithful Renderings: Jewish-Christian Difference and the Politics of Translation. Chicago: University of Chicago Press.

Trezise, Thomas. 2013. *Witnessing Witnessing: On the Reception of Holocaust Survivor Testimony*. New York: Fordham University Press.

Urbainczyk, Theresa. 2018. *Writing About Byzantium: The History of Niketas Choniates*. New York: Routledge.

White, Hayden. 2004. Figuring Realism in Witness Literature. *Parallax* 10 (1): 113–124.

Wiesel, Elie. 2006. *Night*, trans. M. Wiesel. New York: Hill and Wang.

———. 2007. *La Nuit*. Paris: Les Éditions de Minuit.

Wilson, Emma. 2012. *Love, Mortality and the Moving Image*. New York: Palgrave Macmillan.

INDEX

A
Abbasid, 71, 238

Adorno, Theodore, 143, 284

African-American, 77, 83, 86, 88, 155–157, 165, 185

Agamben, Giorgio, 4, 13, 16–21, 29, 30, 111, 113, 114, 124, 127, 128, 156, 197, 198, 289, 290

Homo Sacer, 16, 124, 128

Agnes-Anna of France, 62

Ammonius, 11

Andronikos Komnenos, 62, 243, 266, 280

Auschwitz, 1, 2, 4, 12, 13, 18–20, 22, 24, 27, 29–31, 34, 38, 41, 44, 46–48, 59, 77, 90, 122, 129–131, 133, 143, 189, 200, 213, 284, 291

Austerlitz, 286

autobiography, 13, 77, 79, 83, 88, 89, 93, 94, 172, 173, 178, 274

B
Bari, Italy, 21

Basilakes, Nikephoros, 14, 15

Bergen-Belsen, 201, 289

biopolitics, 16–20, 22, 24, 113–115, 124, 125, 128, 130, 176, 250, 253

biopower, 16, 19, 114, 115, 123, 129, 183, 197

Birkenau, 129

Byzantine Empire, 1, 9, 11, 71, 146, 272

Byzantine Studies, 5, 6, 9, 58, 61, 64, 65, 76

C
Capture of Thessaloniki (Eustathios of Thessaloniki), 8, 10

cattle car, 24, 38

clothes/clothing, 30–32, 34, 35, 219, 220, 250, 251

© The Editor(s) (if applicable) and The Author(s), under exclusive license to Springer Nature Switzerland AG 2021
A. J. Goldwyn, *Witness Literature in Byzantium*, New Approaches to Byzantine History and Culture, https://doi.org/10.1007/978-3-030-78857-5

296 INDEX

Constantinople, 6, 11, 144, 148, 231, 233, 241, 242, 254, 255, 262, 266, 269, 272, 273, 278
Crusaders. *See* Normans

D
De Capta Thessalonica. See Capture of Thessaloniki (Eustathios of Thessaloniki)

E
emotion, 6, 52, 55, 56, 63, 75, 76, 78, 90, 97, 100, 104, 120, 132, 147, 154, 169, 257, 258, 260, 278, 284, 292
Equiano, Olaudah, 88–90, 93–95, 107, 168, 206, 213
Essaka, 88, 93
ethopoeia, 14, 15, 104, 105, 199, 214
Eugenianos, Niketas, 142, 195, 201, 202, 210, 211, 273
  Drosilla and Charikles, 142, 201–204, 208, 210, 215, 217, 266, 267, 273
Eustathios of Thessaloniki, 1–4, 7–11, 13, 21–24, 26, 28–30, 32–36, 40–44, 47–57, 59, 61–63, 66, 78, 99, 100, 107, 141, 142, 144, 148, 149, 153, 154, 159, 162, 169, 184, 191, 195, 203, 213, 217, 235, 240, 242–249, 251–254, 256, 260, 264, 265, 273, 277, 281, 285, 286
  Capture of Thessaloniki, 2, 57

F
Foucault, Michel, 16–18, 123, 124, 128, 156, 157

G
Gangra, 239
Genocide Studies, 1, 4, 5
genre, 8, 57, 64
German, 37, 89
Glykas, Michael, 14
Gregory of Cappadocia, 71, 72, 85–87, 90, 92, 94, 96, 106, 109, 119, 168, 170–172, 192, 217, 220, 288–290

H
Herodotus, 55
History. See Niketas Choniates
Holocaust, 1–6, 8–10, 12, 16, 19, 20, 36, 37, 43, 45, 46, 48, 49, 51, 59, 60, 65, 75, 84, 98, 129, 141–145, 148, 157, 170, 174, 175, 179, 200, 245, 270, 279, 284, 289, 291
Holocaust fiction, 11, 143, 144, 179, 270
Holocaust Studies, 4–6, 9, 49, 58, 83, 84, 98, 142, 170
Homer, 149, 247, 264, 270
  Iliad, xiii, 61, 103, 247
  Odyssey, 207, 220, 247
hunger, 24, 25, 28–31, 35–38, 40, 63, 150, 186, 240, 250, 265

J
Jerusalem, 52
John II Komnenos, 231, 260, 272

K
Kaminiates, John, 2, 8, 11, 27, 29, 51, 52, 66, 71–74, 76–88, 90–128, 130, 131, 133–136, 144, 148, 150, 153, 154, 157, 160–162, 168–173, 176, 178,

INDEX 297

184, 186, 191, 192, 195, 196,
 199, 202–204, 206–208, 212,
 213, 217, 218, 220, 235–238,
 240, 242, 256, 257, 260, 264,
 265, 272, 273, 281, 286, 288,
 290–292
Capture of Thessaloniki, 72, 82, 83
Kapo, 32, 39
Kingdom of Sicily, 1
Klüger, Ruth, 289
 *Still Alive: A Holocaust Girlhood
  Remembered*, 289
Komnenian novels, 11, 88, 104,
 141, 144, 145, 148, 155, 157,
 158, 161, 162, 165, 185, 191,
 201, 205, 232, 235, 241, 266,
 270–272, 274, 280, 286

L
Lager. *See* Auschwitz
Lake Askania, 258
Latins. *See* Normans
Leo of Tripoli, 10, 71, 87, 124, 127,
 128, 131
Levi, Primo, 2, 12–14, 19, 20, 22,
 25–31, 33–42, 48, 53, 111, 122,
 129–132, 146, 156, 171, 175,
 189, 215, 270, 290, 292
 If This is a Man, 2, 12, 25, 36, 37,
  53, 146
 The Drowned and the Saved, 12, 13

M
Maeander (river), 231, 234, 238
Makrembolites, Eumathios, 142, 217,
 218, 220
 Hysmine and Hysminias, 142, 144,
  204, 217, 218, 220, 226, 284,
  285
Malta, 14

Manasses, Constantine, 54, 85, 167,
 169
Manzikert, 147
Mauriac, François, 286–288
Menander Rhetor, 86, 87, 92, 97, 98,
 107, 111–113, 218
Monowitz-Nuna, 129

N
narratology, 15, 74, 90, 95, 97, 100,
 107, 123, 136, 191, 256, 259,
 263
Nicaea, 234, 254, 258, 259, 278, 279
Night, 2, 3, 8, 22, 36, 38, 43, 44, 47,
 48, 60, 73, 88, 136, 278, 286,
 291. *See also* Wiesel, Elie
Niketas Choniates, 11, 66, 103, 142,
 148, 151, 153, 154, 161, 162,
 165, 184, 201, 212, 231–245,
 247–274, 277–281, 285
Normans, 1, 3, 23, 43, 53, 242
nostalgia, 92, 93

P
pathos, 25, 38, 43, 47, 50, 51, 55,
 56, 62, 116, 120, 122, 157, 170
Patzinaks, 235, 237
Peloponnese, 11
Peloponnesian War, 55
Phrygia, 231, 234, 238
Prodromos, Theodore, 9, 142, 149,
 152, 154, 158–160, 163–165,
 175, 177, 178, 180–183,
 185–189, 194–196, 199–202,
 210, 273
 Rhodanthe and Dosikles, 142, 144,
  149–152, 154, 166, 169, 175,
  176, 178, 181–183, 186, 188,
  194–196, 199, 201, 210, 215,
  217–220, 267, 273
Pseudo-Nilus, 11

298 INDEX

R

Rhodes, 144, 149, 158, 171, 178, 184, 192, 200, 217, 273

S

Serbs, 235
shoes, 31, 32, 34, 250
Sighet, Romania, 1, 22
slave narratives, 79, 83, 86, 88, 145, 155–157, 165, 173, 185, 191, 206, 216, 217
slavery, 6, 10, 11, 77, 78, 86, 87, 94, 108, 131, 134, 142, 145, 154, 157, 158, 164, 169, 171, 175, 178, 181, 183, 185, 190, 193, 204, 205, 212, 214, 217, 219, 224, 225, 253, 268, 272, 274, 281, 285, 291
Slaves, 77, 86, 88, 95, 145, 154, 155, 158, 159, 164, 168, 169, 172, 174, 176, 181, 183, 186, 188, 191, 194, 196, 198–201, 205, 211–214, 220–222, 224, 274, 288
Sphrantzes, George, 11
St. Symeon the New Theologian, 13

T

Tarsus, 71
Tenochtitlan, 6
theatron, 11
Thessalonians. *See* Thessaloniki
Thessaloniki, 1, 5–7, 10, 11, 16, 21–23, 26, 29, 30, 32, 36, 41–43, 47, 50, 51, 54, 61, 63, 66, 71, 81, 85–87, 91–95, 97, 99, 103, 106, 107, 114, 117, 122, 124, 133, 135, 136, 141, 148, 159, 169, 186, 204, 208,

213, 217–219, 235, 237, 242, 243, 246–248, 250, 254, 256, 260, 272, 273, 291
thirst, 24–28, 30, 34–36, 39, 48, 63, 130, 265
Thucydides, 53, 55
trauma, 6, 19, 44, 50, 53, 55, 60, 66, 75, 77, 80, 81, 83, 85, 93, 99, 105, 109, 111, 135, 136, 172, 185, 190, 204, 211, 240, 245, 254, 257, 258, 263, 277, 280–283, 285, 286, 289–291
Tripoli, 11, 71, 127, 136, 171
Trojans, 244, 247
Troy, 51, 84

V

Vichy Regime, 286

W

Warsaw Ghetto, 37
Wiesel, Elie, 2–4, 10, 22–25, 28–34, 36, 38, 39, 41–50, 60, 63, 64, 73, 74, 76, 88, 90, 98, 105, 122, 130, 132, 133, 136, 161, 175, 206, 264, 278, 279, 286–288, 291
witness literature, 3, 8, 9, 11–14, 27, 44, 57, 58, 60, 64, 66, 75, 82, 90, 105, 107, 116, 129, 136, 151, 153, 156, 160, 161, 170, 205, 206, 209, 210, 232, 234, 248, 256, 263–265, 272, 279, 280, 284–286, 288, 289, 292
mobile witness, 99, 100

X

Xerxes, 96

Y

Yiddish, 2, 76, 88, 278

Z

Zevgminon, 238, 240, 261
Zonaras, John, 53, 54

Printed in the United States
by Baker & Taylor Publisher Services